WITHDRAWN

The Origins of the
Lloyd George Coalition

David Lloyd George. Photograph by Ernest H. Mills (1912). *Courtesy of the New York Public Library.*

The Origins of the Lloyd George Coalition

The Politics of Social-Imperialism, 1900-1918

Robert J. Scally

Princeton University Press, Princeton, New Jersey

DA
570
S25

Copyright © 1975 by Princeton University Press
Published by Princeton University Press,
Princeton and London

All Rights Reserved

Library of Congress Cataloging in Publication Data will
be found on the last printed page of this book

This book has been composed in Linotype Times Roman

Printed in the United States of America
by Princeton University Press, Princeton, New Jersey

To my mother, Anne

Contents

	Bibliographical Abbreviations	ix
	Acknowledgments	xi
	Introduction	3
I.	Liberal-Imperialism	29
	The Rosebery Revolt	29
	Rosebery and the Fabians	35
II.	The Liberal League and the Policy of National Efficiency	48
	The Liberal League	58
III.	The Coefficients Club	73
IV.	The Tariff Reform Movement: "*Le revenu c'est l'état*"	96
	The Chamberlain-Milner Method	96
	The Compatriots	110
	The Compatriot Doctrine	123
V.	Lloyd George and the Tariff Reformers	133
VI.	The Budget and the Peers	146
VII.	The Lloyd George Plan	172
	The Truce of God	175
	The Criccieth Memorandum: August 1910	187
	October and November 1910: From Conference to Coalition	196
VIII.	The Coalition Plan in the Prewar Crisis	211
IX.	The Rise and Fall of the First Coalition	250
X.	Lloyd George's Estrangement	280
XI.	"Advocates of Another Method"	306
	The Political Crisis of November–December 1916	318
XII.	The Coalition Government	336
	Appendix A. Memo: Campaign Literature	371
	Appendix B. The Criccieth Memorandum	375
	Supplementary Memorandum	384
	Bibliography	387
	Index	409

Bibliographical Abbreviations

A.P.	Asquith Papers
B.P.	Balfour Papers
B.L.P.	Bonar Law Papers
Bev. P.	Beveridge Papers
Br. P.	Braithwaite Papers
L.G.P.	Lloyd George Papers
L.L.P.	Liberal League Publications
M.P.	Milner Papers
N.S.L.	National Service League Publications
P.P.	Passfield Papers
T.R.L.	Tariff Reform League Publications
W.G.C.	Webbs' General Correspondence

Acknowledgments

My work on the Lloyd George coalition began some years ago while I was a graduate student at Princeton University. The original concept upon which the present study was based I owe to Professor Arno J. Mayer; a great part of whatever merit this work contains I owe also to his inspiration, patience, and encouragement. I would also like to acknowledge with gratitude the support of the Woodrow Wilson Foundation, the Davis Center for Historical Research, and New York University for their generous assistance during my research and while I was writing this book. To others, among them my students, colleagues, and the faculties of New York and Princeton Universities, who have provided stimulus and guidance, I will have to express my thanks in person.

For their indispensable assistance, I am also indebted to the staffs of the libraries whose collections I have used during the preparation of this book, including the Bodleian Library; the British Library of Political and Economic Science; the British Museum Reading Room, Department of Manuscripts; the Newspaper Library at Colindale; the Beaverbrook Library; the Library of New College; the New York Public Library; and, especially, the Firestone Library of Princeton University. I would also like to express my thanks to those who have granted me permission to quote from private papers in their possession, in particular to the Warden and Fellows of New College for the Milner Papers; to the British Library of Political and Economic Science for the Passfield and Beveridge Papers; to the First Beaverbrook Foundation and its Honorary Director, A. J. P. Taylor, for the Lloyd George and the Bonar Law Papers; to Mr. Mark Bonham Carter for the Asquith Papers and to the British Library Board for the Balfour Papers.

Although I have made every practical effort to acquire the permission of the owners of the copyright of all the material I have used, I must sincerely apologize to any whom I have overlooked or failed to trace, and would welcome any information which would help me to correct such infringements in any future editions.

Acknowledgments

So far as tolerance, patience, and sympathetic criticism could improve my work over the past ten years, that improvement is due to my wife, whose wit and companionship lightened every hour.

R.J.S.

The Origins of the
Lloyd George Coalition

Introduction

Writing just after the signing of the peace treaty in 1919, Elie Halévy described with strong approval the "Policy of Social Peace" designed by the Lloyd George government to guide the complex process of reconstruction in Great Britain. There were, Halévy claimed, two conflicting approaches to postwar problems that had emerged from the thinking of the war years. The first, the narrow approach, the one most favored by the traditional politicians in the victorious powers, was that the plan of reconstruction should concern itself merely with untangling the confusion caused by the war and, while containing the dangerous turmoil of demobilization as much as possible, return the country to "normal." In the broader sense, reconstruction would not be a mere restoration of the unstable order of 1914, but "the building of a new social edifice" with the tools forged by the war—organization, expert planning, and systematic state intervention. If it could not achieve the utopia of an actual fusion of classes, Halévy hoped, the genius of English politics might still prove potent enough to crown its democratic triumphs of centuries with the harnessing of the twentieth-century struggle of classes to the traditional party system or to some recognizable offspring of it.[1]

Halévy's sentiments were close to Lloyd George's own—both saw in the postwar confusion a perishable opportunity to reanimate the impulse behind the great prewar reforms, the impulse which had apparently been short-circuited by factional feuds, industrial strife, war, and at least partly by Lloyd George's own vagrant ambition. Put beside some of the nostalgic dreams of Edwardian summers which haunted the postwar years, the hope of recharging the Liberalism of 1906 does not seem so grave a delusion or, if Lloyd George had made only a few less grievous errors, so remote a possibility.

If we leave aside the more exotic forms of sheer reaction, mysticism, and pastoralism which also laid hold of the postwar years,

[1] *Revue d'économie politique*, XXXIII (July-August 1919), 385.

there were other compelling memories of Edwardian politics that sought to bend the reconstruction to purposes conceived and refined before the war. The hybrid array of ideas and strategies suggested in the term "Social-Imperialism" emerged in the prewar years as a blueprint for that broader reconstruction—a blueprint lacking something in precision and unity, but designed to erect a similar edifice while sacrificing vital parts of the traditional structure in the building of it. The currency of Social-Imperialist ideas at the turn of the century has been most persuasively described in Bernard Semmel's well-known study, *Imperialism and Social Reform*, and more recently in G. R. Searle's work on the idea of "National Efficiency."[2] But little attention or recognition has otherwise been given to the permeation of these ideas in the politics of the decades between the Boer War and the Peace of Versailles—a period of critical importance in modern English history in nearly every respect, for the empire, the economy, the social structure and, not least of all, the relatively peaceful transfer of political power from the Liberal to the Labour Party. This accomplishment was one which most attracted Halévy's admiration for the English political culture. It is probably the only case in which an entrenched and solvent ruling elite of a great capitalist state yielded a meaningful share of political power, not willingly but without a violent social upheaval. In that process the Social-Imperialists and the Lloyd George coalition played an essential role.

Refined, tested, and adapted by younger men in the acid of succeeding crises, the tentative postulates of the Earl of Rosebery, Alfred Milner, and the Webbs emerged at the end of the period as one of the instruments with which Lloyd George hoped to shape the great postwar reconstruction—as though to revive the ailing democracy, perversely, by controlled doses of its most lethal poison. The plan of reconstruction which had begun to develop even before the fall of Asquith was the direct offspring of the Social-Imperialist formula, a socialism of the Right, of order, social hierarchy, and bureaucratic control which halted access to political power on a line between the prewar middle classes and the radical shop stewards. The ferocious intraparty debacles of the Edwardian years were about the succession to power of the last imperial bourgeoisie,

---

[2] Bernard Semmel, *Imperialism and Social Reform: English Social-Imperial Thought, 1895-1914* (Cambridge, Mass., 1960); G. R. Searle, *The Quest for National Efficiency: A Study in British Politics and Political Thought, 1899-1914* (Oxford, 1971).

the generation of the Great Depression, who were equipped with all the prescribed credentials for upward movement but found the upper levels of government increasingly rigid in yielding to their expectations. The war and the Lloyd George government finalized that succession and delayed the impending upheaval of 1914 long enough to assure that the distribution of power would go no further.

At the war's end, the same resourceful Radical who had done so much to hasten the collapse of the Liberal Party was engaged in filling the resulting vacuum before the forces of the Left could be mobilized. Lloyd George had drawn discriminately from both the personnel and the ideologies of the Left and the Right in erecting his National Coalition. Like the plan of reconstruction, the coalition was a device for carrying over the methods of wartime into the peace; if the reconstruction was to harness the strife of classes which was already devastating the old order across Europe, the coalition would have to continue to suspend the strife of parties and indefinitely prolong the wartime *union sacrée*. Both social progress and order argued strongly in Lloyd George's mind for extending the powers and machinery which had mobilized the resources of the nation during the past four years. To return to the *status quo ante* without that concentration of power would be to plunge foolishly disarmed back into the equally uncertain conflicts of the prewar, a situation which had offered neither order nor improvement.

All of Lloyd George's plans for the reconstruction depended first of all on maintaining a strong coalition of his own forces and the Tariff Reformers. That coalition had come into operation only in the face of the manifest national emergency of 1916 and, as events were to prove, could remain intact only amid continuing crises and plausible imminent dangers short of war itself. If the sense of menace could not be maintained, the rationale for the coalition would eventually crumble. With the removal of the military threat from Germany, and consequently of the imperial and economic rivalry as well, the insurgents who made up the coalition would need new justification—the nature of the crisis would have to be redefined or some new menace would have to be discovered. As in December 1916, Lloyd George returned to the argument he himself had made during the constitutional debacle of six years before for a suspension of ordinary political conflict in order to mobilize against the continuing perils of social unrest, economic decline, and the new international specter of political subversion.

The Lloyd George plan of August 1910, the "other coalition," had invoked threats of this kind and had come near to achieving that powerful "nonparty" alliance which finally coalesced in 1916. Both the arguments and the men marshaled behind the coalition idea in the year of the King's death had been nurtured in the Social-Imperialist movement during its peak years of activity since the Boer War. By 1910, the greater part of the theory of Social-Imperialism had already been elaborated. With the Liberal League, the Tariff Reform movement, and the work of the Fabians, a start had also been made to adapt the doctrine to domestic politics—on the whole without notable success; for by the time of the first coalition plan, the policy of imperialism and social reform had failed either to capture control of one of the great parties or to mobilize a sufficient popular base to challenge the political establishment at the polls. Fabian "permeation" held only the chance of a distant success. With the second failure of the Tariff Reformers to gain control of the Unionist Party in the elections of 1910, the time had come, as Milner put it, for the "advocates of a different method." After years of concerted deprecation, those advocates had at least succeeded (a significant victory) in discrediting "party politics"—construed to mean any putting of party before the national interest as defined by them. The possible fruits of that victory were poorly understood by most Liberal or Conservative leaders such as Balfour and Asquith, who were often perplexed and intimidated by twentieth-century forms of democracy. In the agitated climate of 1910, it was difficult for them to resist overtly the Chancellor's grand proposition, which was energetically heralded by its supporters and the bulk of the press as an "above-party" appeal for unity to meet a mortal national crisis. And few others in a position to influence events understood J. A. Hobson's warning that "in Great Britain the weakening of 'party' is visibly attended by a decline in the reality of popular control."[3]

The jealous contempt of the Social-Imperialists for the party patricians on one side and their unconcealed fear of an expanding and politicized labor movement was shared by Lloyd George and his faction of the Liberal Party and intruded into the writing of the political side of the doctrine—the policy of the "National Coalition of Parties." The coalition idea answered the Webbs' most serious critique of Milner, that he had become infatuated with the idea

[3] J. A. Hobson, *Imperialism: A Study* (London, 1902), p. 147.

Introduction

of nonparty government without having secured any device for achieving it. Educated sons of country doctors, civil and colonial servants, impatient young men of promise, the determined advocates of the nonparty idea saw in the Lloyd George plan a lofty patriotic purpose and an avenue to political power which handily outflanked the tedious old road through the clubs, the caucuses, and the favor of retired scions. Apprehensive of losing control of a changing world with distinguished and jealous amateurs at the reins of the state, they would dismantle the historic parties and thus open the way for the "experts" and the men of ideas.

A feature which distinguishes this insurgency is the almost unqualified confidence of its members in their ability, and thus their right, to serve in positions of power. That was the compelling logic of both the liberal and the imperial ethos in Victorian England. Not unnaturally, when opportunities diminished in a stagnating economy and a static empire that feeling was often attended by the bitter conviction that they were being systematically denied their right by the entrenched and the incompetent. The quality which normally infuriated Europeans, Americans, and Indians, the patronizing arrogance of the imperial civil servant, often translated into domestic politics as a haughty sense of competence, competence to plan and control projects on the grand imperial scale, and a natural impatience to demonstrate the gift in public life.

The leading figures in the Social-Imperialist movement and the coalitions—Rosebery, Chamberlain, Beatrice Webb, Milner, and Lloyd George—all shared that arrogance and, perhaps because it had been frustrated in them, displayed it to a greater degree even than the previous generation. All shared as well the ability to inspire the aggrieved ambition of talented younger men, the kind of men largely from the same kind of backgrounds in the Victorian middle classes whose ambitions had been fairly easily satisfied in the expanding empire of the previous half-century. In the years following the war in South Africa, however, there was decreasing latitude and promise in imperial careers. There was also less plausibility in the loftiness of purpose of the imperial mission. Still educated largely in the traditional classical curriculum, they were prepared almost exclusively to exercise the prerogatives of civilized men among the uncivilized—if not as proconsuls, then as tribunes, if not in Calcutta or Capetown, then in London. There would be danger in their growing number if the right to rule were denied them. Having lost most of the Victorian disdain for foreign methods, recognizing the unmistakable successes of Germany, Japan, and the United States, they tended more and more after the South African fiasco to cast a deprecating eye on all that was traditional and established in British politics, particularly on conventional restraints in social, economic, and military planning, areas in which they felt their talents were urgently required to reverse the ominous stagnation of the empire and the nation. Their criticism consequently tended to focus on what they regarded as the stubborn complacency of the older party and political leadership, slow to change or to accept modern instruction, as well as the institutions which embodied that establishment: the Cabinet system, party organization, the House of Lords, and ultimately parliamentary supremacy itself. These were institutions which most of them felt had not noticeably enhanced the progress of their powerful younger rivals around the world.

Insular chauvinism persisted among the British Social-Imperialists, however, when it came to importing ideologies; some distinction was maintained between emulating German social legislation or American technical education and embracing political dogmas from abroad. Nevertheless, the strong ideological affinity with continental Social-Imperialism which characterized the writings of Karl Pearson and Benjamin Kidd survived to a limited extent in the movement in Britain, mainly through the influential agency of Milner and his circle. As a contemporary movement, British Social-Imperialist thought naturally shared many of the features of the continental models described by Joseph Schumpeter, Franz Neumann, and more recently by Hans-Ulrich Wehler, and should not be viewed in isolation. In these analyses, the Social-Imperialist has been painted as a defensive creature, concerned with engineering a "fusion of classes" or the renewal of an "imperial race," at the same time borrowing arguments from Marxism in an attempt to avert the enactment of a Marxian future. In politics, the Social-Imperialist method often began with the preemptive manipulation of party and parliamentary factions, constitutionally barricading the forces of movement from ministerial control over policy, or with the erection of Center-Right blocs to countervail each surge of growth on the Left. Like the process of *trasforismo* in Italy or *appaisement* in France, the latter tactic generally succeeded in preventing highly factionalized party systems from succumbing to the increasingly strong political pressures from the Left until extraparliamentary agitation and disruption began to force progressively violent confrontations in the streets in the few years before the war. The pattern of Edwardian politics displayed all of these tendencies, including the fragmentation of the two leading parties, an assault on the party system from the Right (and on the capacity of the Socialists to finance its candidates), the coalescence of a Center-Right bloc and a pattern of escalating violence in dealing with social disorder before the war. Moreover, as will be seen, elements of racism, Catonism, and the familiar baggage of reaction adhered to the British Social-Imperialist groups, particularly in the early years. At least in the abstract, this political and ideological syndrome is one which most European historians have included in the study of the origins of fascism; only rarely is such an approach applied to English history before the war. Bernard Semmel's modest suggestion is certainly the exception in this regard, that the fascist excrescence of Oswald Mosley may possibly have been the "fulfillment" of Social-Imperialism in Great Britain.[4]

But, while there were unmistakable undertones of authoritarianism and intolerance in the movement in Great Britain which link it fraternally with such organizations as the Pan-German League and the Action Française, there was also an element, equally visible, of the native Radical and Tory reform tradition in its impulse to organize progress in social reform through the "efficient" allocation of the nation's resources and the opening of careers to talent. Embodied in the contrasting personalities of the Webbs, Lloyd George, and Winston Churchill, that impulse manifested itself in the language of "constructive revolution" by means of which the movement attracted to its banner such antiauthoritarian spirits as Bertrand Russell, H. G. Wells, and William Beveridge. This side of the insurgency also held a more pragmatic than ideological view of politics and influenced the coalition movement in that direction. With the notable exception of that queer trespasser Alfred Milner, the members of the Coefficients Club, the Tariff Reform League, and the coalition were engaged tenaciously in the feasible, that range of practicality between the mere bookkeeper and the visionary. In that prosaic field Milner seldom cared to labor.

The British variety of Social-Imperialism thus showed two faces. Unlike the faces of Janus, however, each bore a mixed aspect of beneficence and enmity which, when ruled by the uglier side, work-

[4] Semmel, *Imperialism and Social Reform*, p. 246.

man and lord alike had reason to fear. For, in the roster of the various Social-Imperialist groups over nearly two decades the movement counted few prominent members (with the notable exception of Rosebery) of that landed class which was the prime beneficiary of protectionist imperialism and as few from its prime victim at the lower end of society, despite the many and ingenious efforts to coax patriotic working men away from the Left. As has been said of the "People's Budget" of 1909, the work of one of the movement's guiding spirits, the Social-Imperialist agitation was to a large extent the "inspired and concentrated clamor of the middle classes."[5] The motif of National Efficiency which characterized the movement, from the Liberal League to the Ministry of Reconstruction, served not only as a critique of established men and methods in government and a warning of the advance of rival younger states, but also embodied the self-serving meritocratic philosophy of the insurgents. Combining the ethic of the civil servant, the imperial bureaucrat, and the self-made man with the ambition of talent without means, the doctrine of efficiency became the hallmark of what H. G. Wells aptly called "the revolt of the competent."

The discussion among historians about this period of European history over the past few years has forced us to reexamine some familiar and, it was thought, well-understood events under a broader circle of light than the traditional national histories had hitherto employed. The widening perspectives offered by the work of comparative historians have made such reexaminations in narrower studies of national history inescapable. We had become accustomed to seeing the turmoil of politics in the Edwardian period, for example, as part of the ongoing constructive adjustment of the most stable and mature democracy in Europe to the final demands of democratization, a process which had been advancing peacefully for a century. On the other hand, it becomes increasingly apparent that at least some of the violent dislocations of the prewar years were systemic rather than passing, problems of a kind similar to those faced throughout Europe at the time and attributable to the blank recalcitrance of ruling or aspiring elites to any further exten-

[5] Samuel J. Hurvitz, *State Intervention in Great Britain: A Study of Economic Control and Social Response* (New York, 1949), p. 117.

sion of democratic institutions—in some cases, even to their continuance. Increasingly, new information and interpretation tends to strengthen the second view, that despite the persistence of what are usually thought of as British democratic values—personal and political freedoms, more or less equal justice, the tradition of parliamentary supremacy, and the legitimacy of compromise—the movement of British society in the period was inexorably in the direction of increasing class conflict and rigidity at the lower levels, increasing erosion from the commitment to democratic and parliamentary methods, and perhaps most important, the ascendancy of a powerful aspiring "successor elite" to the traditional leaders in the party system which militantly argued for a more disciplined and regimented society based on the principles of National Efficiency and for whom the traditional democratic values were merely dangerous impediments to preparing the society for modern modes of production and modern warfare.

That highly vocal segment of the Edwardian Right which encompassed the Tariff Reformers, the Shaw-Webb Fabians, the Liberal-Imperialists, and (after 1910) the Lloyd George Radicals, does not come under the heading "reactionary" in the usual sense, although at various points they were associated and in league with such elements as the Irish landlords, the "Last Ditchers" in the House of Lords, and reactionary intellectuals like Hilaire Belloc and C. K. Chesterton who more properly come under that heading. The Milner wing of the coalition accounts for most of this inclination. Moreover, the term "counterrevolutionary" applies to this combination of forces only if taken quite flexibly in comparing them to their counterparts elsewhere in Europe. Although I have used this expression to describe the Social-Imperialist and Lloyd George combination, it need hardly be said that it must be qualified to exactly the same degree that the description "revolutionary" is in describing the British Left at the various stages of its history during this period. Since there is still much disagreement about the one it is expected that there will also be about the other. The term applies because the behavior of the Social-Imperialists was always in counterpoint to the danger from the Left *as they perceived it*, anticipating and counterattacking as political opportunities arose. Although that perception sometimes varied profoundly from Milner to the Webbs to Lloyd George, they were all moved in the end by the premonition that, without them, British politics would resolve itself into a violent clash between revolution and reaction in which order and progress would dissolve. They saw themselves as the only plausible alternative, combining modernity and stability and able to handle both social change and social order.

It was this aspiring "successor elite," the postimperial leadership of the Tariff Reform and Lloyd George factions in the two parties, which set the strategy and tactics of counterrevolutionary politics in the prewar period. Its ideology and political behavior belonged to the iconoclastic, rebellious class whom Wells called "the competent." As one of the same class, Wells was speaking something very close to their thoughts in *Mr. Britling Sees It Through*, in a famous passage most often used to capsulize the general malaise of the late Edwardian years:

> The psychology of all this recent insubordination and violence is—curious. Exasperating too . . . I don't quite grasp it. . . . It's the same thing whether you look at the suffrage business or the labour people or the Irish muddle. People may be too safe. You see we live at the end of a series of secure generations in which none of the great things of life have changed materially. We've grown up with no sense of danger—that is to say, with no sense of responsibility. None of us, none of us—for though I talk my actions belie me—really believe that life can change very fundamentally any more forever. All this . . . looks as though it was bound to go on steadily forever. It seems incredible that the system could be smashed. It seems incredible that anything we can do will ever smash the system —Old Asquith thinks that we always have got along and that we shall always get along by being quietly artful and saying "Wait and see." And it's just because we are convinced that we are so safe against a general breakdown that we are able to be so recklessly violent in our special cases.[6]

It is deceptively easy to build impressions of popular sentiment on such glimpses, as George Dangerfield and others have done. Well's perception was not, of course, either the perception of the average man or of the "secure generations." But it was assuredly

---

[6] This passage is frequently cited as an illustration of the "Dangerfield thesis." Insofar as it reflects Wells' own sentiments, however, I think it is intended to characterize the mood of the circle of dissidents in which he moved, as in the "Pentagram Circle" of *The New Machiavelli*, rather than the wider social phenomenon which Dangerfield had in mind. There is a good summary of the thesis in Donald Lammers, "Arno Mayer and the British Decision for War: 1914," *Journal of British Studies*, XII, 2 (May 1973), 137-165.

that of a generation which expected and yearned for changes in "the great things in life" without ever finding them, at least not until the war came.

It was partly the recklessness of such expectations, or the frustration of them, which drew men like Wells into the Social-Imperialist orbit and into its fraternal groups like the Coefficients, the Compatriots, and the Round Table. They appealed to idealism and the need for action and offered the illusion of a just and invincible cause. In addition, almost without exception the members of these organizations shared Wells' frustration with the pedestrian political leaders of their time and shared his recklessness in devising methods of replacing them. In a sense their contempt and disenchantment extended also to the general mass of their countrymen. The ordinary man had become, in the words of one of the Coefficients, "sottish and selfish," an unworthy descendant of the stout and hearty yeoman whom their Victorian education had led them to believe awaited their command. It was intrinsic in the imperial mythology that with democracy would come decadence and stagnation. Indeed, the history of their agitation in the decade or so before the war could conceivably be reduced to their desire to create what Beatrice Webb was fond of calling the "imperial race," whose salient virtues would include above all deference, sobriety, doggedness, patriotism, industriousness, physical strength, loyalty, courage (of the sort known as "pluck"), and an assortment of other qualities useful mainly to employers, sergeant majors, and conservative politicians. It is probably no coincidence either that these were much the same virtues which the imperial missionaries labored to instill among the subject races. They were conceived, of course, as the antithesis of the decadent habits widely thought to be on the rise among the working classes, an ominous pattern which many thought to be reflected also in the behavior of the suffragettes, the labor strikers, and to some extent even in the opulent idleness of the once "productive classes" of entrepreneurs. In much of this the Fabians, the Tariff Reformers, and the Lloyd George Radicals shared the feelings of the older elites whose paragons ran the Liberal and Conservative parties. Their attitudes significantly diverged, however, in that men like Asquith, Balfour, Curzon, and Crewe seemed to think that the pattern was regrettable but irresistible and were somewhat inclined to include their own subordinates among those who were losing the ancient virtues, deference and loyalty most of all.

Such differences in outlook, age, and ideology within the various factions of the Edwardian political spectrum must be taken as factors in determining their reactions to the progression of crises before August 1914, and in shaping any disposition to seek a release from internal dilemmas in foreign conflict. Until recent years, the theory of British war guilt had been associated either with the Left war critics like E. D. Morel on one side or with the conservative German apologists like Egmont Zechlin and Gerhard Ritter whose concern was primarily to mitigate the case against Germany by emphasizing the "unreasonableness" of England in dealing with the legitimate aspirations of the German Empire. In different ways, both views indict the Liberal leadership of 1914—they allowed the crisis to go beyond control either from weakness, incompetence, or from more sinister, self-serving motives. On the other hand, the thesis which indicts Bethmann-Hollweg tends to exculpate Asquith and Grey, as in the shattering analysis of German war aims by Fritz Fischer.[7] No comparable set of charges has been, or probably can be, formulated in the case of England. The more formidable and elusive question is whether the men who were in a position to materially influence the decision for war were moved by considerations *other than* those which were conventionally seen as rational and lawful—the defense of national sovereignty, the maintenance of an international order and, in the case of England, the principle of the balance of power. It was largely in the violation of such conventions that the ruling elite of Imperial Germany was judged to be culpable.

Although the examination of the English decision for war does not evoke the same aura of conspiracy and deliberation, it now seems clear that the set of assumptions and expectations which led up to that decision were neither entirely rational nor entirely *responsive* to German aggression, but emanated from a view of international politics now deeply clouded by domestic preoccupations. If lifted from the narrow context of the July crisis, the English disposition towards a war in Europe can only be understood in rela-

---

[7] *Griff nach der Weltmacht: Die Kriegspolitik des kaiserlichen Deutschland, 1914-1918* (3rd ed., Düsseldorf, 1968); also, *Der Krieg der Illusionen: Die deutsche Politik von 1911 bis 1914* (Düsseldorf, 1969). See also his discussion of the thesis of English "war guilt" from the German point of view in *Weltmacht oder Niedergang: Deutschland im Ersten Weltkrieg* (Frankfurt, 1965).

tion to a whole set of new factors which had transformed English politics since the rise of Germany as a great power. Among those operative in the immediate prewar years were the near-paralysis of the moderate leadership in the two parties, the conviction among the leadership that neither the Irish question nor the industrial unrest could be resolved (by them) without resort to force and, perhaps most decisively, the ascendancy in both parties of insurgent forces whose domestic strategy and ideology were rooted in the assumption that a showdown with Germany was imminent and inescapable. These factors forced more than they restrained Asquith's hand in the diplomatic crisis, compelling him and Grey to await some irretrievable step, such as the invasion of Belgium, which would at once overcome the resistance to intervention and at least temporarily restore their waning authority over their subordinates. The passive behavior of Asquith and Grey during the crisis does not suppose any wish to become embroiled even in a limited war in Europe, but it does reflect the extreme vulnerability of their position at home had they held out against intervention—such a position could only have confirmed the charges of complacency and incompetence and advanced the moment of their fall. Much the same situation arose over the question of a negotiated peace two years later. Thus Grey's political weakness at home was a "diplomatic asset," as some have suggested, only in the sense that he could allow the crisis to boil over into war without assuming any direct responsibility for it, and Asquith's famous "detachment" of 1916 could allow him to witness the dismemberment of the Liberal Party thinking it beyond his powers to prevent. Few of the traditional moderates either sought or survived the war because to a large extent their political strength had been sapped in the domestic ferment and polarization of the prewar.

All over Europe the enervation of the traditional Center had been accompanied by the language of decline, decadence, and impending chaos. In the sense already mentioned, the insurgent Social-Imperialists employed the same rhetoric, but the established leaders gave every sign of being bewildered and demoralized by their sense of *epigonentum* and by the increasing aggressiveness of the forces they felt were arrayed against them, feeling more or less powerless to arrest or survive them in the long run. On the other hand, the insurgents did all they could to exaggerate and dramatize the signs of trouble in the society *because of* their unshakable confidence in their ability to reverse the pattern with stern and efficient methods borrowed mainly from the imperialist credo. Needless to say, the more critical the country's problems could be made to appear, the more urgent a change in leadership would seem. It would be a mistake to misconstrue the published alarms of the imperialist press as either panic or fearfulness at the threat of social disorder and economic decline—the most unmistakable and common characteristic of the insurgents was their aggressive, even predatory, self-assurance. For them, the mounting crises of the prewar years were more an opportunity than a menace. It was in part just that quality of aggressiveness which, as though by some primitive scent, identified potential allies to each other and the lack of it in the traditional leaders which engendered the sometimes brutal scorn they showed for men like Asquith. The most discernible anxiety in the leaders of the Social-Imperialist movement, in men like Milner, Amery, Garvin, Carson and, later on, Lloyd George, was that they might fail to achieve the political power and influence they felt their talent and vision entitled them to.

Many of the debacles within the Liberal and Conservative parties in the decade before the war can be understood only in the context of this generational, temperamental, and ideological rift between fear and timorousness on the one side and arrogant disdain on the other. It was the deliberate scenario drawn by the imperialist dissidents in the years between 1900 and the Liberal victory of 1905 to cast Free Traders, Gladstonian Liberals, pacifists, and "good party men" as both antiquated and, because they appeared to be insufficiently alert to the impending menaces from inside and abroad, lacking in patriotism. The same assault was made upon the leadership during the war by the same political forces demanding full-scale military and industrial conscription, the suspension of "politics," and unconditional surrender—it may even be possible to carry the same mentality into the policy of reparations and intervention in Russia, but those questions are somewhat beyond the scope of this study. From the beginning, the insurgents carried a psychology of siege which rooted both their social philosophy and their view of international politics. The most significant fact, however, is that this was a peacetime phenomenon, a product of the deep ideological crosscurrent which had already split the Liberal and Conservative parties as well as the Socialist movement from the time of the imperial crisis in South Africa. The war provided the rationale and the instruments to implement the Social-Imperialist doctrine of a disciplined society and a planned economy and an opportunity for the insurgents to sidestep the constraining parliamentary path to power.

It is possible to see the origins of that crosscurrent in the positions occupied by the principal factions both on the question of war in 1914 and in the division of opinion on how it should be conducted thereafter—on both questions the attitudes of the major actors were formed as much by the internal as by the international consequences of war. Thus, to a somewhat lesser extent than in Germany, considerations of *Innenpolitik* seem to have guided the decision for war and the framing of war aims. To be sure, internal and external contingencies not only were mixed in the strategic thinking of the various governing circles but varied also with objective differences in the prewar internal politics of each state and with the subjective ideological and social affiliations of the decision-makers. Such differences are especially important, and were long thought to be decisive, in comparisons of the internal politics of such diverse societies as England, Germany, and Russia. Nevertheless, in an age in which every European regime was beset by unfamiliar but related problems arising out of the growth of mass politics, some of the uniformities in their behavior may be more illuminating than their obvious differences.

The most recent and provocative description of these uniformities has been offered by Arno J. Mayer in a paradigm which might be summarized as follows: the far Right, mainly the older conservatives of the eastern empires, feared to subject the fragile old regimes to the test of a modern war; the right-wing forces in the western states saw possibilities of heading off the social revolution in their own countries; the liberal and moderate forces tended to fear precipitating domestic revolution; and the republican and radical Left viewed the war as offering more opportunity for reaction than for reform. This was thought to be the lesson of the European wars since 1870, that military victory upheld the forces of order while defeat favored the forces of change.[8] By 1914,

---

[8] Arno J. Mayer, "Domestic Causes of the First World War," in Leonard Krieger and Fritz Stern (eds.), *The Responsibility of Power: Historical Essays in Honor of Hajo Holborn* (New York, 1969), pp. 286-301; also, "Internal Causes and Purposes of War in Europe, 1870-1956: A Research Assignment," *Journal of Modern History*, 41/3 (Sept. 1969), 291-303.

calculations based on such assumptions about the relationship between war and domestic politics had become an essential factor of diplomatic and military strategy.

This paradigm contains both revelations and some distortions when applied to the spectrum of opinion in England. First of all, if we are speaking exclusively of attitudes as they developed during the July crisis, it tends to distort the relative weight and consistency of positions taken by the leaders of Cabinet and party rank and by those other important figures, like Carson, Milner, MacDonald, and Northcliffe, having what might be called special constituencies. Simply counting Cabinet resignations gives an inflated picture of the strength of opinion against intervention—Simon, Beauchamp, Morley, and Burns were figures of secondary importance at best, and their position was far from unified. Opposition from Lloyd Georger or Milner, for example, would have created a far greater problem for the interventionists. Moreover, a high degree of uncertainty and wavering seems to have existed, as in Lloyd George's case, even in some who very quickly afterward adopted the strongest prowar position as well as in those like Simon and Beauchamp who first opposed intervention and later relented.

That uncertain flux of opinion accounts in part for Grey's hesitant diplomacy and for the extraordinary weight given in his thinking to the question of Belgian neutrality; in contrast to the situation in Berlin, the leading figures in the English Cabinet preferred to *react* to events, in effect, to have their decision made for them as the only means of preempting expected opposition. This method of passive response was the way in which the party leadership had threaded their route through the domestic crises of the previous five years. The result is that we find the leaders of the various political factions in England standing astride the suggested spectrum, holding ambiguous and even contradictory feelings about the prospects of war. Figures like Asquith, Grey, Crewe, and their circle, for example, once the leading spokesmen for Liberal-Imperialism, might fairly be said to have harbored at one time or another *all* the fears and intimations described in the paradigm. As we shall see, these Liberal moderates and their Conservative counterparts, committed deeply to the traditional parliamentary and party system, feared for its collapse under any new strains in 1914, whether domestic or diplomatic; they were both tempted and unnerved by the possible prospects the international crisis offered for the violent forces of both the Left and the Right which had become visible in the few years before the war and, probably the guiding emotion in their case, they behaved *as though they were convinced* that the advocates of "stern measures," who had bedeviled them in the prewar years, were already in the process of displacing them and would soon succeed in doing so unless the coming war were a short and victorious one.

One other anomaly occurs when applying the same method to the moderate Conservative leaders, men like Balfour, Lansdowne, and Long who, if we are to measure them by their commitment to the constitutional and parliamentary system, can only be placed with the leaders of the Liberal Party on the eve of the war, sharing much the same sentiments on the prospects of war and, like Asquith, harboring only fragile hopes of a temporary release from the prewar internal pressures which they already felt to be out of their control. This vital center had more or less resigned itself before the war to a spectator's role, awaiting the fated conflict between the political extremes.

The English Center on the eve of the war might thus be seen as the representative of embattled political elites and institutions and their final, hesitant decision for intervention in 1914 as a last assertion of the primacy of the old diplomacy—a decision justified by them in the context of traditional balance of power principles enshrined during the Pax Britannica. Such illusions, which were shared by comparable groups in the other capitals of Europe, tended to carry with them assumptions about a war of limited duration, limited violence, limited cost, and limited aims which were shortly to be overturned along with their adherents. Those who had a better understanding of the potential violence in prewar society often saw through the illusion to both the horrors and the opportunities the coming war would bring.

The application of the method is less ambiguous regarding the formations on either side of the Center in English politics. The major difficulty arises from the general absence of theoretical and ideological definitions of the various factions in the spectrum of Edwardian politics—there is probably no period in modern English history when official party designations had less application to ideological affiliation than in the immediate prewar years. The difficulty intrudes into any of the traditional definitions either of the Right or the Left in England whether based on their class makeup or social policy—the imperialist movement contained more than a fair share of penurious intellectuals and civil servants along with an advanced interventionist social program and the Labour-Socialist leadership was dominated either by men of the same social background or representatives of the conservative "aristocracy of labour," equally concerned with restraining the mass of the labor movement from taking Socialist doctrine too literally. If we are to use the disposition toward the war as a gauge, as it has been by some German and French historians, the question of distinguishing Left and Right appears to remain clouded, since both the imperialist and the labor leadership overwhelmingly supported the decision to intervene. However, their positions in August 1914 had only momentarily converged as they had all over Europe; increasingly, numbers of Labour-Socialists and Radicals moved in the direction either of opposing the war outright or at least towards the policy of a negotiated peace as the war progressed, while the imperialists moved rapidly toward all-out mobilization, unconditional surrender, and aggressive war aims. The positions taken on these so-called "wartime" issues offer much the clearer picture of the ideological conflict. As we shall see, imperialists and Socialists tended to return during the hostilities to peacetime positions on most issues of moment, positions which had emerged during the internal political battle that had been growing in intensity since the Boer War. Since that time the Social-Imperialists had assumed the leadership of the counterrevolutionary forces in politics in shifting alliances with the Fabians, the Tory backwoodsmen, labor reactionaries, and finally with the Lloyd George Radicals. And their influence grew with the radicalization of the labor movement in the prewar industrial troubles, fed by the progressive erosion of the moderates in all parties. The war does not appear to have altered that process.

This pattern, rather than the short-lived truce of 1914, reflected the more fundamental polarization of power in this era between the "forces of movement" and the "forces of order," between mass democracy and counterrevolution, in which the older elites were largely reduced to onlookers, collaborators of the Right or, in some cases, victims of the struggle.

The core of the Edwardian counterrevolution was the Tariff Reform League and its numerous offshoots, many of which recruited from other splinters and factions, like the Fabian imperialists, and the Lloyd George circle, whose place in the ideological spectrum is not so easily fixed. Their attachment to the doctrine of Social-

Introduction

Imperialism separates them ideologically from the traditional Conservatives and consequently from the "Cecil monopoly" which still dominated the Conservative Party at the turn of the century. The main energy of the league, first under Joseph Chamberlain and later under the leadership of the more militant Milner-Garvin circle, was directed towards acquiring control of the Conservative-Unionist Party. They hoped to transform it into a dynamic anti-Socialist instrument with a mass base among those segments of the working and lower-middle classes which they perceived to be more receptive to appeals to social order and imperial security than to militant labor unionism or class conflict.

Before 1910, the strategy of the Social-Imperialists remained mostly within the parliamentary system. But as it appeared that even numerical preponderance in the party, which they had achieved by that time, would fail to guarantee control of party policy or a realistic chance of displacing the Liberals from office, they turned increasingly to extraparliamentary means, first to the idea of overturning both the Conservative and the Liberal old guard at once through the proposed coalition with Lloyd George and the Liberal insurgents and, after that failed, through the erratic series of reckless ventures known as the Tory rebellion in which the army and the Ulster reactionaries were their main allies.

The hub of Social-Imperialist propaganda was the attack on the party system. Around the idea of the "nonparty" government the three main elements of the insurgency gathered—the Tariff Reformers, the Fabians, and the Lloyd George Liberals. The immediate attraction of this idea to each of them is fairly self-evident: the complicated network of local organizations and loyalties which made up the two parties (and increasingly the Labour Party as well) was resistant to sudden changes of leadership or doctrine and would be difficult to capture by arrangements made in London where the insurgents' chief influence was concentrated. The resemblance of this strategy to that employed by counterrevolutionary factions in the rest of Europe, the *Sammlungspolitik* in Germany or the *union nationale* in France, for example, suggests a degree of uniformity in the reaction of imperialist elements in particular to the increasing strength of social-democratic forces. The thesis that the pattern of prewar domestic politics was determined by the defensive strategies of the ruling classes against the process of democratization has been convincingly argued for Germany by the so-called "Kehrite" school, by Hans-Ulrich Wehler in particular.[9] The case must be modified to some extent for both France and England, however, since the process of political modernization had already gone beyond the control of preindustrial elites, leaving the counterrevolutionary response largely in the hands of *aspiring* or bypassed social elements. In England especially, as I have already suggested, the leadership represented a disgruntled "successor elite," impatient but immobilized by the transition from an expanding to a static, and soon to be contracting, empire and economy.

The "nonparty" concept, as we shall see, was also integrated into the body of ideas which emerged from the Social-Imperialist clubs under the title of "National Efficiency." This doctrine had important diplomatic as well as technical, social, and political implications, as was recently pointed out in Searle's study. In particular, the strong anti-German turn of mind on the part of Chamberlain and his circle after the failure of the erstwhile German alliance in 1901 occurred largely because the imperialists in England had previously looked to Germany as the model of "efficiency" they wished to emulate—barring the alliance, then, it seemed that Germany's very efficiency ". . . would sooner or later bring her to challenge the British Empire for world supremacy."[10] That premonition never abated among the imperialists and, through their energetic propaganda on the subject of "National Efficiency," it noticeably permeated the thinking of all but a few of the political leaders who were to make the decision for war in 1914.

The historical and philosophical roots of the doctrine of efficiency appear to be more or less identical with those of the Social-Imperialist movement. The work of both Semmel and Searle suggests that both began to take shape during the ideological assault of the 1880s upon Gladstonian Individualism, blossoming rather naturally under the pressures of both German rivalry and the isolation of the Boer War around the turn of the century. Certain other less specific factors should be mentioned in connection with the appearance of both movements, I think. It should be noted, for ex-

[9] Hans-Ulrich Wehler, *Der Primat der Innenpolitik* (Berlin, 1965); also, *Bismarck und der Imperialismus* (Cologne, 1969). For an excellent summary of the Kehrite approach, see Wolfgang Mommsen, "Domestic Factors in German Foreign Policy," *Central European History*, VI, 1 (May 1973), 3-43; and for the French side, David Sumler, "Domestic Influences on the Nationalist Revival in France, 1909-1914," *French Historical Studies*, VI, 4 (Fall 1970).
[10] Searle, *The Quest for National Efficiency*, p. 56.

ample, that the attraction of efficiency as a political and social idea corresponded in time with what might be called the closing of the imperial frontier. It is not possible to date that event exactly, but for general purposes it might be said that the idea of an expanding empire had certainly lost its currency outside of sentimental and popular literature by the end of the Boer War. That crisis in turn was the primary stimulus for the creation of the first Social-Imperialist political organizations, including the Liberal League, the Tariff Reform League, and the Coefficients, among others. For the first time, imperialism had been put on the defensive.

In addition to a number of the by-products of the crisis of empire which have already been alluded to—the contraction of imperial careers, the internal ideological dislocation in the major parties, and the shift in attitudes towards Germany—there remains the connection between Social-Imperialist ideas and the systemic social, industrial, and technological problems associated with what has been called the "Second Industrial Revolution." The Social-Imperialist movement was consciously a response to that phenomenon, or at least to the symptoms of it which they were able to perceive.

After an early and long-sustained lead as the first industrial power, the English were the only nation on earth to face the overwhelming problems of adjustment to that event before the First World War. The "social" side of the Social-Imperialist program focused primarily on that adjustment in areas like technical education, the training of scientific management, economic planning, the recruitment of experts into government, and a host of other projects conceived as rational and necessary responses to the problem of relative economic stagnation and its attendant implications for national security and solvency. These were unique challenges, for there existed very little precedent or experience in England or elsewhere. At least one of the reasons for the sense of common cause among the otherwise disparate elements of the movement existed in their mutual conviction that they alone understood the nature of the problem and they alone in politics were sufficiently uncommitted to the past to offer the necessary radical solutions to it. The colossal difficulty of forcing or persuading quick adjustment in the long-established private enterprise mechanism or in the thinking of the private and governmental elites which had arisen under the old system accounts for the sometimes furious frustration evident in the younger men's attacks on Gladstonian Liberalism, the title under which they included everything which was unresponsive to their views.

To use a conceptual framework made fashionable by the study of developing nations, the problem facing the British Empire at the turn of the century was one of "modernization," or to be more exact, "remodernization." I have used this terminology mainly to suggest that the process of "remodernization," like the original process of industrialization in England and elsewhere, contained ramifications which could extend to the fundamental organization of the traditional society and all its institutions. Needless to say, all the ramifications were rarely foreseeable until the process was already far advanced. For the most part, the Social-Imperialists limited their thinking to the dominant structures and institutions nearest to them and to their understanding, that is, to party and Parliament, the bureaucracy, the military, the schools and universities, the labor unions, heavy industry, City finance, and so on, and rarely to primary institutions not as clearly visible from London. In short, the instruments with which they expected to accomplish the necessary "reconstruction of society," as they put it, were mainly political. Thus, despite the attention given in their campaign to the social question under the guidance of the Webbs, the ideology was conspicuously lacking a systematic social philosophy or analysis, leaving them to rely rather too heavily on political explanations for their difficulties—the complacency of the older party "Mandarins," the corruption of the party system, the inefficiency of traditional methods of choosing leaders—and most often to discover remedies for the lack of dynamism in the economy in the restriction of popular control over politics.

Without fully understanding the complex technical difficulties facing the domestic economy due largely to the Second Industrial Revolution, the Social-Imperialists nevertheless identified many of the more damaging weaknesses inherited from the years of primacy under the old system. With its sharp denigration of the cult of individualism, the ethic of the nineteenth-century entrepreneur, Social-Imperialism was the ideological carrier in England of the new industrial ethic, that of science, technology, the professional manager, and the corporate society. It was from that ethic that virtually all of the doctrine of efficiency derived.

Few of the Social-Imperialists, with the possible exception of W. A. S. Hewins and William Ashley, had the technical qualifications to address the question of industrial stagnation on economic rather than political grounds. And only later, as in Lloyd George's Ministry of Reconstruction, was there any methodical effort made to deal with practical questions of industrial organization, replacement of obsolete plant, subsidy of growth industries, and the formation of large industrial collectives through which to channel the kind of gross bureaucratic planning which they had long advocated in principle.

Despite the voluminous lip service paid to the principle of "expertise" in government by the imperialist groups, the leading members of the movement remained amateurs themselves, politicians, and their strategies were dominated always by political considerations. Thus, the attack on the stagnation which nearly all parties felt was occurring became for them an attack directed against the political leadership which in their minds represented the old and failing system. The corollary attitude of the Social-Imperialists regarding the rise of the Socialist movement sprang also from their political approach to the problem of remodernization. Perhaps the strongest bond linking the Tariff Reform section of the movement with the Fabian and Radical side was the conviction that, unless they were able to wrest control from the party leadership, it would only be a matter of time before the growing Labour-Socialist forces did. Social-Imperialism was deliberately composed as the *alternative* method of guiding the necessary reconstruction of society to that offered by the Left. They were both aware of the example of Bismarck and the German Socialists in this regard. Of course, the necessary imperative in perceiving their role in this light was that they were thus constrained to counter the Socialist argument (which was shared by a great many non-Socialists in England) that the solution to the nation's problems lay in the direction of increased democratization of the society. Unfortunately, the same notion tended to progressively dampen the reformist element in the movement, eventually even to make Lloyd George seem merely a mouthpiece of reaction. But that was a trap he dug for himself by taking always the narrow political view.

There were strong Catonist and reactionary undertones in Social-Imperialist propaganda, but it cannot be said that the English Social-Imperialist was a reactionary in the usual sense; on questions like reform of the House of Lords, the taxation of nonproductive land, and the reform of patronage and "careers open to talent," they were rarely, and most often reluctantly, defenders of traditional privilege. Their opposition to the process of democratization tended to focus not so much on arresting social movement from below as on heading off the apparent polarization towards increasing class consciousness and rigidity at one end and unproductive wealth, privilege, and idleness at the other. That was their general social prognosis unless the system of laissez-faire capitalism and progressive political democracy which had accompanied the rise of the present ruling elite were brought under rational, efficient control. With the exception of the Fabians, whose attitudes about mass democracy had become deeply cynical during this period, the advocates of the coalition and of National Efficiency bore noticeable populist inclinations, including the conviction that there existed a great mass of discontent, comparable to their own, which felt caught between a rising tide of ungovernable, class-conscious laborers and complacent, self-indulgent nabobs.

The petit bourgeois Milner and Lloyd George together embodied that discontent as well as the instinct for seeking out the language to which such social resentment and frustration would respond—in Milner's case, the almost total incapacity to attract popular affection was largely offset by the formidable talents of Garvin and Carson in that direction. It must be said that their vision of the social strata which they hoped to mobilize was never very distinct or consistent in their minds—Milner usually searching abstractly for the "patriotic working man," as elusive as the missing link until the disruptions of 1916-1917, while Lloyd George shuttled between Whitechapel and the "cities of dreadful knights," the acquisitive captains of industry who first met him at the Board of Trade and returned like mercenary cavalry to rescue (and embarrass) him in the last year of the war.

Although it is not yet possible to speak categorically about the social bases of the coalition, some general features are apparent. It has been suggested in other analyses of the counterrevolutionary and imperialist movements of this period in the rest of Europe that these forces drew upon and attempted to mobilize the "crisis strata" produced by rapid modernization in the various societies. Among those included in this category most often are elements of the nobility and gentry, small shopkeepers, "bypassed" manufacturers and artisans, fixed-income groups like retired officers, civil servants, and pensioners, marginal farmers, status-hungry intellectuals, and the "new middle classes" who are presumed to be undergoing a kind of cultural shock associated with social mobility, a kind of pathology exhibited, for example, in the politics of the California middle classes.

Given the relatively advanced stage of English development by this period, the same pattern appears to me to be appropriate to England with some modifications: the residue of the preindustrial society was both relatively smaller, more homogeneous, and more successfully adapted than in the later modernizers; the nobility was both less cohesive and less agrarian in its economic base than elsewhere; and both the army and the bureaucracy maintained their status more through their imperial than through their domestic role. It must be added that some of these groups in English society displayed differences in their *internal* makeup and consciousness from their continental counterparts, characteristics and relationships such as those of the so-called "black-coated worker" which suggest comparison more with the *déclassé* of postwar Europe than with the bypassed classes of the old regime.

On the whole, I have found that this model is both applicable and useful in discerning at least the parameters of the social base to which the Social-Imperialist insurgents appealed. The most significant variations from the German case are, I think, better understood as differences due to timing rather than to basic dissimilarities in the structure and culture of the two societies. It need hardly be said at this point that the "crisis of democracy" which has been the central theme of European history in the first half of the twentieth century was not a phenomenon restricted to the late modernizers like Germany, Russia, and Japan, although it is still argued that that crisis "had to" produce totalitarian forms of one sort or another in those societies while the older democracies eventually survived. Whatever the merits of that analysis, it is clear that the more advanced capitalist democracies of the west also faced closely related forms of internal crisis in the generation preceding the First World War and that, whatever the strategy of the political leaders, the war either postponed or offered the means for its resolution.

At the political level, the leaders of what Wells called the "secure generations" fared rather badly from the war while the "successor elites" of the Right in the western democracies largely succeeded in their main aim of "drawing the teeth" of incipient revolution. After the fall of Lloyd George, the currency of Social-Imperialist ideas rapidly diminished in politics. But for all intents and purposes the movement's goals had been achieved—the Victorian political elite had been dethroned (perhaps it would be fairer to say diluted) without resort to civil war, the democratic tide had been held back long enough to allow for the *embourgeoisement* of the Labour Party, so that by the mid-twenties the bastion of "MacBaldwinism" stood squarely in the crossroads between revolution and reaction.

I

Liberal-Imperialism

The Rosebery Revolt

"People talk much of the decay of Liberalism," Leonard Trevelyan Hobhouse mourned in 1904. By that date the once triumphant party of Gladstone had been denied office, but for the futile interlude of 1892-1895, for nearly twenty years. Gloomier still for the heirs of Gladstone was the fact that with the debacle over the war in South Africa the party had lost even the solace of unity in opposition. The influential imperialist minority led by the former Prime Minister, the Earl of Rosebery, disdained association with either the Radical "pro-Boer" or the moderate critics of the war, invoking as justification the higher loyalty to patriotism and the empire as above parties.[1]

The title "Liberal-Imperialist," which distinguished those Liberal Members of Parliament who supported the government's policy in South Africa in 1899, had been revived by Rosebery from a term coined fifteen years earlier. As a student at Christ Church and in his first years as a Liberal M.P., Rosebery had attached himself to the imperialist spirit when it was still expansive, when empire and emigration seemed to possess the sanction not only of the economic interests of all classes and of national vitality but even of Christian philanthropy. The word had not yet acquired its pejorative usage. Rosebery described himself as "a Liberal who believes that the Empire is best maintained on the basis of the widest democracy."[2] Liberal-Imperialism thus shared much in principle with

---

[1] Leonard Trevelyan Hobhouse, *Democracy and Reaction* (London, 1904), p. 2.

[2] The term "Liberal-Imperialism" was apparently coined by the press in 1885 and accepted by Rosebery as a proper description of his views; see Rosebery's speech at Sheffield (20 October 1885); also John Roach, "Liberalism and the Victorian Intelligentsia," *Cambridge Historical Journal*, XIII, no. 1 (1957), 58 sqq.

other "parties above parties," such as the Primrose League, which sought, by identifying imperial aspirations with the patriotism and welfare of the masses, to draw on the strength of nationalism for the empire.

J. A. Hobson was among the first at the time to mark the tendency of nationalism and imperialism to mingle, but he noted also the inherent antagonism of the two forces.[3] This contradiction became fully manifest during the Boer conflict. The European nation state, as has often been remarked, is not the best foundation on which to build an empire. The consent and cultural solidarity at the root of its law is not readily expanded, as was Roman law, to assimilate subject peoples without lethal danger to its constitution, particularly if that constitution is democratic. As George Orwell learned as a member of the Burmese police, when the white man turns tyrant over subject races it is his own freedom that he destroys—"He wears a mask and his face grows to fit it."[4]

The inherent and ominous flaw in Rosebery's "Empire . . . maintained on the basis of the widest democracy" would not become fully visible until the process of imperial expansion gave way to the problem of assimilation. While the war in South Africa lasted, the imperialists spoke as of old and succeeded in gathering wide patriotic support. But a fundamental change of principle had taken place. The policy of Chamberlain and Milner in the Cape was not primarily expansive but defensive. Moreover, as orthodox Liberals, Radicals, and Socialists were quick to point out, it could no longer be portrayed as a defense of the interests of all classes in the nation at home—not while the Colonial Office and the governor in the Cape were widely pictured as no more than willing instruments of the Rand mine owners and City financiers. Radical accusations on this score were persistent and unrestrained as the war dragged on, with Lloyd George's infuriating eloquence intoning the lead.[5]

The necessity of answering Radical charges pressed most heavily on just those imperialists of both parties who had all along held the empire above class and party as a kind of transcendent interest

[3] J. A. Hobson, *Imperialism: A Study*, p. 9.

[4] George Orwell, "Shooting an Elephant," in *The Collected Essays, Journalism and Letters of George Orwell* (New York, 1968), I, 239; originally published in *New Writing*, no. 2 (Autumn 1936).

[5] A good example of the pro-Boer charges can be seen in Lloyd George's indictment in the *Daily Chronicle*, 6 July 1899; see also Hannah Arendt, *The Origins of Totalitarianism* (New York, 1960), pp. 126-153.

cementing domestic unity. They had also to salvage somehow the popular glitter, or at least the innocuousness, of the word "imperialism" itself as its connotation became increasingly tainted in African intrigues and scandals.[6] Political idealism, high-mindedness, selfless and ennobling service, patriotism, and the democratic impulse of English Liberalism were the virtues upon which the imperialist catechism drew, the ethos which had sustained that class of men who filled the civil services and parliamentary seats since the Reform Bill. The pro-Boer slings thus appeared to assault not merely a policy but a whole political culture. Faced with the dismaying revelations of the war—incompetence, self-interest, and concentration camps—and the increasingly strident criticism of the Left, new avenues to popular support and new ideological justifications were sought by an important segment of the more dynamic and generally younger imperialists of both parties. Rosebery's Liberal League on the one side and, later, Joseph Chamberlain's Tariff Reform League on the other, first sought to find such a departure through the doctrine of Social-Imperialism. They were, as Lenin noted as early as 1916, the "leading bourgeois politicians" who first comprehended the connection between the purely economic and the "social-political roots" of modern imperialism.[7]

The attempt to recast the image and ideology of imperialism was carried on within the Liberal and Unionist parties by factions which were not in control of the official party machinery but strongly aspired to be. Consequently, in the internal fractures which distracted both parties between the Boer War and the Liberal victory of 1905, there was also an element of the prosaic wrangle for leadership and office in the campaigns waged by the leagues. It was particularly true on the Liberal side during the war, for there the conflict was greatly exacerbated by the personal rancors existing between imperialist and Radical leaders, the growing importance of the Labour-Socialist wing, and the presence of an eloquent former Prime Minister at the head of the disaffected.

Rosebery had returned from a political retirement which had been forced upon him by Lord Harcourt and the National Liberal Federation in order to support the Unionist government's policy

[6] See Richard Koebner, "The Concept of Economic Imperialism," *Economic History Review*, ser. 2, II, no. 1 (1949), 1-29, for a description of the changing connotations of the word up to Hobson's thesis.

[7] V. I. Lenin, *Imperialism: The Highest Stage of Capitalism*, 2nd ed. (New York, 1934), p. 41.

at Fashoda in 1898. On that occasion, and in the Boer crisis which arose a year later, he was able to draw heavily from the Liberal ranks in support of the imperial position, coming quite close (shortly before the "Khaki Election" of 1900) to winning over a majority of the party. The first formal split in the Liberal Party in Parliament occurred shortly thereafter, in July 1900, over a proposed censure of the Unionist government. Sir Wilfred Lawson, who put the motion, was supported by thirty-one pro-Boers, while Sir Edward Grey, leading the Liberal-Imperialists in the House together with Herbert Asquith and Richard Burton Haldane, drew off forty Liberal members into the government lobby to defeat the measure. The moderate and undecided bulk of Liberal M.P.'s (106) abstained, anxious to forestall a final split.[8]

The favorable division on the Lawson resolution encouraged the more sanguine of Rosebery's supporters to attempt unseating the Liberal Party leadership on the war issue. Haldane, a devoted admirer and always the most forward of the group, tried to persuade Rosebery to this course at once:

> . . . if you choose to emerge [he wrote] and lead those Liberals who may be called 'Lord R.'s friends' with Asquith *and* Grey as lieutenants in the House I think this will work out. . . . *We* have the machinery *and* the Whigs *and* the future, *and* this means that we grow *and* become the party.[9]

Although Haldane greatly exaggerated their prospects, it seemed a propitious moment for some decisive action if the Liberal-Imperialists hoped to convert their temporary advantage into actual control of the party. This was Haldane's hope. But, as the large abstention on the Lawson motion showed, there was by no means a consensus even in the generally prowar faction to go to the extreme of splitting the party.[10]

---

[8] Although Asquith himself joined Grey against the motion of censure, both he and Campbell-Bannerman urged the bulk of the moderates to abstain; House of Commons, 25 July 1900.

[9] Cited in Robert Rhodes James, *Rosebery: A Biography of Archibald Philip Primrose, 5th Earl of Rosebery* (London, 1963), pp. 416-417. All italics are in the original unless otherwise noted.

[10] The *Times* (London) estimated the prowar Liberal-Imperialist faction at 81 of the 177 Liberal M.P.'s. Less than half, therefore, may be said to have supported Haldane's more extreme view. *Times*, 6 Nov. 1900.

Moreover, on this early occasion and more critical ones to come, Rosebery displayed a marked tendency to be hard to reach at the critical moment. Even to his most enchanted supporters his political behavior was a puzzle. In a manner which could both inspire and irritate, he exuded the consciousness of being an exceptional man, what he himself might call "a man of acute angles." His highly visible independence, sustained by a great name and fortune, merely exaggerated the ideological image he had projected, in the style of other great eminences in politics, of a man incapable of taking the small view. Naturally, it was the men who did the day-to-day work of keeping the party together who were irritated by the Rosebery *hauteur* and those who despised the discipline of party organization who were inspired.

Among his other obvious gifts Rosebery was an industrious and occasionally brilliant biographer. It would also seem that something of his attitude regarding routine party affairs is suggested in the subjects of his biographical writings: Pitt, Peel, Randolph Churchill, and Napoleon (*The Last Phase!*)—a little of Achilles in them all. Inclined to complain of his tools, he found it difficult either to retire or to return to combat unreservedly. He was, as his closest friend remarked, "not steadfast and unmovable, but unmovable without being steadfast." Such was the character of his response to Haldane's ardent persuasion: "Politics may possibly come to me," he wrote, "but I shall not go to them."[11]

The condition which appeared to favor the Rosebery faction in 1900 nearly evaporated with the government victory at the October elections, in which the Roseberites were inevitably cast in an ambiguous role between the pro-Boers and the Unionists. Furthermore, Sir Henry Campbell-Bannerman, whose personal relations with the Liberal-Imperialists were rapidly worsening, soon after brought over the large moderate center of the party in support of a pro-Boer demand for immediate negotiations in South Africa, thereby leaving the circle of Rosebery's friends a relatively small, though highly distinguished, minority.[12]

[11] Cited in R. R. James, *Rosebery*, pp. 417-419. The description of Rosebery was Sir Thomas Wemyss Reid's.

[12] The National Liberal Federation, the "machinery" which Haldane supposed the Liberal-Imperialists controlled, also passed a moderately pro-Boer peace resolution in December (*Daily News*, 22 Dec. 1900); and again the following June (House of Commons, 17 June 1901). See Halévy's account in *History of the English People in the Nineteenth Century* (London, 1961), VI, 108.

The more ambitious hopes harbored by Haldane were clearly futile after the election and Campbell-Bannerman's emergence as majority Opposition leader. Yet the imperialists neither left the party nor submitted to the now established lead of Campbell-Bannerman. Instead, in February of 1902 they formed the Liberal League which, like the Tariff Reform League and the numerous other extraparliamentary imperialist organizations which appeared at this time all over Europe, had as its original aim the conversion or "permeation" of established parties rather than an overt attack on the leadership or the acquisition of office. Needless to say, however, the leaders of the political parties still had cause to fear the emergence of the leagues.

At the time the Liberal League was founded, the issue dividing the party was still ostensibly South Africa and the question of supporting the government's policy on the war there—including its position on the terms of peace. But as an end to the war came slowly into sight there was increasingly little practical substance in this difference. From the first Campbell-Bannerman had favored, along with conciliation, the annexation of the Boer republics. Even Lloyd George was not opposed to this course. It was also the position of the Rosebery group.[13] The remaining differences on the issue were matters of execution, not of principle.

What then estranged the Liberal-Imperialists from the rest of the party? They disagreed in general on the question of Home Rule for Ireland, but from that Liberal sore they were enjoying a brief respite. The most eminent historian of the period, Elie Halévy, has suggested that at bottom the divisive questions concerned neither the Boers nor the Irish but rather the European policy to be pursued by Liberals after the peace.[14] The German threat and the debate over European alliances did eventually become, as we shall see, a predominant theme in the Liberal League's propaganda. It might even be said that at length the league became obsessed with this single issue. But, in the platform which the Liberal-Imperialists sought to develop with the founding of the league, there was reflected a concern less specific but closer to home.

[13] R. R. James, *Rosebery*, pp. 427-428. Rosebery suggested the initiation of secret talks with Kruger as a first step towards a settlement. He stated the Liberal-Imperialist position, including annexation and full political rights for Boers, in his speech at Chesterfield (16 Dec. 1901).

[14] Halévy, *History*, VI, 110.

Rosebery and the Fabians

A rather vague sense of crisis, much heightened by the public humiliation of the war, marked the utterances of the insurgents of both Right and Left during the last year of the war. Diplomatic isolation, the vehement criticism of the foreign press during the war, and the emergence of American power in Latin America and the Pacific pointed up the presence of larger and younger nations—the United States and Germany in particular—as economic and possibly military rivals in the future. Studies, graphs, and learned prophecies, reinforced by the new authority of social science and statistics, persistently argued the growing superiority of German and American industry, agriculture, and administration; the decline in Britain's birth rate, the degenerating influence of urban slums, prospects of increased unemployment, and endless other proofs of impending collapse filled the journals and tracts of the war years and after.[15] It was a mood which put a timorous gloss on the old text of expansion and progress.

The campaign of Rosebery's dissident group was premised on the existence of this ubiquitous threat of national decline. Its very indefiniteness made for a heterodox appeal which attracted not only some of the most promising Liberal politicians of the day but also a good representation of younger Conservatives and of such new lights in the social and political sciences as W. A. S. Hewins, Halford J. Mackinder, and the Fabians. Rosebery himself maintained a dilettante's interest in the new rigorous methods being applied to social questions and had had some exposure to the work of the Webbs while serving as chairman of the London County Council a few years before, at the time when Sidney Webb was its most vocal member. Asquith, Grey and, more intimately, Haldane had been acquainted socially with the Webbs for several years, but

---

[15] For a sample of the most frequently cited wartime studies by contemporary "experts," see A. W. Flux, "British Trade and German Competition," *Economic Journal*, vol. VII (1899); J. W. Cross, "British Trade in 1898, A Warning Note," *Nineteenth Century and After* (May 1899); Sir Robert Giffen, "The Excess of Imports," *Journal of the Royal Statistical Society*, vol. LXII (March 1899). Arnold White's *Efficiency and Empire* (London, 1901) was the work most often mentioned by the imperialist groups and the Fabians and had a particularly strong impact on Rosebery and the platform of the Liberal League. See also Donald Macrae, *Ideology and Society* (New York, 1958), pp. 21-22.

did not display a practical interest in the Fabians' projects until the latest split began to develop in the Liberal Party. In fact, the first sign that the Liberal-Imperialists' interest in Fabianism had progressed beyond table talk was made by Rosebery himself in his response (in December 1900) to George Bernard Shaw's *Fabianism and the Empire: A Manifesto of the Fabian Society*, stating the position of the proimperial faction of the Fabian Society which had also become divided on the war question.[16]

After writing several notes of praise to the author of the *Manifesto*, Rosebery directed Haldane to arrange a meeting with the Fabians. The fact that the Socialist society had now become an outspokenly imperialist organization, shorn of its orthodox Socialist and Radical elements, certainly made Rosebery's association with its leaders more palatable than previously. The society had always represented a variety of views and had always included highly independent men among its membership, held fragilely together by the very general principles of "collectivism" and expertise on social questions. The split of December, however, had sheared off its most politically aggressive spirits, like Ramsay MacDonald and J. A. Hobson, and most of the union and Radical members, leaving control of the rump in the hands of Shaw and the Webbs. Their ostensible policy was, like the Liberal League's, "above parties." But perhaps more important still in Rosebery's mind was the unmistakable lesson of the past few months, that the position of the Center during a crisis was a constantly diminishing one without a distinct and constructive policy or ideology. Liberalism, Rosebery felt, was being "squeezed out between Socialism and Conservatism," and seemed destined to fall victim to the growing political polarization unless radical renovations were made in its guiding principles.[17]

The Fabians' imperialist *Manifesto* held out the possibility of attracting the best elements from all political circles, that is, from all patriotic-imperialist circles, by combining a strong imperial policy and a dynamic but nonrevolutionary social reform program, thus laying the foundation for what has come to be called a policy of

[16] A poll was taken in the society on the basis of Shaw's prowar speech at Clifford's Inn Hall (23 Feb. 1900), leaving Shaw and the Webbs with a commanding majority. Hobson, Ramsay MacDonald, and the bulk of the radical and union members resigned. Beatrice Webb, "Diary" (9 Dec. 1900), *P.P.*

[17] B. Webb, "Diary" (9 Dec. 1900), *P.P.*; E. T. Raymond, *The Man of Promise: Lord Rosebery* (London, 1923), p. 198; Marquis of Crewe, *Lord Rosebery* (London, 1931), II, 596.

"Social-Imperialism."[18] The predilections of Rosebery and the Fabians in this direction were of a somewhat different origin from the body of thought usually given this name, but overlapped with it at many points. The attempt on the part of the Roseberites to develop a policy of Social-Imperialism at this time also bears a resemblance to the several previous Tory campaigns to find a popular ideological base for imperialism and closely paralleled the direction of the Tariff Reform crusade soon to be launched by Joseph Chamberlain.

Rosebery and the Fabians shared with Chamberlain and his ardent young Unionist disciples three guiding convictions: first, that the prosperity and security of the nation faced immediate peril in the apparent weakening of the empire; second, that somehow the means of meeting that peril lay in a new dynamic approach by imperialists to problems of domestic organization, reform, and planning; and third, that if the lead in this field were left to the muddling incompetence of the old guard of either great party, the political advantage would fall only to the Radical and Socialist Left. It was the presence of these same anxious convictions in the literature of the new imperial Fabianism that attracted both party rebels to them. The only question, as Shaw wrote in the *Manifesto*, was whether Britain would be the "nucleus of one of the world empires of the future" or whether, through complacency and moribund doctrines, it would stupidly lose its colonies and "be reduced to a tiny pair of islands in the North Sea."[19]

Fabian pessimism regarding the future of the empire accompanied an equally gloomy view of the state of things at home, as is evident from the following entry from the loquacious diary of Beatrice Webb:

> To us [the plural is standard form in her diary] public affairs seem gloomy; the middle-classes are materialistic, and the working class stupid, and in large sections sottish, with no interest except in racing odds. . . . And, meanwhile the rich are rolling in wealth and every class, except the sweated workers, has more than its accus-

[18] Bernard Semmel's excellent series of cameo studies in *Imperialism and Social Reform* convincingly argues that such a coherent body of thought existed in the period. But, as some critics have pointed out, his work leaves open the question about whether or not Social-Imperial thought had any discernible influence in Edwardian politics. See Semmel's definition on p. 71 *et passim*.

[19] G. B. Shaw, *Fabianism and the Empire* (London, 1900), pp. 3-4.

tomed livelihood. Pleasure and ease are desired by all men and women: science, literature and art, even social ambition and party politics have given way to the love of mental excitement and physical enjoyment. If we find ourselves faced with real disaster, should we as a nation have the nerve and persistency to stand up against it? That is the question that haunts me.[20]

Among their many busy enterprises, the Webbs had long cultivated that section of the Liberal Party including Haldane, Grey, and Asquith, which fell in behind Rosebery's revolt. These, according to an estimate made by the Webbs several years earlier while Rosebery was with the London County Council, were some chief examples of promising political leaders "deemed to be permeated with Fabianism."[21] In fact, Haldane confided to his Fabian friends before the Boer dispute that they had even "captured Rosebery for collectivism"—though this was partly effusion from Haldane's hyperbolic imagination. The almost passionate intriguing of Haldane had kept the Fabians in close touch with the inner feuds and what he at least felt to be the temper of the Liberal Party through the years in opposition. By February 1902 Beatrice Webb noted with something still short of enthusiasm, "We are at present very thick with the Limps." And when Rosebery at last seemed primed to challenge the Liberal leadership, it was mainly through Haldane's advocacy that Fabian support was to be enlisted.[22]

Rosebery's request through Haldane for a meeting with the Webbs was the first occasion on which he had shown any more than a detached interest in Fabian ideas *per se* or in any form of political cooperation beyond the level of municipal government. Although a meeting did take place shortly after the appearance of the *Manifesto* in December (unfortunately what passed between the participants has not been recorded), it was not immediately followed by further contact on that side. Rosebery's interest was apparently momentary in this first instance, inspired by the language of the *Manifesto* which seemed to embellish the theme he himself was currently stressing in his speeches: practical social reform combined with a consolidating and conciliatory imperial policy.[23] The *Manifesto*, warning of the dire consequences of a collapse in the

[20] B. Webb, "Diary" (31 Jan. 1900), *P.P.*
[21] Ibid.
[22] B. Webb, *Our Partnership* (New York, 1948), pp. 114-115; B. Webb, "Diary" (28 Feb. 1902), *P.P.*
[23] See Rosebery's speech at Glasgow (16 Nov. 1900), cited in R. R. James, *Rosebery*, p. 419; Crewe, *Lord Rosebery*, p. 594.

empire, also echoed his own rather gloomy mood about the future and offered an available and urgently needed complement to his still skeletal understanding of a Social-Imperialist policy. After losses among his supporters in the October elections he had only the unhappy practical choices of a permanent retirement, or of desertion to the Unionist side where the imperialist faction was a good deal stronger, or of drawing off what imperial elements he could into a separate organization (perhaps even a separate party). The latter project, as was obvious from the election results, would be doomed to failure without the force of a distinct and bold domestic program beyond imperialism alone; this, his lieutenants assured him, the Fabians were prepared and at length eager to contribute.

The dispute which developed in the Liberal Party between pro-Boers and the Roseberites coincided closely with the division of the Fabian Society over the same issue. A poll of the heterodox Fabian membership in February 1900, to decide on the imperial question, left the Shaw-Webb prowar faction in control. With the split went most of the society's sympathetic links with the Socialist labor movement, not to be restored until fifteen years and another far more shattering war had intervened. On the other hand, out of the dispute came Shaw's imperialist tract and a door temptingly opened by Rosebery to the highest circles of proven influence and power. At the time, it seemed a favorable exchange for the advocates of permeation.[24]

Rosebery appeared to have committed himself to political action of some kind in a series of public addresses earlier in 1900 denouncing his Liberal colleagues with caustic eloquence. After the first contact had been made with the Fabians, he had even begun to frost these speeches with gleanings from Shaw and Webb regarding imperial organization and the application of method and expertise in domestic social policy.[25] In accordance with their established policy, the Fabians demanded no public credit for the use

[24] The question voted upon in a mail ballot of the national membership of the Fabian Society was phrased by Shaw and Sidney Webb, asking the members simply to condemn or to refrain from condemning the government's war policy. The objections of the pro-Boer members about this procedure contributed to their decision to resign. The results of the poll, however, did allow Shaw to give it a much stronger prowar reading in the *Manifesto* than the wording of the question justified. B. Webb, *Our Partnership*, p. 203; Semmel, *Imperialism and Social Reform*, p. 69.

[25] Rosebery's speeches at Bath (27 Oct. 1900), Chatham (23 Jan. 1900), and Glasgow, already cited. Halévy, *History*, VI, 100.

of their nostrums. Following the same precedent, the Webbs did not at first respond to the Liberal-Imperialist campaign with open support, despite Haldane's industrious liaisons. They were still reluctant to jeopardize remaining Radical and Socialist good will in open association with a man widely mistrusted by the Left and, indeed, looked upon with increasing misgivings by those Liberals outside his own imperialist circle. On the other hand, Beatrice Webb did confess to being attracted by the prospect of writing the domestic side of a Liberal-Imperialist political platform should they actually enter candidates for office.[26]

Remaining true for the moment to the policy of nonpartisan permeation, Beatrice Webb admitted that it suited the Fabian Society better not to fall in with either side of the Liberal argument so as to get whatever hearing they could from both for their collectivist projects. Beatrice Webb and Shaw, who clearly dominated Fabian strategies at this time, were inclined to this course not only by principle but by personality. They were disdainful of politicians of all sorts and always preferred to see themselves in the role of manipulators, movers rather than actors. But the growing polarization of the Liberal faction following the elections divided the now openly imperialist Fabian Society as much as it had the Roseberites from their radical allies. Relations with the Socialists of the Independent Labour Party, with whom they had joined in forming the Labour Representation Committee the previous year, had been strained for several years by Shaw's impromptu sarcasms and the Webbs' pointed indifference to "abstract Economics." The ballot on the war and the resignations which followed, the largest number ever recorded over any issue in the Fabian Society, had merely recognized the basic ideological incompatibility with the Socialists which had existed from the beginning.[27] The consequence for the society was diminished interest among remaining members, at least on the larger questions, and a shortage of funds. In a sense, the "apolitical" Shaw-Webb faction had finally won its point in Fabian tactics by detaching the society from politics; that is, from Socialist and union politics. Moreover, in July of 1901, after months of temporizing, Rosebery finally gave indications of taking the active lead urged upon him by his admirers. In a widely circulated address to

---

[26] B. Webb, "Diary" (9 Dec. 1900), *P.P.*

[27] Eighteen Socialist and Radical members who had formerly served in the Fabian executive resigned after the poll. Margaret Cole, *The Story of Fabian Socialism* (Stanford, 1961), pp. 92-100; *Fabian News* (Dec. 1900).

the City Liberal Club, the former Prime Minister mixed a curious blend of conciliation towards the Radicals, on the subject of a negotiated settlement with the Boers, with a sweeping denunciation of the home policy of Gladstonian Liberalism, raising in particular the contentious matter of Home Rule for Ireland. The speech was his bill of divorce from the party. He had spoken, he declared, from *outside* the Liberal "tabernacle."[28]

Sidney Webb had been urged by Haldane, Grey, and Asquith to attend the address which was to signal the long-awaited break with the Radicals. "We are fighting for our lives," Haldane turgidly protested when Sidney Webb declined to commit himself even to this extent. For Sidney Webb, pro-Boer in sentiment but bound by Fabian practicality to the rationale of Shaw's *Manifesto*, it was something of a dilemma. And he was, as usual, busy with his work. Except on rare occasions, his regard for party politics was like that of the stagehand for the play: it was all rather puzzling and probably irrelevant. Beatrice was less indifferent.

> If Lord R. really means business [she wrote commenting on the address], really intends to come forward with a strong policy, then he has done his lieutenants a strong service by stepping boldly out of the ranks of an absolute Liberalism. . . . R. is bound by no ties and can do the necessary work of the iconoclast of the Gladstonian ideals . . . Whether or not he is to become a real leader depends on whether he has anything to put in the place of a defunct Liberalism. Mere Imperialism will not do: that the other side have. Now supposing he fails, as I think he will fail, to be constructive, then he leaves the field open to Asquith, Grey and Haldane with a good deal of the rubbish cleared away.[29]

Beatrice Webb's remarks show that she at least harbored few illusions about the likelihood of actual political success in any alliance with Rosebery—an attitude which reflected not only her natural cynicism but also a good deal more realism in her than in some of the professionals of Rosebery's group. From the start, Beatrice Webb looked upon a projected association with the Liberal-Imperialists (at least while Rosebery led them) primarily as an additional vehicle for collectivist propaganda and only distantly as a possible avenue to office and power; in principle, however, she

---

[28] Rosebery, "Address to the City Liberal Club," *Times*, 23 July 1901.
[29] B. Webb, "Diary" (9 July, 26 July 1901), *P.P.*

was not indifferent to the latter prospect. With some further prodding from Shaw to plunge in with Lord Rosebery's revolt "as the best chance of moulding home 'policy,'" reinforced by "occasional suggestions" from Beatrice, Sidney Webb began work on an article entitled "Lord Rosebery's Escape from Houndsditch," which was to put the Fabians' endorsement officially on the revolt.[30]

The main thrust of the article, which was published a little more than a month after Rosebery's City Liberal Club speech, was towards broadening Rosebery's attack on the Liberal Party to a general denunciation of "Gladstonian Individualism" as represented by Harcourt and Campbell-Bannerman. The "political force of the old Liberalism is spent.... Its worship of individual liberty evokes no enthusiasm," Webb argued. Not only was the old laissez-faire orthodoxy obsolete in the twentieth century but actually "reactionary" in its resistance to "the higher organization of that greatest of co-operative societies, the State itself...."[31]

Sidney Webb had been well rehearsed in debunking the Gladstonian straw man in previous *Fabian Tracts*. But something of a new twist was added in the current attack in line with the new imperial tone of the Fabian Society and with the sentiments of the Roseberites. This was accomplished in a manner which significantly anticipated the language of the Tariff Reform League two years later and which characterized the style of Social-Imperialism for the next decade:

> During the last twenty years or so [Webb wrote] we have become a new people. 'Early Victorian' England now lies, in effect, centuries behind us.... We have become aware, almost in a flash, that we are not merely individuals, but members of a community.... The shopkeeper or the manufacturer sees his property wax or wane ... according to the good government of his city, the efficiency with which his nation is organised, and the influence which his Empire is able to exercise in the councils, and consequently in the commerce, of the world.[32]

With its attack on individualism (an old Fabian bogey, but significantly refined at this time) and its appeal to efficiency and em-

[30] Ibid. (26 July 1901). Sidney's article did not reach the popular press, appearing at first only in *Nineteenth Century and After* (Sept. 1901), a narrowly distributed but intellectually respected monthly.
[31] S. Webb, "Lord Rosebery's Escape from Houndsditch," *Nineteenth Century and After* (Sept. 1901), pp. 366-368.
[32] Ibid., p. 374.

pire (newly added), the "Houndsditch" article set the leading themes of the projected Fabian-Imperialist alliance. As we have seen, the Webbs were sensitive to the costs they would have to pay, were already paying, in influence with their former Socialist and Radical colleagues for their avowal of imperialism. What compensating source of influence could they or their new associates hope to attract with the joint watchwords "efficiency" and "imperialism"? Haldane, devoted almost as much to melodrama as he was to intrigue, expressed himself on the subject to Beatrice Webb. He was intent, writes Beatrice, on "winning the 'Centre,' a term which he always uses as synonymous with the 'non-political voter' —in whose ultimate power we [too] believe. . . ." What Haldane sees, she recalled, "is the moderate politician: the capitalist or proletarian man who desires little social change and the Empire maintained." Beatrice Webb, quite as interested in permeating the leaders of the "Centre," gave a higher priority to reaching the broad base—the "non-political voter." "The class we wish to appeal to," she felt, "is the great lower-middle class and working class, who want change, but don't know in what direction."[33] For the Fabian Society, which reached a maximum of 800 members in these years and had no official role in advancing Socialist candidates after the split, talk of reaching masses of "non-political" voters was a significant departure in policy, particularly since the Khaki Election indicated that such voters would be those imbued with the highly un-Socialist spirit associated with Robert Blatchford and the imperialist press.[34]

It was evident from the election returns also that a conventional appeal from traditional party policies would yield very little support and enthusiasm from the accustomed voters of either of the great parties. Webb expressed the hope in his article, however, that the great mass of voters—the "weavers, teachers, workers, doctors"—were "not thinking of Liberalism, or Conservatism or Socialism. . . ." What was in their minds, he insisted, was not party, increasingly a word of public contempt, but "a burning feeling of

[33] B. Webb, "Diary" (1 Nov. 1901), *P.P.*

[34] Robert Blatchford, a so-called "Barracks Socialist" and ex-noncommissioned officer, was editor of the *Clarion*, the most widely circulated working-class Socialist paper before 1914. His paper was one of the most vehemently critical opponents of the new Labour Party; see Semmel's chapter on "Lord Roberts and Robert Blatchford," *Imperialism and Social Reform*, pp. 208-225.

shame at the failure of England—shame for the lack of capacity of its governors, shame for the inability of Parliament to get through even its routine business...."[35]

In this argument, Webb made an ingenious embellishment on a complaint to which Rosebery had given a prominent place in his addresses of the preceding months—the complacent and costly inefficiency of the party system, and of "party government." Rosebery had accumulated many reasons for disliking the workings of the party system which added to his aristocratic disdain for the banality of party affairs. He had never succeeded, he had never tried very hard, in winning the full loyalty of the Liberal organization even as its titular leader and the heir of Gladstone, and had therefore found it easier than his successors to "relegate party controversy to a more convenient season," as he put it. Furthermore, he had been vexed, much like Lloyd George in a like situation fifteen years later, by the "partisan" obstacles he saw put in the way of his service to the nation. He would, he said in a speech in Glasgow, have the War Office, the Admiralty, and even the Foreign Office made "non-political" by staffing them with permanent officials attached to *no* party. He admitted it was a "utopian" aspiration, but he warned that government shackled to the unwieldy and divisive party system was not up to the challenges of the new century:

> The development and expansion of the Empire have produced a corresponding demand for first-rate men, but the supply has remained, at best, stationary. Of course we do not employ all those we have; for, by the balance of our constitution, while one-half our capable statesmen is in full work, the other half is, by that fact, standing idle in the market place, with no one to hire them. This used to be in a five year's shift, but all that is now altered. Anyhow, it is a terrible waste.[36]

Rosebery's unhappiness with the party system was neither new nor momentary. His caustic and repeated attacks on the constitution of the House of Lords, begun as early as 1884, were based on the charge of "inefficiency." He had called it "a sort of legislative hydropathic establishment" at that time—"unrepresentative, bum-

---

[35] S. Webb, "Lord Rosebery's Escape," p. 375.

[36] T. F. G. Coates, *Lord Rosebery, His Life and Speeches* (London, 1900), II, 989; House of Lords, 3 Aug. 1900.

bling, and recalcitrant."[37] The conditions which had given birth to the parties, he wrote in 1898, no longer obtained: "The people are more concerned with men than with measures—men whom they trust rather than measures they espouse. . . . Problems are either becoming too large for parties to deal with, or parties . . . are becoming too weak to deal with them."[38]

Playing upon the blows inflicted on the nation's pride and sense of security by the war, Rosebery and Webb were implicitly agreeing on the outlines of an innovation fundamentally pernicious to the constitution—the reduction of parliamentary control over the ministry through reducing the Cabinet's responsibility to party. This was the portent of the attack on the "party system," an attack which was to be persistently renewed and refined by the "parties above parties" under worsening crises during the next twenty years. Rosebery's remarks not only condoned but proposed to accelerate this process towards bureaucratic independence. In the same Glasgow speech, he cited as worthy models to his countrymen the systems of Prussia or Russia, whose government, he admiringly noted, "is practically unaffected by the life of man or the lapse of time—it moves on, as it were, by its own impetus; it is silent, concentrated, perpetual and unbroken: it is, therefore, successful."[39]

The critique of party and Parliament emanating from the imperialist circles and their suggested renovations were not so much proposals to innovate as they were to guide the process of decontrolling bureaucratic power which was already in progress and already being noted and protested by the Left. J. A. Hobson, one of those who had resigned from the Fabian Society a few months before, was engaged at this moment in writing his famous critique of imperialism.[40] His precocious and influential book, which appeared in print a year after the events we are describing, was not only a seminal economic analysis but an impassioned warning about the domestic political impact of imperialism. The complaints of the im-

---

[37] R. R. James, *Rosebery*, pp. 161, 197.
[38] Ibid., p. 403.
[39] Rosebery, speech at Glasgow (16 Nov. 1900).
[40] The development of the "Front Bench System," as Rosebery's critics called the process of increasing independence of Cabinet ministers, was noted by Hobson, *Imperialism*, pp. 145-148, and by James Bryer, *Studies in History and Jurisprudence* (London, 1901), I, 177. An even more vigorous indictment of the ascendancy of the "Front Bench System" was made some years later in a widely read satire by Hillaire Belloc and Cecil Chesterton, *The Party System* (London, 1911).

perialists, including the Fabian rump, and the waning strength of party he saw as "only the first in a series of processes of concentration of power."[41]

> Representative institutions are ill adapted for empire, either as regards men or methods. The government of a great heterogeneous medley of lower races by departmental officials in London and their nominated emissaries lies outside the scope of popular knowledge and popular control. The Foreign, Colonial, and Indian Secretaries in Parliament, the permanent officials of the departments, the governors and staff who represent the Imperial Government in our dependencies, are not, and cannot be, controlled directly or effectively by the will of the people. This subordination of the legislative to the executive, and the concentration of executive power in an autocracy, are necessary consequences of the predominance of foreign over domestic policies. The process is attended by a decay of party spirit and party action, and an insistence on the part of the autocracy, whether it be a Kaiser or a Cabinet, that all effective party criticism is unpatriotic and verges on treason.[42]

Especially dismayed by the defections from the democratic tradition among Fabians and Liberals, Hobson saw the fragmentation brought on by Rosebery in the context of the surrender of Liberalism to the imperialist tide all over Europe. The majority of influential Liberals had, he said, "fled from the fight which was the truest test of Liberalism in their generation. . . ." Most portentous of all the revelations of the war was the apparent decision of those who had presided over the extension of democratic institutions and the enfranchisement of the masses to prevent those same masses "from gaining the substance of this power and using it for the establishment of equality of economic opportunities."[43] The emergent programs of imperialism combined with social reform was the heart of this effort; for the methods projected for dealing with social problems were to be the same methods of independent bureaucratic control designed to manage the empire. Furthermore, Hobson argued, neither the funds nor the will were present to give equal attention to both. Imperialism, and the military, diplomatic, and financial exigencies which pertained to it, had become the paramount concern of government. These considerations "mould and direct the entire policy, give point, colour and character to the

[41] Hobson, *Imperialism*, p. 148.
[42] Ibid., pp. 145-156.   [43] Ibid., pp. 143-144.

conduct of public affairs, and overawe by continual suggestions of unknown and incalculable gains and perils the nearer and more sober processes of domestic policy." In any doctrine of imperialism and social reform which might emerge from the insurgent imperialist groups, the needs of the former would inevitably and disastrously rule in the absence of a unified and effective opposition from the antiimperialist and democratic forces.[44]

[44] Ibid., p. 147.

II

The Liberal League and the Policy of National Efficiency

While Hobson urged the consolidation of all the political forces opposed to imperialism as the only defense of the party system and democratic institutions, Rosebery and the Fabians had yet to complete the skeleton of a Liberal-Imperialist doctrine. Although the area of agreement established by Webb's "Houndsditch" article of September was still extremely general, favorable signs of response from the Liberal-Imperialists encouraged the Webbs, as Beatrice put it, to "insert the Fabian side."

Beatrice Webb especially was skeptical about how far the Roseberites were prepared to commit themselves in the direction of Fabian collectivism. Nevertheless, it seemed to her a reasonable course in the meantime to build up credit for the future with the most distinguished pool of potential Liberal ministers. "The time will come," she predicted, "if they are to be a political force, [when] they will have to fill up the political worker with some positive convictions. Then we think for the needful minimum of nourishment they will fall back on us and not on the other section" (i.e., the Socialist and Labour section).[1] It was with the aim of exploring the base of such "positive convictions" that Sidney Webb proceeded to redraft and expand the September article as a lecture to be delivered a month later to the Fabian Society and for publication as a *Fabian Tract*, under the title, "Twentieth Century Politics: A Policy of National Efficiency."[2]

[1] B. Webb, "Diary" (1 Oct. 1901), *P.P.*

[2] "Twentieth Century Politics: A Policy of National Efficiency," *Fabian Tract* no. 108 (1901). For an excellent discussion of the "ideology" of National Efficiency, especially as it concerned education and science, see G. R. Searle's *The Quest for National Efficiency*.

In the expanded tract Webb was no longer issuing encouragement to the "iconoclasts" but attempting to impart to the revolt the stature of a dynamic ideological crusade. At the same time, he tried to fill in those deficiencies which he believed would hamper the Liberal-Imperialists in winning wider political and, ultimately, electoral support. Webb outlined a model of patriotic corporate collectivism as the modern alternative to a "decadent" Gladstonian orthodoxy, which as before he employed as the principal bogey. "It is not 'Little Englandism' that is the matter with those who still cling to such views," he wrote, "it is, as Huxley and Matthew Arnold correctly diagnosed, administrative Nihilism." The article was not in the scholarly spirit of the familiar *Fabian Tract*—not a review of school board reform or a study of local government in New Zealand—but put forth, as Webb thought, a discovery "as revolutionary as the discovery of America": that "the ordinary elector, be he workman or manufacturer, shopkeeper or merchant, has lost his interest in individual 'rights,' or abstract 'equality,' political or religious. . . . The freedom that he now wants is not individual but corporate freedom."[3]

Webb repeated the theme of the earlier article, that the "average industrious citizen" burns with shame at the "failure of England," of its governors and its Parliament; but he now made the interesting addition, "shame for the slackness of our merchants and traders that transfers our commercial supremacy to the United States."[4] The Liberal-Imperialists, the great majority of whom were still committed to Free Trade principles, Sidney Webb rightly assumed to be especially responsive to such threatening prognoses of commercial and industrial decline as were daily before their eyes in the popular press and leading journals. Webb was neither the first nor the last to use the new authority of comparative statistics on the subject of economic decline in the assault on Liberal principles of government, but he made a more original contribution to this method of subversion by integrating it into the distinctive Fabian approach to social reform. In an earlier *Fabian Tract*, entitled "The Difficulties of Individualism" (1896), he had argued that the continued reign of laissez-faire doctrine would lead to "the breeding of degenerate hordes of a demoralized 'residuum' unfit for social life" which, if left uncontrolled and untrained, would so drain the

[3] S. Webb, "Twentieth Century Politics," p. 7.
[4] Ibid.

vitality of British industry as to allow the more dynamic younger societies "to take your place in the world's workshop."[5]

In his tract of 1896, Sidney Webb first began to draw upon the arguments and the language of the Social-Darwinists and Neo-Hegelians in developing the concept of "social efficiency," later to blossom into the influential Fabian "National Minimum" program. The concept of "social efficiency" was formulated by Sidney Webb in the context of the "race struggle," integrating Fabian collectivism with the currently esteemed theories of Benjamin Kidd, Karl Pearson, and Bernard Bosanquet. Fabian social analysis and prescription was to be scientific, empirical, and unburdened by sacred shibboleths, in the manner of Darwinist biology and the young science of sociology. The ultimate rationale for the suspension of individual freedoms and the laws of nations preached by Kidd and Pearson was, put simply by Webb, "the lesson of evolution . . . that interracial competition is really more momentous in its consequences than the struggle between individuals." Both the necessity and the sole criterion for aggressive state action, therefore, lay in its insuring to the community "the capacity to hold its own in the race struggle."[6]

Shaw's *Manifesto*, which had originally drawn the attention of Rosebery, had found dispensation for a ruthless amorality in running the empire in the same Social-Darwinist imperative for competitive survival. It appeared to answer the Liberal-Imperialists' need to raise their support of the government's war policy above the sordid commercialism and self-interest with which its critics hotly condemned it. "The world is to the big and powerful by necessity," Shaw had written, "and the little ones must come within their borders or be crushed out of existence." The latter fate, as Shaw was at pains to underline, did not exempt the "tiny North Sea islands."[7] Going a step further, Webb's formula of "social effi-

[5] S. Webb, "The Difficulties of Individualism," *Fabian Tract* no. 69 (1896), p. 17.

[6] *Fabian Tract* no. 69, p. 16. Webb describes the "National Minimum" at length in "The Necessary Basis of Society," *Fabian Tract* no. 159. Kidd's *Social Evolution* (1894) and Bosanquet's *The Philosophical Theory of the State* (1899) were the latest and most influential expressions of a body of opinion which reached prominence in academic political theory and sociology during the late 1890s. See Semmel, *Imperialism and Social Reform*, and John Roach, "Liberalism and the Victorian Intelligentsia."

[7] G. B. Shaw, speech to the Fabian Society (23 Feb. 1900), printed as *Fabianism and the Empire: A Manifesto of the Fabian Society* in December 1900.

ciency" was to provide Liberal-Imperialism with an aura of modern social reformism which the Unionists at the moment notably lacked. The Social-Darwinist theories which the Edwardian generation had been exposed to in the universities and press often served the added function of investing their unorthodox political movements with respectable intellectual lineage.

The Fabians' intent had all along been to influence "Home Policy," the area in which they would command the most authority among their prospective clients in the political parties. Accordingly, what Beatrice Webb called the "Fabian side" of the policy of National Efficiency was presented by Sidney in a wide-ranging six-point program of domestic reorganization and reform. The first three points blueprinted a plan of social "reorganization," under the heading "The National Minimum," a theme which became the cornerstone of Fabian propaganda for the next decade. Sidney Webb recapitulated the program some years later as,

> . . . the formulation and rigid enforcement in all spheres of social activity, of a National Minimum below which the individual, whether he likes it or not, cannot, in the interests of the well-being of the whole, ever be allowed to fall.[8]

The National Minimum concept introduced in the "Houndsditch" article vividly expressed the conflicting strains of bureaucratic coercion and impatient reformism in the Fabian Society at the time. Together with Shaw's imperial *Manifesto*, it provided the general basis for the policy of National Efficiency. In somewhat incongruous fashion, Webb argued for the maintenance of the "National Minimum standard of life," as a necessary means of girding British industry in trade competition. Similarly, Fabian reform in the sweated trades, in sanitation and urban housing, the article continued, would serve a higher national purpose. "How," it asked, "can we build up an effective Commonwealth—how, even can we get an efficient army—out of the stunted, anaemic, demoralised denizens of the slum tenements of our great cities?" For Sidney Webb, who had little passion for the empire, it was a remarkable investment of his impressive reputation in the field of social reform in a baited appeal to the imperialists; his purpose being to tie the

---

[8] *Fabian Tract* no. 159 (1911), pp. 17-18. See also *Fabian Tract* no. 131, "The Decline of the Birth Rate" (1907), for another elaboration of the National Minimum program.

imperialists' concerns—an "effective Commonwealth" and an "efficient army"—to the Fabian domestic program. In his clause on housing, for example, he prescribed "swift and ruthless compulsion" by the Local Government Board to provide "three rooms and a scullery as the minimum necessary for breeding an even moderately Imperial race."[9]

The remaining three points of the program dealt with the War Office, the budget, and Parliament. The first merely reemphasized the generally accepted need, in light of the military muddling in the war, for War Office reforms to introduce "a system of scientific fighting to replace soldiering." It was not one of the fields in which Sidney Webb was expert; as he knew well, however, it was of great interest to Haldane. His last two propositions had more substantial content. On the budget, it was proposed to develop a greater tax yield; first, through streamlining the machinery of collection and administration; second, through a tax on unearned increment in urban land values; and, finally, through a general plan of reassessment. Although Webb's fiscal proposals were couched in the same kind of urgent language which colored the entire article, they were strangely timorous for a collectivist pleading for ruthless austerity in all else. Indeed, his proposed patchwork of existing taxing policies was virtually identical to the reforms gleefully unveiled by the Unionists after the war as a possible method of reducing, or even abolishing, the personal income tax.[10] Neither Rosebery nor Webb, even when decrying the maldistribution of wealth and the ostentation of the upper classes, accepted the use of taxing powers to finance social reform; both opposed the Liberal budgets of 1908-1911 on this principle.[11]

In view of the prevailing attitude towards the imperialists' economic argument among the departed Fabians, especially after the appearance of Hobson's study, it is doubtful that Sidney Webb could have defended this new formula without splintering the society a second time. Their division had by now gone beyond the mere question of supporting or attacking government policy in the Cape to a point where the removal of the war issue would not be enough in itself to reunite the Fabians with the Left. It seems that, once having adopted a strong imperialist position, the Fabians

[9] *Fabian Tract* no. 108 (1901), p. 9.
[10] Ibid., p. 15. See debates on the Unionist postwar budgets, House of Commons, 23 April 1903 and 19 April 1904.
[11] See Webb's *Fabian Tract* no. 69, pp. 5-6.

drifted rather naturally towards a more socially conservative domestic outlook, a pattern which Hobson was first to identify.

The final paragraphs of the article related to Rosebery's well-published grievances against the party system and the inefficiency it promoted in the working of Parliament. Webb made two seemingly modest suggestions in this connection: first, to limit "ordinary speeches" (i.e., "political" speeches) in the House to fifteen minutes; and, second, to accelerate the devolution of parliamentary business to committees. The direction of these schemes was precisely that being noted and protested by the Radicals and Socialists in Parliament at the time—another case of the process which Hobson criticized in which various habits of imperialism were "imported" to the home democracy. It was also the persistent theme of Rosebery's attacks on the inefficiency of the House and obviously tended in the direction of his "non-political" Cabinet, unfettered as much as possible by the power of Parliament and the parties to interfere with and impede the presumably more expert administrators—as many thought the parties had done, for example, with the efforts of the controversial commissioner in the Cape.

The Webbs voiced their contempt for the legislative institution less from the kind of intellectual conceit and unhappy memories which moved Rosebery than from the bias of the bureaucrat-expert *par excellence*; the legislative representative, Beatrice Webb once remarked derisively, served little useful purpose other than "as a 'Foolometer' for the expert."[12] Sidney Webb, who was never given to banter on such serious matters, made an attempt to elaborate a "scientific" framework for the complaint, employing again the murky grammar of evolution to show the advantages of expertly planned administration over the hit-and-miss methods of the elected body:

> . . . the lesson of evolution in social development is the substitution of consciously regulated co-ordination among the units of each organism for the internecine competition; that the production and distribution of wealth, like any other public function, cannot safely be entrusted to the unfettered freedom of individuals, but needs to be organised and controlled for the benefit of the whole community; that this can be imperfectly done by means of legislative restriction and taxation, but is eventually more advantageously accomplished

[12] B. Webb, "Diary" (28 Feb. 1902), *P.P.*; see also S. Webb, *Fabian Tract* no. 69, pp. 5-6.

through the collective enterprise of the appropriate administrative unit in each case; and that the best government is accordingly that which can safely and successfully administer most.[13]

The role to be played by the Fabians in such an administration, and more immediately in the councils of the Liberal-Imperialists, was that of a guiding "Brains Trust" in matters of social organization. Accordingly, Webb elaborated on the rather broadly focused expressions of complaint voiced by Rosebery in his speeches, imparting to them overall a sense of purposeful coherence based on the doctrine of "efficiency" in the national struggle for survival, a precept in which Rosebery had developed an interest some years earlier.[14] Moreover, he followed the general design apparently favored by Rosebery and Haldane of drawing sympathy from all imperial-minded elements of the political spectrum by a call to security and authority on the one hand and ordered social reform on the other. This became the catch-all for most of the "above-party" movements of the coming years.

More than a month passed after the appearance of the article before the Webbs learned whether their efforts to stir Rosebery into some kind of decisive action had been successful. The answer came in a speech made by him at Chesterfield on 15 December 1901. There is no record of any further meeting having taken place between the Liberal-Imperialist leader and the Fabians in the six weeks separating Webb's article and the Chesterfield speech. Nor did Haldane, the open wire between them, appear to have had any notice of the content of his chief's address before it was delivered. Nevertheless, the Chesterfield speech was manifestly designed as an endorsement of the National Efficiency program recently outlined by Sidney Webb.

The speech received unprecedented, and apparently unsolicited, advance publicity in the press—it was a masterpiece, as one later observer put it, of "political puffery."[15] The expectation was of some bold plan for a negotiated settlement of the war, since Rose-

---

[13] S. Webb, *Fabian Tract* no. 108, p. 16.

[14] James, *Rosebery*, p. 403. James notes the appearance of the doctrine of efficiency as a basis of Rosebery's critique of the party system as early as 1898: "Problems are either becoming too large for parties to deal with, or parties are becoming too weak to deal with them" (August 1898).

[15] Raymond, *The Man of Promise*, p. 201.

bery's views in this regard had become well known and such an overture might naturally herald a truce in the Liberal Party as well. Rosebery did indeed put forth a conciliatory plan of negotiation, which in general substance was the settlement finally made in 1902. But the overriding tone of the speech was anything but conciliatory to the regular Liberal Party. From the very first lines, he repudiated the principal tenets of Gladstonian Liberalism, including Home Rule and the Newcastle program. The central theme was a "National Policy of Efficiency" with regard to education, housing, and to "combatting the physical degeneracy of our race," to the military and the war, and most emphatically of all, the workings of the parliamentary machinery. He expanded forcefully on the reasons given in July for his alienation from the party. He could not, he reiterated, trust a party bound to the aims of Irish Nationalism in particular or overall to a doctrine which must drag its archaisms with it into a new and ominously different century:

> There are men [he observed] who sit still with the fly-blown phylacteries of obsolete policies bound round their foreheads, who do not remember that, while they have been mumbling their incantations to themselves, the world has been marching and revolving . . . they must march and move with it too.[16]

Although Rosebery seemed eager to assume the aspect of modernity and progressivism proferred by the Fabians, he warned the impatient "not to move much faster than the great mass of the people are prepared to go." His reference here was interpreted, and was thought by most at the time, to be an objection to his party's espousal of Home Rule for Ireland as a policy for the next Liberal administration, a course which was not noticeably in favor with the electorate. But in its context of "National Efficiency" it could be interpreted, and was by some, as a word of restraint for his more advanced supporters—restraint on Haldane in particular and on the Scottish "Limps," Fowler and Perks, who were straining to launch an autonomous Liberal-Imperialist organization.[17] Obliquely, it also responded to Webb's "ruthless compulsion" in the field of social reform, an area in which he was not backward but clearly

---

[16] Rosebery's speech at Chesterfield (15 Dec. 1901); later published as *L.L.P.* no. 1 (1902).
[17] James, *Rosebery*, p. 438; Lord Crewe, *Lord Rosebery*, pp. 472-473.

less comfortable and adventurous than the Fabians. On the other hand, Rosebery spoke with informed conviction on administrative machinery and foreign policy. The greatest area of agreement between the two lay in their desire to curb the influence of the House in favor of greater administrative independence. Accepting the "National Efficiency" label offered by Sidney Webb, Rosebery argued the point as follows:

> My watchword if I were in office at this moment would be summed up in one single word—the word 'Efficiency.' If we have not learned in this war that we have lagged behind in efficiency we have learned nothing. . . . The first thing you have to look to is the efficiency of your machine—your Parliamentary machine and your legislative machine. They say that Parliament is on its trial, and I am not at all sure that the jury have not left the box and are not now beginning to consider their verdict. I will give you only one instance. The great prerogative and usefulness of the House of Commons lie in its control of the national purse. During the last session of Parliament, for reasons which I dare say were perfectly good, I believe that no less than 76% . . . of all the sums voted by Parliament were closured. Can you have any better argument? If I were to speak for an hour I could not show more utterly and more absolutely the impotence, the ridiculous impotency, to which Parliament has been reduced.[18]

Characteristically, he failed to mention precisely what changes or substitutions he was prepared to recommend. But he was in general accord with Webb's suggestions regarding the devolution of business to committees where, Rosebery argued, such questions as military reform could be submitted to "methodical study and planning" by "the best minds."[19] He did not explicitly credit Webb in the address for the proposals and language of National Efficiency, but the indebtedness was clear to those who heard, most especially to Campbell-Bannerman himself:

> Efficiency as a watchword! [he wrote to Herbert Gladstone] Who is against it? This is all mere *réchauffé* of Mr. Sidney Webb, who is evidently the chief instructor of the whole faction.[20]

[18] Speech at Chesterfield, *L.L.P.* no. 1, p. 3.
[19] Ibid.
[20] Campbell-Bannerman to Herbert Gladstone, 18 December 1901; cited in J. A. Spender, *The Life of the Rt. Hon. Sir Henry Campbell-Bannerman* (London, 1923), II, 4.

To a greater degree than Webb, Rosebery was preoccupied with the war in the Cape and the foreign situation in general, and made more use of popular anxieties on these questions to explain the urgency for domestic innovations. Although he renewed his support for the Milner policy in South Africa, both for the conduct of the war and for the eventual settlement of the Boer republics, he issued a separate criticism of the Unionist government for bringing on "a great crisis in the Nation's history," alluding now not so much to Africa as to Europe, Britain's diplomatic isolation, and the alienation of European public opinion. The timely significance of this criticism lay in the fact that it was made at the height of the great Anglo-German press war which marked the end of Joseph Chamberlain's flirtation with the idea of a Teutonic Alliance. Although the German press attacks were directed originally at Chamberlain and the conduct of the war by the High Commissioner and the Unionist government, the leadership of the anti-German reaction in England was soon taken up unexpectedly by the Liberal-Imperialists.[21]

Rosebery himself, as Foreign Secretary and Prime Minister, had been sensitive to growing German ambitions but, like his Unionist successors, he continued to see the greater threat from Russia and France. (It will be remembered that Rosebery returned to politics over the Fashoda crisis of 1898.) Such, however, was not the feeling of either Grey or Haldane, who joined with that single-minded Germanophobe who edited the *National Review*, Leo Maxse, in public denunciations of the government's seemingly pro-German policy.[22] While attacking Unionist foreign policy on the one hand, the Liberal-Imperialists (rising "above partisanship") manfully de-

[21] Ibid., p. 4. Halévy, *History*, VI, 123-124. The campaign began with a series of letters in the *Times* (3 to 6 Sept. 1901) denouncing German atrocities in the war of 1870-1871. It received further impetus from the extreme reaction in the German press to Chamberlain's Edinburgh speech (23 Oct.), citing precedents of European brutality to extenuate British conduct in South Africa.

[22] Apart from the public utterances of Grey and Haldane, a good part of the anonymous and pseudonymous articles appearing in the *Times*, the *National Review*, and the *Contemporary Review* in the winter of 1901-1902 were originally attributed to Liberal-Imperialists such as Arnold White, A. R. Colquhoun, and Archibald Hurd. See Grey of Falloden, *Twenty-Five Years, 1892-1916* (London, 1923), pp. 52-55; Jacques Bardoux, *Essai du psychologie de l'Angleterre contemporaine*, pp. 108 et seq.; Raymond Sontag, *England and Germany* (New York, 1938), pp. 303, 307; Halévy, *History*, VI, 125n.

fended the Colonial Secretary against the abuses of the German press on the other.

Though he apparently was not yet fully persuaded to their anti-German views, Rosebery did nothing to restrain the public activities of his lieutenants on this score. In fact, the spirit of defending the Colonial Secretary was reasserted in the Chesterfield speech, in which he emphasized the "non-partisan," national appeal:

> I am quite sure [he said, concluding the address] that my policy does not run in Party lines, but it is not to Party that I appeal, I appeal to Caesar—from Parliament with its half-hearted . . . majority for the Government and its distracted and disunited Opposition—I appeal to the silent and supreme tribunal . . . the tribunal of public opinion and common sense. . . . Party in this matter can avail little or nothing.[23]

So far as the status of the Rosebery circle within the Liberal Party was concerned, the Chesterfield speech merely broadened the gulf which had opened in July. Immediately afterward, Grey announced in a letter to Campbell-Bannerman that he now "felt obliged to choose between himself and Rosebery," and had chosen Rosebery. Haldane's resignation followed soon after. Asquith, with the prudence that was at once his outstanding virtue and was to become his gravest political flaw, was anxious to keep a door open for the moderate men, mostly by trying to mollify Rosebery's rigid stand against Home Rule. Failing in this, he shortly followed the lead of Haldane and Grey.[24]

The Liberal League

The break with the old Liberalism and "Little Englandism" had finally and explicitly been made; this time it seemed irrevocable. All now waited for Rosebery's call to arms and his strategy. Except as a last resort, few Liberal-Imperialists were contemplating the stroll across the floor that Chamberlain had taken eighteen years before, only to be shackled by another party caucus, perhaps

[23] Speech at Chesterfield, *L.L.P.* no. 1, p. 16.
[24] Spender, *Life of Campbell-Bannerman*, I, 143.

more devoted to empire and security, but one which had proven even more inert and retarded in its methods. Many of the men who had entered the government lobby on the Lawson resolution had severed friendships and preference in the Liberal Party in the debacle of the past two years and had only to hope for Rosebery's reascendancy for their future position. The remaining course was that implicitly suggested by Webb—the formation of an organization which would enter and finance candidates in the constituencies —that is, a rival political party, though that particular designation was to be judiciously avoided.[25]

In a series of unminuted conclaves at Rosebery's Berkeley Square house during January and February of 1902 such an organization was formed by the small circle of Liberals and Fabians and given the name "Liberal League." Though there was much talk but little practical planning of candidates and financing, general strategy and policy based on the Chesterfield speech were discussed prior to the public announcement of the league. Sidney Webb was present at these "little dinners and informal meetings," but it is evident from the statements of policy which eventually emanated from them that his hopes of making the dissident group an instrument of Fabian reform methods, as expressed in the Houndsditch program, were not on their way to fulfillment. On the contrary, the distinctive collectivist formulas of the Fabians were largely absent from the earliest public pronouncements and publications of the league, which were given over primarily to foreign and imperial policy and conventional protestations against Home Rule and the Food Tax.

The failure of the league to take up immediately the domestic Fabian side of National Efficiency in which Sidney Webb had diligently instructed them brought a quick deflation to the Webbs in their first effort to enter partisan national politics. "If we come to throw our main stream of effort into political life," Beatrice noted after the February meetings with Rosebery, "we shall have to choose our comrades more carefully." Unlike Haldane, Grey, and to a lesser extent Asquith, the Webbs had not attached their political future to Rosebery's straying cart. Beyond the surrender of currency with the Left, whom they had effectively alienated more than a year before on their own initiative, the Fabians had spent but little from their plentiful reserve of energy and ideas. But by March

[25] S. Webb, "Lord Rosebery's Escape," pp. 375-378.

of 1902 Beatrice did feel with some annoyance that these had in fact been wasted:

> Two months of 'sampling' of the Liberal Imperialists has not heightened our estimate of them. Asquith is deplorably 'slack,' Grey is a mere dilettante, Haldane plays at political intrigue and has no principle, Perk [Sir Robert Perks] is an 'unclean beast' and as for Rosebery, he remains an enigma.[26]

Despite the habitual use of the first person plural, Beatrice Webb's personal judgments need not be taken for Sidney's—as a rule, his were more generous. But they were probably in their usual agreement about the character of the league in general:

> As for the rank and file [Beatrice noted in her diary], they are a most heterogeneous lot, bound together by their *dislikes* and not by their positive convictions; they have no kind of faith in any of their leaders and are in constant fear as to their 'political future' and 'personal carcus' [sic]. Having done our best to stimulate the Limps into some kind of conviction and having most assuredly failed we now return to our own work.[27]

It is probable that Haldane's zeal to cultivate a great progressive "Centre" on the German model had led him to overstate the conversion of his Liberal friends to Fabian collectivism. Arising out of the false expectation of success in that conversion, Beatrice Webb's abuse of the group was largely unfair and grossly premature, being leveled before any set policy of the league had grown out of the preliminary discussions in February. She showed little appreciation of the severe limitations of the Limps' position, especially of the small group of M.P.'s around whom the league was formed. In the muster on the Lawson resolution two years earlier Rosebery's men counted a small majority, excluding the large abstention, over the pro-Boers; the prospect of capturing control of the party was even then barely feasible.[28] But by the spring of

[26] B. Webb, "Diary" (28 Feb. 19 March 1902), *P.P.*
[27] Ibid. (19 March 1902).
[28] The only attempt by the league to put forth an independent candidate was at a marginal Leeds by-election in July 1902, which was not contested by the official Liberal Party. The Liberal-Imperialists turned a former Unionist majority of 2,500 (Oct. 1900) into a Liberal majority of 800. *Daily Chronicle*, 24 July 1902; Halévy, *History*, vi, 109.

1902 even that modest strength had dissipated. Campbell-Bannerman had moved toward the more radical pro-Boers, bringing most of the moderates with him. Election losses, a number of quiet defections before and after Chesterfield, and the fact that many of those who had patriotically supported the government in South Africa were, like Asquith, reluctant to go to the length of disabling organized Liberalism once the war issue had receded into the background—all these had reduced their strength in the House to a small, glittering corps of about fifteen men.[29] Due largely to Lord Rosebery's erratic moods, the league was brought to life at a moment of vanishing opportunity.

Beatrice Webb's uncomplimentary remarks did, however, point to one important limiting feature of the league's membership which accounted to some degree for its halting interest in Fabian suggestions: that was the relative diversity of views represented among the "heterogeneous lot" which dominated the organization. Apart from the rather vague "imperial patriotism" upon which the league was nominally founded, the only firm and distinct ideological bond uniting the group was a general adherence to Free Trade principles (even that adherence, as we shall see, was not as firm as it had been a year or two earlier). This distinguished them from the majority of Unionists, but explained none of their differences with the official Liberals. It was the odd charisma of a man and, as Beatrice Webb observed, a variety of discontents and anxieties which motivated the league. For example, within the league executive itself Sir Robert Perks (the treasurer) and Sir Henry Fowler (a vice-president), both Wesleyans and onetime Radicals, spoke almost exclusively for an intransigent stand against Home Rule—an opinion not entirely shared by Asquith or Grey, nor probably by a majority of the younger members. The inevitable result was cross purposes and lack of focus in the league's propaganda, blunting whatever force the group might have had with agreement on the larger issues.[30]

[29] Of the original forty members who followed Grey into the government lobby in July 1900, eight had either lost their seats in October or had retired. Only thirteen of the remainder stayed on as active members of the league (an additional two were new members). See *Liberal League Manifesto* (May 1902); *L.L.P.* no. 20, "League Dinner" (July 1902), pp. 18-20; *Constitutional Year Book* (1900, 1901).

[30] Sir Henry Fowler, "The Present Aspect of the Irish Question," *L.L.P.* no. 17 (1902); H. H. Asquith, "Policy of the Liberal Party," *L.L.P.* no. 2 (1902); Sir Edward Grey, "Policy of the Liberal League," *L.L.P.* no. 13

The difference between Fowler and Asquith, which was mirrored in the rest of the group and promoted disharmony in its policies, was equally one of age and education and of the variety of social backgrounds represented among the leading members. In the permanent active corps of the league (rising to a peak of about thirty-two Members of Parliament in the spring and summer of 1902) the largest and most homogeneous segment, though it was not necessarily the dominant one, was that composed of the ten youngest men.[31] Six of these were current M.P.'s, four were former or prospective candidates, and all were of ten or less years political experience. Having held no significant preferment or appointments in Rosebery's administration, for them the element of personal loyalty was not as weighty in their adherence to the league as it may have been for the older members. Among the league's leaders they would appear to have had most in common with Asquith, Grey, and Haldane; indeed, three of Asquith's closest associates in later years, Edwin Montagu, Rufus Isaacs, and H. J. Tennant, were among them. With an average age of thirty-seven, they were only a few years junior to the three leaders and, like Asquith and Grey, most had gone up to Oxford from established middle-class families and directly from there to the bar and into politics. This common pattern, however, did in no way distinguish them from their youthful counterparts in the regular party. Perhaps more important, they were all of the same academic generation of the eighties—the university's most tumultuous and brilliant decade—and had there witnessed the opening of the first great rents in the seemingly eternal walls of the old Liberalism by Thomas Hill Green and Bernard Bosanquet on the theoretical side and Joseph Chamberlain on the political.[32] To this group the elevated style and philosophy of Rosebery was familiar and appealed mightily.

(1902); H. H. Asquith, *Memories and Reflections, 1852-1927* (London, 1928), I, 198.

[31] The thirty-two include those whose names appeared consistently on the league's rolls and petitions, the twelve M.P.'s who temporarily worked under a separate whip in Commons, and authors of league pamphlets. Many others appeared at one or more of the public functions sponsored by the league but otherwise showed no signs of active support. See *Liberal League Manifesto* (May 1902); *L.L.P.* no. 20, "Liberal League Dinner" (July 1902).

[32] Seven of the younger group had attended Oxford colleges between 1885 and 1892; six were solicitors, one a professional intellectual (Halford J. Mackinder, the geographer), and only one, a wholesale textile merchant,

The remainder of Rosebery's group showed both greater diversity and greater age. In addition to the inevitable train of otherwise unoccupied peers (three besides Rosebery), there were seven former ministers of subcabinet rank in Rosebery's previous government, a retired permanent secretary, a former naval commander, and Charles Rothschild, Rosebery's brother-in-law. Overall, the older segment resembled more closely than their juniors the composition of the regular party (excluding the Radicals) in average age and in the fact that most of them were substantially involved in private business. One notable distinction between Roseberite and party Liberal, in view of the Left's charges about self-interest, was the relative concentration of interest among the former in City finance as opposed to the merchants and mine owners who made up the majority of the regular party.

In the parliamentary Liberal Party of 1900, businessmen, the merchants and mine or mill owners, were in a dominant majority (about 70 percent). Of the nineteen older league members (Asquith, Grey, and Haldane again excluded), approximately one-half were directly engaged in private business, but only two in their own firms. There were no less than seven board chairmen of City investment houses and fourteen board members among the thirty-two active league regulars, corresponding to a much lower proportion of about 40 percent in the regular party.[33] That elusive "personal union" of banking and industrial capital which Lenin saw as the cement of the bourgeois political monopoly and the wellspring of domestic imperialist politics was not notably present among the Liberal-Imperialists, though the soon-to-emerge Tariff Reform League would make strenuous efforts towards realizing that union. The absence of employers of industrial labor among the Liberal-Imperialists perhaps also allowed for their relatively detached and sometimes farsighted views on certain important domestic ques-

---

drew his primary income from his own business. *Constitutional Year Book* (1896 and 1902). *The New Parliament* (January 1902), House of Commons Report, pp. 18-34.

[33] *Constitutional Year Book* (1902), pp. 132-36. The Unionist percentage was slightly higher, according to the *Constitutional Year Book*. The absolute accuracy of the *Year Book* regarding the financial connections of M.P.'s has sometimes been questioned. Where possible, therefore, its reports have been checked with other available biographical sources. See also *Directory of Directors: A List of the Directors of the Joint Stock Companies of the United Kingdom, and the Companies in Which They Are Concerned* (London, 1907).

tions, such as in the heated controversies which followed the Taff Vale decision; it would also seem to account to some extent for the league's critical attitude toward the competitive failings of British industrial management.

Between November 1901 and the January of the Berkeley Square meetings, the *Times* ran a widely discussed series on "The Crisis in British Industry," which argued that the main obstacle to the development of British industrial productivity and competitiveness relative to American was the unreasonable demands and excessive strength of trade unionism.[34] The response to the *Times* articles was not limited to labor or the left-wing press. In fact, the series provoked an unexpectedly prolonged public debate on the "industrial crisis" in which virtually every shade of opinion and every depth of gloom was heard. The employers' charge, as stated by the *Times*, was answered first by the unions with the argument that improvement in wages, hours, and work conditions, far from impeding productivity, had invariably stimulated mechanization and innovation and thus increased competitiveness in the long run.[35]

In the ensuing debate, which occupied the months between the Chesterfield speech and the announcement of the league, a flood of comparative industrial studies and statistics were produced to bolster the arguments of both management and the unions. The Webbs and Roseberites, through the *Daily Chronicle*, not only plunged into the controversy largely on the union side but soon incorporated a good deal of the prounion case into developing the National Efficiency program.[36]

[34] The *Times* articles of November-January 1901-1902 were a continuation of a series begun earlier by Edwin A. Pratt, the *Times*'s industrial correspondent, entitled "American Engineering Competition" (13 June, 10 July 1900), which also argued that militant trade unionism was at the root of Britain's industrial lag. The later series were republished by Pratt as *Trade Unionism and British Industry* (London, 1904); see also Henry Pelling's *America and the British Left* (London, 1956), pp. 72-75.

[35] A refutation was issued by the Management Committee of the General Federation of Trade Unions and printed by the *Times*, 20 Dec. 1901.

[36] The Webbs first countered the *Times* series in an article in the *Times* itself of 6 Dec. 1901. The *Daily Chronicle* also took an advanced position against the *Times*; cf. especially the leader of 16 Nov. 1901. The *Daily Mail*, though generally sympathetic to the employers' case in the early stages, reversed itself to some degree in February and March (cf. *Daily Mail*, 1 Feb. 1902). Shortly thereafter, Harold Harmsworth, a close friend and neighbor of Rosebery, subscribed both his name and newspaper to the

The league drew most of all from the reports of the Mosely Industrial Commission.[37] The general conclusion of these studies was that, beyond the obvious natural advantages, America's industrial efficiency and its openness to the introduction of laborsaving innovations were largely due to the superior education of the American worker. Similarly, in the league's pamphlets and in the writing of the Webbs, the question of popular education and vocational training was almost invariably linked to the improvement of industrial competitiveness. Such, for example, was the argument of a *Fabian Tract* sent by Webb to 750 M.P.'s in March ("The Case for the Factory Acts"). Reform, an accompanying letter urged, was needed to provide educational opportunities for the young in order to "stop the degradation of character and physique caused by sweating . . . , increase industrial efficiency . . . , and enable us to meet Foreign Competition."[38]

In the year-long debate which filled parlors, union halls, and Parliament as well as the press, the Liberal League, despite its heterogeneity, displayed a far greater capacity than the established parties to recognize the need for departures in the method and tempo of state interference in domestic problems. A number of league publications which appeared during the year (especially those authored by the younger members) revealed the gradual emergence of a precocious plan of government action in social and economic reform based on the general precepts of National Effi-

---

league. He resigned a few months later, exasperated with Rosebery's lack of decision. R. R. James, *Rosebery*, p. 440; *L.L.P.* no. 20 (July 1902); George Harmsworth and Reginald Pound, *Northcliffe* (London, 1959), pp. 225-226.

[37] Alfred Mosely, a South African mine owner impressed with American industrial efficiency, sponsored a commission of union leaders and industrial and educational experts to travel to America. Its reports, appearing in print during 1902, were published together as *Mosely Industrial Commission: Reports of the Delegates* (London, 1903). See also *B.O.T. Memorandum on the Comparative Statistics of Population, Industry and Commerce in the U.K. and some Leading Foreign Countries* (1902), pp. 5-6.

[38] "The Case for the Factory Acts," *Fabian Tract* no. 109; B. Webb, "Diary" (12 March 1902), *P.P.* Educational reform became one of the main themes of the early league pamphlets (March through July) and was, perhaps under the instruction of Webb, urged with the same emphasis as industrial efficiency. See *L.L.P.*'s no. 5, "The Education Bill" (May); no. 10, "Liberalism and Labour" (June); no. 16, "The Education Bill" (July). See G. R. Searle's discussion on efficiency and education, *The Quest for National Efficiency*, pp. 138-175.

ciency as laid down by Webb and Rosebery. Some of the arguments made in these, notably the ones pertaining to vocational and technical education and industrial modernization,[39] raised critical questions which, to the serious detriment of the postimperial economic adjustment, were not taken up again until the next war forced the issue.

What most distinguished the league's literature during the debate was its prominent display of the most current "expert opinion" (marshaled mostly by Sidney Webb and the younger members). Moreover, as the economic question began to revolve increasingly around Tariff Reform in 1903, the league's argument focused on the recognition, first, that the increased competitive pressure from abroad was in fact related to the lag in domestic industrial productivity rather than to foreign protectionist policies; and, second, that tariffs and the restriction of union organization urged by most Conservatives, though they might reduce immediate anxiety, would not provide the means for the necessary long-range reconstruction of the nation's aging industrial system.[40] Indeed, there was a precocious recognition in some of the league's propaganda that the socially regressive policies urged by some Conservatives concerning unionization and public education were less a means of achieving modernization and competitive strength than a method of delaying it.

Some elements of the league had begun to show themselves more receptive and forward than Beatrice Webb had expected. Without going the whole way to "ruthless compulsion," the Limps' evolving format of National Efficiency was moving towards an inclusive doctrine of planned economic, social, and political reform which contained a glimmering foresight of the "remodernization" of British

[39] *L.L.P.*'s no. 7, 10, 16 (cf. n. 62); no. 33, "Administrative Efficiency" (1902); no. 64, "Wanted! Efficiency, not Tariffs" (1903).

[40] See especially *L.L.P.* no. 62, "Mr. Chamberlain's Conjuring Trick" (1903), and no. 64 above. It is generally agreed that a large part of Britain's postwar economic stagnation was due to the general failure of industry, in the growth period 1896-1914, to reinvest inflated profits for the sake of increased productivity and modernization. The result was, as the Limps sensed, a sensational inferiority in industrial rate of growth vis-à-vis the "later starters." C. P. Kindleberger, *Economic Growth in France and Britain, 1871-1950* (Cambridge, Mass., 1964), pp. 12-13, 291; R. S. Sayers, "The Springs of Technical Progress in Britain," *Economic Journal*, vol. 60, no. 238 (June 1950), pp. 276-279; W. W. Rostow, *British Economy of the Nineteenth Century* (Oxford, 1948).

society. However, due partly to the inertia of the older majority and partly to the unpopular dogmatism of Fabian collectivism, the National Efficiency program sketched by the publications of the Liberal League in the first year never went the whole of the way mapped out by Webb. Yet, largely under his tutelage (he attended league meetings until the end of July despite Beatrice's earlier defection), the league advanced a sampling of seminal ideas in the role of government in social planning, in education and housing, and in industrial regulation by "expertly advised" administrators—ideas which not only broke into political dialogue at the highest level but inevitably became part of the governing attitude of their authors, five of whom were to become Cabinet ministers in the great period of reform following the Liberal victory of 1905.

From the long-term point of view the Webbs had made a success of their "permeation" of the Liberal-Imperialists, especially of the younger men. Their disappointment arose out of what they regarded as the league's neglect of the "Fabian side." In the league *Manifesto* drawn up in July, for example, the order of issues was listed as follows: (1) Naval Supremacy; (2) Army Reform; (3) National Efficiency in education, housing, and temperance; and (4) Reform but NOT Home Rule for Ireland.[41] It was as Hobson diagnosed—in any movement of imperialism and social reform, the former would be the ruling passion.

The clear emphasis on defense over domestic reform rankled the Webbs who, as we have seen, threw in with the imperialists mainly in the hope that they would perform "the necessary work of iconoclasm," of reigning Liberal principles. Theirs was an essentially different obsession, with the nation rather than the empire, while the imperialists were inclined to ramify all domestic questions into their world view and, indeed, to compose their views on domestic problems largely upon extranational criteria. While also making use of the threat from abroad to illustrate the failure of Liberal principles at home, the Webbs still hoped to see the fate of Liberalism hinge primarily upon the social question.

Rosebery saw the role of the league somewhat differently, or at least less clearly. Despite his appeasement of the conventional anti–Home Rule and Big Navy prejudices of the older Liberal-Imperialists (whose views he shared anyway), the enigmatic league president had also demonstrated his genuine interest and fluency in the

[41] *Manifesto*, attached to *L.L.P.* no. 20, "Liberal League Dinner: Speeches given at the Hotel Cecil" (31 July 1902).

bureaucratic aspects of Webb's gospel of efficiency.[42] In addition, his evasiveness on the details of "efficiency in education, housing, and temperance," though it seemed to the Webbs a deplorable return to the imperialists' old indifference to social reform, was sufficient to attract a young progressive element and thereby absolve Liberal-Imperialism somewhat from the stamp of mere Whiggish reaction. Such an appearance was to be avoided at all costs if, as Rosebery put it, the great stabilizing yet progressive force which Liberalism had represented under Victoria was to escape being "squeezed out between Socialism and Conservatism"—between the emergent "predatory elements in society" and "those who wish to keep things as they are."[43]

Both Liberal-Imperialists and Fabians agreed that the Liberal Party had ceased to function as that stabilizing force in politics. Although there was disagreement as to whether Liberalism had drifted too far to the Left or to the Right, the idea persisted that a new doctrine of Social-Imperialism was somehow to reverse the polarization of political and social forces in the nation by occupying a central position based on neither class nor party but on ordered social progress and security within the empire—an updated version of Rosebery's "Empire based on the widest democracy."

A "Centre bloc" based on this appeal, as Haldane and Webb indicated, would seek popular support from the so-called "nonpolitical voters" thought to reside in the "non-Socialist working class," the "great lower-middle class," and that segment of capital which saw its interests in the maintenance of the empire on an intelligent, pragmatic, and therefore peaceful basis. To these Fowler and Perks promised to add large numbers of Nonconformist voters unhappy both with the Liberal attachment to Home Rule and with the Conservative policy in church, education, and temperance.[44] Over all, the popular base at which the Liberal League aimed bore a remarkable resemblance to that which later coalesced under the expert orchestration of Lloyd George. It was of this diverse mass of opinion that the league optimistically spoke in their July *Manifesto*, at the height of the league's fortunes:

> People are apt to think that the country is divided into two political parties . . . [but] there is a great volume of opinion, not very expres-

[42] The best example is Rosebery's "Administrative Efficiency," *L.L.P.* no. 33.
[43] Cited in E. T. Raymond, *The Man of Promise*, p. 198.
[44] See Fowler's "The Irish Question," *L.L.P.* no. 17 (1902).

sive, that does not make itself heard very much on platforms, but which has often a decisive effect in the electoral battles of the country, which does not greatly sympathize with the extreme men of either party. . . .[45]

The existence of this great untapped pool of silent "non-political" votes was in part only a hopeful assertion based upon the results of a solitary by-election victory in July for a league candidate.[46] However, it was also a recognition, similar to that made by the Primrose League and later by the Tariff Reform League, that the "industrious classes," whose enfranchisement was just beginning to be felt and understood, were not a homogeneous mass accessible only to the predatory promises of radicalism but a stratified collection of interests and sentiments part of which would rally as eagerly to the cause of order and patriotism as to the assault on property.

Rosebery had enlisted the aid of the Fabians and young Liberal-Imperialists almost reluctantly, in the faint recognition that neither the threat of imperial decline nor a menace from Europe were sufficient to mobilize the moderate elements in society and politics—and thus to reverse the trend towards polarization which was his most anxious concern. To avoid being squeezed out between Left and Right, the new "Centre" needed an alternative and compelling system—an ideology for ordering the future less fraught with change and disturbance than the Socialist yet not so stupidly intransigent as the Conservative. National Efficiency, with its mixture of expertise and patriotism, bureaucratic authority and abuse of parties, was an attempt to create such an ideology of the "Centre" and thus to restore the sense of social unity, purpose, and political stability which imperialism and primacy no longer seemed to assure. Like both English Liberalism and English Socialism, the embryonic doctrine of Social-Imperialism was theoretically unfocused and politically fickle when compared to some continental varieties. While it displayed the same irritation with the defections of the Left from the enthroned liturgies of race and destiny, it felt a lesser need to offer a systematic alternative to the Marxian scenario for the future. Nor at this early stage in its development

---

[45] *Liberal League Manifesto, L.L.P.* no. 20 (31 July 1902).

[46] I.e., the election at Leeds. It was a poor test case of the league's appeal since it was fought almost exclusively on education and local issues and was not contested either by a party Liberal or a Socialist. *Daily Chronicle*, 24 July 1902.

was Social-Imperialism consciously entering the modern debate over what to do with a nation without an empire. Yet it contained inklings of both which would be distilled in the mounting crises to come.

Once the Radicals had captured control of the party apparatus, it was doubtful that the league could seriously have challenged the electoral strength of either of the great parties. Moreover, the continued irresolution of Rosebery, who might otherwise have given the body coherence and unity, virtually extinguished any chance of success for the league as an independent political force. This was especially so after the peace of Vereeniging retired the most passionate issue of the moment. The league's effective life ended at about the time of its first electoral success in July 1902. The Fabians, who had been the source of its most distinctive and persuasive ideas, were disillusioned again by the July *Manifesto* and ceased to collaborate actively.[47] Though the league continued to publish pamphlets on specific issues, Rosebery reverted after that time to his luxurious solitude, leaving his associates the choice of retiring (as some of the older men did) or of decorously drifting back into the regular party, which was the way taken eventually by Asquith, Grey, Haldane, and most of the younger men.

Another alternative, possessing curious appeal, briefly presented itself in the fall of 1902. At several points in the interval between July and Chamberlain's Tariff Reform revolt the following spring, Rosebery considered the possibility (as Haldane described it) of "accepting a coalition with the Younger Tories" (i.e., the Chamberlainites).[48] The possibility of a reunion of the older Liberal-Imperialists with their onetime colleagues first arose in July when a serious rift in the Conservative-Unionist coalition was opened over the succession to Lord Salisbury. Chamberlain had not only been passed over in the selection of a successor, but was not even consulted on the appointment of Arthur James Balfour, a humiliation to his ardent supporters which poisoned their view of the

---

[47] The league's meeting of 31 July (*L.L.P.* no. 20) was the last at which Sidney Webb's name appears among the list of members; nor did he contribute to any league publications after that date.

[48] Reported by Haldane in a conversation with the Webbs on 21 July 1902. Rosebery's thoughts about a coalition did not apparently include persuading the entire league to come over with him. Haldane and the Webbs suspected, in fact, that it was his intention to "leave his lieutenants in the lurch" (i.e., Asquith, Haldane, and Grey) by joining Chamberlain. B. Webb, "Diary" (21 July 1902), *P.P.*

"Cecil monopoly" for years afterward. Though their leaders were as far as possible apart in temperament, the Rosebery and Chamberlain factions held common views on a wide range of questions including Ireland, education, imperial union (before the tariff revolt), and above all they shared an apprehension about the nation's social and economic future should the Left increase its strength and the feeling that they represented the only viable response to that possibility. However, the absence of Chamberlain on his momentous tour of South Africa during the winter of 1902-1903, added to Rosebery's continued dalliance, held off the possible fruition of this new departure. Then, almost immediately on his return, Chamberlain imposed the barrier of Protection between himself and the Liberal-Imperialists, still predominantly Free Traders. Although Rosebery himself had never felt the Free Trade doctrine to be, as he put it, "part of the Sermon on the Mount," and seemed near to conceding to the imperial tariff at one point, the league eventually pronounced itself opposed to it, ending the thought of that potentially formidable coalition.[49]

Rosebery's neglect of the Fabians and even of his closest Liberal followers, his reversion first back into his "lonely furrow" and, finally, towards alliance with the "Younger Tories," appeared to be merely further evidence of his erratic moods. But was not a powerful coalition of imperialists, once the fragmentation of parties provided the occasion, the logical political outcome of "National Efficiency" with its abuse of party politics, its insistence on nonpolitical Cabinets, on the full use of the few "first-rate men" available in both parties, and on reducing parliamentary opposition? Was not such a coalition of imperial civil servants, in fact, a more direct means (and one more congenial to the ardent imperialist) of occupying the gap between the "extreme men of either party" than the minority union with the politically powerless Fabians and the young Liberals whose devotion to the empire took second place, at best, to their interest in national problems?

Wartime governments, as the next war was to show, are often inclined to exercise the same means in the name of national unity. Efficiency, "ruthless compulsion," suspension of "politics," and government by experts is the historic means of cementing the *union*

---

[49] Rosebery was clearly undecided in his speech at Burnley, 19 May 1903. The Limps soon after stated their opposition. See "Mr. Chamberlain's Conjuring Trick," *L.L.P.* no. 62 (1903), and *L.L.P.* no. 64; Halévy, *History*, VI, 344.

sacrée in the visible presence of the enemy. And invariably in war such powers have been used either to foster or to frustrate the forces of domestic change. Lacking a visible enemy, beyond the diminutive Boer republics, the apostles of Social-Imperialism merely began to simulate the state of permanent warfare which exhilarated the empire-builders and guided their rule over subject peoples into a method of rule at home.

III

The Coefficients Club

The end of hostilities in the summer of 1902 brought a temporary subsiding of tension and activity among the imperialist politicians. Between the signing of the Treaty of Vereeniging in June and Joseph Chamberlain's ignition of the tariff question the following May, Rosebery expended only random efforts in advancing the policy of National Efficiency. He had had the distinction of standing for patriotic Liberalism during the war but, while this had not been the only issue dividing him from the official party, he seems to have been at a loss to maintain the advantage of that position and the ardor of his cause once wartime fears and passions relaxed. He had neither joined the "Younger Tories," as some had anticipated, nor had he progressed very far towards building the great "Centre Party" which Haldane envisioned. He had lost the fascination of the Fabians by neglect of their domestic program while at the same time being preempted of a major foreign policy issue by the government's reversal of course towards France and Germany in the last months of the year. Finally, there was some thought among his friends that Rosebery's leisurely politics also cost Liberal-Imperialism what might have been a most potent source of new support—that source which Chamberlain tapped in May. For it was Grey's belief that Rosebery was contemplating just such an apostasy on the tariff prior to Chamberlain's return from the Cape.[1]

Although it was difficult for his closest associates to know Rosebery's mind at this as at any time, the feeling of Grey, Haldane, and Asquith that he was close to a pronouncement on Tariff Reform indicates the direction in which Liberal-Imperialist thought was running during 1902. Haldane, still persistent and sanguine,

---

[1] Grey to Milner (16 Feb. 1907). *M.P.*, Letters, A. III. After a brief hesitation, Rosebery and the Liberal League declared themselves against Chamberlain on the tariff; cf. Rosebery's speech at Burnley, 19 May 1903.

believed Rosebery's intention was to ally with Chamberlain's Liberal-Unionists to form that elusive "Centre Party" which would galvanize the forces of order and be strong enough to defy both the Tory and Liberal machines; Grey and Asquith agreed he was leaning in that direction.[2] And Beatrice Webb, having lost her always provisional hopes for Rosebery, also felt that he was about to "leave his lieutenants in the lurch" by joining with the Chamberlain faction.[3]

These thoughts occupied the minds of the Roseberites in the summer and fall of the year, when the fortunes of the Liberal-Imperialists appeared to be reaching their lowest ebb. In the absence of a lead from the master, Haldane, Grey, and the Webbs made some attempts to keep alive the body of Liberal dissent and imperialist solidarity that had been aroused. Not only had Haldane and Grey continued to cultivate the Fabians, but in the prevailing mood they renewed their ties with the Cape governor, Alfred Milner, the archvillain of the pro-Boer tableau and for years after the *éminence grise* of the Tariff Reform movement.

Milner, himself a Liberal-Imperialist when he first entered politics in the eighties, had already experienced the kind of estrangement from traditional Liberal doctrines which the Liberal Leaguers now appeared to be undergoing and had thereafter moved into close connection with the Unionists. Like Chamberlain, as well as many of the imperialists who had remained in the Liberal Party, his defection from the guiding principles of the party had been a product of the shattering crisis which attended Gladstone's efforts to enact Home Rule for Ireland. A man of somber and eccentric illusions, his reaction had followed a more unorthodox course than either the Liberal-Imperialist or the Liberal-Unionist. Yet as the leading imperial *fonctionnaire* of his day and the butt of the anti-imperialists, he always commanded a certain respect from both groups, a respect often mixed with anxiety, however. Since he had also evolved a similar interest in the kind of forceful state action and bureaucratic "efficiency" which attracted Rosebery to the

[2] Milner to Asquith (13 Sept. 1901), *M.P.*, Letters, vol. 28; Grey to Milner (30 Oct. 1902); Milner to Synge (1902); and in Headlam (ed.), *The Milner Papers*, 2 vols. (London, 1931-1933), II, 331. Asquith's and Grey's correspondence with Milner at this time strongly suggests that they would quickly have followed Rosebery had he developed a protectionist position. Haldane all along viewed Free Trade and Ireland as almost insignificant issues compared to the urgency of linking up with the Liberal-Unionists.

[3] B. Webb, "Diary" (21 July 1902), *P.P.*

Webbs, he shared with the Liberal peer a contempt for the kind of Radical individualism and planless methods widely associated with Gladstone and his successors. But to the rather restrained elegance of Rosebery's attacks on the "party system" he added an unforgiving intransigence of which Rosebery was incapable, denouncing it as the sole, sordid agent of Liberalism's excessive longevity.[4] In any possible imperialist political front, Milner's name would be a magnet for extremists and crusaders for a hundred odd causes.

While Commissioner in South Africa, Milner had begun to acquire extensive prestige and influence among the more ardent imperialists of both parties. And while many, including Rosebery, felt his political style to be on the rough side, the loathing in which he was held by the pro-Boers made of him a symbol of resistance to Radicals and Little-Englanders, not only in the eyes of his Tory admirers but among many Liberals and Fabians as well. With more plausibility than Rosebery, he had linked his name with the kind of dynamic bureaucracy and modern imperialism to which all these groups wished to attach themselves, maintaining also an appearance of disinterest as to party and political ambition which the Liberal League leader could not convincingly affect. The agency of Milner's powerful image, therefore, also served to maintain some of the cohesion among the advocates of the "new imperialism" which Rosebery's halting energy had done so much to dissipate.

It was in the hope of retrieving something from the Rosebery wreck that the Webbs and Leo S. Amery, a Milner disciple, a former Fabian, and the *Times*'s military correspondent in South Africa, conceived the idea of forming the "Coefficients Club" in November of 1902. One of the immediate aims which the club was to serve was to maintain the dialogue between parties by regularly assembling the more talented and willing imperialists from both sides. There was the obvious likelihood that with the peace the bulk of the Liberal insurgents would return to the party fold, abandoning the revolt and the incipient doctrine which legitimized it for the sake of survival—or, with the waning of the league, merely for lack of a practical political alternative. Moreover, Asquith led a number of the moderate league members who wished not to sever themselves permanently and he had already begun at the end of the war to repair the bridges back.[5] But, Amery later recalled, "a more nat-

---

[4] An excellent discussion of the Milner style in politics is offered in Eric Stokes's "Milnerism," *Historical Journal*, v, no. 1 (1962), 49 sqq.

[5] See Roy Jenkins, *Asquith* (London, 1964), pp. 133 et passim.

ural outcome, many were inclined to think, would be some coming together of Liberal-Imperialists with the more progressive wing of the Unionist Party." The latter alternative, he admitted, held special attraction for himself and for his collaborators in the founding of the club—those "two ingenious minds, forever planning and scheming as one."[6]

The strategy of "permeation," the political style of the Fabians, had been that of the gadfly—to ask embarrassing questions to which they possessed studied and instructive answers. Fabian tracts and lectures were calculated for an audience, actually or potentially in power, which could take their ideas and language for their own without acknowledging, perhaps not even realizing, their indebtedness. Quite early the Webbs had added distinct personal embellishments on that method, particularly through their "little dinners and informal meetings." Consequently, their work as Fabians had been both part of and apart from the Fabian Society's, a circumstance which occasionally made for surprising divergences. Beatrice especially, with wide social contacts and skill, was given to cultivating the small group, mostly of the promising and interesting young men who yearly flowed into political society from the universities:

> The trick of forcing on the party [i.e., the Liberal Party] an advanced program, and then calling them traitors because they did not carry it out, is played out so far as we are concerned. It served its purpose; it was a wedge driven into the party and has discovered the true line of cleavage between the old and the new. . . . Now we collectivists have to assert ourselves as a distinct school of thought. . . . Our special mission seems to be to undertake the difficult problems ourselves, and to gather round us young men and women who will more or less study under inspiration. . . .[7]

The capably managed home of the Webbs at 41 Grosvenor Road was the most active political salon in London in 1902. Over the preceding ten years the industrious pair had firmly established their authority in matters of municipal and industrial reform among an important segment of receptive bureaucrats and politicians of both major parties through their books, pamphlets, and their work in local government. But in furthering the aim of permeation the reputation of their little dinners was undoubtedly one of their greatest

---

[6] Leo S. Amery, *My Political Life* (London, 1953), I, 221.

[7] B. Webb, *Our Partnership*, p. 128.

assets. Captains of industry, artists, union leaders, scholars, journalists, naval officers, aspiring politicians in large numbers, and more than one Prime Minister-to-be gave an open ear to Fabian collectivism in exchange for the congenial hospitality and stimulating company of the Webbs' table—and, not least of all, the repute in official circles of being up with the latest ideas in the currently fashionable "science of government."

With the wartime split in the Fabian Society and the secession of most of the Radical elements, the Webb-Shaw imperialist section was free to mingle more openly with the political Right and even to engage actively in imperial politics, as they were doing in connection with the Rosebery revolt during the late months of the Boer War. Never before had such a splendid parade of guests crowded Beatrice's engagement lists and never had the Fabians' collectivist formulas commanded such an attentive and illustrious audience.

Shaw, cordially unimpressed by his colleagues' rapid rise in London political society, viewed the new affinity between Fabians and imperialists (a tendency which he had done much to stimulate) with characteristic skepticism.

> Why are Fabians so well spoken of in circles [in] which thirty years ago the word Socialist was equivalent with cut-throat incendiary? . . . because they believe that the Fabians, by eliminating intimidation from the Socialist agitation, have drawn the teeth of insurgent poverty and saved the existing order from the only method of attack it really fears.[8]

Despite the considerable harmony of view achieved at one point in their association with Rosebery, Shaw and the Webbs had maintained something of this cynical attitude in all their dealings with his exalted circle, or at least with the man himself. The complaisance of the informal meetings and dinners through which the alliance had mainly been nurtured did little to remove their reservations and, when differences over policy and priorities arose—when, in fact, Rosebery showed signs of exerting any distinctly independent view—it disposed them to the quick disenchantment which dissolved the partnership in the summer of 1902.[9]

Sidney Webb broke formal contact with the Liberal League in

---

[8] G. B. Shaw, *Man and Superman* (New York, 1916), p. 249.

[9] The Webbs broke with the Liberal League in July, immediately after the appearance of the second *Manifesto*, *L.L.P.* no. 20 (July 1902).

July and thereafter appeared at none of its public functions. Naturally, the Webbs did not sever their friendship with Haldane, Grey, and the younger faction of the league, many of whom were intimate friends of long standing. In fact, it was largely from this younger element that the Webbs recruited the Liberal side of their next "non-party" enterprise—an extraordinary political discussion group christened by them the "Coefficients Club," which met for the first time in November.[10]

On this occasion, it was Beatrice rather than Sidney Webb who played the more forward role. Indeed, several of the founding members of the Coefficients understood that both the conception and the organization of the club were her doing.[11] Although there was later to occur a sharp dispute over the practical purposes of the club, the Webbs had apparently reached some agreement with Leo Amery on its general nature and goals before choosing from among their friends the dozen men who were to be invited to the first meeting. The idea at the start was an extremely ambitious one, mixing the sober-sounding language of the Fabians with the radical-imperial illusions of Amery. As Amery understood it, a carefully selected company was to meet at regular intervals "for serious discussion and the subsequent formulation of policy," directed ultimately towards producing a "well thought out programme combining Imperialism and 'semi-socialism' with a 'Brains Trust' or 'General Staff.' "[12]

The criteria applied by Amery and the Webbs in choosing the personnel of the "Brains Trust" arose directly out of these goals. All of the twelve were imperialists (or were thought to be, since one exception was discovered with dismay only later) and all of them were associated with one of the so-called "progressive" factions which had appeared during the war in both major parties and in the Fabian Society. Moreover, each was selected for his demonstrated expertise in an essential field of public or intellectual life—

[10] W. A. S. Hewins, one of the charter members, recalls from an undated diary entry that the club first met "around the beginning of 1902." Hewins, *Apologia of an Imperialist* (London, 1929), I, 65. All other sources, however, indicate November or thereabouts; e.g., H. G. Wells, *Experiment in Autobiography*, 2 vols. (London, 1934), II, 761, and Amery, *My Political Life*, pp. 223-224.

[11] All descriptions of the founding of the club, except Amery's, attribute its conception to Beatrice Webb. Amery, *My Political Life*, p. 223; Hewins, *Apologia*, I, 65-66; and Wells, *Experiment*, II, 762.

[12] Amery, *My Political Life*, pp. 52-54.

a quality which would, hypothetically, equip him for the role of "expert planner-administrator" in a particular department of state as envisioned by the authors of the club. Accordingly, each was to contribute from his special knowledge toward the construction of a workable "semi-socialist," imperialist program capable of appealing to the advanced, reform-minded sections of all parties. Since the general idea had been bruited by the Webbs (to W. A. S. Hewins) as early as February, when the meetings with the Liberal-Imperialists were in progress at Rosebery's home, it seems possible that the club was originally imagined as the "Brains Trust" of Rosebery's National Efficiency program. It will be remembered that the project, too, was to adopt the "above-party" character always projected by the Liberal-Imperialists.[13]

Thus the twelve original Coefficients constituted a kind of nonparty Shadow Cabinet of experts, roughly paralleling the general structure of departmental functions as follows: Sidney and Beatrice Webb (Local Government and Labor); L. S. Amery (Army); Sir Edward Grey (Foreign Policy); R. B. Haldane (Law); Sir Clinton Dawkins (Finance); W. A. S. Hewins (Economy); Bertrand Russell (Science); W. Pember Reeves (Colonies); Commander Carlyon Bellairs (Navy); Halford J. Mackinder (Empire); Leo Maxse (Press); and H. G. Wells (a kind of Cultural Minister without Portfolio).[14] It would seem likely that the allotment of personnel and posts was not the ideal makeup imagined by the founders; a more impressive authority on the navy than the obscure Commander Bellairs, for example, might have been preferred. Described by Russell as "a breezy naval officer," Bellairs was a Lib-

---

[13] Ibid.

[14] Halford J. Mackinder, the famous exponent and author of the geopolitical theory, joined the Liberal League in June, at which time he made his first contact with the Webbs. B. Webb, "Diary" (5 June 1902), *P.P.* His seminal article, "The Geographical Pivot of History," *Geographical Journal*, XXIII (April 1904), was published only two years after joining the club. Hewins, an academic economist, was a former Fabian and Director of the London School of Economics until 1903, when he resigned to work for the Tariff Reform League. Pember Reeves was New Zealand's Agent-General in London and the Fabian specialist on colonial issues. See "The State and its Functions in New Zealand," *Fabian Tract* no. 74 (1896). Dawkins, the oldest member, was also attached to the National Service League, as were Amery and Milner. Dawkins to Milner (25 April 1902), *M.P.*, A. III; Milner to Dawkins (n.d.); in Edwin Crankshaw, *The Forsaken Idea* (London, 1952), p. 135.

eral League member and Liberal M.P. from King's Lynn in 1902. His most notable achievement in an undistinguished political career was to retake the King's Lynn seat as a Conservative in the first general election of 1910 after having crossed the floor against the Lloyd George budget.[15] Or in Wells' case, though his presence was desired, his evasive title suggests that there may have been some difficulty in classifying his eclectic talents as "expert" in any given field. Nevertheless, all but one (Bellairs) were qualified in the important particular that they were generally free of commitments to either of the official parties and their leadership.

The twelve also constituted a fair representation of the dissident factions of both major parties and of the Socialist movement. Grey, Haldane, Mackinder, and Bellairs were members of the Liberal League. Amery, Dawkins, Hewins, and Maxse were Unionists of the Chamberlain-Milner faction, which was then preparing its assault on the Cecil leadership; and the Webbs (always counted as one), Russell, Wells, and Pember Reeves were Fabians.[16]

Such were the affiliations of the members only at the moment of their first meeting. They did not by any means represent permanent commitments to a party or a leader in the usual sense. On the whole, the Coefficients were young and highly talented men whose erratic behavior bespoke the widespread disaffection with conventional politics and leaders which had been gathering force since the upheaval of the eighties and had been much accelerated by the war. Mackinder and Bellairs, for example, had enthusiastically enlisted in the Rosebery revolt, had shared the Webbs' disenchantment, and both eventually moved over to the Unionists. Amery and Hewins had cast their first votes as Liberals, both entered the Fabian Society in the nineties, and both fell finally under the spell of Chamberlain and Milner during the war. Maxse, Wells, and Russell, the freest spirits of the fraternity, veered unpredictably during the course of their careers from one passionate cause to another across most of the political spectrum without settled commitment to leader, to party, or to ideology. The kind of maturity sometimes asso-

---

[15] Bertrand Russell, *Portraits from Memory* (London, 1956), p. 76; B. Webb, "Diary" (5 June 1902), *P.P.*

[16] Chamberlain's formal opening of the tariff debate did not take place until late May 1903; House of Commons, 22 May 1903. The best general discussion of the debacle in the Unionist Party over the tariff is still Halévy's "The Decline of the Unionist Party" in *Imperialism and the Rise of Labour* (London, 1961), pp. 285-356.

ciated with consistent political behavior was not the dominant feature of the group.

The Coefficients were thus a reflection in cameo of the rife unsettlement of both parties and of the Socialist movement at the close of the war. The appearance in quick succession of the Fabian split, the Liberal League, the National Service League (February 1902),[17] a revived Tariff Reform League, and working-class jingoism of the Blatchford variety, all of them contemptuous of older leaders and rebellious towards traditional policies, was symptomatic of the decomposition of old party loyalties—perhaps even, as many thought and some hoped, of the decline of the party system itself.

Each of these extraparliamentary groups was represented in the Coefficients Club by one of its major spokesmen: the Fabian imperialists by the Webbs; the Liberal League by Haldane and Grey; the National Service League by Maxse and Amery; and the Tariff Reform League by Hewins. Although there was no official status to this representation, the assembled voices of the dissenting right wing of each of the major political forces of the time around the Coefficients' table furnished the only sustained converse among these influential groups—the primary carriers of Social-Imperialist ideas—during the Edwardian decade.

The Coefficients Club was a peculiar experiment in English politics and poses some unusual problems in description. Appearing in the heyday of social, academic, and political clubmanship and of the league movements in England, the Coefficients shared some of the features of all but does not properly belong to any of these traditional categories. It served a familiar social purpose—"interesting little dinners" overseen by Beatrice Webb, the accom-

[17] The National Service League has not been extensively covered in the secondary literature. Founded by Earl Roberts in February of 1902, it attracted large numbers of the younger Unionists, including the Coefficients —Amery, Dawkins, Maxse and, later, Milner and Henry Birchenough. Cf. Amery's *The Problem of the Army* (1903); Birchenough, "Military Training and Industrial Efficiency," *National Service Journal*, I, 5 (March 1904). These left a distinctive Coefficients' mark on the literature of the league from the start. Cf. *National Service Journal*, I, 1 (Nov. 1903).

plished hostess—yet this aspect was certainly secondary or even incidental to the permeation of potential leaders by Beatrice, the Fabian. But, as we have seen, it was something of a departure in the Fabian style as well. The club was to provide a regular forum for the discussion of ideas of common interest to the members, somewhat in the manner of the horticultural or scholarly clubs; yet, as the declared aims of Amery suggest, discussion would hopefully lead to the formation of a coherent "programme" and, presumably, to some kind of political action. Finally, unlike any of the leagues of the time, only passing attention was given to the thought of reaching the public or to organized lobbying, the main reason for this being that the members had either dim or divergent ideas of what cause the club was meant to represent and further. The circumstances of its founding were not greatly different from those of the numerous "cause" societies, promoting anything from winter squash to psychical research, which were endemic to the country. Under the political circumstances of 1902, however, and in light of the affiliations of its members, the cause for the Coefficients was surely both less circumscribed and more immediate.

Amery's idea that the meetings were to produce "a well thought out programme combining Imperialism and 'semi-socialism' with a 'Brains Trust' or 'General Staff' " was a design as clear, and certainly as ambitious, as any held by the other members. Whether all were aware from the start that they were being singled out especially for their qualifications to sit on the "Shadow Cabinet" seems unlikely. Though that officious division of labor appealed later to Wells, it was apparently discussed at first only between the Webbs, Amery, Hewins, Haldane, and Grey, significantly those who were most deeply involved in the two party insurgencies. Wells remembered a "curious little talking and dining club" which met monthly to discuss the future of "this perplexing, promising, and frustrating Empire of ours."[18] Russell first met Wells at the "small discussion society" christened by Sidney Webb (as Russell thought) the "Coefficients," in the hope that "we should be jointly efficient."[19] To the economist, Hewins, the club's purpose was more tangible and serious: to discuss the "aims and methods of Imperial policy," which quite naturally meant to him plying the Liberal members with the debits and credits of Tariff Reform.[20]

[18] H. G. Wells, *Experiment*, II, 761.
[19] Russell, *Portraits*, p. 76.   [20] Hewins, *Apologia*, I, 65.

The heterodox and at least half-suspecting company convened for the first time in the dining room at 41 Grosvenor Road one evening in early November 1902—shortly after the denouement of the Webbs-Rosebery venture. After the founding dinner the group's regular meetings moved to the Ship Tavern in Whitehall Court and later to the St. Ermin's Hotel, which became the usual monthly rendezvous of the club until its dissolution in 1908.[21] Though the "larger design" had been generally discussed at a smaller dinner given by Grey a week before,[22] the idea of a select "Brains Trust" of talents, independent of party, could not have been entirely novel to any of those present. Indeed, Amery had been a very recent witness to such an experiment in Milner's "Kindergarten" in the Cape. Nor could the fresh memory of Rosebery's National Efficiency Cabinet—the "best minds" regardless of party —have been far from the minds of the Liberal-Imperialists.[23] For all, with the exception of Wells and Russell, the primary interest in such a device would be to sharpen the methods of bureaucracy, imperial and domestic.

For the Webbs, the Coefficients fitted into a larger deliberate framework. There had long been an articulate distaste among the Webbs-Shaw circle of Fabians for the planlessness of English democracy—"the sham," as they called it, "behind which civil servants ruled."[24] Their entire policy of permeation, moreover, was premised upon the gullible pliancy of the elected representative, the "Foolometer" of the expert. That policy and sentiment, which was not necessarily that of the Fabians as a whole, aimed at the creation of an elite of what they called "social engineers," independent both of political loyalties and institutional restriction; it was a fairly typical example of the progressive technocracy envisioned by many who came of age in the waning years of Positivism. The Rosebery interlude had been one of the first attempts by the Fabians to carry permeation beyond the stage of the dinner table and lecture hall into the realm of active politics; and the experience, though it may

[21] L. S. Amery, *My Political Life*, p. 224; Wells, *Experiment*, II, 762.

[22] The original scheme was apparently discussed also at a dinner given by Grey in November, attended by the Webbs, Amery, Wells, and Haldane (Wells, *Experiment*, II, 761). The first meeting of the twelve, however, did not occur until 8 December (Amery, *My Political Life*, p. 224).

[23] Rosebery at Glasgow (16 Nov. 1900); and on the "non-party" Cabinet, see House of Lords, 3 Aug. 1900.

[24] B. Webb, "Diary" (17 April 1902), *P.P.*

have left some annoying aches, had added a new refinement to the technique. The Coefficients were not, like the Webbs' past protégés, fresh graduates who might one day sit on royal commissions, but politicians, economists, and intellectuals, most of whom had already gained some foothold in one of the corridors of power.

Together with Russell, H. G. Wells was somewhat out of tune with the dominant mood of the club. He was an irrepressible enthusiast whose flighty political visions were a constant source of irritation to the methodical Webbs. He apparently took up the Coefficients idea as a possible foundation for one of his most cherished oriental fantasies (for the Webbs one of his most annoying, since they were never quite sure he didn't enjoy caricaturing their beloved asceticism). He proposed the remodeling of the Fabian Society into what he called an "Order of the Samurai" which should "embody for mankind a sense of the State."[25] That eccentric project would appear again in various guises in Wells' later works, but in the back of his mind at this moment was the wish to create a "constructive social stratum" which would become the new directive element of the empire—an idea which he admitted drew him, too, toward the Younger Tories and the possibility of building a "new aristocracy" out of the better elements of the old.[26]

Despite a widespread current fashion among British intellectuals of admiring Japanese and German styles, usually attended by righteous disgust at their countrymen's "decadence," Wells' visions were not of necessity shared by the company. Nevertheless, despite his bitter falling out with the Webbs a few years later over both principles and personalities in the Fabian Society, be believed that they were less offended originally by the substance of his proposal than by the gusty manner and odd language in which he advanced it. In *The New Machiavelli*, a pseudonymous autobiography in which the Coefficients appear as the "Pentagram Circle," he recorded their enthusiasm on the subject in language closer to their own:

> The more complicated and technical affairs become, the less confidence will the elected official have in himself. We want to suggest that these expert officials must necessarily develop into a new class

[25] Wells, *A Modern Utopia* (London, 1906), p. 660.

[26] Wells, *The New Machiavelli* (London, 1911), p. 317. The book covers the years 1900-1909 and is apparently accurate in most details. The Coefficients appear in it as the "Pentagram Circle."

and a very powerful class in the community. We want to organise that. It may be the power of the future. They will necessarily have to have very much of a common training. We consider ourselves as amateur unpaid precursors of such a class. . . .[27]

The New Machiavelli was the first of several parodies which Wells made of the Fabian leaders. Before he finally resigned from the Fabian Society in 1908, Wells had become critical of the authoritarian streak he had detected in the Webbs. Much later, during the flirtation of Shaw and the Webbs with both fascism and communism, he reiterated his belief that they had always tended towards "just such a qualification of crude democracy."[28]

Wells' penchant for amplifying language does not obscure the harmony of sentiment behind the "Samurai" idea and the Webbs' recently refined "missionary" role of the expert. Though the Liberal-Imperialist members were not as replete with models of a new order, they had been caught up in Rosebery's National Efficiency crusade and did not find it difficult to fall in with the mood of the Coefficients. That mood was colored, Wells thought, by "the undeniable contraction of the British outlook" at the time:

> Gradually the belief in the possible world leadership of England had been deflated by the economic development of America and the militant boldness of Germany. . . . As a people we had got out of training, and when the challenge of these new rivals became open, it took our breath away at once. . . . Over our table at St. Ermin's Hotel wrangled Maxse, Bellairs, Hewins, Amery and Mackinder, all stung by the small but humiliating tale of disasters in the South African War, all sensitive to the threat of business recession and all profoundly alarmed by the naval and military aggressiveness of Germany, arguing chiefly against the liberalism of Reeves, Russell and myself, and pulling us down, whether we liked it or not, from large generalities to concrete problems.[29]

Though Wells' impressions of the group were naturally shaded by his own dramatic reading of events, the prevailing mind of the

---

[27] Ibid.

[28] Wells, *Experiment*, II, 661; see also *A Modern Utopia* and *Machiavelli*, p. 199 sqq. The reasons for Wells' resignation and his defense against the Webbs are found in *Faults of a Fabian* (1906). F. E. Loewenstein, "The Shaw-Wells Controversy of 1904-1908," *Fabian Quarterly*, no. 41 (April 1944), 15-20.

[29] Wells, *Experiment*, II, 763-764.

members about the future was gloomy by all accounts. Indeed, that gloom itself, which was so prominent a feature of political life for the past two years, was in a sense the common bond of the Co-efficients and the main subject of conversation during the first months of the club's life. On the other hand, the reasons why the members felt drawn to the group varied widely. In Haldane's case, for example, an admitted affinity for the well-laid table may have sufficed alone to sustain his interest in the project. He himself successfully launched the club, from the gastronomical point of view, by hosting the first regular meeting on 8 December (this time in the Ship Tavern). The early conclaves, at least until the spring of 1902, proved satisfying socially and a high level of attendance was kept up—both Haldane and Beatrice Webb were acknowledged masters of the "little dinner."[30]

The agreeableness of the social side, however, was not matched in the discussions. These were governed by a fairly strict regimen, oddly incongruous with the indulgent surroundings. A prepared statement on a topic previously designated was presented by one of the members, after which discussion was to be general, another member refereeing when necessary (as it often was in the early meetings). These procedures were managed casually since most of the members were fully at ease in such small discussions, if not through undergraduate clubs then from their professional and political life. Wells, whose background and education made him a comparative newcomer to these circles, was an exception. These talks, he later recalled, played an important part in his education: "They brought me closer than I had ever come hitherto to many processes in contemporary English politics and they gave me juster ideas of the mental atmosphere in which such affairs are managed."[31] Unfortunately, neither minutes nor written agenda were kept. This was the common practice and obviously a stimulant to freer discussion of the unconventional topics which Amery and the Webbs wished to introduce.[32]

The meetings held between December and May 1903, concentrated on that area in which the Coefficients had hoped to find the largest common ground: the aims and methods of imperial policy. Since all looked upon themselves as imperialists in their own style,

---

[30] Amery, *My Political Life*, p. 224; Wells, *Experiment*, II, 762.

[31] Wells, *Experiment*, II, 761.

[32] See the rules governing discussion in the Pentagram Circle in Wells' *Machiavelli*, p. 314.

it seemed the ideal subject to launch the club on an agreeable and timely note. However, Amery's introduction of Imperial Preference, the cause simultaneously being broached to Chamberlain by the Cape governor, immediately aroused warm divisions.[33] The general principle of closer political and cultural ties within the empire—the object of the Imperial Conference just having met in London—could be supported by all present. Economic union, over which always hung the shadow of Protection and the Food Tax, was a Pandora's box. Preference necessarily introduced into the discussion a host of contentious domestic issues and prejudices: taxation, military training and finance, the City interests, unemployment, education, the price of bread, union organization—over which few bridges had been prepared between the parties.

All were eager to take a "new look" at the empire, all more or less from the common belief that the existing national structure was part of an era that was passing, an era made obsolete by the world of giant national unions like the United States and Germany and the rise of a powerful new maritime power in the Pacific. Brought together by the prevailing prophetic mood, there was a conscious willingness among the members to be farsighted, and to entertain grand designs. Amery and Hewins tried to focus discussion on the idea of a British Imperial *"Zollverein"* in which England would play the Prussian part, a self-sustaining unit which could compete effectively with the new industrial empires.[34] The essential prerequisite for such a union, they argued, was some abridgment of the strict Free Trade principles of the past and the wasteful dogmas which they supported. The majority listened sympathetically, with Wells and Russell the main dissenters (though his feelings were not recorded, Pember Reeves, the Liberal-Fabian, was probably with the minority). The Imperial Tariff Union was too exclusive an idea for Wells and, for Russell, too deliberately provocative towards Europe. These imperialists, Russell felt, "looked forward without too much apprehension to a war with Germany."[35] Wells, a true but slightly dislocated son of the Victorian century, pictured the future

---

[33] Amery was obviously informed of the general nature of Chamberlain's coming speech as early as the meeting of January 1903; four months before the public announcement. His source was probably Milner, who was in touch with both Amery and Chamberlain at the time. Amery, *My Political Life*, p. 224; Hewins, *Apologia*, II, 68-69; Wells, *Experiment*, II, 762-763.

[34] Wells, *Experiment*, II, 762.   [35] Russell, *Portraits*, p. 77.

English-speaking world community as a "Free-Trading, free-speaking, liberating flux for mankind . . ."—the precursor of an enlightened "world-state" or nothing. The oddly enchanted apostles of Tariff Reform in the club, thought Wells, "found it impossible to distinguish between national energy and patriotic narrowness."[36]

To his disappointment, the assembled "Brains Trust" did not find Wells' world vision seductive or even plausible, dispite the imperial sensitivities they held in common. He ascribed this to that mood of "contraction" and alarm which he had first noted in them; there was idealism enough in the club, he thought, to respond to the idea of a generous, benevolent, and "liberating" empire but for economic panic, wounded patriotism, and Joseph Chamberlain's Pauline conversion to protection on the African veldt.[37]

Chamberlain's "national commercial egotism" was outmoded to Wells and repulsive to Russell. But, nailing his colors to the mast and himself to the Coefficients' table, Wells stayed on as a dissenting but loyal regular for the life of the club. Russell was an early casualty. Disturbed by the bellicose mood towards Germany and then denouncing Grey's advocacy of a French and Russian Entente, he stormed out of the February meeting with Hewins, Amery, and Mackinder incanting "My Empire, right or wrong." From this early experience, Russell seems to have formed a lasting suspicion that the Webbs were "fundamentally undemocratic," an inkling confirmed in his mind, as in Wells', by what he later saw as their "undue tolerance" of the dictators of the thirties.[38]

Unhappy that Russell, "like the ego-centred Whig he is," had not consulted him before exiting, Wells felt he should remain as the "one voice" against "this imperialist nonsense" until he was thrown out. Until his final estrangement from the Webbs six years later, Wells obviously attached a great deal more value to these high deliberations than did the aristocratic Russell and, after the first bumpy sessions, he found the group got on very well together.[39] If it was as Wells recalled, we might take it to mean that the discussions moved on from Germany to more general issues.

Thus, by the spring of 1903, with Russell flown and Wells acting an irksome but useful minority of one, the Coefficients appeared to have cleared some of the obstacles in the way of forming

---

[36] Wells, *Experiment*, II, 763-764; *Machiavelli*, p. 315.
[37] Wells, *Experiment*, II, 763.
[38] *Ibid.*, II, 765; Russell, *Portraits*, pp. 100-101.
[39] Wells, *Experiment*, II, 764.

Amery's "well thought out programme." The stubbornest of these questions, however, was yet to arise from the shadow of Chamberlain which had lain across the cups and menus from the start. His introduction of the tariff as a party issue in May basically altered the character of the club. The four club Unionists (Amery, Dawkins, Maxse, and Hewins) rallied to Chamberlain's call with the incongruous ardor that soon became the mark of the Tariff Reformer. Mackinder, formerly a Liberal with a bright future in the party, joined them presently and, with Hewins, became a leading theoretician of the Tariff Reform movement. Like many of their party colleagues, the four Liberal Coefficients (Grey, Haldane, Bellairs, and Mackinder) were flexible and by no means doctrinaire on the Free Trade principle; had Rosebery acted on a moderate revision of that doctrine as he was contemplating a few months earlier, there is no doubt that these four would have followed him. But the kind of thoroughgoing reversal demanded by Chamberlain's May proposals would necessarily have meant a trip across the floor and the immediate sacrifice of long-cultivated party priority. It was an adventure Mackinder and few others (including Winston Churchill passing in the other direction) were prepared to embark upon.

Chamberlain's announcement had about the same effect in the Coefficients Club as in Parliament: to rally the divided Liberals in defense of sacred Free Trade principle, or at least to use that dying cause once more as a means of uniting the party. As we have already seen, Rosebery hesitated before opposing Chamberlain, but when he did the Limps in the club followed suit. They issued a manifesto arguing with some force that Protection would not only undermine the welfare of the working classes but would, as they argued in the league pamphlets, erect a permanent obstacle to developing the competitive efficiency of British industry, thereby increasing rather than reducing the ultimate threat from its foreign rivals. Asked to join the Liberals in their manifesto, Hewins upbraided his dinner companions, adding gratuitously an abusive harangue against the Liberal Party. The most constructive work for them to do, he said, would be to smash it. By the June meeting the founding "non-party" spirit of the club appeared to have dissolved.[40]

[40] The dispute began at the meeting of 12 June 1903. Hewins, *Apologia*, II, 69. Hewins to Sidney Webb (31 May 1903), *W.G.C., P.P.; L.L.P.* no. 62, "Manifesto: Mr. Chamberlain's Conjuring Trick" (June 1903).

The Webbs found themselves between the two groups, somewhat puzzled by the rhapsodic vehemence of the Tariff Reformers and piqued by the regression of their Liberal-Imperialist friends into what seemed cowardly defense of the decrepit Liberal tablets. Shaw, still one of the leading voices of the Fabian Society, declared for Chamberlain right away. The Webbs were staunchly assured by Hewins, who was now the Director of the London School, that "the Liberal Party as we know it will never come into office again." More persuasive still was his pledge that the Tariff Reform program would necessarily include a "social and labour policy," one which the Webbs could no doubt take a hand in writing should they choose to join the Chamberlain bandwagon.[41] The temptation for the Webbs to do so was great; feeling in the Coefficients Club was lopsidedly in that direction, as it probably was in the rump of the Fabian Society as well. Moreover, the excitement of the Younger Tories seemed to highlight the tiredness in the rest of non-Radical politics.

In the few months after May the Webbs more than once considered Hewins' course and, in fact, were persuaded for a time that with their help the Chamberlainites would be headed for dramatic success. "If Joe were to take up the 'National Minimum,' " Beatrice noted in her diary, "he would quite romp in after 'a few months propaganda.' " Nor did they share any of the Liberals' outrage at Protection; if Chamberlain showed sufficient interest in the collectivist social and labor policy, more dynamic interest than had Rosebery, they would willingly "throw in the Import Duties as a willy and expensive ornament to attract the employing classes to the policy of State Regulation." On the other hand, to commit the remaining prestige of Fabianism openly to Tariff Reform, which inevitably meant public involvement in inter- and intraparty squabbles, was to pursue the departure from the old policy of frank opportunism which had proved a failure once and to sacrifice their essential reputation for nonpartisanship.[42] The Rosebery revolt could be construed as a continuance of their assault on the old Liberalism; Tariff Reform at the moment was party politics.

As for the future of the Coefficients Club, Chamberlain had irretrievably doomed the prospect of a "Brains Trust" of talents from all parties acting independently. Whatever course the Webbs now

---

[41] Hewins to S. Webb (31 May 1903), *W.G.C., P.P.*
[42] B. Webb, "Diary" (18 Nov. 1903), *P.P.*

took, this could not be altered. What then was to be the future role of the Coefficients, if any? Most of the original members considered the club, so far as its original aims were concerned, to have become defunct in May 1903. Hewins, Amery, Mackinder, Maxse, and Dawkins, all possessed by the tariff, now began to look upon Chamberlain and the Tariff Reform League as the sole voice of the new imperialism. Haldane, Grey, and Wells sensed quite rightly that their brand of Liberal-Imperialism had suddenly been made obsolete as a political force. Moreover, the dogmatism of the Tariff Reformers left no further room for ad hoc collaboration with imperialists of other parties. That had been the purpose of the club; it now seemed pointless to continue.

It is hard to say how much influence might have been exerted by the Coefficients had the tariff question not divided them so soon after their founding. Whatever their potential, the division of May greatly sobered the sanguine, and rather pretentious, expectations of the would-be "General Staff." Apart from the oddly religious emotions surrounding the Free Trade–Protection controversy, many hard obstacles stood in the way of their acting together as an "above-party" group—not least of all the live political ambitions of most of the members. The original idea necessitated either a strong cohesion of personalities, an agreed-upon sphere of action, or a clear and binding idea. The first, once Russell left and the rest got used to Wells's fancies, was sufficiently strong to keep up "a high rate of attendance" for several years.

It must be remembered that individual members and the various political factions present in the club had their own reasons for being there and continuing to attend over the years. And only for the Webbs and Wells was the club a primary means of engagement in political life after 1903. For Haldane and Grey the Coefficients Club lost its political significance after that time and remained only as a monthly diversion from the regular business of the Liberal Party to which they had become reconciled (both, of course, served in Campbell-Bannerman's first ministry). During the low ebb of their fortunes in the party, the club provided for them a sense of continued activity and contact and for a time was their main source of ideological stimulation. Although it would have been a difficult thing to confess, they clearly shared in Liberalism's much-abused planlessness and lack of assurance. Grey expressed that state of mind plaintively: "Politics have completely changed . . . , formerly you had your cause made for you: all the politician had to do was to preach it; now you have to *make your cause.*"[43]

Despite their protestations, neither Grey nor Haldane ever possessed such a "cause." It was in search of a clear and compelling doctrine, a "well thought out programme," that they had joined with Rosebery, who seemed to promise one, and with the Coefficients, whose professions of expertise seemed to embody one. Their rather prosaic performance in the next Liberal government, however, clearly suggests that they had drawn no such potent doctrine from either source, though they did demonstrate a memory of Fabian instruction in their handling of numerous small issues. Hobson's clearheaded observation that imperialism and domestic Liberalism were unmixable agents seems substantially borne out in the careers of these two Liberal-Imperialists. The case was not necessarily the same for the Tariff Reformers. These now had a clear idea and a consuming passion, though a very odd one among history's multitude of fervent causes. The charismatic leader, Joseph Chamberlain, inspired and personified the movement, but the Liberal League had also had its prophet. Ironically, Chamberlain's paralyzing stroke and Rosebery's temperamental immobility gave both movements a disembodied head—each of them more a legend than a leader. The Liberal-Imperialists dissipated their energies in broad criticism and unfocused discontent, however, while the Tariff Reformers imparted to the ledger of imperial trade duties the mystical certainty of evangelists. Around that particular issue the Tariff Reformers attempted to marshal a harmonious economic, social, political, and racial doctrine, to systematize the nascent and scattered principles of Social-Imperialism. For the Tariff Reform Coefficients, that was the purpose of their presence in the club and the main source of their interest in the bureaucratic "semi-socialism" of the Fabians.

What might be called the organizing principle of the Coefficients was still quite far from being an ideology around which a Jacobin, Bolshevik, or fascist "vanguard" might coalesce. Even in the flexible context of English political theory, the doctrine of "efficiency" was still slightly more a fashionable attitude than a system. Yet such episodes as the Liberal League and the Coefficients Club were symptomatic of the growing tendency within the ruling political organizations, together with such sympathetic factions as the

[43] Grey to Beatrice Webb, "Diary" (28 Feb. 1902), *P.P.*

Webb-Shaw Fabians, to search out and refine a modern "counter-ideology" to both traditional Liberalism and Marxist Socialism. Rosebery's irritation with the ruling parties is indicative of this mood: "I am inclined to think that the disgust of the country with both front benches will aid the extremists—Socialists, Labour, Independent Labour, or what not—and I don't blame the voters for this."[44]

The attempted transformation of the Liberal Party into a party of Social-Imperialism was in compliance to the need felt for such a counterideology. Needless to say, the eclectic maxims of National Efficiency lacked the substance and passion to move masses, despite its considerable appeal among younger imperialists and civil servants. In an important sense, the Coefficients Club was the recognition, by the Webbs particularly, of the need for greater refinement and system in the imperial movement. The short history of the club between November 1902 and June 1903 marks the shift of the Webbs and the doctrine of Social-Imperialism from the Liberal to a Conservative orientation. This new affinity reflected the most fundamental ideological precepts; unlike the Liberalism of Gladstone, Wells, or even Rosebery, Fabianism at this moment and the Tariff Reform movement in general were emphatically not "about equality."

Had Amery and the Webbs realized their handicaps from the beginning and been satisfied merely with bringing the Coefficients together in an atmosphere of open and exploratory discussion, the club would have enjoyed a longer career intact, very possibly with far-reaching effects in the next few years of unprecedented social reform and fierce ideological conflict. Even so, the more realistic potential of the club was not drastically diminished by the schism over the tariff. Its original promise lay merely in drawing into contact, precisely at the right moment, some of the more thoughtful and dynamic younger spirits in empire politics, all of them likely to exercise great influence in the near future. It might still serve this function.

The Coefficients Club survived the May debacle of 1903 as a "dining club for the formal discussion of serious topics" (Amery's description), meeting monthly until the great budget crisis six years later. As the "Brains Trust" of November, there were to have been twelve members only, "all contributors, no passengers."[45]

[44] Cited in R. R. James, *Rosebery*, p. 448.
[45] Amery, *My Political Life*, I, 223.

That prospect now shattered, the dining club ranged more widely. The roster of new members recruited over the next three years indicates considerable success, as well as a progressive waning of Liberal representation in the circle. Before 1906, the Coefficients were joined by Sir Henry Birchenough (chairman of the British South Africa Company), Lord Milner (advanced to viscount on his return from the Cape), Julian Corbett (the naval historian), J. L. Garvin (the volatile editor-to-be of the *Observer*), and John Hugh Smith (chairman of Hambro's Bank). By 1908, the membership was expanded by seven, the most important acquisitions being F. S. Oliver ("Pacificus" of the *Times*), C. F. G. Masterman (the first member of Lloyd George's "Brains Trust" of 1910-1911), W. F. Moneypenny and Colonel Repington of the *Times*, and Josiah Wedgwood (then a member of the Liberal League).[46]

Needless to say, in the expanded club attendance was not kept up as regularly as before. This was in keeping with the more informal regimen of the group. Moreover, a number of selected "passengers" were periodically invited. Both Lloyd George and Winston Churchill, for example, attended a number of club dinners in this status between 1903 and 1909.[47] Such guests were not necessarily aware that they were attending a regular meeting of a club which, at least at one time, had been designed for a political purpose. Most of the minor duties of host, such as the writing of menus and invitations, were left almost entirely to Beatrice Webb after 1903. This pattern naturally left the impression, especially with the transient guests, that the club meetings were nothing but more of the Webbs' famous "little dinners." And since they tended more and more to choose the subjects for conversation if not to dominate the actual discussions after 1903, the Coefficients Club did in fact become something of a Fabian vehicle, a useful variation on the tried practice of permeation.[48]

Previously, the Fabians had dined and cultivated the young So-

[46] Ibid. Wells adds Lord Robert Cecil to the list of new guests, but does not specify whether he attended as "passenger" or member. The former is the more likely, since Cecil was of the Unionist Free Trade faction. Wells, *Experiment*, II, 762.

[47] Lloyd George was first invited in March 1903. B. Webb to Lloyd George (26 March 1903), *W.G.C.*, *P.P.*; B. Webb, "Diary" (10 June 1904), *P.P.*

[48] What appears to be a fairly representative roll of the club's guests is contained in the *Webbs' General Correspondence* (July 1903) which notes the invitations sent out between January and July of that year.

cialists, the union men, and Liberals primarily in the hope of moderating some and stimulating others with their collectivist social prescriptions, to which the Left might logically have had some susceptibility. Now, sequestered from the Left (including most of the reunited Liberal Party), who remained to be permeated? The answer is fairly clearly suggested by the composition of the Coefficients Club after 1903. Of the ten new regular members recruited from that time, all but three were protectionists, engaged in the work of the Tariff Reform League either as active members or as vocal sympathizers. Together with the five original Tariff Reform Coefficients, they were demonstrably the largest cohesive faction of the club.

Hewins, Amery, Mackinder, of the charter members—joined by Milner, Garvin, and Oliver later—were the leading voices of the Tariff Reform movement in its most aggressive period between 1906 and the elections of 1910. During that time, the Tariff Reform League, like the Liberal League before it, began to develop and disseminate a program based upon a strong united empire and "regenerative" social reform at home.[49] That ambitious sphere of action as the "General Staff" of political Social-Imperialism eluded the club from the beginning. But, as we shall see, by bringing into company the leading practitioners of that ideology in both parties over the next few years, the Coefficients helped not only to give form and language to the methods of government but to change the language of ideological conflict in English politics until the war.

[49] In April 1909, the league reported its circulation record as follows: 1906—1,603,000; 1907—3,225,000; 1908—6,034,900; 1909—53,169,716 (its bookkeeping more exact now). See Macnamara, *Tariff Reform and the Working Man* (London, 1910), p. 9; "Monthly Notes on Tariff Reform," *T.R.L.*, x, 4 (April 1909). The primary authors of the latter were Amery, J. L. Garvin, Hewins, and Austen Chamberlain.

IV

The Tariff Reform Movement:
"*Le revenu c'est l'état*"

The Chamberlain-Milner Method

Between Lord Rosebery and Joseph Chamberlain there was very little personal resemblance or affinity: Rosebery, the model of aristocratic tradition, a contemplative and private man for whom politics was a mere obligation, and the Birmingham manufacturer, clamorously middle-class, self-consciously a public figure and active and ambitious by nature. But if the quality of leadership in late Victorian politics grew out of the habit of being admired, envied, and listened to, then both might be said to possess the right to rule men. Within their respective circles the position of the two men was strikingly similar in some significant respects. Their close admirers tended to be slightly younger men than the average in Parliament and the press and, perhaps partly for that reason, they invested more than the usual fervor in their leaders. Moreover, at the high point of their popularity during the life of the two leagues which they headed, both left an unmistakable impression of not being physically present, of presiding over the battle in disembodied form. Rosebery's cultivated aloofness created that illusion while Chamberlain's invalidism permanently elevated him above the tarnishing banalities of politics. Ironically, his stroke beatified the Chamberlain name, magnifying and prolonging its influence in politics in the Edwardian years, until it was thought not at all excessive to invoke the "Chamberlain spirit" among the Tariff Reformers. In comparing such movements as Liberal-Imperialism and Tariff Reform, it would seem that the muter the prophet the more ardent were his priests.

Excepting the protective tariff itself, the resemblances of the

Liberal-Imperialists and the Tariff Reformers are worth noting. Both were headed by aging crusaders of a previous political generation whose political careers were frustrated just short of complete success; both elaborated a "new imperialism" based on efficiency, authority, and bureaucratic dynamism; and both movements were given life by the war crisis. The two league leaders also sought to capture political power by a distinctive appeal "above parties" to the young, uncommitted men just emerging into prominence around Westminster. Although Chamberlain's men carried through the revolt in the Unionist Party behind the banner of Tariff Reform (finally winning over their party where the Liberals had failed), their campaign was never restricted merely to the tariff issue. Like the Liberal League, the Tariff Reformers worked upon a public already sensitized to the language of decline and decadence. And from the beginning of their long and industrious crusade they attracted, as had Rosebery for a time, many shades of opinion from within the two parties and accommodated numerous anxious causes from outside of party politics. For some of their allies, such as the Fabians and the National Service League, reform of the tariff was no more than a secondary, sometimes even an unpalatable, issue. Moreover, both groups of rebels were keenly aware, once the war was ended, of the poverty of popular issues in the platforms of the major parties which could hold any promise of capturing, or even of retaining, the strength of the enfranchised masses.

Mere imperialism, after the unglorious conclusion of the Boer War, was seen by both Rosebery and Chamberlain as an inadequate defense against continued Radical victories at the polls. Rosebery and Grey, with the help of Maxse and a powerful section of the press, had added something to this defense by focusing attention on the growing threat from Germany and America in industrial, technical, and educational sectors as well as the military. But it had been mainly the Fabians who had streamlined Rosebery's imperialism by embossing it with a Fabian "social and labour policy." Amery's amalgam of "imperialism and semi-socialism" was much the same blend. Social legislation was not especially new to Unionist platforms either; it was a powerful subtradition of Tory conservatism and had been a prominent part of Unionist campaigns as late as 1895. Both the municipal "semi-socialism" of Chamberlain and the broad Tory democracy of Balfour recognized the utility of a prudent social policy in countervailing agitation from the

Left: "Social legislation," Balfour remarked in 1895, ". . . is not merely to be distinguished from Socialist legislation, but it is its most direct opposite and its most effective antidote."[1]

Chamberlain fully subscribed to this thesis and had firmly associated his name with Unionist social reform long before the war. Beyond the campaign rhetoric, Conservative-Unionist social policies had never exceeded a very moderate Bismarckian measure of accident and old-age insurance for deserving workers—far short even of the mundane municipal "Socialism" of Chamberlain's Birmingham. Yet the failure of Liberal governments in this field combined with Chamberlain's nationwide reputation were enough to win working-class votes from the Liberals and to attract the interest of the reform-minded, including the Fabians and a segment of the growing numbers of social scientists.[2]

Although Chamberlain's image as a man of modern social ideas was somewhat tarnished by the current legislative record of the Unionist government in this area and his own obsession with Colonial Office affairs, it remained sufficiently strong after the war to keep in his train such men as Hewins, Mackinder, Charles Booth, and Sidney Webb, all of them inclined to look to him for a viable alternative to the social policies of the Socialists and Liberals. His apparently dormant interest in the social question only began to revive after the war. This process was no doubt quickened by the success and obvious promise of the Labour Representation Committee, notably by the sensational by-election victory of Will Crooks in Woolwich, one of the safest Tory constituencies, on the very day that Chamberlain stepped off the boat from the Cape.[3]

The conjunction of Crooks's election and the rebirth of the Tariff Reform movement was not fortuitous; it symbolized the appearance of labor as an independent and aggressive political force and the simultaneous reaction of the Right. Responding to the threat implicit in Crooks's victory, the Tariff Reform League openly en-

---

[1] Arthur James Balfour, speech at Manchester (16 Jan. 1895).

[2] A good example of Chamberlain's overall policy on the social question and one which attracted much favorable attention can be found in his article of 1892, "The Labour Question," in *Nineteenth Century and After*, XXXII (Nov. 1892), 677 sqq.

[3] Crooks's election at Woolwich was the fourth success for the L.R.C., but by far the most significant until then, since it was conducted for the first time with the full cooperation of the unions and the committee, whose membership for the year had shown its first sensational rise (450,000 to 750,000). L.R.C., *Report of the Third Annual Conference* (1903), p. 7.

gaged to challenge the hold of the Left on the votes and loyalties of the British working man. Though no striking success was to be achieved before the war, continuous efforts were made to evolve an ideology and tactic to reach this goal under the auspices of the Tariff Reform League. Early in 1904, a National Free Labour Association was organized by the league to "represent the overwhelming numbers of working men unconnected with Trade Unions or Socialistic associations."[4] The National Free Labour Association was a prototype for a succession of such projects sponsored by the league and its appendages between 1903 and 1918. Tariff Reformers directed (and to a large extent financed) the Unionist Labour Representation League, the Conservative Working Men's Association, the Unionist Social Reform Committee and (during the war) the British Workers National League.[5] In addition, the Tariff Reform League maintained a permanent Trades Union Branch which had the function of recruiting and organizing non-Socialist working men and, theoretically, of speaking for them in the making of league policy. Apart from the Labour Party and the trades unions themselves, the Tariff Reform League was by far the most active political labor organization in the country during these years. There was no comparable Liberal effort.

The working men's association was an idea obviously borrowed from the Left in a manner that became increasingly common in Tariff Reform strategy before the war. Often, the working men's groups organized by the Right were treated merely as a matter of form—the creation of a suitable title (like the Unionist Labour Representation League) and the election of a secretary from among the small number of bonafide working men active in the league. There was little faith in the regular Conservative ranks that the working classes could be weaned in great numbers from the Socialists and Radicals, except in the minds of the Tariff Reformers

[4] "Monthly Notes," *T.R.L.*, I, 5 (Nov. 1904), 238.

[5] The National Free Labour Association apparently lasted only till the 1905 election, at which time the reports of its activities in the "Monthly Notes" ceases. Cf. "Monthly Notes," *T.R.L.*, I, 5 (Nov. 1904); II, 3 (March 1905); IV, 2 (Feb. 1906). For the U.L.R.L., which seems to have been largely under Milner's personal direction, see "Memo": U.L.R.L. to Milner (9 Dec. 1907), *M.P.*, A. I. For the U.S.R.C. (1911) and the B.W.N.L. (1917), see chapters XI and XII. Another such group, the Trades Union Branch of the T.R.L., is described in Semmel, *Imperialism and Social Reform*, pp. 114-115; also in "Monthly Notes," *T.R.L.*, VI, 2 (Aug. 1907).

behind Chamberlain and Milner. These, together with the Liberal-Imperialists and the Fabians, had begun to see the possibilities of the Social-Imperialist approach. In the aftermath of the Boer War there was the obvious need felt to respond to radical charges that imperialism, Tariff Reform, jingo patriotism, and even the war itself were nothing more than the cause of fearful special interests. Even those who took the leading interest in organizing labor support, like Alfred Milner, had scant experience in popular political organization; like the Fabians, the Coefficients, and Milner himself, the majority of Tariff Reformers desirous of reaching large masses of working men had finer skills in the writing of memoranda than in the writing of pamphlets. Several years passed before mere practice and the brilliant instruction of J. L. Garvin (the editor of the *Observer* after 1906) sharpened the Tariff Reform League spokesmen in the esoteric craft of modern propaganda. Just as Rosebery had, the Tariff Reform League leaders recognized the need of a clear "social and labour policy" in competing with the Left for a popular following, but like him they also found the passage between lip service to the "patriotic poor" and substantial relief in housing, health, and prices cluttered with novel and unpleasant questions.

Their experience with the Trades Union Branch was typical of their confusion over the question; the branch, founded expressly to canvass and represent the view of working men in the league, was immediately besieged with protests over the so-called Food Tax, and when the branch's spokesman conscientiously argued that point at the general meeting it was greeted by consternation and shock that such a fundamental axiom of the movement should arise for debate at all. Though such incidents did not noticeably shake the confidence of the leadership that a social policy could be integrated into the tariff program, they revealed the distance yet to be traveled in the strategy and skills of the league, as well as in the instruction of its membership, in dealing with labor and social issues. As the details of a social policy evolved, numerous experiments and alterations were made in the working of the various Tariff Reform League labor associations, while their ultimate purpose remained in focus and unchanging: to delay or to prevent the feared political monopoly of the Left in the labor movement.

Much of the organizing and ideological work in connection with labor was carried on by Milner who, after Chamberlain's invalidism, became the guiding spirit of the Tariff Reformers. The vacuum left by Chamberlain could never be completely filled by Milner; a morose and introspective bachelor, Milner had the sort of humorless intelligence which invariably awed small groups of serious young men but was far too dogged and intolerant ever to win a broad political following. Edwardian politics were full of biographies such as his: sons of mid-century families enjoying a Victorian respectability which made their poverty the more bitter and intolerable. He brought neither family nor joy with him to his extraordinary personal success, merely that industrious loneliness which had raised him up. Milner's complicated personality combined with the autocratic habits of a colonial governor made him a most unlikely candidate to succeed to Chamberlain's charisma. Both his style and his philosophy, according to the many critics of his rule in South Africa, stood for all that the country abhorred[6] —it was, as Hobson noted, an attitude commonly inspired by the returning colonial civil servant.

Milner frequently professed a devotion to what he called a "nobler Socialism" than that of the class struggle, of a kind which would substitute the consciousness of nation and empire for that of class.[7] Partly because of his German birth and background, Milner's ideological utterances were frequently ridiculed by his critics for their "alien," metaphysical quality. Indeed, he is often thought of still as an exotic aberration in modern British politics and no example of a significant native attitude.[8] Nevertheless, the idea of an integrated nation and empire which might generate a sufficiently strong anti-Socialist spirit to subsume class had substantial currency among his contemporaries on the Right. It rested on the not completely naive hope that, despite the divisive efforts of the Cobdenites and Socialists, materialism and class hatred had not yet displaced patriotism as the dominant intuition of the working classes of Great Britain. In addition to Milner's own numerous protégés, this hope was diligently nurtured by the immensely influential "barracks Socialist," Robert Blatchford of the *Clarion*,

---

[6] Cited in Alfred Gollin, *Proconsul in Politics* (London, 1964), p. 4.

[7] Alfred Lord Milner, *The Nation and the Empire* (London, 1913), pp. 139-140.

[8] A. P. Thornton is one prominent example of the school of thought which holds that such minority views as Milner's, not being widely shared by the British public, were therefore alien aberrations or personal "quirks." See Thornton's remarks on Semmel's thesis in *For the File* (London, 1968), p. 28 et passim, a witty but none too serious collection of pot shots.

and by the Fabians, both of whom maintained a sympathetic communication with the Tariff Reformers during the Edwardian period.[9]

The efforts of the Tariff Reform League to divert labor from its radical course and from the kind of internationalism they feared in the form of the Second International were stoutly applauded by the Shaw-Webb Fabians who continued in control of the major Fabian propagandist organs. And, since the method of achieving that purpose had come primarily from their contacts with the Fabians since 1901, it constituted an important and sustained link between the two groups. Shortly after the launching of the Tariff Reform League pamphleteering campaign in December 1904, the *Fabian News* outlined the strategy that soon became the dominant refrain of the Tariff Reform movement: "Socialism is anti-Liberal . . . the typical working man is more Tory than Liberal. . . . Probably he is at heart a Protectionist . . . and certainly a Jingo."[10] The league's pamphlet for that month ("Monthly Notes," December 1904), in an article signed by the Coefficients' W. A. S. Hewins, echoed the theme: ". . . Tariff Reform is preeminently a working man's question . . . [and] the working man naturally rejects Cobdenite principles."[11]

The picture of Liberalism held by the Tariff Reformer had not yet become that of the Trojan Horse through which the predatory and alien forces gained entry into national politics; rather it was portrayed at this time in Tariff Reform League literature as a oncegreat national institution whose senile complacency was infecting the nation's vigor and whose life was being prolonged through an unnatural infusion of Radical and Labour strength. Liberalism, not Socialism, was still seen as the immediate enemy. The other view began slowly to emerge after the next general election, but in 1904 the strategists of the Right still held to the belief that it could challenge Liberalism for at least a competitive portion of the growing political strength of the working classes and that the traditional political methods and institutions still offered a means of containing that strength. That conviction and the strategy which derived from

[9] "Socialism and Tariff Reform," *Clarion*, 21 Jan. 1910; cited in Semmel, *Imperialism and Social Reform*; also, Blatchford to Milner (n.d., 1909), M.P., A. III; Blatchford, *My Eighty Years* (London, 1931), p. 200.

[10] *Fabian News*, XIV, 4 (Dec. 1904), 47.

[11] "Monthly Notes," *T.R.L.*, I, 6 (Dec. 1904). The "Monthly Notes" at this time had a limited circulation and was designed mainly for distribution among active league members rather than to the public.

it came in one part from the imperialists who dominated the movement and in another from those circles which had been primed by the Fabians and the Coefficients. The league's design in the first few years was to juxtapose the patriotism and economic interests of the working man, as the Tariff Reformer saw it, to the supposed internationalism and individualism of the Liberal Party. "Tariff Reform," the league's pamphlet of March 1905 proclaimed, "stands for the principle of State-assistance to the individual, whilst the present system leaves the individual to his own resources."[12] The resultant content of the Tariff Reform League propaganda disclosed more of an ideological caricature than a systematic philosophy, but still contained clear marks of the well-developed Fabian critique of Liberalism. It was precisely the stance in which the Fabians had tried to pose the Liberal-Imperialists two years before without great success. The dynamic interventionist-reform posture in which the pamphlets of 1904-1905 depicted the movement is attributable much less to Chamberlain, whose increasingly rare public utterances were restricted generally to parliamentary and imperial issues, than to the two Coefficients who became the theoretical mentors of the league, Hewins and Mackinder. Both of these "Shadow Ministers" of the Coefficients' Brains Trust (Hewins as the economist and Mackinder as imperial expert) had become interested in the Liberal League through the Webbs, both became directors of the London School through their contact with the Webbs, and both finally resigned that post to devote their time to the campaign for Tariff Reform. Though it is incorrect to call either of these distinguished intellectuals Webb's creatures, their close association with the Fabians in all of these projects does help to explain the presence of the Webbs' characteristic mark in their writings and, consequently, in the formative propaganda of the Tariff Reform League.[13]

[12] Ibid., II, 3 (March 1905).
[13] Hewins left the L.S.E. in 1903. He was succeeded there by Mackinder until he too left to join the league in 1908. That Milner was, in fact, the responsible director of the league at that time is clear from Mackinder's correspondence with him, in which the terms of employment, including salary, are approved by Milner. Mackinder to Milner (22 May 1908), *M.P.*, Letters, A.II. See also B. Webb, "Diary" (10 May 1908), *P.P.*: ". . . the man I shall be working with most closely will be Milner. . . ." Mackinder had apparently to be interviewed by Amery before speaking of the post with Milner. Amery to Milner (4 March, 15 May 1908), *M.P.*, Letters, A.II; Mackinder to Amery (22 May 1908), *M.P.*, Letters, A.II.

The Tariff Reform League thus inherited from its leading theorists the Fabian-composed lexicon of State Socialism—contemptuous antiindividualism, social "engineering," efficiency, expertise, and bureaucracy—which Rosebery's Liberal League had also adopted from its contact with the assiduous Webbs. In Mackinder's first general exposition of the Tariff Reform argument, *Money-Power and Man-Power: The Underlying Principles rather than the Statistics of Tariff Reform* (1906), Rosebery's vision of the "Imperial Race" was restated axiomatically: "A great trade can alone supply much wages and support a great and efficient population. A great and efficient population is the only firm source of great power."[14] Through Mackinder, too, many of the pet projects of the Liberal League in temperance, slum reform, and education, its alarm at the decline in the birth rate and at international trade statistics, and its constant preoccupation with the "German menace," were all smoothly transposed into the script of Tariff Reform.[15]

That there should have been strong similarities in the language of the two movements whose overriding concern was the decline of the empire is perhaps not remarkable. But it was more their increasing *integration* of imperial and domestic "reconstruction" which gave both the Liberal League and the Tariff Reform movement their distinctive character and significance—what has been called their Social-Imperialist ideology. It has already been noted that the Fabians were the first to instruct the Liberal-Imperialists in the crucial interlocking, and the political possibilities, of imperial and domestic policies. Primarily through the agency of the Coefficients Club, this tutorship had continued into the formative period of Tariff Reform thinking. "The dominant note in our intercourse with these people (i.e., the imperialist politicians) is Social Reconstruction," Beatrice Webb noted of the club in 1904; ". . . in all the little dinners at Grosvenor Road and the tête à tête talk at other people's dinners—it is always around some [such] project that the conversation ranges."[16]

[14] H. J. Mackinder, *Money-Power and Man-Power: the Underlying Principles rather than the Statistics of Tariff Reform* (London, 1906), pp. 13-14. See also "Man-Power as a Measure of National and Imperial Strength," *National Review*, XLV (March 1905)—a culmination of a series of articles for the T.R.L. during 1903-1904.

[15] Ibid. For T.R.L. views on Germany, see "Monthly Notes," *T.R.L.*, III, 5 (Nov. 1905); VIII, 4 (April 1908).

[16] B. Webb, "Diary" (n.d., May 1904), *P.P.*

Tariff Reform Movement

By the time the Tariff Reform campaign had gotten fully underway in 1904, the Webbs had more or less abandoned their education of the Liberal Party, or at least of its older members and leadership, as an investment with diminishing returns. With Campbell-Bannerman and the older Gladstonians in the ascendant, Beatrice mourned, "Little Englandism, crude democracy, economy, secularism, are all again to the front in the official Liberal Party. . . ." With the doggedness that sprang from their unshakable certainty, the Webbs plied the other side—the Unionists and protectionists conveniently assembled each month in the Coefficients Club. This was of course in keeping with their policy of opportunism and permeation. It did not mark any sudden disillusionment with their accustomed friends, whether Liberal or Socialist; they had few illusions there since the war and the Rosebery experiment. Neither was there any intention of permanently severing what connections they retained with the Left. "A man who has brains and is willing to lend them freely to anyone who can use them," Beatrice still believed, "will sooner or later have his share of real power."[17] As in the break with the Left over the war, they had merely misread again the flow of political power and had inadvertently narrowed the scope of their political influence to the Right for the time being.

The Tariff Reformers who made up such a large part of the club membership proved gratifyingly receptive to the Social-Imperialist formulas, perhaps none more so than Alfred Milner. Having attended several meetings of the Coefficients after his final return from South Africa in 1905, Milner was impressed. Writing to Sidney Webb after one of these encounters, he expressed what appears to have been the harmony of views at the previous night's gathering:

> There is an unfortunate division between two sorts of people, both in their way patriotic and unselfish, of whom the one party is attracted by what is called 'social reform' and the other by 'Imperial' problems. It is quite true that in the vast field of national politics, no man can be an expert all round, and every man is, rightly, most interested in the branch of which he has most experience. But it ought not to follow . . . that he undervalues the importance of the other side. Personally, I always resent the suggestion that, because I am what is vulgarly known as an 'Imperialist,' I am therefore in-

[17] Ibid. (1 March 1904).

different to and callous about those domestic reforms—real reforms .... I know that you and Mrs. Webb are among the few people, who, like myself, try to see our national position as a whole.[18]

After Chamberlain, the Webbs could not have won over a more favorably placed Tariff Reformer than Milner. Not only was he the central personality in the movement after Chamberlain's removal, but he commanded the most intense devotion of his many disciples and protégés, including Amery, J. L. Garvin, and the graduates of the Kindergarten, many of them strategically placed, capable, and determined to possess the policy-making apparatus of the Unionist Party.[19] Moreover, during their first contacts, Milner and the Webbs found that they shared much in their political philosophy. Both passionately belabored the mechanical individualism and the divisive "abstract rights" of traditional Liberalism, popular indolence, middle-class materialism, and parliamentary muddling while extolling service, efficiency, bureaucratic expertise, and national solidarity. The Webbs never fully reconciled themselves to the "crude democracy" created by a century of reform while Milner felt himself—with the ruination of his career and his life's work for the empire—to be the principal victim of what he labeled with disgust "the System."

Like many another repatriated proconsul, Milner brought back with him to the home democracy the bearing and the stern manners of colonial rule. The Webbs and most of their faction saw similar virtues in other overseas models. Impressed by the success of Japan against the Russians, they frequently noted the possible lessons to be learned from that other island society—as Beatrice Webb described it:

> ... the Japanese; the Idealist, the self-abnegation of all classes to the community in a common cause. ... Their success will tell against

[18] Milner to S. Webb, *W.G.C.* (19 Oct. 1906). Milner begins to attend club meetings regularly from 14 Oct. 1905; he is mentioned in the Webbs' correspondence to have been at the meetings of October, November 1905; September, October 1906. For Milner's position on social reform, see his address, "Unionists and Social Reform" (19 Nov. 1907, *The Nation and the Empire*, pp. 250 sqq.

[19] Milner's recent biographer implies that he gave up plans in 1907 to direct the T.R.L. after long negotiations regarding expenses, etc. This picture does not correspond with the impression of Amery's and Mackinder's correspondence of early 1908 (see n. 13 above) in which Milner holds the decision of clear authority. Gollin, *Proconsul*, p. 207.

Christianity as the One Religion, against materialistic individualism, vs luxury, in favour of organisation, collective regulation, scientific education, physical and mental training—but on the whole not in favour of Democracy. . . .[20]

Milner, with the sympathy of his circle, nurtured a bitter personal resentment against the Parliament for its public rebuke of his actions in the Cape. Even "Joe," whom he had been accustomed to trust, had been made to give way in that instance to the pressures of "parliamentary necessities, of Party, of a rotten public opinion." It was "the System," the party system, which had ruined him and threatened to do the same to the empire. "What can you expect," he wrote at the time of his connection with the Coefficients, "with the system of government in such a mess. Here is everything dependent on this *Rotten Assembly* at Westminster and the whole future of the Empire may turn upon the whims of men who have been elected for their competence in dealing with Metropolitan Tramways or country pubs."[21]

Such a critique was most congenial to the kind of grievances behind the stillborn "Party of National Efficiency" of Rosebery and the Fabians; while among the Coefficients, despair with the party system was a sustaining common emotion. It appears that Milner's part in the conversations at the Coefficients' table was an unrelenting and well-received harangue against the party tradition and all that it supported in the constitutional framework. During one of the early meetings attended by Milner, Beatrice marked that he was "obsessed . . . with a vision of non-party government without having invented any device for securing it."[22] Although Rosebery shared something of that vision with him too, Milner was clearly prepared to go much further than he in realizing it; where Rosebery would prune, Milner wished to uproot: "You will have to abandon 'party government' to me for plenary execution before you have done," he wrote to Sidney Webb after another Coefficients meeting. Even his close admirers felt the jarring extremism of his views on the subject. There were moments, one of them remarked, when he would have thought the suspension of the ancient constitution itself

[20] B. Webb, "Diary" (22 Dec. 1904), *P.P.*
[21] Milner to George Parkins (24 July 1905), *M.P.*, A.I.; Gollin, *Proconsul*, p. 46. Though more restrained, Milner's public remarks on the party system were in the same vein; e.g., Milner, House of Lords, 26 Feb. 1906.
[22] B. Webb, "Diary" (14 Oct. 1905), *P.P.*

"a wholesome step towards the more efficient developement [sic] of the Empire."[23]

There was a degree of romance attached to the figure of the censured proconsul, industriously fostered by imperialist critics of Parliament and his own circle. For the more ardent imperialists he was a symbol of the selfless public servant betrayed, victim of the perfidious "politicians" of Westminster and the party clubs. His case had some of the makings of the myth fostered by the German military after the defeat in 1918. In this instance also the myth contained a malignant potential for the democracy, whose direction is visible in the following correspondence between Milner and F. H. Congdon, founder and secretary of the Colonial Section of the Tariff Reform League (known outside of England as the Imperial Federalist Association).

> I believe you to be [Congdon wrote] the one man at present in public life who possesses the ability, patriotism and *hatred of sham* necessary in him who shall lead the way in saving the Empire from the very *imminent dangers* which menace it. . . . I believe the Association to be the only possible instrument with which to lead up to the formation of the *Patriotic Party*, by which such salvation shall be affected. . . . I feel so deeply the dreadful condition of Public affairs, brought about by this cursed *Party system*, that I am little better than a fanatic . . . fools . . . scoundrels!
>
> . . . I hold that man to be the most traiterous [sic] and despicable of scoundrels who for Party or selfish ends or yet to gain cheap notoriety—clings to a position of public . . . trust which, he must know, he is wholly incapable of properly filling. . . . Your letter [17 November 1904] shows that we entirely agree that Party Government—in its present form—is the immediate cause of the dangers which threaten the Empire. . . . How to render the system harmless? . . . I wrote [in a previous letter to Milner] that I should labour to create such a Party which should be a weapon in your hand, when someday you assumed your rightful position in Public Affairs.[24]

Although Congdon's language appears to mark him as something of an extremist—in his own words a "fanatic"—his vision of

[23] Ibid.; Julian Amery, *Life of Chamberlain* (London, 1932), IV, cited in Gollin, *Proconsul*, p. 47.

[24] F. H. Congdon to Milner (24 Dec. 1905), *M.P.*, Letters, A.I. Milner's correspondence with Congdon on the subject of the "Patriotic Party" ranges over the entire year 1905; cf. 18 March 1905, 27 Oct. 1905, in *M.P.*, Letters, A.I.

a Patriotic Party was by no means out of tune with current imperialist thinking, especially in Tariff Reform circles, both inside and outside the mother country. Implicit in the behavior of imperialists like Congdon was an anxious need for a clear and compelling new cause, or at least for a dynamic contemporary language in which to clothe old ones. The Liberal-Imperialists had been in that same quest and came up, a little uncertainly, with National Efficiency. Grey's confessed bewilderment with the changes that had taken place in political life was shared by many of his contemporaries, including the leadership of the Tariff Reform movement who evidently felt, too, that in the looming conflicts of twentieth-century politics you would have to "make your cause" in order to survive.

From the day Chamberlain launched the tariff campaign, the protectionists had been pursuing such a cause with even greater urgency and went at first to the same source as Rosebery had. "The position at home is rather gloomy," Milner sadly reported to a friend in the Cape:

> There is a sort of blight on men in both parties, and indeed on public life generally. We are flogging dead horses, mumbling the formulae of the past. I can see no realisation of the facts of the present: there are certainly no big ideas—in fact I don't see any ideas of any kind—with regard to the future. Not among politicians I mean. There are occasional spasms of VITALITY in the press and outside, which the party organisations on both sides seek to suppress.[25]

The Tariff Reformers did not find the "big ideas," indeed they did not even look for them, in the platforms or from the leaders of the Conservative-Unionist coalition; no more than did Rosebery seek inspiration from Liberal orthodoxy. For both, however, the seemingly assured and militant logic of Socialism contained a kind of illicit appeal as of forbidden fruit; and when expounded patriotically and congenially by the Fabians it also lost most of its predatory menace. The conspiratorial undertones even of the Fabian variety bore a romantic attraction to the growing number of young and unaffiliated men in and around Westminster, or those who had broken ties during the many debacles since the war. In the small

---

[25] Milner to Lionel Curtis (25 Aug. 1905); cited in Gollin, *Proconsul*, p. 102.

exclusive political group they could find the form, if not the substance, of a clear ideological purpose. Such close, militant, and determined cabals were consistently Milner's preferred way of conducting political affairs. From his Kindergarten in South Africa, to the Coefficients, the Compatriots, the Confederates, and the Round Table—groups with which he became affiliated during the next few years—all were of this secretive character, organized around the imperial cause, and all drew the unstinting fascination of the proconsul.[26]

The Compatriots

The Compatriots, one of the groups through which Milner hoped to reenter home politics after his return, were a continuation of the political style set by the Coefficients. Founded by Amery in January 1904, the Compatriots were rather obviously modeled on the Coefficients Club of two years before. Five of the original nucleus of twelve Compatriots were, in fact, still active members of the Webbs' group: Amery himself, Maxse, Mackinder, Hewins, and Milner. The significant difference in the two groups lay in the fact that the Compatriots' roster was to be strictly limited to leading members and associates of the Tariff Reform League and its affiliated organizations. Thus the new group would distinctly bear the mark of the Unionist Party. Much like the earlier circle of twelve Coefficients, the Compatriot members were to be chosen discreetly by Amery and the Tariff Reform members of the Coefficients on the basis of ability and imperial ardor, with political popularity and position playing no part in the selections.

When Amery invited Milner to join the Compatriots in February, the nucleus of the group had already met several times in Amery's rooms in the Temple, but as yet they had not fully refined their purpose:

> . . . I have been engaged lately [Amery wrote] in trying to get together a small League or association of people who think con-

[26] The Round Table was another small circle of imperialists, graduates of Milner's Kindergarten, organized by Lionel Curtis, Philip Kerr, and F. S. Oliver in 1910 to disseminate information of imperial interest through a monthly journal named for the group, *The Round Table*; see chapter III.

structively and Imperially.... So far, though there has been plenty of revolt against laissez-faire and Little Englandism, there has been *no coherent general outcome to put in its place*.... At present, no doubt we shall mainly think and worry about the economic side, but there are lots more in the background, from compulsory [military] service and demolition of the Treasury to the construction of an Imperial Council and the putting of the House of Commons in its proper place.... Fossils, even if 'whole hog' Chamberlainites, protectionist manufacturers, Parliamentary place hunters, and all that clan, will be ... kept out.[27]

The Compatriots were to play a more active political role than the Coefficients. Except in the sense that Amery saw no immediate political outcome emerging from the Webbs' circle, the new group was in no way intended as the successor of the older one; most of the joint members kept up their attendance at the Ship Tavern simultaneously. Amery had organized the Compatriots at the outset as a conscious application of the Coefficients' "Brains Trust" idea to the organization of the Tariff Reform League. The patent failure of the Coefficients to constitute themselves as an "above-party" General Staff, as well as the now clear intention of the Coefficient Liberals to ease their way back to the official party fold, led the Tariff Reformers back to their immediate goal of capturing control of the Unionist Party through the growing organization of the Tariff Reform League. As his letter to Milner suggests, Amery's hope in founding the Compatriots was to prevent the influence of those protectionist manufacturers and office seekers who had quickly attached themselves to the league from diluting the high "Imperial Tone" of the Tariff Reform movement, a process he distastefully sensed was already in motion by 1904. His patent disdain for the business interests which provided not only the financial prop but a good portion of the membership of the league he helped to lead reveals something of the gulf between the supporters and the leadership of the movement.[28] In excluding the vested interests of Tariff

---

[27] Amery to Milner (26 Feb. 1904), *M.P.*, Letters, A.I. My italics.

[28] The financial report of the Compatriots Club from Amery to Milner quotes a total budget of £2700 *for four years*, out of which Mackinder's salary as editor of the T.R.L. literature was to be paid. The major contributors were the Duke of Westminster, Lloyd George's Limehouse whipping boy, C. S. Goldman and G. C. Sellar, a protectionist manufacturer and a Tariff Commissioner. Amery to Milner (4 April 1908), *M.P.*, Letters, A.II; L. Corbally to Milner (20 Dec. 1907), *M.P.*, Letters, A.I.

Reform, the Compatriots group would array itself with the nobler mission of maintaining the theoretical purity and idealism of the imperialist cause; that is, of formulating that "coherent general outcome" to put in the place of laissez-faire and Little Englandism. Indeed, this was the objective of Amery as well as of Mackinder and Hewins in composing the policy of the Tariff Reform League: to arrive at some coherent ideological statement of the imperialist faith which, by removing the taint of class privilege and private interest, could rival the purposeful and transcendent logic of the Left.[29]

The role in which the Webbs had cast Rosebery and the Coefficient Liberals, as "iconoclasts" of Liberal principles, would now be played by the Tariff Reform members of the group in the Conservative Party tableau, and with a good deal more force. A number of factors which had appeared to favor the Liberal-Imperialist insurgents in their bid to win control of the Liberal Party were not present at first to assist the Tariff Reformers in their attack on the Conservative-Unionist leadership—the so-called "Cecil monopoly." First of all, behind Rosebery in 1901 and 1902 was the most distinguished group of Liberal ministers-designate, men like Asquith, Grey, and Haldane, who could expect to be part of any future Liberal Cabinet. As the Webbs had correctly estimated, the Rosebery circle of those years was bound to become a leading force in any Liberal government whether or not Rosebery himself endured. Thus, although the actual number of Liberal dissidents even at the height of the Liberal League was never very large compared to the bulk of the party in Parliament, a revolt led by this small influential group had to be taken seriously by the party. Moreover, with the Liberal Party in opposition, and deeply fragmented over war issues, the real possibility existed that at any moment the Limps would carry off the moderate center of the party in a patriotic reaction to the excesses of the pro-Boers and Socialists during the war.

The situation was more or less reversed for the imperialist bloc on the Unionist side. In this instance, the pool of ministerial talent

---

[29] Ibid. Semmel presents a good discussion of the economic bias of the T.R.L. membership inside and outside of Parliament, but does not note the patent separation from the theoretical leadership of Amery, Hewins, Mackinder, Milner, et al., all relatively penurious and none of whom can be closely associated financially with the export industries. Semmel, *Imperialism and Social Reform*, pp. 102-105.

and status was one-sidedly in Balfour's camp and most of them looked upon Chamberlain's crusade for the general tariff as a dangerous aberration. Although the majority of Unionist ministers favored some form of Imperial Preference, or tariff retaliation, they regarded the sweeping proposals of Chamberlain and the Tariff Reform League as a revolutionary threat comparable to that from the far Left, the threat of "protection, socialism, and the antagonism of classes."[30] Thus, fearful of radical polarization, the weight of the Conservative-Unionist leadership was strongly opposed to the Chamberlain forces within the organization and, along with the small but highly-placed group of Unionist Free Traders, they seemed capable of standing off any direct challenge at the top. In contrast to their fellow insurgents on the Liberal side, however, the Tariff Reformers not only had succeeded in winning over nearly half of the Unionist M.P.'s in the House (172 to Balfour's 171 before the elections of 1905) but also held control of the Liberal-Unionist Association and the growing Tariff Reform League, whose combined strength in the constituencies assured them of an ever-increasing majority of Conservative-Unionist representation in Parliament. The portent of that strength bore out the fears of the Balfourites when, in the elections of 1905, the Tariff Reformers won about two-thirds of the greatly diminished Tory delegation in the House. Although it was to take the Tariff Reformers more than five years' more agitation to unseat the "Cecil monopoly," the forces of the Tariff Reform movement had clearly become the dominant voice of Unionism in the country by this time. The consciousness of that strength added much to the resentment of the insurgents against the accustomed leadership in the party and exacerbated the fears of the Balfour circle that these energetic dissidents, by "democratizing" the party, would bring down traditional Conservatism and its supporting pillars—property, the Established Church, and the privileges of the governing classes.[31]

The Compatriot nucleus represented the most radical voice of the Tariff Reform insurgency and embodied the increasing alienation of the younger rank-and-file Unionists from the Salisbury-Balfour establishment. In both respects, their common views were considerably in advance of even Chamberlain himself. Neither Jo-

[30] Peter Fraser, "Unionism and Tariff Reform: the Crisis of 1906," *Historical Journal*, v, 2 (1962), 150. This is the best discussion of the question within the Unionist Party during the Chamberlain period.
[31] Ibid.

seph Chamberlain nor his son and successor were ready to lead the kind of no-quarter assault on Balfour which the advanced league members urged upon him. And Balfour, ruled at all times in the tariff controversy by his rather smug "plain sense" and expediency, generally handled the Chamberlain family with diplomacy and recognized the claims of the Birmingham faction on major Cabinet posts, particularly in the Colonial Office and the Exchequer. The ascendancy of Milner and his *enragés* after Chamberlain's retirement worsened Balfour's position dramatically.

Joseph Chamberlain's name did appear on Amery's list of founding members of the Compatriots Club but the titular leader of Tariff Reform was present in name only—or in spirit. As in so many of the activities emanating from the Tariff Reform movement during his confinement, his name was invoked as the guiding spirit as a matter of course. Most of the other eleven founding members, whose midnight convocations in Amery's rooms in the Temple had hatched the idea of a vanguard committee for the movement, enjoyed no such favor or recognition from the party in the matter of appointments. The one exception was Alfred Lyttleton, an old fellow "Soul" of Balfour's, who succeeded Chamberlain at the Colonial Office to take up the controversial defense of Milner's South African policy (Lyttleton's tenure with the group was short-lived, however).[32] Amery, Maxse, Mackinder, and Hewins—the Coefficients—were outside the higher councils of the party, as were their fellow Compatriots. Those remaining, J. L. Garvin, John Buchan, F. S. Oliver, and C. S. Goldman, were of Milner's circle, always the most advanced and aggressive imperialists in the movement. They were, therefore, of that major disgruntled faction of British Conservative-Imperialists whose influence and careers would find little promise in the Unionist Party so long as the Balfour moderates remained in command.

Among the numerous offspring of the Tariff Reform movement, the Compatriots are probably the most revealing of that characteristic certainty in the ultimate triumph of the just cause which possessed all the younger imperialists. They felt themselves to be distinctly apart from the "defensive" imperialism of Salisbury, Curzon, Balfour, or even of Rosebery and they reacted to the gloomy inertia with which those older men now viewed the future of the empire with a conscious sense of their own dynamism and creativ-

---

[32] E. T. Raymond, *Life of Arthur James Balfour* (Boston, 1920), p. 135.

ity. At the outset, the Compatriots Club was not designed to bring about the overthrow of the party leadership (although they would later assist in that effort) so much as to nurture and refine the doctrine and to keep alive the spirit of the young imperialists towards the moment of their inevitable triumph. This was the light in which Amery saw the founding of the club:

> After much eloquent discussion to a late hour we decided to constitute ourselves as the nucleus of a club to act as an energizing and propagandist body and as a meeting place and forum for mutually strengthening each other in the faith.[33]

As a propagandist body the Compatriots were extraordinarily well equipped to expound the doctrine of Social-Imperialism among the growing ranks of protectionists in the Tariff Reform League and in the Unionist organization in the country. In Garvin, Oliver, and Maxse (later joined by H. A. Gwynne) they had a most talented and industrious corps of propagandists who were to exert strong influence in political journalism over the next decade. And in Mackinder, Hewins, and Amery (to whom J. W. Ashley and Dr. William Cunningham were added within the year) the Compatriots were in a position to dominate the shaping of a new imperialist ideology and a new conservative doctrine in the decade of crises to come.[34]

In the ten years before 1914 the Compatriots Club remained, as Amery put it, "a very live and effective body." Indeed, though that decade was its most active period, the club survived both World Wars, holding meetings several times each year for imperialist M.P.'s "to talk Empire" and, as Amery recalled nostalgically, "to drink the toast of *Communis Patria*, our wider home."[35] In their first few years, however, the Compatriots devoted themselves to more mundane matters. At the inaugural meeting (18 March 1904), J. L. Garvin quickly established himself in the eyes of the group as one of the most promising and dynamic spokesmen of the

---

[33] Amery, *My Political Life*, pp. 224-225. See also J. E. Kendle, *The Colonial and Imperial Conferences, 1887-1911* (London, 1967), p. 265.

[34] Ashley first appeared in the Compatriots Club on 19 May 1904, when he delivered a lecture on "Political Economy and the Tariff Problem." Cunningham was invited in January of 1905 and spoke on "Tariff Reform and Political Morality." Both addresses were soon after printed in *Compatriots Club Lectures* (London, 1905).

[35] Cited in Kendle, *The Colonial and Imperial Conferences*, p. 265.

Tariff Reform movement. Even at this early stage in the career of this contentious and tough Irish journalist, he displayed a talent for the crisp, simple, and stunning reduction of complex questions which was to make him indisputably the most effective political propagandist of his time in Great Britain. The moguls of the new journalism who rose in this generation on both sides of the Atlantic all had to depend on such innovative and volcanic editors as Garvin. Men like Garvin were neither equipped nor inclined to construct the theoretical systems—the compelling, systematic ideologies demanded by the mass political formations for which they spoke. In his more than thirty years of writing for the British Right, Garvin contributed practically nothing to its fundamental policy or ideology; that is, to the theoretical "antidote" to Socialism toward which the Social-Imperialists had been laboring. He could "sell" the article with great ingenuity and persuasion, but he could not manufacture it. His recommendation to the Tariff Reformers in his first address to them was to "simplify": statistics, the stock in trade of protectionist speeches and pamphlets up to the time he joined the Compatriots, "made speeches cold, meetings dull, and democracy depressed," he warned them. If imperialists were to learn from their enemies, the Manchester School and the Socialists, they must recognize the kinetic force in the "definite and compact" quality of those creeds. He urged the Compatriots to "substitute one creed for another, principles for principles, ideals for ideals" to construct a "leading Idea" which would "come straight of itself in the mind of a plain man."[36] This was the classic axiom of political journalism which the new mass media were now to refine exquisitely.

Garvin found it as difficult to cast Social-Imperialism into such simple and imperative language as had Chamberlain and Rosebery. But more vividly than they, he stated the necessary linkage between an effective imperialist social and economic policy and a consciousness of the threat from newly developing powers in Europe, Japan, and the United States. As we shall see, he was to become a master doomsayer—creator of goblins and bogeys. But, unlike those older men among whom it had become fashionable to speak fatalistically of the end of civilization "as they knew it," he invariably offered a ready proposition to avert disaster at the last moment. Menace

[36] J. L. Garvin, "Principles of Constructive Economics as Applied to the Maintenance of Empire," *Compatriot Club Lectures*, pp. 1-2. The following material is all derived from the same address.

and foreboding were woven into one such proposition, what he called "the Doctrine of Development," which he expounded in his address to the club. It comprised four main points: (1) ". . . that the security and peace interests of nations depend upon the efficiency of their war apparatus"; (2) ". . . that the one thing worse than war is being beaten . . . that there is no economic injury more penetrating than defeat, . . . that there are no economic factors so potent, so creative, as national strength and the sense of it"; (3) that abandoned colonies would mean lost markets, a broken empire, and the permanent weakening of national spirit and energy at home; that the "Doctrine of Development," whether applied in the empire or domestically, thus started from the direct denial of laissez-faire; and (4) ". . . that under modern conditions the economic progress, no less than the political preservation of the State, must largely depend upon the conscious purpose and efficient action of the State itself. Government, in a word, should be the brain of the State, even in the sphere of commerce."

No political economist, even by the standards of that still young social science, Garvin nevertheless displayed a superior breadth of intuition regarding the elemental changes taking place during his decade in the international balance of power and possessed some insight into the increasingly defensive position into which his own nation's economy was being forced. The broadly drawn "Doctrine of Development" was consciously based on his amateur observation of the "new State techniques of growth" (as he called them) being employed in Japan, Germany, and the United States. Naturally, he pointed out to the Compatriots the obvious uses to which tariff protection had been put in recent years in advancing these younger rival economies. They had all heard and expounded that precedent before; the economists W. J. Ashley and Hewins were soon to expand on the theme to the club and the Tariff Reform League and make it one of the leading themes of Tariff Reform propaganda. State subsidy and protection had, he noted, also played their role in Britain's development during its own "national" period. But now, given the advanced state of British industry and the home market, Great Britain was in "a completely different class from the methods of 'new states' still in the process of developing the home market." The issue for Britain was confused, he argued, by the fact that large parts of the empire were still in the early stage, without fully developed home industry and markets, and had thus inclined the home country to depend more and more on food imports, a process which had by now not only put novel strains on commerce and industry at home but put "strains on political areas, also in various stages of development between Britain, the colonies and her rivals." The interplay of those forces, imperial and international, brought two urgent political questions to a head in Britain. Garvin raised them rhetorically in concluding his address: first, could the "consent of democracy be secured for a proposal so daring" as the tax on imported food?—the one measure essential to imperial unity. And, second, if imperial federation was to play a role comparable to the recent unification movements on the Continent (movements which were in large part responsible for Britain's present predicament), how would that role "react" on political institutions at home? Thus, rather ironically, Garvin and Hobson were in general agreement as to what was the essential political question of their time: which way offered the best hope of achieving an acceptable and viable international system in the coming century, expanding imperialism or expanding democracy? There was substantial agreement between them that the future must exclude one or the other.

Garvin's design in this address was clearly not to lay out the specific terms of a protectionist economic policy nor to blueprint exact measures for "positive state interference," but to lend a broader political purpose and urgency to that policy—to write merely the key and tempo to a score which could then be orchestrated by the movement's "experts," Ashley, Hewins, and Mackinder. Like the rest of the imperialist avant-garde and in keeping with the propagandist role of the Compatriots Club, his interest was almost exclusively political rather than economic. Although the Tariff Reform League membership at this point, both inside and outside of Parliament, displayed a variety of vested economic interests in protection, that pattern is not readily discernible among the leadership, particularly not among the Tariff Reform League's "intellectuals" assembled in the Compatriots Club.[37] Indeed, as Amery resolved in forming the group, the "protectionist manufacturers . . . and all that clan" were to be rigorously excluded. The driving force of these Tariff Reform militants and, through their efforts, of an ever-increasing share of the Unionist Party sprang more from their political instinct than their economic interests, more from a conscious sensation of cultural and military vulnerability than from any rational and deliberate reading of trade and production indices. Even

[37] See note 29 above.

the qualified economists among them, like Ashley and Hewins, showed the tendency to subject objective data to the communicable fear shared by the rest. "Statistics," as Garvin warned, "made speeches cold, meetings dull, and democracy depressed."

There were several directions in which the Compatriots' energies could be directed if they could first settle among themselves the broad questions raised by Garvin. The first of their functions—that of a "Brains Trust" for the Tariff Reform movement—they had already begun to serve; their membership would dominate the making of policy in the Tariff Reform League over the next six or seven years. In this role, the Compatriots had already surpassed the Co-efficients, whose early efforts had been largely misdirected towards the now ineffectual Liberal League. Then, through the Tariff Reform League and its "Monthly Notes" (which the Compatriots monopolized), they possessed an open line to the growing protectionist majorities in the Unionist constituencies. Through the same channels, by the spring of 1905 they had a nearly captive audience for their propaganda in the Liberal-Unionist Association (nearly unanimous for Protection and the Tariff Reform League) and the National Union of Conservative Associations, which passed Tariff Reform resolutions in their annual meetings of 1904 and 1905.[38] This was the traditional route of agitation within the party system followed with indifferent success by Peel, Randolph Churchill, and Rosebery, and it led inevitably towards a direct conflict with the Balfourites and very possibly to the kind of division which would foolishly leave the way open to the lurking radicals. However, there was no great taste among this advanced section of the movement for "politics"—the "rotten party system" as Milner never ceased to call it. And after Joseph Chamberlain no longer offered that element of charismatic unity with which the movement had so auspiciously started, there remained no single personality (apart from the admired but politically impossible Milner) behind whom to contest for party position and government office. That lack of leadership at the top of the Unionist Party and parliamentary organization was to become a persistent force driving the Tariff Reformers

[38] "Monthly Notes," *T.R.L.*, II, 4 (April, 1905). The Liberal-Unionist Association had swung so strongly behind Tariff Reform in its 1904 meeting that Joseph Chamberlain published an open threat to run "third" candidates if the Unionist leadership failed to endorse his tariff position. See J. Chamberlain to Mr. Rowland Hill (chairman of the Greenwich Conservative Association) in "Monthly Notes," II, 4.

both towards their attack on parliamentary parties, "the System," and towards their search for a national, "non-party" leader outside the Conservative-Unionist camp.

The intellectuals of the Tariff Reform movement were thus in a relation to the established party system similar to that of the Fabians. They saw their role as "educational." They showed general contempt for those of their allies whose interest lay in seeking office, since they had largely resigned that method themselves; their power resided not in the parties nor in Parliament but in the press, in their own extraparliamentary organizations and in their conspicuous pool of talent. The influence both of Milner and, through the Coefficients, of the Fabians also inclined them towards a critical rather than participatory role in domestic party politics.

The Compatriots were superbly equipped to carry out their role as imperialist propagandists; for in addition to their control of Tariff Reform League pamphlets, they had a voice, through Maxse, in the *National Review*, through Amery and Oliver in the *Times*, through H. A. Gwynne in the *Morning Post*, and in the most relentless advocate of all, Garvin, as editor first of the *Outlook* and later of the *Observer*. The former of the papers on which Garvin served was purchased (by Sydney Goldman, also a member of the club) specifically for Garvin to become the Compatriots' first exclusive mouthpiece.[39] If they could arrive at some kind of coherent policy, as Amery hoped, or discover a prophet to replace Chamberlain, the Compatriots would thus be in possession of the strongest unified voice in the political press. Even lacking that unity of purpose, they inevitably constituted a force which had to be reckoned with by all of the parties.

The task yet remained, however, of developing the coherent imperialist doctrine—of "strengthening each other in the faith." Several methods of achieving this end were tried in the first two years of the club. None of these, as it turned out, produced what was hoped for. The first experiment entered into by the group, the purchase of the *Outlook*, came to nothing when Garvin moved over to the *Observer* to begin his long career as editor.[40] From that point the *Observer* became the most authoritative regular advocate of the Conservative Social-Imperialist point of view. Before the elections of 1905, the Compatriots also published a large bound collection

[39] Amery, *My Political Life*, p. 267.
[40] See Gollin's outstanding study of Garvin, *The Observer and J. L. Garvin* (London, 1960).

of articles, representing both addresses given at club meetings and numerous contributions on various imperial subjects from Compatriots enlisted in other parts of the empire. The collection, entitled *The Empire and the Century,* could not have been intended to reach a wide public audience. Its printing, just a little more than a year after the launching of the club, appears to have had the purpose of officially celebrating the founding of fraternal Compatriots Clubs throughout the empire. The organization of these clubs, mainly in Canada, Australia, New Zealand, and South Africa, was an attempt to further a cause which Chamberlain had adopted some years before and which had become one of the cherished ideals of the Tariff Reformers—imperial federation. Since the time (in 1900) when Chamberlain had espoused the well-worn idea of federalism in the empire by recommending a process of "naturalization" for the colonies, a great deal of effort had been given by the imperialists to devising a workable means of integrating imperial and home policy, particularly around the question of coordinating economic policy and defense planning for the empire as a whole.[41]

Contributors to *The Empire and the Century* and members of the imperial Compatriots Clubs, such as William Courthope, G. S. Clarke, W. Pember-Reeves, and C. S. Goldman, had been especially active in the few years before Amery's founding of the Compatriots in 1904 in creating interest in the colonies for an imperial conference to discuss problems of tariff and defense policy. While Chamberlain was in South Africa, Courthope had proposed a "Central Consultative Council" for the empire which would hold regular meetings, serve an "educational" role on imperial affairs, and maintain a staff of imperial experts "which in time of danger might be granted large executive powers."[42]

From the summer of 1902, with the denouement of the war, a movement towards integrating the government of the empire through some kind of centralized body attracted greatly increased attention among both Liberal-Imperialists and Tariff Reformers, as well as among the large variety of "sentimental" imperialists in Great Britain and in the colonies. In an address to the Royal Colonial Institute in the spring of 1903 Haldane argued the necessity

---

[41] Chamberlain's best exposition of the federation principle is in his "Domestic Parties and Imperial Government," *Quarterly Review* (July 1900), pp. 421-469.

[42] W. J. Courthope, "The Society of the British Empire," *National Review* (July 1902), pp. 747-758.

of "gradual and cautious changes in the modes in which the Sovereign was advised in imperial affairs."[43] In light of the discussions then taking place in the Coefficients Club, it is not surprising to hear Haldane advocate "relying on a body of experts independent of party" to guide the integration of the empire; experts who would, in his words, make up a "Cabinet of Empire" much like the Webbs' General Staff of experts to guide domestic policy. It was merely the principle of efficiency applied to the empire.

One of the early products of this renewed interest in imperial federation after the war was a commission set up under the direction of Sir Frederick Pollock. Like so many other such enterprises of this period, the Pollock Commission on imperial organization grew out of discussions at "mixed dinner parties"—like the Coefficients' dinners or the meetings at Amery's rooms, these parties were "mixed" in the sense that imperialists of all political parties were welcomed. Socialists, regular Liberals, and pacifists were not. Meeting during the same period as these other two groups, the Pollock Commission contained active members of both: Haldane and W. Pember-Reeves of the Coefficients were joined by the Compatriots' Milner, Alfred Lyttleton, and Bernard Holland (another contributor to *The Empire and the Century*).[44] Following the suggestion of Haldane and Courthope, the commission concentrated its efforts on devising a centralized body to plan and coordinate policy for the entire empire, a "Secretariat" attached to a permanent Imperial Council which would "discuss, thresh out and report" to that body and in general, in Pember-Reeves' plan, serve as "an intelligence department for the civil affairs of the Empire."[45]

The discussions of the Compatriots and the various projects launched by them during the first few years suffered somewhat, as had the Coefficients', from an overabundance of "expertism," that quality which both groups prized so highly. There appeared in their schemes of "Brains Trusts" and "Imperial Intelligence departments" the tendency which Karl Mannheim found present in all bureaucratic thought to turn all problems of politics into prob-

[43] Cited in Kendle, *The Colonial and Imperial Conferences*, p. 58, from Haldane's "The Cabinet and the Empire" (June 1903), *Proceedings of the Royal Colonial Institute*, XXXIV, 325-352.

[44] The other original members of the Pollock Commission were Churchill, Balfour, Wyndham, Robert Giffen and, a regular Liberal, Herbert Samuel. See Kendle's discussion of the Pollock Commission in *The Colonial and Imperial Conferences*, pp. 56-60.

[45] "Pollock Commission Report," *Times*, 17 Oct. 1904.

lems of administration. Although both the Webbs and the Compatriot members were to find some recognition in royal commissions and in imperial administration later on, the central thrust of their incipient ideology and of their critique of traditional politics was inevitably diverted in the process. Having soured on the conventional political methods and become contemptuous of the "office seekers" who had not, these imperialists failed to come to grips with the problem of political power, beyond an occasional infatuation with prophets past their prime. Milner exemplified their failing best of all—he lacked, said Lloyd George, the "political nostril." It is no mere irony that Lloyd George later became the man best qualified to know how much of a handicap contempt for politics could be to a politician.

The Compatriot Doctrine

"Why does Socialism make such great progress, and why are we not making the progress we ought to do?"—Austen Chamberlain wrote to Balfour, urging him to throw his full weight behind the Tariff Reform program as the best means of reversing that trend.

> All my experience, the letters I receive, the reports from agents, and so forth, agree in the answer—because Socialism speaks with a united and decided voice and because it has an active and positive policy, which (mischievous as we know it to be) is very attractive to the ignorant and rouses hope and enthusiasm among the masses. We, on the other hand, speak still with a divided voice, and, except in so far as fiscal reform is preached courageously, and *definitely*, our policy is purely critical and negative. 'Why, you're not even agreed among yourselves. Anyway, the Socialists have a policy and you have none.' This is the constant answer which our canvassers get, and its profoundly discouraging effect on them and all our workers cannot be exaggerated.[46]

As we have seen, that absence of an inspiring and coherent ideology had created despondency among anti-Socialists and imperialists of both parties. In the inconclusive explorations of Rosebery, the Coefficients, and the Compatriots, considerable effort had been spent to discover the desired antidote to the Radical and So-

[46] A. Chamberlain to Balfour (24 Oct. 1907), *B.P.*, 49736-787B, 26.

cialist doctrines before the electoral fiasco of 1905. The Tariff Reform movement, now being guided largely in its ideological utterances by the Compatriots, had taken upon itself the burden of rousing "hope and enthusiasm" among the masses through its pamphlets and the press. After the blow which the general election inflicted on the strength of the imperialists in Parliament, there seemed little alternative but to leave the renovation of Conservative policy to these determined avant-garde protectionists. This, in effect, was the course being urged upon Balfour by Austen Chamberlain—and in the defeated ranks of the Balfour party following the general election there was scarce will and energy to resist giving in.

Austen Chamberlain, though he bore the great name, had not automatically inherited the affections of the Tariff Reformers nor had he taken his place among the advanced men of the movement. In the demoralized atmosphere of the postelection, he shared the feeling of most Conservatives that the Liberal and Radical tide had swept over an abandoned fortress, that until such a "united and decided voice" as he mentioned to Balfour spoke for the forces of order, that tide would continue to overwhelm them. Thus the advanced Tariff Reformers had made at least one point in their debacle with the party—since the lumbering efforts of the old party leaders had patently failed, it was time, as Milner put it, for the advocates of a "different method." Whether or not such an alternative method did, in fact, exist and whether or not it was capable of rousing any greater enthusiasm than conventional party platforms would now have to be tested against a reforming Liberal-Radical-Socialist coalition at least temporarily united in a massive parliamentary majority.

The Liberal landslide of 1905, although the Tariff Reformers took it merely as the expected defeat of antiquated Conservative thinking and the fulfillment of their repeated warning, was to have delayed but far-reaching effects in developing the ideas and tactics of the movement itself. They had been accustomed to looking upon the Liberal Party as a rickety amalgam of factions dominated by much the same sort of complacent shibboleths as their own party but within which resided a large body of imperialists sharing widely in their own beliefs and fears. It was also felt that a significant area of agreement had been discovered with the Liberal-Imperialists and the Fabian section of the Socialist movement in the preelection years regarding the dangerous condition of the nation and the empire. Those links which had been established between the dissident factions of both parties at least encouraged the hope among the Tariff Reformers—a hope which in the end was sustained from a most unexpected quarter—that with imperialists like Asquith, Haldane, and Grey in the Cabinet, radical caprices of the Left would not be allowed to run completely unbridled under Liberal rule.

Imperial unity, non-Socialist reform, economic planning, defense, expertise, and efficiency had been the catchwords of the Social-Imperialist movement between the Rosebery revolt and the Compatriots—all of it cast in the sacred benediction, "nation above party," the issues being so momentous and grave as to supersede the sectarian interests and the competence of the party system. The latter theme came to play a larger and larger role in Tariff Reform thinking as Milner's influence began to be felt and after the Liberals had achieved power, but the basic idea was present from the start. "This question [i.e., the tariff] is above all party politics," was the preamble to the very first Tariff Reform League pamphlet.[47] It was not an unlikely ploy for either Rosebery or Chamberlain, whose insurgency depended largely upon whether they could break down the standing loyalties to party organization and leadership. It possessed the added premium of furthering the invidious "national" image which both leaders wished to engrave on their cause in contrast to the party hacks and the special interests. However, first through the agency of the Coefficients and later through the Compatriots, the "nonparty" concept took on a wider and more positive meaning.

Rosebery and the Webbs had erected the argument for "nonparty" government upon the principle of "efficiency," a highly generalized method of handling national problems in which the "expert" would be raised to a level of autonomy more or less free from the impediments of the party system. The expert had, of course, to be unencumbered by sectarian loyalties himself and must presumably be recuited into the proper bureaucratic post irrespective of all considerations but his special skills (in practice, the lack of party ties often constituted the *sole* qualification as expert in one or another of the clubs' slots). In Rosebery's "Government of National Efficiency" this process would avoid the wasteful "rotating unemployment of the best men" inherent in the traditional party and Cabinet system. In itself efficiency was a politically innocuous term—as a puzzled Campbell-Bannerman had once put it, "Efficiency! Who is against it?" But when fitted into the Social-Imperial-

[47] "Monthly Notes," *T.R.L.*, I, 1 (July 1904).

ist schema, it portended basic mutations in the traditional political process. An early example of that potential is evident in a proposition introduced by Sidney Webb in a meeting of the Coefficients in April 1905. Speaking of the inefficiency of local government, Webb's assigned province in the "Brains Trust" and an area in which he possessed genuine expertise, he suggested the transfer of crucial administrative powers from the elected bodies to "ad hoc authorities" composed of trained experts. Claiming to speak for his fellow members and himself, Hewins expressed his delight with Webb's scheme of "stripping existing authorities of functions they now discharge" and handing them over to such experts chosen by present local bodies which could then be diminished to "mere electoral colleges." Thus, he wrote to Webb, "you would . . . take the power of 'consent,' for practical purposes, out of the hands of the electorate," which would be unable to oversee the intricate process of decision-making.[48]

In such innovations as that suggested by Sidney Webb, Hewins apparently saw the way to escape the pernicious hold of parties:

> All the forms of government under such a system remain unchanged [he concluded to Webb]. But a given measure when introduced would not be that of the Progressive, the Moderate, the Liberal or the Unionist Party, but of the expert whose business it is to take account of the various currents of opinion and to harmonise conflicting interests.
>
> In fact, constitutional developement [sic] in this country appears to be on the lines I have indicated, and though the ancient forms are retained much of the business in the country in reality . . . [is] done in this way. *Imperial Consolidation must materially hasten this movement.*[49]

As J. A. Hobson had foreseen several years before, the influx of imperial men and ideas into domestic politics held a great erosive potential, as Hewins put it, for the "constitutional developement" of the home democracy. Much like the indefinable notion of "Americanism" in the United States after 1945, the imperialist idea of service above party required the presence of a plausible external or internal menace, or more often a conjunction of the two—as in wartime, the suspension of domestic sectarian conflict had to be grounded and sanctioned in a psychology of siege. Thus, the most

[48] Hewins to S. Webb (18 April 1905), *W.G.C.*
[49] Ibid. My italics.

frequently used catchwords of Social-Imperialism—efficiency, expertise, austerity, discipline, race survival, unity, fitness, etc.—were invariably accompanied by forebodings of military, economic, or civil disaster. It is only in light of the pervasion of this mentality in both major parties that the erratic political patterns of the period between the greatest victory of the Liberal Party and its dissolution in the First World War can be understood.

While it would seem true, as Hannah Arendt said of the Primrose League, that such "above-party" crusades were nothing more than the rallying calls that had always led people to war, it must be remembered that the doctrine as developed by these Social-Imperialists between the Boer War and the death of King Edward VII had been designed as a *response* to a humiliating war. Perhaps more importantly, the idea acquired its greatest appeal and refinement at a time before the crises of 1911-1912 when domestic anxieties took a clear precedence over the as yet insubstantial threats of war in Europe. Thus, their attack on parties and the calls for national unity were not at first prompted so much by a fear of imminent external menace as by long-standing anxieties regarding the patterns of domestic change. Needless to say, the two were invariably linked—the insolvent and unstable society, as their literature repeatedly warned, was the one most vulnerable to outside force. The recent Japanese coup over Russia was the most frequent object lesson cited. Just as Sidney Webb had seen the greatest threat to the old ways—to democracy, capitalism, and Christianity—in the example of Japanese discipline and "collectivism," the Tariff Reformers pointed to the Japanese model as the means to security and order for Britain and the empire.

Contrasting the "slovenly" habits of political thinking in Britain with the coordinated discipline of the Japanese, Amery recommended (in his role as defense expert among the Compatriots) a sweeping revision of defense planning and philosophy:

> It is essential that we get rid of this vicious attitude of mind . . . and endeavor to realize [sic] that not only our naval and military preparations, but our foreign and domestic policy, our political and social customs, our industries, the distribution of our territories, of our population, and of our trade, *all have their defence aspect*, and form part of the general problem of defence. . . .
> The truth is that between the different factors of national life it is impossible to draw hard and fast partitions, *each is continually in-*

teracting upon the other. . . . The political and social freedom and stability which we prize, and for the sake of which our State is most worth defending, are, at the same time, the most effective means of securing the full development of national power in time of war. The war in the Far East has brought out clearly the intimate connection between those two aspects of the same question.[50]

The reorganization of broad aspects of national life along military lines, or at least in a martial "spirit," became an increasingly dominant note in the thinking of the Compatriots and therefore in the propaganda of the Tariff Reform movement after 1905. The impressive military and economic advances of Japan provided an obvious model for that objective. Garvin had used that example in composing his "Doctrine of Development" before the Compatriots. Amery, combining in a sense the thinking of Garvin and Sidney Webb on Japanese society, concocted a formula for defense policy which, though it reflected a shocking ignorance of the differences between British and Japanese society, clearly illuminated the dark road upon which the Social-Imperialists were traveling.

> We begin to realize [he argued in his treatise on defense for the Compatriots] that defence need not be a diversion of the national energies from higher and better aims—a mere payment of insurance, necessary, perhaps, but essentially undesireable [*sic*]—but can be used as a motive power and a stimulus in the development towards a higher form of national organization.[51]

No departure from traditional ways was required to restore military priority and prestige to their proper place in national policy. For two centuries at least, he suggested, the whole of the nation's import and export trade had been regulated to create the excess of exports which would accumulate precious metals in the island. That policy, according to Amery, "was not the outcome of mere mistaken economics, but the result of *intelligent preparation for war.*" It was also that policy, the securing of markets for those exports, which led to the acquisition of the colonies and stimulated the or-

---

[50] L. S. Amery, "Imperial Defence and National Policy," *The Empire and the Century*, pp. 174-175. See also Garvin on Japan, "The Maintenance of the Empire," *The Empire and the Century*, pp. 99-100.

[51] Amery, "Imperial Defence," pp. 175-194. All of Amery's remarks which follow are from the same source.

ganization of the empire. The "new danger," as he saw it, had come not from the pursuit of that proven strategy but from its neglect and abuse by the "selfish interests of the English export trade." The latter, as in the case of India, tended to regard the colonies as foreign countries to be treated in the same way as the rest of the foreign market. The fact was, Amery insisted, that most of the colonies were indeed poor countries whose economic development would in the end determine the development of empire and therefore the solvency and strength of the nation as well. It would be impossible for them to contribute to the costs of defense without crippling their growth—"every penny they can raise is required for their internal administration and for their development."

It is not surprising to find Amery, one of the leading protectionist imperialists, dissociating Tariff Reform thus from the protectionist "interests" even though those interests were still the financial bulwarks of imperialist politics at home. There is even a strong suggestion in his writing that, in the short run at least, where there occurred a conflict between domestic and imperial economic needs the former should sacrifice its priority to the imperial future. Like the notorious Food Tax, such a position was hardly designed to win political support at home; it was, like much of the Compatriots' prescription, self-consciously austere and disinterested, a pose much favored among the imperialists at the time. Amery had also been the one to lay down the rule excluding protectionist manufacturers, place seekers, and "all that clan" from the Compatriots Club at its founding. The new leaders of the Tariff Reform movement were to be a kind of secular sacerdotal class, guided alone by the ideal of service, eschewing party, place, and favor. The idea, though in reality it never acquired any significant practical organization, was not far in conception from the "Order of the Samurai" which Wells had rather whimsically imagined for the Coefficients. The binding vows, in a clerkish parody of Japanese feudalism, were service, efficiency, discipline; these were the virtues which would preserve the nation and empire from their enemies if they could also be grafted onto the habits of the population and the working of its institutions.

> The new danger can only be met in the same spirit as the old [Amery urged]. No army reorganizations or naval schemes, no mere increases of our defence budgets will permanently solve it. We must go back

to the old view, and remember that defence is an essential part of the national life, a thing which must be kept in mind in everything that we do or leave undone, a part to which every other must, in a sense, be subordinated for the development of the whole.

Amery and the Compatriots shared deeply the feeling of the Webbs that all classes had become enervated of the vigorous qualities which had made them rulers of the greatest empire and most industrious nation on earth—the middle classes were materialistic and self-indulgent, the workers physically degenerate and "sottish." Compulsory universal military service, as currently being preached by Lord Roberts' National Service League, received the strong support of the Tariff Reformers as one means of restoring the health and discipline of the nation. Amery, one of the many Tariff Reform leaders who were also active in Roberts' campaign, fully incorporated the main points of the National Service argument into the Tariff Reform League's defense policy:

> National Service will not only provide the reserve for our armies, and increase the efficiency of the voluntary armies raised in the midst of a warlike nation, . . . it will infuse a spirit of discipline and organization into our masses; while at the same time it will be democratic, bringing every class together to the same common work, and inspiring them with a common sense of duty.[52]

Military training, he pointed out, would afford the opportunity to spot "physical degeneration" in time to cure it. In the tracts of the National Service League and the Tariff Reform pamphlets, "physical degeneration" was generally meant to denote the "sottishness" that the Fabians constantly denounced and reflected the widely held opinion in the governing and reforming circles that many workers were converting each small increase in earning power into an increase in their consumption of alcohol. As we shall see, they were to find some unexpected allies on the question of "Drink" and physical fitness among Chapel-going Radicals and the enemies of the big Tory brewing interests. As on a growing number of such issues, the advanced men of the Tariff Reform League were finding themselves out of step with the official thinking of the Unionist Party and its traditional positions.

[52] Ibid., p. 194. See also H. W. Wilson, "Tariff Reform and National Defence," *Compatriots Club Lectures*, pp. 113-115.

One major issue of great concern to the Compatriots, as it was to the Liberal-Imperialists and the Fabians, lay in the improvement of popular education around which there remained strenuous controversy after the reforms of 1902. The Liberal League under the prodding of both the Fabians and Mackinder had stressed the need for extending technical and scientific training at all levels, taking the examples of Germany and the United States as their models. Amery added a recommendation for extending the duration of public education by raising the school-leaving age and introducing instruction in military matters into the curriculum at all levels. It was necessary to integrate a consciousness about defense into everyday affairs in order to bring about a change in the negative public attitude which he saw as the main barrier to any sweeping reform of the military establishment—"to have an efficient defence we must have a nation interested in defence," he pointed out with some frustration. All who received education at public expense, therefore, must also receive military instruction as "an essential part of the citizen's education in his political duties."[53] Popular ignorance and indifference about defense, as well as fiscal and imperial questions (as shown in polls taken by the Tariff Reform League), were a matter of continuing frustration to the movement. William Cunningham, in a Compatriots' article ("Tariff Reform and Political Morality") expressed one of the more extreme reactions of the Tariff Reformers to a London poll on the fiscal question indicating the apparent failure of the league pamphlets to get their message across. The public was apathetic and ignorant of the question, he thought, with "no real sense of their duty as citizens." It might surely be doubted, he thought, "whether a community which contains many such men, is, after all, really fit for parliamentary institutions."[54]

Despite the willingness of the Compatriots to lend their support to piecemeal reforms in the naval budgets and army reorganization, they were adamant that long-term security lay only in a fundamental conversion of the public and government attitude towards defense and towards the empire. It is revealing of the character of the Tariff Reform movement that a good deal more stress was placed

---

[53] Ibid., p. 194. Amery noted with disgust in the same article the "national disgrace" that neither Oxford nor Cambridge maintained a chair of Military Strategy.

[54] William Cunningham, "Tariff Reform and Political Morality," *Compatriots Club Lectures*, pp. 302-303.

upon their critique of the laissez-faire spirit than upon its particulars in the movement's literature. The doctrine of laissez-faire, C. S. Goldman wrote, while it might once have been valuable as a conscious and reasoned policy, is "extremely dangerous and futile as a temperamental attitude."[55]

Sharing a common feature of European conservative movements of the period, the Tariff Reform critique of Liberal and Socialist ideology and policy tended frequently to slip over, ad hominem, into a critique of the character, morals and, ultimately, the patriotism of rival leaders. Among the imperialists, the weightiest factor in choosing political allies thus became some conspicuous devotion to the nation and the empire rather than adherence to a particular party or ideology, even in some cases (as with the Fabians) when that ideology was a Socialist one. This was the temperamental basis of the Social-Imperialist "above-party" affectation which, in the time since the movement began during the war period, had been reinforced by numerous personal contacts and friendships in the various clubs and imperialist organizations. Under the bitter influence of Milner among such a group of ardent men frustrated by powerlessness, a psychology of "we" and "they" easily emerged—on the one side the adherents of a new patriotism, as Goldman put it, "in which the nation takes the place of the old Medieval Church"; and on the other, those whose "antinational bias" Milner once compared to the "subsidized traducers of Great Britain in foreign lands." Somewhere between lay the ruling party majorities and their leaders, in the minds of the militant imperialists equally despicable and dangerous in their muddling complacency and narrow self-interest. When Amery insisted that "we must Imperialize our policy, the attitude of our Government departments, and the personnel of our services," in order to insure the national defense, he was in effect opposing party with patriotism and calling for a kind of coalition of patriots whose unifying bonds, as well as its right to power, would be the guiding virtues of the Social-Imperialist movement. The keystone of that coalition would be defense and the essence of its defense policy would be a principle which Amery transposed from imperialism, "a capacity for almost unlimited expansion."[56]

[55] C. S. Goldman, "The Imperial Ideal," *The Empire and the Century*, XXI.
[56] Amery, "Imperial Defence," pp. 188-191.

V

Lloyd George and the Tariff Reformers

> Democracy is a woman which is always wanting a man! The dictator in dead earnest, like Roosevelt, is accepted by the mob because he dares (not too often!) to tell it to its teeth it is wrong.
>
> J. L. Garvin to Lord Northcliffe
1 Dec. 1906[1]

If mere patriotic ardor and energy were enough to move masses and to acquire political power, the Compatriots might have made of the Tariff Reform movement the greatest single force in British political life. As we have seen, once the need was felt for a compelling Tariff Reform doctrine, they went about erecting one with feverish industry—though perhaps with a good deal more hammering than design. In the short history of the Social-Imperialist movement, in which the younger men were always the most forward, a number of prominent figures had been recruited in the role of the architect and had momentarily enjoyed the adulation of the youthful imperial idealists. Rosebery had briefly radiated the necessary light but soon glimmered out leaving most of his supporters embarrassed at their hasty enthusiasm; Chamberlain entered forcefully, seeming to fulfill most of the jilted expectations raised by Rosebery, but he too retired prematurely, leaving less recrimination but the same disenchantment. To many of the younger imperialists Milner had always been the one who most faithfully embodied their outlook and emotion; particularly after his censure he symbolized, as Rosebery and Chamberlain had not, their isolation from the sources of power and influence. Whether or not that experience had marred his personality as it had his public image, isolation, aloofness, and contempt for conventional political ambition remained part of his character from that time on. In this he also embodied at least one side of his followers' attitude and thus could not betray them—but by the same token he could never lead them to power without some dramatic and unlikely transformation of the political

---

[1] Headlam (ed.), *The Milner Papers*, II, 477n.

system. It would need a national calamity to make Milner a feasible political leader.

Failing to find a man to focus and discipline their activity, the imperialists thought to fill that gap, as had the Socialists, with a powerful gospel. Except for the occasional excesses of Milner, Garvin, and the more passionate spokesmen of the Social-Imperialist cause, no methodical, permanent, or revolutionary overturning of the constitutional order had been seriously contemplated. Between the Coefficients and the Compatriots, their deliberations ranged from a fairly extensive tinkering with the parliamentary system and its supporting bureaucracy to transforming the "spirit" of imperial and party politics. In neither instance had a counter-system come clearly into view; indeed, most of the plans and proposals to come out of the imperialist caucuses still bore a distinctly defensive tone and a frustrated consciousness of lacking such a system: that feeling which was tersely summed up in Austen Chamberlain's question, "Why does Socialism make such great progress?" remained their propelling emotion.

The tone set by Joseph Chamberlain, the founder of the movement, in his now famous homecoming address to the people of Birmingham, that the fierce party squabbles at home could only be seen in true perspective when viewed through the clear air of the South African veldt, had harmonized with the postwar mood. That clear and simple call of empire above party and above class interests had held strong political appeal to sections of both parties, the one obsessed with a sense of its own obsolescence and the other racked with radical dissension. By offering a new program and survival to one side and relief from boisterous insurgents to the other, Chamberlain touched upon ground in which an imperialist "Centre" might take root. As we have seen, the Tariff Reformers had found occasion to treat with Liberal-Imperialists on a range of domestic issues on which a wide sharing of convictions and fears was discovered. It was this background which made the idea of the "party above parties" plausible. Even now, after the Liberal victory, with Asquith, Haldane, and Grey in high Cabinet posts (all imperialists and the latter two Coefficients) and Roseberites scattered through the Liberal ranks and administration, the hope persisted. None were dogmatically opposed to Protection and each of them had demonstrated considerable independence from Liberal Party pressure. Haldane had conspicuously abstained from the

1904 vote of censure against Milner, the only Liberal to do so, while both Grey and Asquith pledged their intention at least to soften the blow.[2]

The possibility was still felt to exist, then, that the years these men had spent out of power working for the imperial cause and their long association with Rosebery, the Coefficients, and the various "non-party" projects of the preelection years would keep their ears receptive to suggestions from outside the government and, in the minds of the more sanguine Tariff Reformers at least, make of the small imperialist clique in the Liberal Cabinet something of a fifth column in the ranks of the detested Radicals and Socialists. Referring to this possibility, Milner was one who felt confident that the Radicals could at least be prevented from doing any "positive mischief" during a Liberal administration.[3] Nor did the three Liberal ministers give their former associates cause to abandon their hopes during the first two years of office. Grey, as Foreign Secretary, not only set to work immediately on the diplomatic realignment against Germany resolved upon in the Coefficients discussions (the occasion on which Bertrand Russell grumpily shuffled out of the club), but he also spent unusual energy for a Foreign Secretary in cultivating imperial relations. On his first official visit to the imperial Compatriots Clubs in Canada, that project which C. S. Goldman and the Compatriots had recently launched, he invited Milner to collaborate with him in the effort to foster this base of imperial unity: "These clubs," he urged Milner, "provide a splendid pulpit for those who wish to focus the energies of the rising generation on the contemplation of National Ideals, and not party interests." This was the spirit which the Tariff Reformers had accustomed themselves to expect from the Liberal-Imperialists in the new government. They were not disappointed by Grey.[4]

Haldane's work at the War Office was no less encouraging. Both the Tariff Reformers and the Fabians joined behind the former Coefficient in his effort to reform the reserve system by the creation of a Territorial Army based, in his original design, on the concept of universal compulsory military service. It will be remembered that compulsory service had been a central part of both the Co-

[2] For the T.R.L.'s reaction to the elections, "Monthly Notes," *T.R.L.*, IV, 2 (Feb. 1906).
[3] Milner to Curtis (25 Aug. 1905), *M.P.*, A.I.
[4] Grey to Milner (n.d., 1906), *M.P.*, A.I.

efficients' and Compatriots' projects of social and health reform. Though Haldane soon was obliged to press for a less sweeping voluntary system of service, he received the willing support of the Webbs, who did their best to sell the idea to various party and "County big-wigs," as Beatrice put it, at their little dinners in Grosvenor Road, Sidney afterward being appointed to a War Office committee to work out an implementation of the conscription scheme with local authorities.[5] To a rather modest extent, the Co-efficients' "Brains Trust" idea seemed to be on the way to blossoming in the first years of the new Liberal regime.

Milner, Amery, Maxse, and Dawkins were all active in Earl Roberts' National Service League, another crusade whose banners carried the "above-party" device and whose language was permeated with the Social-Imperialist jargon. Like so many of the conservative and imperialist organizations which proliferated in this decade before the war, Roberts' National Service League seems to have depended on the same rather limited pool of tireless Tariff Reform ideologues of the Chamberlain-Milner-Garvin circle. A little deflated over Haldane's eventual acceptance of the voluntary system, these Coefficient and Tariff Reform members of the National Service League nevertheless supported the War Minister in the protectionist press, by contributing the aid of the extensive national Tariff Reform network in the creation of the Territorial Force Associations, and by sometimes useful advice in a busy unofficial correspondence with the minister.[6] In the short space of three years, Haldane's consuming effort—a "missionary effort" in his own words—to establish a strong line of defense against the continental threat (by now unequivocally German) came to fruition with the presentation of colors to the first Territorial Army battalions in 1909. In a process which foreshadowed the unorthodox administrative methods of the war years, both Grey's diplomacy and Haldane's military reform had been accomplished against the often vociferous objections of the ruling majority of Liberals in Parliament; it was looked upon as a triumph of the national,

[5] B. Webb, "Diary" (6 April and 19 June 1906), *P.P.*

[6] "Memo to Haldane on National Service ('rough draft')" (n.d., 1909), *M.P.*, A.III; "Crossfield Memo," signed by Amery (14 May 1907), *M.P.*, A.III. Crossfield was chief of the Warrington section of the National Service League, see *National Service Journal*, I, 1 (Nov. 1903). "Scheme for a System of Compulsory Military Training applied to Mr. Haldane's Proposals," *N.S.L.* (1907), based on the Crossfield Memo.

"non-party" principle and a manifest example of the possibilities of joint effort among imperialists in the government and the Opposition.[7]

Although the initial cooperative enterprises of the early years of the Liberal regime were moderately consoling to the Tariff Reformers, the crucial test of the nonparty principle could only be decided by the behavior of the Liberal Chancellor of the Exchequer. Though Asquith had been a leading Liberal-Imperialist, he had not been prominent in Rosebery's revolt nor was he a member of the Coefficients. He had kept up much less intimate ties than his two colleagues in the new Cabinet with the Tariff Reformers and Fabians and, consequently, maintained a firmer reputation in the regular party. Nevertheless, during his tenure at the Exchequer, Asquith was still far from being the despised "Squiff" of later years, the prime whipping boy of the protectionists. His first budgets and statements of policy were eagerly scrutinized by the Tariff Reformers for hidden leanings toward Protection and the signal words of the Social-Imperialist script. Like an overardent suitor, they seized upon innocuous and ambiguous words dropped by the chancellor, seeing in them unmistakable signs of affection. Thus, in one case, after a casual public remark by Asquith concerning industry's need for "more guidance and help from the State," the very next league pamphlet triumphantly announced, "Mr. Asquith throws over Cobdenism."[8]

Asquith's private views on Free Trade at the time of his chancellorship were something of a mystery. His own description of them to a friend, a strict Free Trader, in 1908 was typically equivocal:

> ... I have realised from the first that if it could not be proved that Social Reform (not Socialism) can be financed on Free Trade lines, a return to Protection is a moral certainty.
> This has been one of the mainsprings of my policy at the Exchequer. ...[9]

---

[7] There is a good description of Haldane's army reform in Cyril Falls's "The Army," in S. Nowell-Smith (ed.), *Edwardian England* (London, 1964), pp. 530 sqq.

[8] "Monthly Notes," *T.R.L.*, VIII, 4 (April 1908), referring to Asquith's speech at Manchester of 14 March 1908.

[9] Asquith to St. Leo Streachey, editor of the Free Trade *Spectator* (9 May 1908).

While his words have been read as the confession of a secret protectionist, one who felt the Free Trade line was bound to fail, they might as easily be read as antiprotectionist, viz., that Asquith meant to devote his efforts to proving that a modern social reform program could be financed without resort to Protection. Where Asquith is concerned, however, such a statement might as well be taken as a confession of private ambivalence. In any case, it would seem from Asquith's last budget, in 1908, which balanced major new expenditures for defense and social reform (including his own old-age pensions plan) with old-fashioned economies rather than new tariff revenues, that he felt that, for the moment, the proof for Free Trade did still exist.[10] Asquith could never be accused of dogmatism.

It was not strictly over the Liberal government's pension plan and its other reform efforts that Tariff Reformers were finally disenchanted with the Liberal-Imperialists but, as Milner complained, over paying for these measures "by starving the Army and the Navy." Concisely summing up the Social-Imperialist argument, Milner insisted that the question of social reform was not merely one of relieving humanely the victims of uncontrolled change in Britain, but of *asserting* an order and discipline into the social chaos: of equipping the young with usable skills and physical training; of regulating the random movement of the population by halting the depopulation of the countryside and the "influx of foreign paupers into overcrowded towns"; and of discouraging the undermining of established British industry by unfair foreign competition.[11] Such programs called for long-range and integrated plans such as the Compatriots claimed to offer rather than piecemeal palliatives, no matter how urgent or humane. As always, the Tariff Reformers linked reform with order and discipline—always, social reform had to be governed by some *idée force* strong enough to vie with the Left. Leaderless, they listened for the clarion call. The tentative hopes placed in the Liberal-Imperialists were producing no compelling vision, no plan which could be either supported or opposed with enthusiasm. To their eyes, the opening of the greatest period of Liberal reform showed instead only an unfocused and uncoordinated effort which merely exacerbated their sense of dispersal and aimlessness.

[10] Gollin rather surprisingly reads this single remark as simple proof that Asquith felt the tariff to be a "moral certainty." *Proconsul*, p. 152.
[11] "Monthly Notes," *T.R.L.*, v, 5 (Nov. 1906).

Before the protectionists had abandoned their more sanguine hopes in the Liberal-Imperialist ministers, however, their attention was aroused from another and unexpected quarter in the Liberal government, the pro-Boer president of the Board of Trade. Covering a speech delivered by Lloyd George in Birmingham, the Tariff Reform League pamphlet for November 1906 noted for the first time what they called "the struggle for mastery between the two Lloyd George's." In his address, dealing mainly with the tariff vs. Free Trade question, he generously conceded to the wary Birmingham audience that the election had not necessarily settled the issue against a reform of the tariff. He further confided to them something he was to avow publicly and often in subsequent years, that he was not by nature given to dogmatism, even with regard to such a sacred Radical doctrine as Free Trade. It did, however, work satisfactorily for the present, he added.[12]

By itself, the Birmingham speech would not seem to have warranted the significance given to it by the Tariff Reform pamphleteer (either Amery or Garvin in this case). As the most galling of the pro-Boer critics of the war, Lloyd George had naturally been on even less congenial terms with the protectionist circles than had Asquith. Yet, as we have seen, both he and Churchill, the detested apostate, had at least been introduced to the leading protectionists through the Coefficients Club prior to 1906. Neither Lloyd George nor his successor at the Board of Trade had been frequent visitors either at the Coefficients' table or at Beatrice Webb's little dinners before the Liberal victory, but they both became well informed of the thinking of those industrious circles through the platoon of bright young assistants which they recruited to work on their monumental social reform projects. Charles Masterman and William Beveridge, in particular, provided a useful and sustained liaison during the reform period. Whether or not these slender contacts had given the Tariff Reform pamphleteer any foreknowledge of Lloyd George's thinking, his intuition was substantially confirmed by the activity of the Board of Trade during the ensuing months, which saw its president's popularity among the Tariff Reformers surpass that of the erstwhile Limps in the Cabinet. The shift in affections was brought about both by the disappointing orthodoxy of Asquith and by the emanation from Lloyd George's office of a series of bills of a decidedly protectionist flavor, culminating in the

[12] Ibid.

Merchant Shipping Patents and Design Bill which reached the House in March of 1907.[13]

The cautiously friendly mood of the Tariff Reformers is clearly visible in the league's response to the new bills:

> The responsibilities of office, it is becoming increasingly evident, are producing the effect *we have always anticipated they would have upon the mind of Mr. Lloyd George.* . . .
>
> Every Tariff Reformer will congratulate the President of the Board of Trade upon his welcome change of front. It proves that Mr. Lloyd George is too able a man to content himself long in office with the ostrich-like defiance of the facts which won him the cheers of the Cobdenite Party. . . . He has already won the cheers of the Tariff Reformers by his Industrial Census Bill. . . .[14]

Over the next few years the Tariff Reformers had numerous opportunities to observe both the belligerent and the friendly faces of "the two Lloyd George's." To them as to others, the man remained a puzzle which both fascinated and frustrated. Though at the time of the Patents and Design Bill he did nothing publicly to acknowledge what could turn out to be embarrassing applause from the sidelines, his actions were not designed to discourage it. The high point of this novel affinity of imperialists for the pro-Boer which had grown up during the winter of 1906-1907 was reached when Lloyd George introduced the bill on the floor of the House of Commons in March. "I am not afraid," he proclaimed, "of foreign competition so long as British Trade is free to fight, free from impossible conditions abroad and from equally stupid tariff systems at home. Many British industries have been wiped out by privileges conceded over our own institutions to foreigners."[15]

No language could more effectively have stirred the affections of the protectionists or, needless to say, the suspicions of his Liberal Free Trade colleagues. Whether it was deliberately designed

---

[13] The main B.O.T. bills to be considered of a protectionist coloring were the following: the Industrial Census Bill (1906), the Merchant Shipping Patents and Design Bill (1907), Assay of Foreign Watchcases Bill (1907). See H. duParcq, *Life of David Lloyd George*, 3 vols. (London, 1913), III, 498, on the composition of the bills.

[14] A T.R.L. article in response to Lloyd George's exposition of the Patents Bill at Walsall in February, before its introduction in Parliament; "Monthly Notes," *T.R.L.*, VI, 3 (March 1907). My italics.

[15] Lloyd George, House of Commons, 19 March 1907; reported in "Monthly Notes," *T.R.L.*, VI, 4 (April 1907).

to endear himself to the Tariff Reformers after their kind words is impossible to say: it is just as likely that Lloyd George's "political nostril" was beginning to scent the advantages of that national "above-party" image he increasingly tried to project as social reformer. It was good political sense not to squander good will from any quarter; once having reached national prominence, Lloyd George lavished his considerable charm rather indiscriminately, bewitching friends and enemies alike. After his work at the Board of Trade, the most powerful and vocal of the Unionist Party were never fully able in the ferocious battles to come to denounce either the man or his works unreservedly, without an undertone of admiration, of what could have been achieved if only he shared their idealism. Needless to say, being unpredictable also helped to guard his independence within his own party, a point over which he was both to gain and to lose a great deal in the years to come.

There is some indication that the suggestive quality of the admiring articles in the protectionist press since the fall of 1906 did not pass completely unnoticed by the precocious Welshman. Characteristically, the Tariff Reformers defended their praise of the Radical minister with the argument that such matters as the health of the nation's industry, like the strength of the empire, were after all beyond the scope of party politics and prejudices. It was an argument quickly adopted and frequently used by Lloyd George. "The question of the trade of this country ought to be non-political," he argued in defense of his Patents Bill against the opposition of his Liberal colleagues. Similarly, in a speech to the colonial conference soon after, loudly applauded by the Tariff Reform League for its "flashes of insight," he called for the raising of imperial issues "above parties."[16]

Nonpartisanship was, of course, also the language of the Coefficients, with whom not only Lloyd George but Churchill and Charles Masterman, his closest associates, had established amicable social ties. The gregarious Churchill was a more frequent guest at club dinners than was his friend, and Masterman, Lloyd George's chief aide, had been a regular member for several years before join-

---

[16] Lloyd George's speech at Walsall; "Monthly Notes," *T.R.L.*, VI, 3 (March 1907); Ibid., VII, 5 (Nov. 1907). Following the Boer War, Lloyd George had apparently recouped his reputation with the imperialists of his own party well enough to be offered, and accept, a post in the next Liberal-Imperialist government (by Rosebery); cf. Wilfred Scawen Blunt, *My Diaries* (New York, 1923), p. 216.

ing his staff. What influence the Coefficients were able to exert on the thinking of the future Chancellor of the Exchequer, therefore, probably came more by way of the two younger men than directly. The Fabian tactic of permeation meshed quite smoothly with the pragmatic opportunism of the Radical reformers. Little prodding, it seems, was needed to interest Lloyd George's "emissaries" in the various projects broached at the meetings. On the contrary, Beatrice noted of a meeting attended by Churchill and Masterman that

> ... the net impression left on our mind is the scramble for new constructive ideas. . . . Every politician one meets wants to be 'coached'—it is really quite comic—it seems quite irrelevant whether they are Conservatives, Liberals or Labour Party men—all alike have become mendicants for practicable proposals.[17]

The two came away from the encounters richly laden, Masterman with the outline of an "Insurance Scheme" for unemployment and sickness; Churchill with the Port of London Bill (to which Milner contributed) and the Labour Exchanges plan which became the most heralded achievement of his tenure at the Board of Trade.[18]

The net effect of Lloyd George's work at the Board of Trade and his colleagues' receptiveness to constructive schemes of non-Socialist reform was to rekindle among the Tariff Reformers the conviction that on the momentous questions the true conflict was not between the old parties—which reflected the "mere husks of dead controversies" (Milner's words)[19]—so much as between the old guard of both parties and younger men of vision to be found in either camp. The increasingly visible cleavage which existed between themselves and Balfour, whom Beatrice Webb now described as "the Prime Minister of the little white people,"[20] was projected with some accuracy on the warring factions of the Liberal

[17] B. Webb, "Diary" (10 Feb. 1908), *P.P.*

[18] For the development of the Insurance and Labour Exchanges plans, see B. Webb, "Diary" (11 March, 24 March, 22 April, 16 Oct., 15 Nov. 1908), *P.P.* Beatrice's claims to authorship are largely corroborated by Masterman and by William Beveridge (assistant to Lloyd George on the National Insurance Plan of 1911). Cf. Beveridge, *Power and Influence* (London, 1953), pp. 39, 56-61, 63 et passim; Tom Jones, *Lloyd George* (London, 1926), p. 36. Churchill thanks Milner for his aid on the Port of London Bill in a letter of 3 January 1909, *M.P.*, A.III; and Churchill to Milner (17 May 1909), *M.P.*, A.III.

[19] Milner to Clinton Dawkins (n.d.), *M.P.*, A.III.

[20] B. Webb, "Diary" (16 Sept. 1906), *P.P.*

Party, with the Radical reform group occupying the advanced role formerly filled by the Liberal-Imperialists.

Always somewhat envious of the unremitting energy of the Left, the Tariff Reformers were deeply impressed by the sense of dynamism and assurance in Lloyd George. They had hoped to imbue Unionism with a similar drive, rooted in the language of Social-Imperialism. But, after two years of Liberal government and a lethargic Opposition, they seemed near to abandoning the effort:

> I am meditating a bold move [Milner confided to Amery] which is to cut myself quite adrift from 'anti-Socialism.' It means going into the wilderness, but I have come to the conclusion that Unionism in its present lines is hopeless, that the only chance—any way a poor one—is to have a new policy, root and branch, and 'trust to luck' and the future to reform . . . our present party, with perhaps a strong contingent of the saner workmen, on a broader basis than that of Conservative Mandarinism and middle-class timidity, lethargy and narrow mindedness.[21]

In Milner's tortuous logic, giving up "anti-Socialism" implied merely a search for a more effective antidote to the revolutionary threat than he felt either Unionist or Liberal orthodoxy could provide. The inevitable conflict, he confided to Mackinder, would be between Tariff Reform and Socialism, with no middle ground. It was the hope of the Tariff Reformers before the budget of 1909 that the "New Radicals" might after all be marshaled in that coming struggle on the patriotic side of the barricade.[22]

Such was the implication in one of the last Tariff Reform pamphlets composed by J. L. Garvin prior to the opening salvos of the budget debate:

A POLICY OF NATIONAL COMBINATION

> . . . the advanced Liberals, who repel any suggestion of changing the antiquated practice of 'laissez-faire,' are simply conservatives of the type that would conserve even chaos. The twentieth century, in spite of them, is going to be dominated in politics as in trade by the widest and strongest combinations of the most efficient individuals. . . .[23]

---

[21] Milner to Amery (25 Sept. 1907), *M.P.*, A.III.

[22] In a conversation repeated by Mackinder to Beatrice Webb, "Diary" (19 May 1908), *P.P.*

[23] J. L. Garvin, "A Policy of National Combination," in "Monthly Notes," *T.R.L.*, VI, 1 (Jan. 1909).

Garvin's emphasis is upon individuals whose political imagination was not blinded by the traditional political dogmas. While president of the Board of Trade, Lloyd George was surely close to qualifying himself as such a one of those "efficient individuals." Quite as much as the protectionists, he had been elevated by the promise of nonpartisanship during his period of tenure. "In politics as in trade . . . ," as Garvin said, was the theme and spirit of Lloyd George's administration at the Board of Trade. It was the first extended contact of this impatient son of obscurity with the ordered and practical world of business, of competent marine engineers and confident industrial managers, much the same "efficient society" the Webbs had in mind and much the same men whom Lloyd George looked to when forming his own government a decade later. He felt that things were getting done at the Board of Trade without excessive fuss and debate and, perhaps more important, without the tension brought on by conflicting social styles and accents. Out of the public eye in the conference rooms of the B.O.T., less time need be wasted in being a gentleman. The atmosphere suited him. There was a "repose" about it to which he had been unaccustomed, he reminisced on becoming chancellor.

> After years of strife, politically, I found myself at peace with all my neighbors. I met men of all political parties and of no political parties—because there are a great many people who care very little about any political party in this country; and I met these. And . . . they all did their best to help me to administer the affairs of the Board of Trade in the general interest of the trade and commerce of the country; and it was quite a delightful experience to be able, for two or three years, to work in a department where there was really no political feeling, no political bias, and no political prejudice. . . . When I got to the Board of Trade I felt exactly like a mariner who had been all his life in stormy trades in a very frail craft and who had been appointed to the position of the harbour master. There was a calm, a peace about it that was soothing.[24]

In introducing the monumental budget on 29 April, Lloyd George knowingly forsook his repose—inaugurating his chancellorship with the distracting fanfare he brought to all his offices. During the year-long ruction which ensued, however, the tentative friendliness of the protectionists for the conciliatory president of the Board

---

[24] Lloyd George, speech at the Law Society Hall, 29 Jan. 1909.

of Trade was displaced by bitter fear and mistrust of the new incendiary Chancellor of the Exchequer. For in a stroke he persuaded a good part of the nation, if not all in the Liberal Cabinet, that other means than the tariff existed for the financing of both progressive reforms and defense. The budget was all that the Tariff Reformers had feared from Liberalism, or so it seemed to them at first; it was the antithesis and the antidote for their brand of Social-Imperialism. If it could be shown that punitive taxation of property and wealth could support expensive social reforms and even more expensive military and naval modernization, it would be the undoing of all their efforts and the defeat of the conservative solution to the condition of England. While the fury over the budget lasted, the "Red Budget" was in their minds—the coming of the Socialist revolution. Nor did the bellicose language of the chancellor do anything to moderate that view. In a quieter climate a year later, in the summer after the King's death when open political conflict was suspended, it was possible to distinguish the bite of the famous budget from the barking of its author.

Ironically, this instance of the fiercest confrontation between the chancellor and the Tariff Reformers marked a notable advance in their eventual coalescence. Both attempting to nudge a reluctant party into bold positions and adamant causes, they found by the time the yelling had been silenced by the death of King Edward that on the deepest issues of the state's role in reform and defense they shared more with each other than with their more squeamish party colleagues.

VI

The Budget and the Peers

The budget debacle of 1909 contained two simultaneous assaults, apparently moving in opposite directions; one by the activist Tariff Reform section of the Unionists, strong in their party but leaderless, against the entrenched Liberals; and by Lloyd George against the "Dukes." Garvin on one side and Lloyd George on the other represented insurgent blocs which were considerably in advance of the main bodies of their parties. The Tariff Reformers were forced to rely heavily on extraparliamentary agitation and propaganda because they had never succeeded in getting an open endorsement of Protection from Balfour and the party, who feared the "dear bread" taunt at the polls. Similarly, Lloyd George and Churchill played at demogogy to goad a reluctant party into the battle against the Lords for a supreme elective assembly and an open field for an aggressive social reform program.

An enormous increase in the activity of the Tariff Reform League, now the recognized vanguard of the attack on Liberalism, registers the intensity of the campaign undertaken in 1909 over the budget. Following a temporary eclipse after the defeat of 1906, the league's publications expanded steadily from slightly more than 1.5 million in 1906 to 6 million two years later. That was due in part to the successful fund-raising done by the Compatriots. But in the single year preceding the first elections of 1910 (January), more than 53 million leaflets, pamphlets, and posters were distributed.[1]

The provocative budget served to focus the energies of the league and, by polarizing all political discussion, it also drove many previously uncommitted Unionists and some Liberals into the league's camp. Naturally, the corresponding increase in funds re-

[1] See chapter III, note 49, for the exact figures.

flected in the dramatic expansion of the leaflet campaign significantly enhanced the strength of the Tariff Reform organization in the party and put further pressure on the Balfour wing to give in to the protectionists. In the league's campaign of 1909, Protection was deliberately and explicitly advocated as the only alternative to the budget and Socialism if the admittedly necessary increase of £20 to £30 million in revenue was to be raised.[2] "Either Tariff Reform or Socialism had to be adopted," Garvin admitted. Moreover, if the "red flag Budget" were to be defeated, the tariff would have to support the necessary measures of social reform, including unemployment insurance, housing, and Poor Law reconstruction along the lines of the Webbs' *Minority Report of the Poor Law Commission* while at the same time guaranteeing the national security by maintaining the "two-to-one" standard in naval construction.[3]

Spurred on by the competitive dynamism of Lloyd George and Churchill, the Tariff Reformers gave first place in their literature to their policy of social reform. The strategy was brought up to date by Garvin under the banner of "Tory-Socialism." The imperialists had been tutoring themselves for years in this language with the help of the Fabians. With the polarization of 1909 it seemed to them that their time had finally come. "The world is moving towards organization," Benjamin Kidd proclaimed in the stylish jargon of the time, and "constructive thinking has passed for the time to the Socialist and Conservative Parties." Many Unionists and some Liberals were coming to recognize the tactical advantage against the Liberal platform such an encircling movement might hold; it had long been the established policy of the Social-Imperialists, from the time when Gladstonian Liberalism was still seen as the main enemy. Even Balfour, who had always to beware of of-

---

[2] This was the line taken by the advocates of a "general tariff" for the purpose of raising revenue as opposed to the "preferentialists" and "retaliationists." The former represented a majority of the Unionist Free Traders (sixteen) after 1906. Cf. Fraser, "The Unionist Debacle," *Journal of Modern History*, 69/4 (Dec. 1963), pp. 154-155.

[3] "Monthly Notes," *T.R.L.*, xi, 4. The leaders and the main contributors to the Tariff Reform program besides Garvin at the time were F. E. Smith and A. Chamberlain. Cf. Gollin, *The Observer and J. L. Garvin*, p. 110. The manner in which the *Minority Report* came to be adopted by the Tariff Reformers is discussed in chapter II. Cf. also, Garvin's *Tariff or Budget: The Nation and the Crisis* (London 1910), a reprint of his *Observer* articles during the budget fight, 3 August to 12 December 1909.

fending the less precocious section of the party, reluctantly conceded "some form of Tory-Socialist" policy to be vital to the defeat of the budget. As the crisis deepened, nearly all were learning to sing Garvin's tune.

If the moment was indeed ripe for Tory-Socialism, the long-flourishing connections of the leagues and the Tory "outsiders" with the Fabian Society insured that preparation in a social policy would not be lacking. Nor would strangeness stand in the way of a more intimate friendship, for as Shaw had remarked with familiar cynicism, the Fabians were now welcomed in the salons of the great and the legislative commissions of the government because they had proven the gentility of their variety of Socialism and perhaps even offered a method of domesticating the more dangerous kind.[4]

It was this double-edged policy of anti-Socialism plus tariff-financed social reform and defense which the Tariff Reformers urged upon the party during the budget fight prior to the elections of January 1910. Garvin insistently prodded Balfour to "summon the country to the supreme struggle against Socialism, a struggle which must begin now in England [if], of all the countries where the thing was thought most impossible, [it] is not to surrender without a blow."[5]

As Garvin and the Tariff Reformers had repeatedly pointed out to Balfour and those still unconverted, Socialism of the sort portended by the budget would never be repulsed until it was met by "an ideal as great but nearer and clearer" and by "a faith as living." In this, they asserted, lay the great strength of their fiscal vision:

> That ideal resides in the Imperial vision of the Tariff Reformers alone; that energy of belief only in their ranks. Our fiscal Adullamites can not fight the red Crusade . . . Tariff Reformers can fight it and they will.[6]

Balfour's eventual decision to defer to the ardor of the Tariff Reformers and to commit the party officially to their policy was made reluctantly. His choice had been so narrowly circumscribed on the one hand by the power of the league in both numbers and élan and on the other by the half-formed conviction in his own dis-

---

[4] G. B. Shaw, *Man and Superman*, p. 249.

[5] In a letter from Garvin to Jack Sandars, Balfour's confidential secretary, Sandars to Short (21 Sept. 1909), *B.P.*, Add. Mss. 49766-787C.

[6] "Monthly Notes," *T.R.L.*, VIII, 1.

tinguished but disheartened circle that for the moment opposition to the triumphant Radicals was hopeless.⁷ He was also obliged to accept Garvin's tutorship by the fact that nearly the entire Unionist press was behind Protection, with the *Observer* itself at the height of its influence in the party and in the country.⁸

When Garvin first sought to persuade Northcliffe of his rare qualifications as a political editor three years before, he described to him his passion "to mould national opinion and address large masses and move them." He had been disgusted by the petty partisanship of both parties, he said, adding on behalf of Northcliffe's ambitions as well as his own that "until the newspapers command and cease to follow the opinions of conventional parliamentary people always years behind their age, nothing will be well with this nation. . . ."⁹

It was precisely this reversal which the flamboyant young editor attempted to bring about during the budget debacle, and with general success so far as forcing the Tariff Reform platform on the Unionist leadership was concerned. But the simple adoption of a reform of tariff policy was only a part, and not necessarily the most important part, of the course he urged upon the party. In an extraordinary series of letters to Balfour just prior to the January elections of 1910, Garvin outlined with great forcefulness and even brilliance his plan for the campaign which was to vindicate Tariff Reform and dish the "red flag Budget."

At this point in their relations it would appear that Garvin looked upon the famous older statesman much in the way the master of an ironclad steamer might look upon that of an aging square-rigger, with a combination of reverence and impatience, with a sense of inferiority but some contempt. The man was impressive, graceful, and represented a noble tradition, but Garvin was sure of

---

⁷ The Unionist Free Traders, led by Balfour's cousin Lord Hugh Cecil, George Hamilton, and the Duke of Devonshire, were strong in ex-ministers but weak in numbers since 1906. The Tariff Reformers were incomparably stronger in the country and in control of the Liberal-Unionist Association. See Fraser, "The Unionist Debacle," pp. 154-155.

⁸ At the opening of the election both the *Daily Mail* and the *Times* were solidly behind Garvin's strong line, with both Jones and Buckle personally urging Balfour to follow the *Observer's* proposals. Cf. Sandars to Short (21 Sept. 1909), B.P., 49766-787C; Gollin, *The Observer and J. L. Garvin*, p. 104.

⁹ Garvin to Northcliffe (1 Dec. 1906), cited in Gollin, *The Observer*, p. 17.

himself and of the timeliness of his cause. The scions of the party finally had to come to him; he would instruct them in the new political method. This he began to do in a voluminous correspondence with the Unionist leadership at the peak of the budget debate in the two months before the first elections. Among this correspondence was a "Memo" (see appendix A) ostensibly dealing with the character of the campaign literature being prepared for the elections, a subject upon which Garvin could command a good deal of authority together with the experienced staff of the Tariff Reform League. But it went considerably beyond this purpose, presenting an elaborate scheme of tactics and issues which, if employed, would have unconditionally committed the Unionist Party to the most extreme utterances of the Tariff Reform League and polarized the imminent political conflict to an unprecedented degree.[10]

He suggested a radical simplification in the style of Unionist political leaflets to suit the "inconceivably crude" mind of the masses —simple, provocative arguments in short words and "big black type." In content, the campaign was to be equally blunt and spectacular and must have, "like the other side," a "Dream" and a "Bogey." The dream of "Imperial Strength and Industrial Security" must be substituted for the Socialists' "earthly paradise"; and as for the bogey, the "foreigner" instead of the landlord. Most of all, the "real feelings" of the uncommitted voter must be exploited:

> ... they dread dimly an Imperial and Social catastrophe. *That dread has got to be developed and defined in their minds.* We have got to show them that the Budget does represent the Spirit of the Socialistic Revolution; and that the Limehouse speech is a firebrand's signal for a class war. The argument that the nation is prepared for is that the Radical-Socialist method means revolution, chaos and peril, while the Unionist party stands for *power, union and security*.[11]

Balfour and probably a majority of the regular Conservatives had been strongly disinclined to encourage the kind of free-for-all opposition tactics advocated by the Tariff Reformers up till now. Balfour suspected that such a fight would play into the hands of Lloyd George by stirring the Liberals, Labour, and the Irish into a spirit of unity which they demonstrably lacked at the moment.

[10] Garvin to Sandars (29 Nov.–1 Dec 1909), *B.P.*, 49795-787E.

[11] Ibid. These remarks will be found in sections v and vi of appendix A.

Moreover, Garvin's method naturally included a flat rejection of the budget by the House of Lords, an act which Balfour opposed since he strongly suspected that the Radical chancellor had posed precisely that challenge to the upper house so that it might invite its own destruction.[12] Lloyd George would either have his budget or, if the Lords vetoed, would have the solid support of the anti-budget Irish for an all-out attack on the upper house. Balfour understood the daring gambit, perhaps better than did Garvin. On the other hand, Garvin's belligerent counsels offered the only method of preventing a serious demoralization and possibly a split in the party.[13] To the rejoicing of the Tariff Reformers, however, the budget was rejected by the Lords in December. Where even the mighty Chamberlain had failed, the young editor succeeded; the Tariff Reformers would now have the long-awaited chance of conducting a general election with a more-or-less united party behind Protection—the only available option to the hated budget to cover the costs of a modern social and defense program.

The naval construction schedule and the unexpectedly high costs of the new welfare projects made the 1909 budget the highest in history, for peace or war. The Chancellor of the Exchequer, still a pacifist in the public eye, had been compelled to increase the naval estimates after a battle of interoffice memorandums with the equally volatile head of the Admiralty, Lord John Fisher. But with his accustomed ingenuity, he soon made of his defeat an invaluable ploy to justify a more explosive aspect of his program—the overt, punitive assault on unearned wealth from the land.[14]

The Land Tax which so outraged the Tory backwoodsmen tended to be mildly confiscatory, yet it would neither destroy

---

[12] There is some dispute as to Lloyd George's intentions on this score. However, even if he had no design to discredit the upper house, the challenge would at least, as the sequel proved, serve to divert the Opposition's attentions from the budget to the constitutional issue. Roy Jenkins, *Asquith*, p. 196.

[13] The dispute over whether the Lords were to reject or amend the budget resurrected the rift between the protectionist and moderate wings of the Unionist Party which had plagued Balfour since 1903. For a statement of the moderates' case, see the speech of Balfour of Burleigh in Roy Jenkins, *Mr. Balfour's Poodle* (London, 1954), p. 48 et passim.

[14] Asquith's 1908 budget of £154,350,000 was also a record high, but he drew upon the surplus of three years of commercial boom. It was the last Gladstonian budget, based as it was on "retrenchment" and leaving a surplus of £5 million as compared with Lloyd George's £16 million deficit, to which must be added a base increase of £10 million.

landed property as some of its critics charged nor raise sufficient revenue to materially affect the budget crisis. Nevertheless, both Garvin and Lloyd George unsparingly laid on the red paint; in the manner presented by Lloyd George at Limehouse and Newcastle-on-Tyne it seemed boldly and avowedly revolutionary—although it may have been more in the style of Monk than of Marx. It was, as its author described it, a "War Budget," a red herring brandished in the faces of the "Dukes" to incense them into imprudence and thus confront his timorous Liberal colleagues with a challenge from which they could not shrink without intolerable public embarrassment. The hopes of both the chancellor and his most determined enemies were realized when the Lords threw out the budget. A dissolution was called for 15 December, with the elections to follow early in January. Asquith, and even a majority of the Cabinet, feared an election because of the string of Unionist by-election victories. But Lloyd George and Churchill feared equally to postpone until the unpopular Whisky and Tobacco clauses of the budget were put into operation; an immediate election, Churchill insisted, "would save the Government from certain defeat" later on.[15]

The election returns, despite a record poll, were surprisingly anticlimactic. The two leading parties returned nearly equal numbers (272 Unionist, 275 Liberal), enabling Asquith to form a government only with the support of the Irish Nationalists (82 seats) and the Labour members (40 seats). Consequently, passage of the budget depended entirely on the good will of the Nationalists; or, in the very possible event of an Irish abstention, on the Socialists. The Irish had already abstained on one budget division because of the Whisky Tax (increased by 6d./bottle) and this provision had not been altered in the final version of the bill.

To add to Asquith's burdens, the Irish demanded a heavy price for their aid: immediate passage of a Home Rule Bill over the corpse of the House of Lords. Despite the fact that they were themselves ailing from serious internal divisions, the Nationalists were bargaining from a position of great strength vis-à-vis the embattled Liberal government; they were immovable and the most that Asquith could gain at length was an agreement for immediate passage of the budget (because of the delay, the government was technically without funds), on the condition of an open avowal to override the Lords' inevitable veto of Home Rule. The much-

---

[15] Cited in Blunt, *My Diaries*, 2 Oct. 1909.

maligned Redmond was inclined toward a softer line but he feared the rising challenge of more extreme Nationalist and Republican sentiment in Ireland.

Asquith's position was extremely embarrassing. It seemed to some indeed that the frequently uttered taunt of its enemies, that Liberalism was "played out," was close to being confirmed. An often reluctant party had acquiesced in four years of unorthodox Radical reform and even on the budget had appeared to go along merely for the aura of progress it attached to the party, at a loss to bring forth an alternative. Now it would appear, with the Irish demand for Home Rule and Labour's expectation of reversing the Osborne Judgment, that they were being driven unwilling to the overthrow of the constitution by their fanatic and, as it seemed to some, subversive allies, thus creating a situation which held bleak prospects for all but the extremists.

Something akin to the fragmented political situation of 1902-1903 appeared to be recurring during the budget debate. Fragmentation and divided leadership was again plaguing the Liberal Party; again the Tariff Reformers, straining themselves under slow-moving leaders, tried their best to exploit it by driving a wedge between their former Liberal-Imperialist friends and their Radical allies. Asquith, himself a member of the small group of Liberal-Imperialists who had broken from the party on the former occasion, had had to bear the onus of alienating his former friends—including not only his onetime chief, Rosebery, but his son-in-law, Sir Edward Tennant—by committing the party to support the new budget. Rosebery, Tennant, and four other Liberals, including Carlyon Bellairs, the "naval expert" of the Coefficients, had crossed the floor when the budget was introduced in June of 1909.[16]

Asquith was nevertheless able to maintain temporary discipline in the great mass of the party over the budget, especially because the need for greatly increased revenue was generally conceded, while no effective alternative short of Protection was bruited.[17] But

[16] The six Liberal Members who crossed over at the introduction of the budget in June 1909 were, after Rosebery, Tennant, and Bellairs, Lord Joicey, Harold Cox, and Sir J. Dickinson-Payner. See *Daily News*, 16 June 1909.

[17] Rosebery did bring forth a timid method of saving funds involving "retrenchment" in civil service and the Irish Administration. A review of both parties, however, judged it a "hopeless" expedient in raising the nearly £20 million needed. Cf. "Monthly Notes," *T.R.L.*, xi, 4, p. 222.

the election results and the subsequent demands of the Irish and Labour sections made his task of keeping the peace in the government infinitely more difficult.

At Garvin's suggestion, the Tories had made a good deal during the elections of "letting the Labour tail wag the combination dog." The embarrassing imputation would seem unanswerable should the government now attempt to pay the price of holding office by destroying the Lords' veto, thus opening the way for Home Rule and a reversal of the Osborne Judgment.[18] Such a course, as Garvin was well aware, would find anything but a wholehearted consensus in the Liberal Party. But the possible alternative of calling another election, despite its many attractions, raised another serious problem, as Sir William Harcourt indicated to Asquith in January:

> Well! the Elections are a disappointment to you and me: I had hoped not to lose more than 80 seats on the balance. Now we are not quite our own masters. Everything seems to point to an inevitable second Election this summer: *but has Pease* [the Liberal Chief Whip] *got or can he get the funds to fight it*? I know that before Christmas the Tories were reckoning on exactly this situation and that they would break us financially.[19]

Even if Asquith were able to dissolve and run a second election campaign on the moderate proposals for the internal reform of the upper house and removal of the veto in finance alone—measures which had the support of most of the party—he had no assurance and small hope of emerging with any more independence than he already possessed.[20] On the contrary, he was assured by J. A. Simon that even the current majority was secured only by the belief among the working classes that the government was to "deal drastically with the power of the Lords forthwith." Reporting in February on his own constituency, Simon wrote to Asquith,

---

[18] Garvin, *Tariff or Budget*, p. 11.

[19] Harcourt to Asquith (26 Jan. 1910), *A.P.*, Dep. 12.

[20] There were several methods proposed for overcoming the obstructions posed by the House of Lords to Liberal reforms short of depriving it of the veto. These "internal reforms" varied from the wholesale appointment of Liberal peers to secure a majority, to the "self-reform" proposal of Rosebery and Lansdowne by which the upper house would voluntarily restrict its voting members to give each party equal representation. Cf. House of Lords, 14 March, 13 April 1910.

I was supported by the I.L.P. (though I definitely refused to accept their 'Right to Work' proposals) and by every Trade Unionist (though I declined to pledge myself to vary the Osborne Judgement). The only reason these people have worked so hard for the Liberal cause is because they believe the hour to deal with the Lords is at hand and I am certain that if the line which is now taken is regarded by them as wanting in definiteness or courage, neither their approval of the Budget nor their dislike of tariffs, will keep them straight.[21]

Lloyd George bore much of the responsibility for raising popular expectations of drastic action against the Lords. Determined to win the greatest challenge of his political career, he had hitched Home Rule and the Osborne Judgment to the budget and set that truck full of passions rolling towards the recalcitrant upper house. Wittingly or not, Lloyd George had committed the future of the Liberal Party to the attack on the upper house and at the same time had made himself the kingpin of a fragile Liberal majority coalition; without him, it would surely come apart. One can begin to speak at this point of the breakup of the old Liberal Party.

The new balance of power exercised by Labour and the Irish pleased few Liberals. The majority of ministers, including Asquith himself, desired some method of reform for the upper house that would remove its hereditary character and break the Tory monopoly rather than the outright abolition of its veto power as the Irish demanded—a step which would virtually reduce it to the innocuous position of an advisory council.[22] With the uncertain discipline of the major parties, lacking a clear majority or any prospect of one, and with the adamant blocs on both the Left and the Right, a supreme lower house held out a darkly unpredictable future.

The renewal of Redmond's ultimatum—"No Veto Bill—No Budget"—to the Cabinet in February did not further endear the increasingly impatient Irish to the Liberal ministers.[23] Even Lloyd

[21] J. A. Simon to Asquith (5 Feb. 1910), *A.P.*, Dep. 12.

[22] The reform largely preferred at this time involved the abolition of the political privileges of peers and the substitution for the old house of a new, smaller (about 200) upper chamber with perhaps a minority of distinguished or expert life members. Cf., for example, plans proposed in H. Samuel to Asquith (3 Feb. 1910), *A.P.*, Dep. 12; Grey to Asquith (7 Feb. 1910), *A.P.*, Dep. 12. For Asquith's position, House of Commons, 4 Feb. 1910.

[23] Redmond frankly issued the ultimatum to the Cabinet on 25 Feb.; Cabinet Memo: Asquith to H.M. Sec. (25 Feb. 1910), *A.P.*, Dep. 51.

George and Churchill, the chief authors of the party's present conundrum, were a little perplexed with their work. Churchill was horrified by some of the more unrestrained attacks on the historic constitution. Lloyd George, despite his recent ferocity regarding the "Dukes," was inclining now towards the relatively moderate method of reforming the House of Lords internally, making it smaller and elective and thus improving rather than destroying its effectiveness as a legislative institution.[24] This sentiment was in line generally with some of the suggested methods which had broad bipartisan support, including one which Lord Rosebery had long advocated, in the interests, as he still put it, of "National Efficiency." There was an element of such constructive criticism, though unkindly expressed, even in Lloyd George's more sensational taunts of the Lords during the angry latter stages of the budget fight:

> ... here is the Assembly which is supposed to be dispassionate, to be calm, to be judicial above everything; this is the body that is to stand between us and anarchy; here is the fire brigade that is to quench the flames of revolution when it comes—why they cannot put out a little fire in the Sunday Edition of the *Daily Mail*. [A Garvin article calling for all-out resistance to the Budget].[25]

It was with almost unanimous displeasure, then, that the Cabinet received the demands of Redmond. The "anti-Irish prejudice ran very high" in the Cabinet, Lloyd George confessed to a friend. Lord Grey and others argued, without specifying an alternative, for an assertion of independence against the extremists. "The future belongs," Grey wrote to Asquith, "to whichever party inspires confidence in itself before another appeal to the country. We cannot inspire this by patching up working arrangements with the Labour or Irish parties or with both."[26]

Given the formidable arguments against an immediate second election, Grey's objection must have remained futile were it not for an offer of assistance from a most unexpected quarter. Soon after

[24] The feelings of Lloyd George and Churchill on the veto and the ultimatum were recorded by Charles Masterman, the chancellor's assistant on social questions at this time; cf. Lucy Masterman, *C. F. G. Masterman: A Biography* (London, 1939), p. 159.

[25] Lloyd George's speech at the National Liberal Club, 3 Dec. 1909. *Daily Chronicle*, 4 Dec. 1909.

[26] Cited in Lucy Masterman, *C. F. G. Masterman*, p. 159; Grey to Asquith (7 Feb. 1910), *A.P.*, Dep. 23.

the election returns revealed the government's predicament, Garvin, apparently without previous consultation with his party, made the following proposition to Asquith in the pages of the *Observer*:

> If he is wise, he will disregard the extremists of his own party and frankly enter into counsel upon the question of the Second Chamber with the Unionists, who would maintain him in power against Mr. Redmond's followers until the Constitution is placed upon a firm and fair basis.

This was not to be the last offer of cooperation to be made during the looming constitutional crisis, but it was the source from which all the others flowed and in some ways it was the oddest. Garvin was obviously not authorized to speak officially for the Unionist Party at this stage and it is doubtful that he spoke to anyone besides his circle of intimates of his surprising proposition; though that is not to say that interest was lacking for such a solution to the Irish problem among the party's leaders. Naturally, the idea would have been insanity for Asquith to entertain openly at this stage—there was no workable majority without the Irish and Labour should the Unionists leave him in the lurch, and an immediate election was inevitable if the plan failed, an election which he was desperately trying to avoid. It seems clear, then, that Garvin could not have been strictly in earnest nor could Asquith have taken such an offer seriously in the manner in which it was presented. Why then did Garvin raise such an apparently futile and distracting proposal? And more strangely still, why should he have addressed himself to Asquith, whom he and his circle had long looked upon as the personification of the most mindless and dogmatic Liberalism? If Garvin can be taken as representative of the Tariff Reform section of the Unionists at this time, being its main public spokesman, his proposal suggests very much the same attitude toward the Asquith Liberals as the Social-Imperialists held toward the old-line Conservatives: men whose capacity to govern had perished with the rise of a powerful and vocal Left and who must inevitably come to rely on the younger and bolder men to stave off the impending revolution. In this, Garvin was not far from the fact; he played upon a consternation which was painfully conscious in the Liberal ranks. The editor, with what he felt to be persuasive premonition, added to his proposal that if the government after all chose to "dragoon" the country with the votes of the "antiimperialist elements," it would "plunge the nation into convulsions of which no man can see the end."[27] His instinct struck remarkably close to the private mood of the Liberals.

The first conciliatory overture by Garvin, though unauthorized, nevertheless seems also to have reflected accurately the mood of many Unionists after the election. The party conflict since the introduction of the budget had reached an intensity beyond the experience of any of those involved. Home Rule, "The People v. the Peers," and unrestrained demagogy on both sides had stirred up a tempest of feeling which, it was feared, only the extremists would ride out. Some Tory irreconcilables, of whom the editor had been a gleefully willing leader, had been prepared for war to the knife and to "damn the consequences"; but even Milner, the author of the phrase, paused at this point. "The gravity of the times," he recollected of this postelection period, "produced a different response from some conservatives, who thought that circumstances demanded a diminution rather than an intensification of party conflict."[28]

For Milner, who had recently resolved to cut himself adrift from anti-Socialism, the political game had suddenly taken on a new interest, new possibilities. He was somewhat better prepared than the party leaders for the dilemma which arose in the early spring of 1910, it was just the kind of aimless muddle he had always said to be inherent in the party system. He stood always aloof from the parties and his disdain for "politics" had not abated. In South Africa, as he ceaselessly reminded everyone, he had accomplished remarkable work with a highly disciplined and competent cadre of young bureaucrats—his disciples, the "Kindergarten"—many of whom returned to England after the union to exert an extraordinary influence on British politics, all bearing the imprint of the master. Through the *Round Table*, an imperial journal and political club, the remnants of that cadre were reconstituted in 1910 and provided another effective platform for the broadcast of Milner's distinct political philosophy: among them were Geoffrey Dawson and F. S. Oliver of the *Times*, Philip Kerr (later Lord Lothian), and Lionel Curtis, who were the founders of the group, joined by the core of Milner's "regulars"—Amery, Garvin, Mackinder, and Maxse. Continuity with their original fraternity was maintained

---

[27] *Observer*, 23 Jan. 1910.

[28] Milner, *The Nation and the Empire*, p. xxxi; see also R. B. McDowell, *British Conservatism* (London, 1959), p. 178.

throughout the empire, where they overlapped frequently with the Compatriot organizations, and through the financial underwriter of the journal, Abe Bailey, the South African millionaire and longtime friend of Cecil Rhodes.[29]

Milner and his circle had built up the most elaborate body of criticism of the party system in the years since his repatriation; and it was ready to hand when the trend of thinking began to turn in this direction in the 1910 crisis. He summed up the defects of "the System" once more in the following four points:

> (1) Ultimate power in all matters, without appeal, with an ignorant people, without regard for trained knowledge and capable of the same levity with regard to the biggest things as with regard to trifles. (2) Party Politics at their worst, i.e. the old divisions of parties no longer corresponding to any real differences, and representing the mere husks of dead controversies . . . hence a pure struggle of ins and outs without any inner meaning, or principle in it whatever. (3) A huge, unwieldy Cabinet, in which half a dozen men of Cabinet rank are swamped by twice the number of second-rate men, who are mere ballast. (4) Above and Before All. No grading of the 100,000 questions . . . the great and the small, but all ultimately centering in that same unwieldy Cabinet, which . . . may be shaken in its dealings with a national question of the first moment, and in any case cannot give 'continuous thought and study' to the 'vital' . . . order of questions.[30]

Amery, one of the oldest members of the circle in point of service and cofounder with the Webbs of the Coefficients, restated the proconsul's case to suit the current crisis. The "dangerous situation" created by the elections, he suggested, illustrated the "grave underlying weakness of . . . [the] political system." The "two-party system," he declared, "by subordinating all other considerations to the single aim of keeping office, gives, from time to time . . . dangerous power to any substantial block of M.P.'s who are determined to achieve a certain policy regardless of all other considerations, however revolutionary that policy and however contrary to the general wish of the nation."[31]

Milner's "diminution" of party conflict by the method offered

[29] See Walter M. Nimocks, *Milner's Young Men: The 'Kindergarten' in Edwardian Imperial Politics* (Durham, N.C., 1968).
[30] Milner to Sir Clinton Dawkins (n.d., 1910), cited in Crankshaw, *The Forsaken Idea*, p. 133.
[31] L. S. Amery, *My Political Life*, pp. 358-359.

in the pages of the *Observer* meant, of course, a détente only between the two *traditional* parties in the state. As such, it was a course which offered not only a tempting respite from extreme pressures to the beleaguered Cabinet but an opportunity for the Tories to rise from the frustrating position of mere spectators to what they felt to be the most dangerous crisis of their generation. For, as Garvin proposed, if the Nationalists' demand be conceded, "why not the Welsh demand for Disestablishment . . . or the Socialist demand for the 'Right to Work Bill?' "[32] To thwart Redmond and all that impended should he succeed as taskmaster of the Liberal Cabinet, therefore, Asquith must be bailed out. In addition, the current crisis seemed to offer the attractive opportunity of separating the ruling Liberal-Radical coalition. This was the persuasion employed by Austen Chamberlain on Balfour. Labour "has come to stay," he reminded Balfour just after Garvin's article appeared, and its continued association with the Liberals greatly "reduces our advantages from the 'swing of the pendulum.' "[33] The imperialists, in short, were ready to move a little from their earlier position of trying to win a share of the working-class vote through their ambitious but rather futile "conservative working men's" organizations, to the more tactical maneuver of detaching anti-Socialist Liberals from the alliance with Labour.

The Garvin proposal was attracting a widening range of interest. The decisive effort to persuade Balfour seems to have been made by Lord Lansdowne, former Foreign Secretary and currently the Unionist leader in the House of Lords. He proposed to the leader that the Lords reform should be the work of "both parties, acting in consultation and in a spirit somewhat different from that which now prevails."[34] Balfour's response was characteristically circumspect, but encouraging. He agreed that if arbitration "would strengthen the hands of the King and of the moderates in the Cabinet in resisting unconstitutional pressure by the extremists," some attempt should certainly be made. Thereupon Balfour issued a Memo to the King which, though it carefully avoided any hint of compromising the union or the House of Lords, suggested that some royal initiative be taken to bring about the "co-operation of both parties in the State" in settling the constitutional deadlock.[35]

[32] *Observer*, 20 March 1910.
[33] A. Chamberlain to Balfour (29 Jan. 1910), *B.P.*, 49736-787B.
[34] Ibid.
[35] "Memo," Balfour to the King (15 Feb. 1910), cited in Lord Newton's *Lord Lansdowne* (London, 1929), pp. 386-389.

The delicate operation of opening an avenue of negotiation was conducted with extreme discretion, and some uncertainty, on both sides in order not to bring down prematurely a charge of surrender or even worse either from the extremists or from the rank and file still fired with the emotional partisanship of the elections. Asquith witnessed this danger a week after Balfour's Memo, when, after a long private debate, he announced in Parliament his desire to withdraw his earlier demand that the Crown appoint sufficient peers to allow the passage of the Veto Bill through the upper house.[36] It was a tacit guarantee to the Opposition that no assault would be made on the Lords' veto until a second election should be held and it immediately drew a storm of outraged protest from the Left. Moreover, the proposal was an alarming blow, and perhaps a fortuitous one, to the Redmondites and an unmistakable signal to Balfour that further pacific overtures from the Opposition would at least not be met with outright hostility.

The first substantial attempt to bring the negotiations to a head, not too surprisingly, was undertaken by the distraught Liberal leadership, not long after Asquith's announcement. On 29 March, a "Secret" memorandum was drawn up by A. C. Murray, Master of Elibank and the Liberal Chief Whip, with the knowledge and approval of Asquith, which outlined a project to summon a conference on the constitutional issue under the mediation of King Edward. The plan, first revealed to the Prince of Wales, was to appear to originate with the King "as if the suggestion was the product of cogitation on his part and not one he was being induced to follow." This was Elibank's language, of course, not Asquith's. To the proposed conference the Irish were to be invited as well as Labour, which might help to show, Elibank added pointedly, how "invaluable the Crown can be at critical moments and that Labour is recognized, consulted and that [the] Crown is in sympathy." It argued the urgency of such a conference in Elibank's peculiar telegraphic, Mr. Jingle style:

> The one force that is irresistible in the country is the electorate. If it returned same number of members of all parties Government could not carry on. . . . U. [Unionists] *could not* govern—with Irish against.

---

[36] Asquith, House of Commons, 11 March 1910; and Asquith's speech at the Oxford Town Hall (18 March 1910); *Annual Register* (1910), p. 273. The protest which met Asquith's reversal is described in Jenkins, *Balfour's Poodle*, p. 100.

Alliance with Irish would break up U. Party—none too solid now. Always preserve in discussion preliminary essential that veto must be *abolished* in Finance and *curtailed* otherwise.

Room for negotiation and compromise in second—NONE in first.

THAT IS THE KEY OF SITUATION

Bear in mind also
Socialists and
Labour and
Irish and
Extreme Radicals if joining in one party would make Liberalism impossible. . . .[37]

Elibank, who had only succeeded Pease as Chief Whip in early February, had been thought by his predecessor "a bit too scheming" to be trusted with the powerful and delicate position at such a time.[38] But Elibank, if he merited the description, was admirably fitted to the task before him upon taking up the office—he would find a broad scope in which to practice his dubious talent. The proposition contained in his Memo departed from Garvin's by including the Irish and Labour sections, but added an ingenious embellishment to the rather straightforward betrayal of the minority factions suggested by the editor.

The new whip had acted as the party's liaison with Labour during the election campaign and had gleaned from this experience, as he related in a letter to Garvin, what he felt to be the "secret of tactics" in dealing with the Left. Labour's success, he wrote, would be

> detrimental to both the great parties . . . as they create the nucleus of a solid Socialist vote which is liable to expansion should a leader be thrown up at a time of national excitement.
>
> If Unionists and Liberals allow Labour and its various trades to consolidate they are done. '*Detach; Detach*' has been my guiding principle. . . . There are many matters upon which you and I are on common ground, because we do not pursue a party rut but try to unravel situations as they arise and look ahead.[39]

---

[37] "Memo" (29 March 1910), *Elibank Papers*, cited in Gollin, *The Observer*, p. 183.

[38] Pease to Asquith (4 Feb. 1910), *A.P.*, Dep. 12.

[39] Elibank to Garvin (n.d., 1910), cited in Gollin, *The Observer*, p. 328.

Elibank's "guiding principle" shrewdly anticipated the sort of tactics which were used to hamstring Labour in the war years and on some occasions thereafter. As we have seen, the Tariff Reformers had also been fascinated for some years by the idea of winning over the "patriotic" section of Labour, such as those whom Robert Blatchford was thought to represent, but had been so far unable to arrive at a successful formula for doing so. In regard to the "detachment" of the nearer fringes of the Labour coalition and working-class votes, Elibank and Garvin were indeed on common ground. That seductive prospect had been earnestly pursued in Social-Imperialist activities and in the work of the Tariff Reform League during the past seven years. "Why not Unionist Labour M.P.'s," Milner had asked, sensing strongly, as did Garvin, that the "working classes . . . [were] not the unpatriotic, anti-national, down-with-the-army, up-with-the-foreigner, take-it-laying-down class of Little Englanders, that they are constantly represented to be."[40] Milner's inimitable lyrics!

The failure of their previous efforts to muster working-class interest had dampened their hopes somewhat and reduced their efforts in that direction over the past two years and the Osborne decision seemed at first to make the prospects even dimmer. But, as we shall see, the opportunities of the year 1910 set the Tariff Reformers back on that scent with renewed energy and a good deal more realism. In the formation of the Unionist Social Reform Committee in that year, the Tariff Reformers began to discover a policy which would govern, with great long-term success, the approach of the future Conservative Party to the non-Socialist laboring classes.

Whatever the long-range hopes harbored by either side of "detaching" dissident members of the Labour section, which was increasingly susceptible since its political funds had been cut off by the Lords, the more immediate problem was how to deal with Redmond. Appeals to patriotism and the national welfare would find

[40] Milner, speech at Rugby, 19 November 1907, "Unionists and Social Reform," *The Nation and the Empire*, p. 250. The attempt of the Tariff Reform League to develop a labor policy is discussed in chapters II and IV. The beginning of several attempts on the part of the Tariff Reformers to implement the Milner policy, in the formation of the Unionist Social Reform Committee and later the British Workers National League, are also to be found in 1910; e.g., cf. *Reports on Labour and Social Conditions in Germany* (1910), the first publication of the U.S.R.C.

little response in this quarter. To deal with the Irish Garvin advocated a tactic again similar to Elibank's. If he were able to persuade Asquith, Grey, Haldane, and the Liberal League section of the government to resist Redmond to the point of resigning, a choice he believed them beleaguered enough to make, an entirely new situation would arise regarding the Irish.[41] He outlined the plan to Balfour as follows:

> If Asquith and Grey refused to continue then the King's Government having to be carried on and the House of Commons entertaining a majority in principle agreeing with Unionist views on Education, licensing, Tariff Reform and above all the food tax, it would be our . . . duty to exchange views with Mr. Redmond, Mr. William O'Brien and Mr. Healy . . . it might just be possible to make what I have called the Unionist majority in principle, a real working majority in practice. . . .[42]

There were elements in the Irish group also, he pointed out to Balfour, that were sufficiently hostile to Socialism to look favorably upon a compromise with its staunchest opponents; especially those connected with the Irish church who were in "dread of being left alone in an anti-cleric movement." Milner, having been asked by Balfour for his thoughts on the situation, also advised him that some concession on "Provincial" rather than "National" Home Rule might bring out the potential of the Irish Party as "a conservative force in U.K. politics standing for Tariff and private property—as against collectivism. . . ."[43]

As ingenuous as Garvin's scenario might appear at first glance, with the Nationalists deeply and publicly committed to, and expecting, a final settlement of Home Rule, it contained intuitions into the temperament of Irish Nationalism beyond the sight of more orthodox political men. Although the situation was to change rapidly in the next few years, the more socially conservative Nationalists were still dominant in the Irish parliamentary delegation and still retained control of most of the Irish press. Whatever else the move-

---

[41] Garvin specifically states that his appeal was directed to "the representatives of the Liberal League" in his editorials of 10 and 17 April 1910 (*Observer*). His hopes in this direction were no doubt stimulated by the close cooperation of Rosebery and Lansdowne at the time in the House of Lords; cf. Newton, *Lord Lansdowne*, pp. 392-393.
[42] Garvin to Sandars (27 Jan. 1910), *B.P.*, 49795-787B.
[43] Ibid.; Milner to Balfour (17 April 1910), *M.P.*, Letters, A.III.

ment for Irish self-government was to become, Garvin was right in thinking that it would retain a strong anti-Socialist inclination.

During the postelection deadlock in the early months of the year many played at reshuffling the various parliamentary factions in search of an advantage—the Unionists in hope of cleaving the rickety ruling coalition and the Liberals hoping to prolong their conditional majority without binding themselves indefinitely to the demands of their junior partners. In most cases, the method of "detaching" advocated by Elibank and Garvin held the strongest attraction. Such maneuvers naturally lent themselves somewhat better to private discussion than to public debate, particularly so for those party leaders who in such a delicate equilibrium had to avoid most gingerly the many chances of offending the wary and by now rather skeptical political minorities. The demands of this situation explain in part the almost paralytic torpor of both Asquith and Balfour in the months between the two elections of 1910 as well as the unceasing industry of men like Garvin, Elibank and, eventually, Lloyd George. These were not only better suited temperamentally to such a situation but were also less strictly governed by orthodox parliamentary methods and discipline. Lloyd George and Garvin in particular shared remarkably similar instincts throughout the crisis, bearing out to some degree Garvin's remark of a few years before regarding their common "Celtic" outlook. On the problem of detaching the more amenable Irish Nationalists, for example, Lloyd George was apparently contemplating a course parallel to Garvin's—though of course the end in mind was not the creation of a Unionist-Irish majority. Anticipating his tragic but rather successful handling of the Irish a decade later, Lloyd George was weighing recent intelligence which he had received from private sources in March regarding dissention between the O'Brien-Healy and the Redmondite factions in Ireland. One report, marked "Quite Confidential" and unsigned, which crossed the chancellor's desk at about the time Elibank drew up his Memo, suggests the direction in which both he and Garvin were looking. O'Brien was portrayed by his informant as the one man in Ireland capable of galvanizing moderate sentiment, including the Irish Tories, and standing off the extremists. O'Brien, the report argued, had "a hold on Irish hearts immeasurably beyond any other living politician." O'Brien's policy, resistance on the budget and conciliation on Home Rule, had already gained wide sympathy, it went on, "sympathy which will be increased indefinitely if a reconciliation with

J. Redmond does not take place. . . ."[44] Moreover, the condition of O'Brien's success against Redmond would depend largely upon his ability to finance the moderate press in Ireland and sustain a prolonged public campaign—an important factor which might be exploited in any dealings with the Irish factions. Like the Liberal Party in England, both Irish factions were short of funds; this would be a continuing consideration for the rest of the year in deciding on the date for a second election.[45]

Prevailing Irish views on the budget and Home Rule would seem to have ruled out any significant cooperation with the Tariff Reformers on one side or with the Lloyd George Liberals on the other. Moreover, it is unclear what either Garvin or Lloyd George were in a position to do regarding the Irish even if they could somehow reconcile their momentous differences (though both were to show astonishing flexibility on both great issues in the months to come). There was obviously no lack of inventiveness on either side for ways of gaining some advantage out of the stalemate of the early spring. But the necessary precondition of all the schemes had not yet been achieved; the leaders of the major parties had as yet agreed upon nothing, neither to meet, nor to arbitrate, nor to let the electorate break the deadlock in a new election. Two months and more had thus passed after the election and no substantial initiatives could yet be taken with discretion regarding Labour or the Nationalists until the question of a negotiated settlement had been decided—Asquith and Balfour were moving slowly and uncertainly.

Since the conciliatory representations from both sides had thus far been made through the Crown rather than directly, the initiative seemed to lie with the King. This was as both Asquith and Balfour would have it in order to disarm the inevitable charges of surrender and collusion that would arise from inside and outside their own parties once a conference had been publicly announced. Both leaders, as we have seen, had had serious trouble with recalcitrant and undisciplined sections of their parties and the necessary discretion and indecision of this period did little to reassure those who felt left out of the inner circle.

The King was extremely anxious to arrange a compromise in the

---

[44] Untitled and unsigned Memo (31 March 1910), *L.G.P.*, C/20/2/1.

[45] Ibid. The report based its conclusions mainly upon the O'Brien-Redmond struggle in County Cork, seeing this as the critical arena of the internal Irish dispute at the moment.

reform of the House of Lords, having been gravely upset by the "extreme direction of feelings between the Houses" during the election, and had even added to the growing ledger of proposals with a compromise plan of his own.[46] Although he was willing to act personally in settling the constitutional question, he was naturally hesitant to inject the Crown imprudently into a heated partisan conflict. It was partly to allay this fear that those Unionists who were desirous of an arrangement with the Liberals began to ply the political journals with the argument that a negotiated settlement between the two major parties initiated by the Crown, far from being a sordid party artifice, was a solution "above parties"; in fact, the only truly "national" solution. Such, for example, was the line taken by the protectionist Liberal-Unionist Association in its April report, published a few days before the King's death:

> When parties are divided by different notions and principles concerning some particular ecclesiastical or civil institution, the constitution, which should be their rule, must be that of the prince.
> This may be done by him without fomenting division; and far from forming or espousing a party, he will defeat party in defense of the constitution . . . and lead men from acting with a party spirit, to act with a national spirit.[47]

This line of argument, deploring the "grubby struggle of parties" in the name of the national interest, which had been preached by Milner and publicized by Garvin so often in the past, was repeated throughout the protectionist press with increasing force as the crisis deepened. Other strong voices of Tariff Reform—the National Service League, Northcliffe's *Daily Mail*, and especially the *Observer*—reinforced the plea of the Liberal-Unionist Association that squalid factional advantages be sacrificed to the nation. This, it became clear, was to be the patriotic exoneration of any compromise that could be reached between the parties and the response to any protests from the "extremists."[48]

During the lull which followed the submission of the conference proposals to the King in late March, Garvin devoted his editorial

[46] James Pope-Hennessy, *Lord Crewe* (London, 1955), p. 108.
[47] "Liberal Unionist Memoranda," *Liberal Unionist Publication*, VII, 5 (May 1910).
[48] "The Patriot," *National Service League Publication*, II, 10 (Feb. 1910); cf. also "The Patriot," II, 11 (March 1910); *Daily Mail*, 10 Jan. 1910; *Observer*, 3 and 10 April, 1 May 1910.

energies to extracting the Liberal Leaguers in the government from the clutches of the "Irish Dictator" (as Garvin now characterized Redmond). It was clear in his April articles that he had been keenly disappointed by his failure to bring about a rupture in the government before the final budget vote, which was scheduled to take place at the end of the month. It was thought, he grumbled on 10 April, that the "representatives of the Liberal League, Mr. Asquith, Sir Edward Grey, and Mr. Haldane," would prove strong enough to curb the "Celtic hysterics" of the chancellor and the "neurotic brilliance" of Mr. Winston Churchill. But this hope had vanished into thin air, he lamented, with the whole of them being dragged by the Irish along the road of "sham, shuffle, and shirk. . . ."[49]

Despite the willingness of the Liberals whom Garvin was addressing to arrange a détente in the conflict over the upper house, there had been no indication from them, despite Garvin's dogged harangues, that they contemplated any desertion on the budget. On the first, he had not unreasonably inferred that the desertion of Rosebery and Carlyon Bellairs indicated the mood of the former Liberal-Imperialists in general—Rosebery also came up with an attractive plan of *internal* reform for the Lords founded on his famous principles of "National Efficiency" which Garvin assumed still held some of their old magic for the Liberal Leaguers. If Rosebery had still held even the spiritual sway which he had possessed nearly a decade before, the editor's expectations might well have been realized—as it was, Rosebery was a lonely raven in 1910, his projects had lost currency and were largely ignored. Garvin's hopes for desertions on the budget from this quarter were even less well founded; like most of the party, the old Liberal-Imperialists had misgivings on many aspects of the controversial budget and had made them known, but had committed the government in the end to its passage, being at a loss for any alternatives. Garvin was soon to recognize that he had badly overestimated the remaining vitality of Liberal-Imperialism. Furthermore, he seems from his article to have harbored still another misapprehension; this one regarding the mood of Lloyd George and Churchill. The revolutionary fires of both cooled abruptly when confronted with the new power of Redmond and Labour since the elections. Indeed, without

[49] The editorials of both 3 and 10 April made the same point and were also explicitly addressed to Asquith, Grey, and Haldane. *Observer*, 10 April 1910.

the knowledge of Garvin, his appeal to resist the Irish seems ironically to have received its most sympathetic hearing in these very unexpected quarters. Churchill retained enough of his Tory heritage to view the destruction of the House of Lords with some distaste, preferring that the entire question, as he confessed to a friend, be somehow "shunted."[50] And the Nonconformist chancellor, who had been embroiled with Redmond over the Whisky clauses in the budget, had less inclination than most of his colleagues to strain under a situation which committed the great opus of his career to the arbitrary discretion of the Irish.

The crisis which induced Asquith, Grey, and Haldane to temporize seems to have struck new springs of enterprise in the volatile Welshman. At a Cabinet meeting in mid-April, Lloyd George suddenly turned on the Irish. Asquith had opened the meeting with some remarks about the Whisky Tax and the Irish demand for its repeal. Churchill was preparing to follow the Prime Minister when he was passed a note from the chancellor announcing to his "joy and astonishment" that there was to be no surrender to Redmond after all; whereupon the both of them turned menacingly upon Redmond (who was apparently present only to discuss the Whisky Tax), challenging him with great success on both the royal guarantees and the tax. In effect, they were defying the Irish to kill the budget, topple the government, and thereby hazard if they dared the promised reward of a Home Rule Bill for the sake of twopence a quart.[51] Short of funds, his party and the movement in Ireland fragmenting to the Right and the Left, Redmond had few resources to rely on, whether to bargain with the government or to defy them. He was the first only of many Irish and British leaders to be suddenly hamstrung by Lloyd George's startling turnabouts.

Although Garvin seems to have remained ignorant of the chancellor's change of heart, the proceedings of the stormy Cabinet meeting quickly reached Balfour. He was informed, through Runciman, another minister who had been delighted by the spectacle, that Lloyd George had turned on the Irish "with the ardour of a convert" in announcing his decision to push the budget intact "without concession." Furthermore, far from wanting to conceal

---

[50] Lucy Masterman, *C. F. G. Masterman*, p. 176.

[51] A description of the meeting was given by Churchill to Charles Masterman shortly afterward and was recorded by Lucy Masterman, *C. F. G. Masterman*, p. 161.

this new source of disunity in the government from the Opposition, Lloyd George himself quickly made his new views known to Bonar Law and to Balfour, through his secretary, Jack Sandars.[52]

These few weeks of March and April prior to the last reading of the budget were apparently a period of reflection and some perplexity for the chancellor. He had ample reason to suspect some of his colleagues of coolness towards his controversial projects, even jealousy of his having captured the initiative in forming party policy. In addition, he was certainly aware of the recent flirtation with the Tories, an affair in which he had not to this point taken any substantial part. Both these considerations were probably in his mind when in April he expounded to Masterman one possible solution to the present crisis. On a bench in St. James's Park, he explained to his friend that the whole of the "Cabinet left wing" would probably have to resign. Although he admitted that he did not know what men he personally could count on, he suggested the possibility of forming a government with himself as Prime Minister and the departments headed by "business men" such as Sir Christopher Furness and Alfred Mond. Such a Cabinet, he proposed, "would carry enormous weight in the country." As for the businessmen, he said, "they are very simple people, these Captains of Industry. I can do what I like with them. I found that out at the Board of Trade."[53]

Although it was not to be apparent at the time to all who witnessed it, the chancellor was in the midst of a personal political transformation. It was a change, as one observer aptly put it, from "radical agitator" to "manipulator of power"—a perhaps inevitable process in a man of his gifts and temperament in which the half-formed projects he toyed with in St. James's Park were only the first inklings. He had passed from the "repose" of the Board of Trade to the emotional and draining agitation of the budget fight—one cannot help but feel from his behavior during 1910 that he had lost enthusiasm for the position of chancellor after the completion of the budget; though he was to accomplish more lasting works in that office, he never again brought the same inspiration and emotion to

---

[52] Sandars to Balfour (16 April 1910), *B.P.*, 49766-787C.

[53] The conversation, which took place sometime shortly after the April Cabinet meeting on the Whisky Tax, is reported in Masterman, *C. F. G. Masterman*, pp. 159-160. It may be anachronistic, it is not corroborated in any of the scanty personal sources on Lloyd George at this time, but it represents what seems to have been his general mood during the spring.

it; something of him hibernated until the time he took over the Ministry of Munitions. The year 1910 was one in which he wished to make great decisions and policy on the grand scale, no longer in the guise of agitator but as statesman. Lloyd George's political face, with the menacing grimace of his earlier radicalism conspicuously lifted, did not emerge fully at this early date; but as his embattled budget finally approached enactment, the Limehouse firebrand began discreetly to disclose a new demeanor, as unfamiliar to his friends as to his enemies.

VII

The Lloyd George Plan

The King returned from Biarritz on the day the budget was carried in the House of Commons. Two weeks later he was dead. Two days after the royal death on 6 May 1910, Garvin published an elaborate plan for an immediate Constitutional Conference, warning that the bitter conflict over the budget and the Veto Bill was "threatening the very bases of the nation's institutions." Expressing a widely felt anxiety, he added that "social unrest at home and the German menace abroad were national dangers which the politicians could no longer ignore, whatever their constitutional differences."[1]

On the same day, newspapers all over the country, most of them bordered in black on the front page, issued similar calls for armistice, for the nation to pull together in its hour of grief. The front page of the *Times* featured such a plea composed in verse by the current Poet Laureate, Alfred Austin, entitled, "The Truce of God, a King's Bequest." The same entreaty was made here, in slightly creaky hexameters, for an end to internal conflict and a display of solidarity to meet the nation's approaching peril.[2]

The death of Edward struck a genuine note of bereavement in the country; he had been a popular monarch—neither austere nor, like Victoria, fastidious in his personal habits. He was a well-publicized sportsman and traveler; a king to suit the tastes of his time. Nevertheless, not even the most nostalgic of king-watchers or Tory backwoodsmen could seriously have thought the passing of King Edward VII a political calamity of any great consequence, at least not for any direct political role he had played during his reign. Yet, the event was seized upon with undissembled relief in the Unionist press and in government circles as a signal to halt the violent parti-

[1] *Observer*, 8 May 1910.   [2] *Times*, 8 May 1910.

sanship over the budget, which had anyway passed the House of Commons two days before, and for a postponement of debate over the impending Veto Bill. Edward VII's most adroit political maneuver was merely to expire at precisely the right time.

The death of Edward was an opportunity, the occasion only and not the cause, of the forebodings expressed by Garvin and Alfred Austin. Such feelings had taken root long before the budget and the constitutional crisis had made them specific and clear. The assured peace and security of the Pax Britannica had come to an end almost before it had come into existence; the same forebodings had filled the pages of late Victorian journals and, as we have seen, was the primary emotion upon which the Social-Imperialist movement played since the *fin de siècle*. With its fetish of the classics, its divided Christian conscience, and its guilty materialism, the Edwardian empire was obsessed with the scent of its own decline at the height of its power. A decade of pessimistic social scientists had morally bludgeoned the public into the vague conviction that the country, like Rome and Pithecanthropus, was about to face its moment of trial in the "struggle for survival." Closed frontiers in Africa and Asia, menacing realignments in Europe, vigorous economic rivals, declining birth rates, foreign immigration, industrial and agricultural decadence, military incompetence, homosexuality, opulence and scandal—this was the dismal glass through which the English public had been asked to view the future since the chastisement administered by the Boers.

It is easier to gauge the mood of officials, journalists, and politicians than to characterize the sentiments of an entire nation. It is probable that what was a pressing concern of editorial pages and political salons was a matter of the smallest consequence to the daily passage of life in the factory, office, and farm. Except at moments of great crisis or celebration—Mafeking night or the August days of 1914—mass "moods" are elusive, perhaps even nonexistent. At no point in the year 1910 was such a climax reached, certainly not at the news of Edward's death. Indeed, the supposed public indifference to the great affairs of state was just one more indication of approaching disaster to those haunted by gloomy forecasts—a disaster which would be fully earned, as Beatrice Webb had put it, by the general selfishness, materialism, and debauchery of the current generation. This was the reasoning behind a good part of the numerous projects of social reform advocated by the Social-Imperialist movement over the past decade, and the conviction was present in one form or another in virtually all their literature and private debates.

The specter of moral and physical decay, the loss of ancient virtues, the decline of "racial" vitality, were themes common to all the Catonist movements of this period throughout Europe and in parts of North American society as well. That state of mind was laced with a good quantity of myth and metaphysics, but it was also related to quite real shifts, mostly gradual but momentous, in the balance of world power and wealth and the progressive turbulence of domestic life.

"Seldom has the Empire been nearer to disintegration," Cecil Chesterton wrote early in the year, "seldom has the country been nearer to overthrow, spoliation, and subjection than it is at present. For the first time for at least a hundred years a great European Power has definitely set itself to challenge our command of the seas."[3] Before the worst of the Anglo-German crises of the next four years, there had been at least two minds about the rising arrogance of German power. Most agreed by now that she was a threat to the European balance, an economic and naval threat, and an imperial rival. On the other hand, since the Entente, with France and Russia apparently prepared and watchful, was it really necessary to do much more than fortify the island, continue the reform of the reserve, and maintain a few ready regiments to reinforce the French line? And was the historic naval ratio to be continued by building eight dreadnoughts, or would four do for defense while the difference was spent on health, housing, education, and pensions?

The set of emotions building up with regard to the situation at home was equally grim and divided. Sir George Askwith, the Liberal government's labor-management troubleshooter, a sensible and perceptive pioneer in this young profession, recalled the fears of the government as well as the trades union executives in 1910 due to the alarming incidence of unauthorized strikes forced upon them by the "new" men—a pattern which was to peak sensationally three years later. In his reports to the government, he dwelt on the "real possibility" of a general abandoning of constitutional means by the rebellious shop stewards and membership. They had been put into this mood, according to Askwith, by the feeling that wages had lagged behind rising costs amidst an unprecedented parading of opulence on the part of many of their more favored

[3] Cecil Chesterton, *Party and People* (London, 1910), p. 104.

countrymen. It was a mood which seemed badly out of tune with the spirit of *la belle époque* and one which the muddle of national politics, the agitation over the budget, the Osborne Judgment and the continuing vacillation of the government on the Veto Bill did little to mollify.[4]

As the debacle which came with the reading of the budget was reaching its climax, Lord Curzon, who was then vice-president of the National Service League, tried to depict the dark turn which feelings had taken. "I am afraid we live in an age of self-depreciation," he said. "The pessimists are abroad in the land. We can hardly take up our morning newspaper without reading of the physical and moral decline of the race . . . beaten in cricket, then in polo." He added sadly, and with deeper perception, "Every man over fifty years of age is a Cassandra."[5]

Curzon was admittedly speaking as one of the older men; he might as well have said that he spoke for the last Victorian generation, whose scions were still in titular control of most of the nation's institutions. The despairing mood which he ascribed to the age is probably one of the reasons for the often mystifying behavior of the older leaders in the course of the events which filled the rest of the year. While the younger men in both parties also engaged in the same public foreboding and doomsaying, they appeared to be less numbed by the prospects. The impact of events which produced pessimism and passivity in some called up energy and inventiveness in others. Then, as the constitutional question reached ever more critical stages, the reins of control began perceptibly to slip from the hands of the last Victorians.

The Truce of God

The *Observer*'s article of 8 May calling for a "Truce" and a conference was an inspiration which, Garvin explained rather implausibly, "came in a flash with absolute conviction as the new policy for

---

[4] Lord George Askwith, *Industrial Problems and Disputes* (London, 1920), pp. 145-146; see also the article by Standish Meacham, " 'The Sense of an Impending Clash': English Working-Class Unrest before the First World War," *American Historical Review*, 77/5 (Dec. 1972), 1343-64 for a summary of labor sentiment between 1910 and 1914.

[5] Speeches of Lord Curzon of Kedleston, *Subjects of the Day* (New York, 1913), p. 163.

a wholly new situation."⁶ In fact, as far as the editor was aware at the time, nothing very much in the situation of the early spring had been altered by Edward's passing. The monarch had had little personal influence on the issues at stake and would quickly have passed out of the picture even if he had agreed to play the part written for him by Elibank. His occasional injunctions regarding the tone of radical speeches and the mounting abuse of the upper house were cordially ignored and were indeed more embarrassing to the Lords' defenders than to their critics.

The "wholly new situation" of which Garvin spoke did seem to arise, however, on the day following the appearance of his article, and from a direction that was genuinely unexpected. The "hysterical Celt," the incendiary author of the hated budget and Garvin's most formidable antagonist, had himself read Sunday's "flash of inspiration" and arranged for a personal emissary to convey to the editor that he was "much impressed."⁷

Lloyd George communicated to Garvin through another journalist, W. T. Stead of the *Review of Reviews*. The message he delivered on Monday morning instantly revived the editor's hopes of heading off the Irish before the Lords' veto was destroyed, the act from which Home Rule and the Osborne reversal would inevitably follow. Now that the budget had passed, the chancellor intimated that he would be satisfied with a reform of the second chamber "on some principle of nomination," in which case its constitutional powers might remain much as the Unionists wished. All that he wanted in his new pacific mood, he assured Garvin, was that his party "have their chance of a majority" in the upper house.⁸ Thus the Liberal promise of a Home Rule Bill still stood, but Lloyd George had now emerged both with his budget and, after his open defiance of Redmond in the Cabinet, with grounds for a certain moral latitude on the manner in which Home Rule was to be achieved. If some agreement with the Opposition could be arranged for dealing with the Lords' veto, he would then have rescued the government from its dilemma and established a position which offered considerable freedom of action on both the Home Rule Bill and on any revision of the Osborne Judgment.

⁶ Garvin to Northcliffe (8 May 1910), cited in Gollin, *The Observer*, p. 185.
⁷ Garvin to Sandars (10 May 1910), *B.P.* 49795; W. T. Stead to Garvin (9 May 1910), cited in Gollin, *The Observer*, p. 186.
⁸ Garvin to Sandars (Empire Day, 10 May 1910), *B.P.*, 49795-787B.

The Lloyd George Plan

Lloyd George's discreet overture to the Unionist editor was a timely invitation to the Opposition to reopen the preliminary discussions of a negotiated settlement which appeared to have lapsed during the few weeks before the death of the King. Furthermore, this new initiative was apparently also taken in collaboration with the Master of Elibank, though it is unlikely that Asquith was informed of it at this point. On the same afternoon Stead transmitted another message to Garvin, this time from Elibank, urging that in the new and promising situation the Tories should take the next step to further the projected conference.[9] This Garvin himself was prepared to concede; but despite the chancellor's unexpectedly conciliatory, and unauthorized, proposition on the reform of the upper house, he could not guarantee that the Unionist leadership would risk the wrath of its stalwarts by making the first overt gesture of appeasement.

Balfour was in doubt, and remained so all during the negotiations which were to follow, as to how far the various sections of the party would acquiesce in privately arranged understandings with the government. Since being informed in March of the possibility of negotiations on the question of the second chamber, he had been quietly sounding out a few close associates for opinion regarding a compromise and had even reached the point of drafting a Reform Bill which he felt might command a general consensus. His draft, completed sometime in early May, allowed for an equal Liberal voice among the peers based on a combination of nomination and election. It was a conservative but flexible plan which, if Lloyd George's proposition was sincere, may well have formed a basis for negotiation of the Lords' veto. Nevertheless, Balfour took no further action on Garvin's information, not trusting the quicksilver moods of the Welshman, and preferring to await some advance by the leader of the Liberal Party himself. The unauthorized activities of Lloyd George and Elibank may also have been an upsetting reminder of the restless indiscipline within his own party and an inducement to keep the negotiations in official channels as much as possible.

The slowness and hesitancy with which both party leaders approached the subject of a constitutional conference reflected limitations of which both were aware in their control of party discipline. Garvin and the Tariff Reformers, like Lloyd George, had succeeded in making the party leader a virtual captive of their ad-

[9] Ibid.

vanced positions during the preceding months. The pressure on Asquith had been somewhat relieved by the passage of the budget but Balfour still labored under the commitment to Tariff Reform, wrung out of him mainly by Garvin before the January elections. The prospect of at least a temporary lessening of the crisis which the conference could afford was clearly in the interests and to the liking of the beleaguered party leaders, but the intrusion again of the two adventurous personalities—the same two whose blustery intransigence had brought the parties to the present impasse—cast the shadow of extremism even over their councils of moderation. Balfour's pronouncement on Tariff Reform before the January elections had been seriously qualified by his insistence that it be submitted to a referendum if the Unionists won. The main result, therefore, was that neither the Tariff Reformers nor their opponents in the party were satisfied. Now he feared to impose a policy of conciliation on the party, a course which would seem to the Unionist Free Traders another surrender to the Tariff Reform wing dictated again by Garvin and the protectionists.

Although the encounter with Lloyd George had no immediate sequel, further advances were received from Haldane and Elibank during May urging the necessity of a meeting of party leaders which they felt could most plausibly be broached to the Unionists through Garvin, both privately and through the *Observer*. Consequently, encouraged by his Liberal friends, Garvin accelerated his journalistic efforts in this direction through the rest of the month and early June, priming his arguments more towards persuading Unionists now that the other side seemed eager for a compromise.[10]

Garvin's articles of May and June were considerably warmer towards his former enemies. "Since we wrote last week," he announced on 15 May, "we have had the strongest evidence and from some very unexpected quarters, that the overmastering sentiment of the country at large . . . [is] for conference between responsible statesmen" of both parties. Lloyd George, it must have startled his readers to learn (and puzzled many a Liberal), was also to be praised for his wise moderation. In the same article, Garvin introduced into the discussion a proposal that went significantly beyond the previous idea of conferring to settle the House of Lords dispute. As a further lure for the chancellor he suggested that an interparty conference with authority to settle the constitutional issue might also be able to deal efficiently with such complicated

[10] *Observer*, 15 and 22 May 1910.

projects as national insurance and Poor Law reconstruction.[11] This proposal, which Garvin appears to have tacked on mainly as an afterthought and on his own initiative, was in fact a radically new twist in the original conference idea. Should the new addition be made part of the proposed truce, the conference would in effect be transformed from an ad hoc constitutional committee into a new parliamentary coalition of a very unusual variety—unusual at least in peacetime, in that the conference would presumably be working outside the parliamentary and party apparatus.

Although the editor's idea was a natural derivation of the years of talk about "non-party" methods and legislative "efficiency," it is quite probable that Garvin did not weigh all the immediate implications of his suggestions at this moment. Indeed, it was several weeks before even Lloyd George, for whose eyes the suggestion was printed, grasped its full potential. The chancellor was engaged at the time in laying the groundwork for his monumental Insurance Bill and one of the more formidable obstacles he faced was the political effect of displacing about 80,000 private insurance canvassers—an adventure no party could lightly undertake alone. This was one of the charms of the editor's proposal for Lloyd George. A joint program sponsored by both parties could survive the protests of the insurance agents, the Friendly Societies, the doctors, and the other powerful lobbies involved. Although there is no definite evidence that Lloyd George's subsequent plan for a coalition government was specifically inspired by Garvin's article of May, the prospect of carrying the Insurance Bill by this expedient method was certainly one of the contingencies he had in mind.[12]

Garvin's remaining task was to precipitate some positive action from his Unionist colleagues. This he endeavored to do mainly by painting in sensational strokes the danger from the Socialists and the Irish. Without an understanding between "responsible statesmen" of the two historic parties, he argued, the nation could look ahead to a "period of disastrous tumult and incalculable peril." He pointed accusingly at the Irish and Labour factions as the main

---

[11] *Observer*, 15 May 1910.

[12] Lucy Masterman's diary, from which her husband's biography was written, is one of the few intimate sources of information about Lloyd George for this period. She asserts that the problem of the insurance agents "was the first thing that attracted Lloyd George towards the idea of a possible coalition between parties." Unfortunately she offers no further substantiation. Masterman, *C. F. G. Masterman*, pp. 163-165.

opponents of compromise. (There had actually been very little public response from either to the published reports of the conference proposals.) The nation's historic institutions were threatened, he declared, by these "irresponsible, almost anarchic" elements concerned only with their own narrow and unpatriotic motives.[13] As Garvin had advised Balfour before, the Socialists and Irish must be dressed in the costume of extremists whether they wished to play that part or not.

Garvin was seconded in his campaign in May by the editorials of "Pacificus" and "Historicus" in the *Times*. "Pacificus," the pseudonym of F. S. Oliver, a member of Milner's circle and the major propagandist of imperial federation for the *Round Table*, was himself canvassing the Unionist Party in support of a two-party conference to "write" a constitution for the United Kingdom "with a full regard for all Imperial interests." Their joint efforts, Oliver was able to inform Garvin late in May, had finally "done the trick." Salisbury was spreading the word among the Unionist peers; Milner and Curzon were now in full and active support, as was Chamberlain and the all-important Northcliffe. "Surely the mere fact that the Labour Party is furious," he wrote to the latter, "indicates what Unionist opinion should be...."[14]

Unionist opinion had thus been well primed by the Tariff Reform section at the time when Asquith finally broke his silence at the end of May. In a printed Cabinet Memo of 31 May, a unilateral effort to bring about a political truce was recommended to the Liberal ministers. It was argued first that

> ... there is a general reluctance to press constitutional struggle of the very gravest kind and of the utmost difficulty, involving the prerogative of the Crown in its most delicate aspects during the first ... week of a new reign.

It seemed hopeful, Asquith continued, that a "settlement by consent" could be found for the Liberal grievances concerning the upper house without risking the injury to national interests which a protracted controversy would entail.[15]

---

[13] *Observer*, 15 May, 29 May, 5 June 1910.
[14] *Times*, 23 May 1910; *Observer*, 29 May 1910; Garvin to Northcliffe (n.d., 1910), cited in Gollin, *The Observer*, p. 195.
[15] "Cabinet Memo: 'Secret'" (31 May 1910), *A.P.*, Dep. 23.

These were the general arguments being mustered by all those advocating the Constitutional Conference (it was about this time, the end of May, that the proposal acquired capital letters). The Unionists concentrated on the danger from the "extremists" while the Liberals, at least in their public pronouncements, invoked the more general unsettlement of the times. The case for the truce was couched always in the tone of grave crisis and peril, a tone which had been established by the antagonists in the budget debate and one which became both graver and more urgent as the possibilities of the conference unfolded. Asquith's closing remarks in the memo made several substantial points which aimed at dissolving the remaining qualms in the Liberal Cabinet. "The most cogent of all reasons," he reminded his ministers, was that they themselves needed time before facing another general election; there remained the financial problem after the exhausting campaign just past and, no less important, the matter of the Irish. "It would," he concluded, ". . . be fatal to the Liberal cause if we were thought to yield to pressure against our own better judgment, especially when the pressure is not always free from the appearance of an attempt at dictation."[16] Probably unwittingly, Asquith had now conceded the core of the Unionist charge regarding the Labour-Irish "extremists" in the Liberal coalition.

What finally decided him to act on the conference idea Asquith only hinted at in the memo. He had received word from the Royal Secretary during his deliberations that "any contingent guarantees," as had been agreed upon with the dead king, would not be asked for or granted during this Parliament. The Crown wished to avoid the charge of partisanship which the use of the prerogative would almost certainly bring down upon it and, like the Prime Minister, wished also to avoid the appearance of dictation by a parliamentary minority—the actual Liberal majority of two was not a sufficient mandate to warrant such extreme action, Sir Arthur Bigge informed Asquith.[17] Asquith was not able to regain those guarantees, which were his only means of conducting government once Home Rule was introduced, without threatening resignation. Since the Liberal Party could not afford such a course in May, the conference seemed a most convenient opportunity to put off a crisis

[16] Ibid.
[17] Sir Arthur Bigge to Vaughan Nash, Sec. P.M. (n.d., May 1910), *A.P.*, Dep. 23.

until after the summer recess. As we shall see, his misjudgment was to have a considerable impact on the eventual shape of the Parliament Bill and on the ultimate failure of Home Rule for Ireland.

Delay, therefore, was among the foremost reasons that the two party leaders entered upon the Constitutional Conference; both hoping rather bewilderedly to restrain the centrifugal flights of their younger colleagues without losing in them their only source of dynamism and inspiration for the future. Consequently, the terms upon which Asquith and Balfour finally agreed to enter the conference were limited in scope and somewhat evasive of the crucial issues at stake. Asquith made the proposal to meet Balfour in a letter of 9 June. The letter was a formality necessary to save the Unionist chief the embarrassment of taking the initiative as was suggested by Elibank. The projected conference was portrayed, no doubt to Balfour's liking, primarily as a means of enforcing a respectful hiatus in the political controversy so that the "early months of the new reign" at least be spared what all expected to be a violent partisan struggle.[18] At the meeting which took place between the two men a few days later, it was agreed that the tentative agenda for the conference would include (1) the relations of the two houses in regard to finance; (2) machinery to deal with persistent disagreement between the two houses, whether by limitation of the veto, joint sitting, referendum, or other; and (3) proposals for changes in the composition and numbers of the second house.[19]

In addition to Asquith, Lloyd George, Augustine Birrell, the Secretary for Ireland, and Lord Crewe, Liberal leader in the Lords, were selected to speak for the government; Balfour, Lord Lansdowne, Lord Cawdor, and Austen Chamberlain for the Unionists. The agreed terms of reference carefully circumscribed the scope for agreement on crucial issues. Only the second clause of the agenda touched upon a truly live problem, since what the Tories most feared was a tampering with the Lords' veto which would open the way for Home Rule or reversal of the Osborne decision by virtue of the Irish-Labour leverage in the House of Commons.

Both the agenda and the personnel of the conference were indic-

[18] The Cabinet had decided in favor of the Constitutional Conference on 6 June; Asquith to H.M. (7 June 1910), *A.P.*, Dep. 31; Asquith to Balfour (9 June 1910), *B.P.*, 49692-786A.

[19] "Extract from a letter to the King: 'Secret'" (14 June 1910), *A.P.*, Dep. 23.

ative of the two leaders' approach to the idea from the start—both wished to buy time until order could be restored in their parties and both attempted to appease disgruntled elements by participating in a show of nonpartisan statesmanship. Neither trusted in this unorthodox method of handling important questions and, consequently, they strove to pitch the conference in the lowest political key possible under the circumstances and to confine its work strictly to form rather than substance. The agenda was innocuous and superficial; there were any number of plans in both parties for tinkering with the constitution of the House of Lords, most of which engendered more scholarly than political fever. They had the added virtue of complexity sufficient enough to occupy the entire summer in a most unnewsworthy discussion, even if the meetings were held publicly. Every device had thus been used to make the Constitutional Conference a temporary soporific to quiet tempers until, by some means neither leader had as yet discovered, politics could return to "normal" channels when Parliament reconvened sometime in the fall or when they were ready for a new election. Despite their cautious delicacy, however, the mere agreement on the terms of the conference had profoundly altered the situation before the first meeting convened; the Lords had escaped the outright abolition of the veto (permanently, as it turned out) and both Labour and the Irish had been isolated from the Liberal coalition at least temporarily. Nor could their conspicuous exclusion from the nonpartisan conference have helped to strengthen their wavering commitment to constitutional means of redress, for despite the moderation of the Labour and Irish leadership at this point, that commitment was to undergo severe tests by their rank and file over the next few years.

Partisan sentiment in the rank and file of the two major parties had reached a high pitch in the preceding months and, because the deliberations of the eight were to be conducted in complete secrecy, there remained a constant suspicious pressure from below against concession. The position of both leaders was extremely delicate. Asquith's pledges to the Irish and Labour still stood, but for the time being he was without the power to fulfill them, being still unable to extract the guarantees from the new king and his advisors. And while sitting in conclave with their staunchest enemies, Asquith's personal assurances that none of their interests would be traded away carried decreasing currency among the Irish the longer the issue was put off. The chances for moderation on Home Rule were dissolving in the grasp of both Asquith and Redmond and, as they entered this summer of apparent compromise and negotiation, the hands of leadership were increasingly forced by rank-and-file agitation in all parties. While Asquith, who had entered the conference without optimism, had always to fear being estranged from both Irish-Labour and Liberal support alike, Balfour was also under pressure from some extreme elements in his own camp. For example, Leo Maxse's *National Review*, which was to initiate and lead the "Balfour Must Go" insurgency a few months later, excitedly denounced the conference. "It is not time for Unionists to talk compromise," Maxse protested. "Those who begin negotiating with Mr. Asquith will find themselves sold to the Molly Maguires before the end of the chapter."[20]

Apart from the inevitable press leaks, the proceedings of the conference were scrupulously withheld from the public. The few public speeches that were delivered by the participants during the four-month life of the meetings also avoided allusions to the constitutional question beyond reassuring constituents that no sacrifice of principle was being made or contemplated. Such reassurances naturally did little either to assuage those who suspected a betrayal or to lessen the fear among the leaders that any substantial agreement would immediately bring this charge down upon them.[21]

The conference began with a series of thirteen sessions between 17 June and 29 July, when Parliament rose. These were devoted to a wider-ranging and inconclusive discussion of procedural novelties proposing to settle "constitutional deadlocks" such as existed over reform of the upper house and the veto. It was the kind of limited, uncontentious technical proceeding envisioned by Asquith and Balfour in the original agenda and seemed to promise no more than the hoped-for postponement of a climax. Since Parliament was not to reconvene until November, the conference succeeded at least in providing a peaceful interval of nearly six months which was most welcomed by Asquith and Balfour. Indeed, even in the regular sessions of Parliament, the conference seemed to have a

---

[20] *National Review* (June 1910).

[21] Asquith's anxieties on this question were expressed in a strongly worded Cabinet Memo condemning leaks to the press of conference proceedings; Memo: "Secret" (22 July 1910), *A.P.*, Dep. 23; Sir Charles Petrie, *The Life and Letters of the Rt. Hon. Austen Chamberlain* (London, 1939), I, 255. Austen Chamberlain reports suspicion among the rank and file to Balfour in a letter of 23 Sept., *B.P.*, 49736-787B; Jenkins, *Balfour's Poodle*, p. 107.

The Lloyd George Plan

sedative effect. Lloyd George presented a statement outlining the budget for 1910-1911 which, though it contained notice of the national insurance plan and increased pension allotments, was markedly pacific in tone. More important, despite a flurry of heated speeches from the Labour benches on Indian and naval expenditures, the most serious divisions took place over the Civil List provision for the Royal Family. The Osborne Judgment, payment of members, and women's suffrage were left dormant.

A second series of meetings were to take place during the fall into which those pointed questions, as well as Irish Home Rule, would inevitably intrude. In fact, at the moment any of these issues was broached, the conference began to crumble. Once the talks had served their original purpose, the uninspired efforts of Asquith and Balfour were dull weapons against the stern immovability of Irish tempers, Nationalists and Ulstermen alike. They represented a barrier which translated itself into deadlock at this conference as at all those that followed. Balfour could even less afford to sacrifice the support of the Irish Unionists and their English sympathizers than Asquith could the Nationalists. Both had chosen the method of arbitration primarily to put off the day of a second election and the internal reckoning it would bring and to recapture control of dynamic forces within the parties which both feared. Since mere delay failed to achieve that end, indeed had further undermined their authority, the two leaders called upon their parties to return to normal party business and prepare for an election in December. Theirs was a deception in a season of deceptions and was costly for both.

Soon after the breakup of the conference in November, Balfour tried again to suppress the Tariff Reform platform upon which the previous Unionist campaign had been run, thinking to shift the emphasis in the coming election from finance to Ireland and the constitution. He was forced to resign in title the leadership he had effectively lost earlier in the year.[22] Asquith's fall was not so prompt, but his prospects at the end of the conference looked almost as dismal as his counterpart's. The weaknesses of his position were comparable in nature to Balfour's, dependent as he was on the progressive élan of the Radicals and on Socialist and Irish numbers, a combination which he could neither lead nor dispense with.

---

[22] See Peter Fraser's excellent description of the fall of Balfour in "The Unionist Debacle of 1911," *Journal of Modern History*, 69/4 (Dec. 1963), pp. 335-336.

Garvin, who was as we have seen an unusually well-informed if biased observer, placed him "somewhat in the position held by Lord Hartington and his friends in 1886," likely to be left with no option save a dark-futured alliance with the Unionists. In the same July article, ominously entitled "The Break-Up of the Old Party System," Garvin suggested into whose hands the Liberal succession would fall. He noted three potential factions erupting in the Liberal camp: the first, wildly far from the mark, "prepared to be led over under Mr. Churchill's leadership to Socialism; another, and much the largest, which looks to Mr. Lloyd George, and still hopes, while combining democratic finance with Non-Conformist aspiration, to keep the Labour element in tow"; and a third, Asquith and the old guard, inching wearily towards a Tory alliance, merely having no place else to go.[23]

The editor's prophetic miscalculations reflected the situation in July, as he thought, when some optimism remained about an agreement in the conference. He obviously mistook all three men, one absurdly, but his errors bespeak less his lack of perception than the magnitude of the changes in the ensuing months—in particular, Lloyd George's stunning surprises. During August, while both the conference and the Parliament were in recess, Garvin's editorials maintained the friendly détente which had arisen between himself and the chancellor on the King's death. He reiterated his support for the proposed national insurance plan, linking it as before with the warning that no truly great reforms could be carried through while the Irish could shackle them to Home Rule or Labour to the reversal of the Osborne Judgment and the remaining host of minority interests.[24]

Garvin does not appear to have been in direct touch with the chancellor during the summer sessions of the conference. Lloyd George made no open response to his friendly overtures in the *Observer* and remained unusually unobtrusive in the conference as well. Although Lloyd George had advocated the conference idea in the Liberal Cabinet in May, he had entered the discussions with neither noticeable enthusiasm nor hostility. Moreover, since he honored the unspoken agreement that members of the conference would refrain from public comment while the meetings lasted, there is little indication of his mood during the two months of technical

[23] Garvin, "Break-Up of the Old Party System," *Fortnightly Review*, 94 (July 1910), DXXIII, p. 5.
[24] *Observer*, 14 Aug., 2 Oct., 9 Oct. 1910.

The Lloyd George Plan

discussions preceding the August recess. It was not the sort of milieu in which he was at his best. The complex preparations for the Insurance Bill were also in full progress at this time—it was the manner of work which previously offered the "repose" that he so often spoke of and might explain in part his general silence during the conference. But it is evident from what followed the breakup of the first round of talks that his fidgety mind was far from restful during the truce. Spending the month of August in his native hills, he contemplated a stroke that would startle the conference out of its sluggish track when it reconvened in the fall.[25]

The Criccieth Memorandum: August 1910

On 15 August 1910, Haldane escorted the chancellor on a tour of army maneuvers in Wales, hoping to gain a favorable estimate of military needs in the new budget. Lloyd George had not been notably receptive in the past to such approaches, but Haldane found him a good deal more sympathetic on this occasion and, as he related to a friend, had received assurances for all that he wanted. Haldane was elated and surprised but feared that the promises he had received would come to nothing since the government, he was told during his conversations with Lloyd George, was in immediate danger of breaking up over the conference.[26] Together with the Exchequer "Brains Trust," Lloyd George was spending these summer weeks at his home in Criccieth composing a draft of the National Health Insurance Bill which he hoped to introduce in the next Parliament. It was to be a monument of reform legislation and had already taken nearly two years of research and preparation. Now that the great budget had survived its ordeal, the insurance plan replaced it as the chancellor's all-consuming effort. If, as Haldane was given to understand, party divisions were to cause the conference to collapse, throwing the parties into another bitter elec-

[25] Lucy Masterman credits Lloyd George as the sole author of the conference idea, having introduced it into the Cabinet in May purely to "mark time." Masterman, *C. F. G. Masterman*, p. 163. However, Garvin's article of 23 January, specifically proposing a conference, shows that even though Lloyd George did support the idea he was several months behind the editor in thinking of it. *Observer*, 23 Jan. 1910.

[26] Reported by Lord Esher, Haldane's correspondent, in a letter from Esher to Balfour (16 Aug. 1910), in Esher, *Journals and Letters* (London, 1934-1938), III, 14.

tion fight, Lloyd George's new enterprise would very likely be tossed into the partisan mangle together with Home Rule and the Lords' veto. He was prepared to go to some length to insure against this possibility; he had already sought and received private assurances from Garvin of the Tariff Reformers' help in keeping the bill "above party" at least during the committee stages. He had already been in private contact, through the ubiquitous Elibank, with the O'Brien-Healy Nationalists and was assured of their cooperation on condition that the elections be postponed to no later than September or October.[27] Thus Lloyd George had begun to put by some tentative resources in expectation of a fall election, though such tacit assurances would only be negotiable if the Liberal Party either achieved a sufficient majority to escape the hold of Redmond and Labour or if the conference could arrive at a satisfactory compromise. If the Unionists should win or the existing balance recur, the Insurance Bill would obviously become an early casualty of renewed partisanship and Labour hostility to the insurance plan. With the party and the conference breaking up, as he informed Haldane, the future of the great piece of social reform consequently became uncertain.

On 17 August, two days after Haldane's visit, Lloyd George completed a long memorandum setting forth an unprecedented plan by which all the difficulties which seemed to baffle the parties and overtax traditional parliamentary methods might be resolved without risking further political turmoil. The circumstances which prompted him to write it were summarized by him some years later:

> In the year 1910 we were beset by an accumulation of grave issues —rapidly becoming graver.... It was becoming evident to discerning eyes that the Party and Parliamentary system was unequal to coping with them. There was a jam at the legislative dock gates and there was no prospect of the growing traffic being able to get through. The shadow of unemployment was rising ominously above the

[27] Masterman, William Beveridge, J. W. Braithwaite, and Wilfred Greene, who drafted the first bill, were the most active of the chancellor's "Brains Trust" at the time. Both Braithwaite, a permanent Treasury employee, and Mrs. Masterman record that the hope of nonpartisan treatment for the insurance plan was what first attracted Lloyd George to the coalition idea. Cf. Braithwaite, typescript of *Lloyd George's Ambulance Wagon, Br.P.*, II, 155; Masterman, *C. F. G. Masterman*, p. 163; Elibank to Lloyd George (1 May 1910), *L.G.P.*, C/6/5/1.

horizon. Our international rivals were forging ahead at a great rate and jeopardizing [sic] our hold on the great markets of the world. . . . Our working population, crushed into dingy and mean streets, with no assurance that they would not be deprived of their daily bread by ill-health or trade fluctuation, were becoming sullen with discontent. . . . The life of the countryside was wilting away and we were becoming dangerously over-industrialised. . . . The Irish controversy was poisoning our relations with the United States of America. A great Constitutional struggle over the House of Lords threatened revolution at home, another threatened civil war at our doors in Ireland. . . .[28]

Although Lloyd George's recollection draws liberally on the hindsight of later events, his résumé corresponds extremely well with the main points as well as with the tone of the original memo which bore the title, "Coalition against Party Government for dealing with social reforms." He proposed in the memo that a period of "national reorganization" (sic) and "reconstruction" be launched through a coalition of "*both great parties* in the State" (the Irish and Labour are pointedly excluded in the memo). A situation had arisen at home and abroad, he argued, with which the nation had never before been confronted. The consequent threat to British supremacy—the danger of "national impoverishment" brought about by the rise of dynamic foreign competitors—called for a bold and determined effort which could be undertaken only by such a coalition of the "enlightened" elements in the two most powerful parties in the state. If a truly "national" program were undertaken by a single party it would have to give way to the factious demands of "extreme partisans" and "rival faddists"—"the least responsible, the least well-informed" and the most "selfish interests." Joint action by the overwhelming strength of the two parties, on the other hand, would sink these "undesirable elements" to their "proper insignificance."[29]

In keeping with the "non-political" stance of the entire memo, it is not surprising to find that first place in the suggested reconstruction program was given to social reform, under the headings

---

[28] Lloyd George, *War Memoirs*, 2nd edition, 2 vols. (London, 1934), I, 21.

[29] "Confidential Memo; Coalition against Party Government for dealing with social reforms" (17 Aug. 1910), *L.G.P.*, C/16/9/1, dictated by Lloyd George at Criccieth. The material which follows is taken from this copy of the memo.

of Housing, Drink, Insurance, Unemployment, and the Poor Law. The housing clause in the original draft was very brief, merely underlining the "devitalisation" of the population in the great urban slums. His brevity on this point can probably be ascribed to the general consensus of ideas regarding the social and moral effects of cramped urban housing; housing reform was already a plank of the Fabians, the Tariff Reformers, and the National Service League, as well as of the Radicals and Labour. It is worth noting in his section on housing the occurrence of the familiar Fabian and imperialist vocabulary of social reform—"degenerative," "devitalising," "demoralising," etc.—which Lloyd George affects throughout the memo. Although, as we have already seen, the language of National Efficiency formulated by the Social-Imperialists since the Boer War period eventually permeated the general political dialogue of the time, it did not appear prominently in Lloyd George's vocabulary until the Criccieth Memo. Its use now was the product of conscious deliberation on his part; packaged in the plan for a coalition of the "responsible elements" in the two parties, it was clearly designed to appeal to the Tariff Reform Unionists.[30]

"National Sobriety" had long been a Radical crusade. But Lloyd George now offered to temper the often virulent Nonconformist abuse of the brewers—the "vested interests" referred to in the memo—with "fair, or even generous" treatment. This was the first of the series of startling turnabouts performed by the chancellor in the memo. Through a coalition, he maintained, the currently "rigid and sterile plan" of the Radicals could be rationalized and moderated to allow some accommodation with the Conservative liquor interests.

Naturally, the section dealing with health insurance set forth his own contributory scheme. As Garvin's articles of May and June indicated, there was already an area of agreement between the major parties on the question of state insurance, since the Tariff Reformers had endorsed the Webbs' *Minority Report of the Poor Law Commission* to which the chancellor's plan owed much. Indeed, like so many of the great Liberal reforms of the period, it had

---

[30] Ibid. Housing became a very live issue between parties only in 1918, when again Lloyd George received Unionist support against the noncoalition Liberals for a state housing scheme. Paul Thompson, "Fabian Socialism," *Past and Present* (July 1963). For the Fabian housing scheme, see *Fabian Tract* 108 (1909); for the National Service League, Curzon, *Subjects of the Day*, his speeches for the N.S.L., p. 166.

sprung from seeds scattered by the Webbs around dinner and committee tables. Although there were points of conflict between the Webbs' plan and Lloyd George's which later impelled the Fabians to oppose the bill in the society's tracts, they were compatible in principle at this point, both having been based on the model of the German system of compulsory insurance. The difficulty, as Lloyd George went on to point out, was the improbability of a single party's overcoming the "bitter hostility of powerful organisations," presumably both private and union organizations engaged in insurance collection, especially since adequate compensation to them would not be possible.[31]

Lloyd George's remarks on unemployment and the Poor Law continued in a similar vein. He saw nothing in the principles of either party that need conflict on these questions. An important step towards bipartisan agreement on unemployment had already been taken with the passage of the Labour Exchanges Act sponsored by Churchill in 1909—a reform which again borrowed freely from the *Minority Report*. Poor Law reconstruction raised thornier problems which the memo deftly evaded. Like so many of the other obstacles the coalition was supposed to overcome, Poor Law reform as formulated by the Webbs could more easily be enforced by ignoring factious "minority" opposition, which in this case was expected to come from orthodox Socialists who hotly contested several key aspects of the Fabian plan.[32]

A sixth heading, "National Reorganisation," dealt with education, in particular with raising the age for leaving school. The enforcement of a minimum leaving age was urgently needed, it maintained, "if the youth of the country . . . were to receive a training which . . . [would] enable them to cope with the workmen of Germany and the United States. . . ." He freely borrowed from the

---

[31] The growing opposition to contributory national insurance from the trades unions is described in Henry Pelling's chapter "The Labour Unrest, 1911-14," in *Popular Politics and Society in Late Victorian Britain* (London, 1968), pp. 163-164.

[32] The Webbs' unemployment plan can be found in their *Break-Up of the Poor Law*, pt. II: "The Public Organisation of the Labour Market" (1909). The plan adopted by Lloyd George and Churchill also owed much to William Beveridge, who had been appointed by Churchill to the Board of Trade at the Webbs' suggestion; cf. Beveridge, *Unemployment: A Problem of Industry* (London, 1909), pp. 239 et passim. For the Socialist position, see "Report of Debates between George Lansbury and H. Quelch," *Poor Law Minority Report* (1910).

familiar protectionist text and then subtly departed from it: a major obstruction which only a joint effort of the parties could clear in this area would be the opposition "amongst sections of its own supporters who benefit . . . largely by boy labour" and from other such "ignorant and selfish prejudices." Such remarks were again keyed to the minds of the Tariff Reformers whose propaganda, as we have seen earlier, had for years decried the competitive inefficiency of the British workman and the "glorified grocers" and protectionist manufacturers of their own party who resisted all attempts at improving their own efficiency or technical education. Moreover, they were the first clear indication that the author was appealing only to limited sections in either party; for as Lloyd George knew well, the opposition which could be expected from the "selfish prejudices" in the ranks of both parties would inevitably put a heavy strain on party unity should his scheme be carried out.

The six remaining headings concerned National Defense, Local Government, Trade, the Land, Imperial Problems, and Foreign Policy. Lloyd George's unambiguous espousal in this section of compulsory military service and his softening on protective and preferrential tariffs were undoubtedly the most striking *volte-face* committed in the document. But only when taken together with the whole do they reveal the truly radical character of this coalition plan, as well as a few strands of consistency with the chancellor's past behavior in office. He had been a belligerent antimilitarist throughout his career; his sudden espousal of conscription and of expanded army and naval budgets naturally came as a surprise to those who read the memo. But from the start of his tenure of office in 1906 he had consistently championed direct interference by the state in trade, commerce, industry, and the social question, ignoring or openly flouting what remained of orthodox Liberal principle. As he often reminded his colleagues, he was never a doctrinaire. One may note, for example, his treatment of the "Drink" issue above or his high degree of "flexibility," indignantly chided by many of his Liberal colleagues, on Free Trade doctrine when composing the Merchant Shipping and Patents Bills of 1906. As we have seen, on the latter occasion Lloyd George had won considerable praise from the protectionists and from various sections of the business community; and his ruminations in May about forming a government of "business men" recalled his days at the Board of Trade where he had flourished in the atmosphere of cooperative improvisation and pragmatism. To a large extent, then, the wording of the memo

The Lloyd George Plan

tended to refurbish his former image of undoctrinaire statesmanship which had for a time led some members of the Opposition to look upon him as a "second Chamberlain in the making." Well aware of the growing tensions between Balfour and the powerful Tariff Reform bloc in the Unionist Party, Lloyd George recognized the obvious opportunity such an image might help to exploit; if carefully fostered, it could make him the kingpin of the proposed coalition.

In the local government, trade, and land clauses the motif was streamlining, central direction, and efficiency. On the first, he proposed a reform again taken from the *Minority Report*, which would restrain the excessive proliferation of small local bodies while reducing responsibilities of the imperial Parliament in local government. This is precisely the Webb plan of the Coefficient days, modeled in both cases on the London County Council.[33] His brief proposals on trade and land were of a similar character: more active state interference with greater powers of compulsion, more central direction, and more expert planning. On these notoriously sensitive and complex issues the memo again creates the impression that the only thing standing in the way of "intelligent and judicial impartiality" was party rivalry and the "duffers" on both sides of the House who held fast to outmoded prejudices and selfish interests. The purport of his remarks on trade and tariffs was clear: the whole question would have to be considered as to how, rather than whether, state assistance could be used to promote foreign trade; with the German system as the model, the door to the protective tariff was left wide open.

Besides the heavy dependence upon Fabian-conceived projects, another consistent theme in the latter sections of the memo was the frequent reference to continental precedents, predominantly German. One notable departure was a proposal to consider the Swiss system of compulsory training and military service—a model to which Haldane often referred and one currently in vogue in Lord Curzon's National Service League.[34] Lloyd George had traveled to Germany more than a year before to study the state insurance system, being then in the early stages of planning his own scheme. The influence of his brief trip stands out nearly everywhere in the

---

[33] S. Webb, *Minority Report*, I, 499-500, "Scheme of Reform," section D (iii), "New Machinery."

[34] See Curzon's address to the National Service League at Victoria Hall (21 Oct. 1910), *Subjects of the Day*, p. 262.

memo; not only in insurance and unemployment, but in the trade and land clauses as well. "In Germany," he noted in the trade section, "the railway is one of the most important weapons of the State for the purpose of promoting the foreign trade of the country." He suggests that as in Germany the question of tariff protection be coupled with the overhaul of inland transport in which the government could take a direct part. Similarly, land reform would profit from a more direct role on the part of the state. "After all," he argues, "farming is a business." Therefore, the doctrine current in both parties—the "small holdings craze"—is of doubtful utility since the community would be more likely to gain from "farming on a large scale by competent persons with adequate capital" than from a system which parcels the land among a myriad of "more or less incompetent smallholders." Only under the larger system, he pointed out, could competent "guidance, direction, and State assistance" be fruitfully administered. Once more, the memo's language held up efficiency, concentration, and planning in a business spirit against traditional ways, local interests, and smallness—who could resist rational demands of modern efficiency but the backward or the fanatical?

The most vexing and pressing issues were left to last. Under the heading of "Imperial Problems," the memo treats two points very briefly: first, imperial unity and a "scheme for uniting together the Empire and utilising and concentrating its resources for defense as for commerce"; and second, the Irish question. Of the latter the memo merely observed that the proposed coalition "might deal with it without being subject to the embarrassing dictation of extreme partisans, whether from Nationalists or Orangemen." Realizing that the success of the entire project would inevitably turn on finding some acceptable resolution of the Irish question, Lloyd George wished to maintain the appearance of openmindedness on this issue above all, without conceding so much, however, as to make the memo intolerable to the bulk of his own party. Nevertheless, his very brief remarks on the issue implicitly made at least two significant concessions to the Opposition: first, that if the coalition were formed, the Liberal pledge to the Nationalists could be voided; and, second, that Home Rule for Ireland would be treated only as part of a general reorganization of the empire, that is, some version of the "Federalist" solution which the imperialists had long advocated. As he explained this part of the memo to the Tariff Reformers a few weeks later, such a method of dealing with Home

The Lloyd George Plan

Rule would redeem the Liberal pledge and allow them, "if a scheme agreed on between the two great Parties were rejected by the Irish, . . . [to] wash their hands of the whole affair and leave the Irish to stew in their own juice."[35]

The memo was first of all a positive response to Garvin's published invitations to cooperate on the Insurance Plan in exchange for a harder line towards the Irish. Indeed, the proposal for bipartisan support of his insurance plan against its opponents was the only significant concession asked of the Tories in the original draft. The chancellor was no doubt concerned about the success of his greatest reform if a new election were fought over Ireland and the prospect of guaranteeing its easy passage would seem to have played a central part in inspiring his coalition scheme.[36] But the scope of the plan laid out in the rest of the memo suggests a more far-reaching vision. His unprecedented magnanimity on compulsory service, the tariff, Home Rule; his sweeping abuse of "selfish" and "irresponsible" minorities; his repeated emphasis on national unity and the threat from abroad—all packaged in the plan for an overpowering Center coalition, do not seem to have been the products of a cool reconsideration of the issues during the few months since the King's death, nor a merely ambitious political maneuver. It has more of the quality of a manifesto, a consciously historic testament of conversion from Radical gadfly to national statesman. Lloyd George had come by another road to the same compelling mystique of nation and empire which moved the Milner-Chamberlain section and, like them, he wished to imbue it with the spirit of controlled reform, efficiency, and modernism.

It was the unmistakable emotional force of this conversion in his argument which, perhaps even more than the tempting breaches it offered in the Liberal alliance, allayed the suspicions of most of his long-time detractors in the Unionist camp and lent plausibility to his plan. Above all, Garvin was persuaded. He had fervently espoused Chamberlain's Social-Imperial vision because it seemed to provide the best means of defying the nation's rivals abroad and at the same time allow reform at home towards a "contented,

---

[35] This was an explication of the Home Rule clause given by Lloyd George in a conversation with F. E. Smith and recorded by Austen Chamberlain. Chamberlain to Lord Cawdor (21 Oct. 1910), in Chamberlain's *Politics from Inside* (New Haven, 1937), p. 287.

[36] Masterman, *C. F. G. Masterman*, p. 163. Jenkins, *Balfour's Poodle*, p. 110.

healthy and energetic population." Now, in the Lloyd George plan he discovered with hopeful enthusiasm the same element of vision, strength, and idealism. "You are Merlin," he would say later, "you follow the gleam."[37]

October and November 1910: From Conference to Coalition

Lloyd George put off giving the details of the Criccieth Memo to any but a few close associates during the recess of August and September. Instead, as he continued his work on the insurance plan, he quietly sounded out opinion among intimate friends on the project, adding somewhat to the original draft in the form of a "Supplementary Memorandum" (dated 29 October) which dealt with sixteen areas in all where bipartisan cooperation might be possible as a basis for the coalition.[38]

In addition to Masterman, one of the few who had conscientious misgivings about the political side of the plan, and Churchill, who fell in enthusiastically with the entire idea, Lloyd George consulted Sir Robert Chalmers of the Inland Revenue Department through whom discreet soundings were made to ascertain the reaction that might be expected of business leaders outside of Westminster. Although the results of Chalmers' canvassing are unfortunately not available, it would appear that they were favorable enough to encourage the chancellor to pursue his project as soon as the conference reconvened in the second week of October.[39]

The conference was to meet again for the final series of talks on 12 October in Asquith's room at the House of Commons.[40] On the day before, Lloyd George asked Balfour to dine privately to hear

[37] Quoted in Gollin, *The Observer*, pp. 208-209.

[38] The "Supplementary Memorandum" of 29 October was more of a summary than a supplement. Only the last seven numbered paragraphs of the sixteen in this version of the plan are actually new, since although the wording is altered the earlier topics are treated almost exactly alike in the original. The version described by Lucy Masterman (*C. F. G. Masterman*, pp. 170-172) is clearly of a later date.

[39] Masterman, *C. F. G. Masterman*, p. 165.

[40] A last series of nine meetings took place between 12 October and 21 October. The method under discussion when the conference recessed was that of the "joint sitting" for cases of disagreement between the two houses. The Unionists insisted on a minimum majority of eighty, against the Liberal offer of forty, for the settlement of disputes by this method. Cf. Masterman, *C. F. G. Masterman*, p. 175.

"some important suggestions" he wished to put to him. He added the dubious assurance to Balfour that "the servants are Welsh and could not follow the conversation and the only other person present would be my little daughter of eight summers."[41]

Asquith had not yet been informed of the existence of the memo, much less of the extraordinary proposition which it embodied. Indeed, he remained in the dark regarding the details of the plan until a week after Lloyd George had met with Balfour at least twice and had spoken to the Tariff Reform leaders and the press about it. Moreover, since Elibank again acted as the chancellor's Mercury, gleefully bustling between Downing Street and the Carlton Club, many others heard rumors of the document before the Prime Minister. For Asquith, it was a sadly prophetic audition for the part of the knacker's horse he was to be cast in six years later. From the moment he first received the memo from his minister's hand, in the week the conference reconvened, he was skeptical and bemused; indeed, he was almost incredibly indifferent. He made no unusual sign of either interest or annoyance. Through the weeks of discussion which followed the introduction of the memo, as he later recalled, he merely watched with "detached amusement" the "lively seekers after new things."[42] Whether amused or uncomprehending, the Prime Minister made no move to restrain or prohibit the chancellor who immediately proceeded to canvass support for the coalition idea after canceling a partisan speech timed to signal the end of the conference and of the six-month truce.[43]

Asquith's tolerant and condescending view of Lloyd George's activity may well have been justified by the sheer improbability of the coalition plan, at least as it seemed to him; the plan may also have seemed a harmless expedient for gaining a further stay before the election. Balfour's reaction suggests much the same frame of mind. Neither expected the kind of reception it would receive from their colleagues. Lloyd George had, of course, already won Churchill's exuberant support; indeed, the two spoke of the coalition almost as though it were already in being. "I cannot tell how such an arrangement (as spoken of with Balfour) might ultimately affect democratic political organizations . . . ," Churchill wrote to Lloyd George. "But if we stand together we ought to be strong

[41] Lloyd George to Balfour (11 Oct. 1910), B.P., 49692-786A.
[42] J. A. Spender and Cyril Asquith, *Life of Lord Oxford and Asquith* (London, 1932), I, 287.
[43] *Daily Mail* (15 Oct. 1910). Jenkins, *Asquith*, p. 217.

enough either to impart a progressive character to policy, or by withdrawal to terminate an administration which had failed in its program."[44] This was Churchill's kind of political stage—the gathering storm, the eleventh-hour crisis, the unexpected and historic stroke. He was generally left out of the more serious discussions which ensued.

At Asquith's suggestion Lloyd George consulted Lord Crewe, who responded favorably. The reaction of Crewe, the minister personally closest to Asquith in the government at this time, reveals to a great extent the dilemma of the Prime Minister himself and also perhaps something of his reasons for allowing the chancellor to introduce his extraordinary formula into the deadlocked situation that had arisen. Crewe wrote to Asquith on the 22nd:

> Lloyd George sent me his Memo. . . . It is a clever document, but the important point at the moment is to consider the situation created by its production—a very strange one. I have thought for some time that we have got not far from the end of our tether as regards the carrying of large reforms. I do not see what inspiration in normal circumstances the Party is to receive in order to bring them about. That, so far as it goes, is the strength of Lloyd George's position, and also the strength of our opponents in the Conference.[45]

Like Crewe, Grey somewhat despairingly assented when informed of the proposal as the only acceptable means out of a dismal situation:

> I am favorable to it [he informed Asquith], though there are many difficulties. If the Conference breaks up without agreement I foresee the break-up of the Liberal Party and a time of political instability, perhaps of chaos, to the great detriment of the country . . . behind us there are explosive and violent forces which will split our Party, and I do not believe that we can resume the old fight against the Lords by ourselves without division.

Haldane, who had gotten an inkling of the plan at Criccieth, added his approval to complete the small circle of Liberal ministers who were consulted.[46]

Such unanimous assent might not have been forthcoming had

---

[44] Churchill to Lloyd George, "Private" (6 Oct. 1910), *L.G.P.*, C/3/15/1.

[45] Crewe to Asquith (22 Oct. 1910), *A.P.*, Dep. 12; see also J. Pope-Hennessy, *Lord Crewe*, p. 118.

[46] Grey to Asquith (26 Oct. 1910), *A.P.*, Dep. 12; Lloyd George, *War Memoirs*, I, 34.

Lloyd George kept his colleagues fully aware of the development of his plans; certainly Crewe would have been less encouraging. To the Liberal ministers it appeared that the chancellor was merely offering an honorable, temporary way of retreating from a dangerously advanced position to which he himself had forced them over the past year. His discussions with them dwelt mainly on assurances to safeguard Liberal principles on the Welsh church, compulsory military service, education, and the Lords while his negotiations with the other side ranged far more widely. He was playing a tortuous double game, improvising and shifting the ground rules as he moved from one side to the other. But even Asquith believed himself to have been "fully informed of all that was going on." Lloyd George had indeed revealed the general scheme to his chief, though it is not certain that Asquith saw the actual August memo at this or at any other time. Lloyd George first spoke to him about the plan on or about 13 October, approximately a week before Crewe and the rest of the government were approached, but at least a day after the chancellor had met with the leader of the Opposition for a second time.[47] He had also renewed his liaison with Garvin at about the same time, again through Stead. On 11 October, the day before the conference was scheduled to reopen, Garvin wrote to Northcliffe, "I think we are going to have a weird time in politics. The Conference seems hopeless but final efforts are being made to save things at the eleventh hour."[48] The editor followed a few days later with the first public announcement in the *Observer* that a "Larger Settlement" was being sought. The article, generously praising Lloyd George's "patriotic energy and determination," included a spirited harangue by the chancellor himself on the threat from abroad and the consequent need, as a "matter of life and death," to spend without stint to maintain naval supremacy. Such a public statement from Lloyd George might help his prospective allies to gain support among rank-and-file Unionists and at the same time prepare a patriotic defense of the coalition against the inevitable protests that would arise from some sections on both sides.[49]

[47] Spender and Asquith, *Life of Lord Oxford and Asquith*, p. 287. Lloyd George himself informed Crewe that the Prime Minister had learned about the memo sometime during the week preceding 20 October. Pope-Hennessy, *Lord Crewe*, p. 119.

[48] Garvin to Northcliffe (11 Oct. 1910); cited in Gollin, *The Observer*, p. 203.

[49] *Observer*, 16 Oct. 1910.

The author of the memo could not have expected the Liberal Cabinet to accede without division to a reversal on tariffs, military service, Home Rule and local government; he must also have expected some recoil from former allies in the Cabinet from his new stance on naval estimates. His public statement on the latter question, in fact, indicates that he was also prepared to estrange that section of the Cabinet which included McKenna and Burns in order to forward the coalition. The necessity, perhaps the desirability, of such a break he had apparently seen from the start, since at no time during the discussion of the plan were any but the original five ministers (Asquith, Grey, Haldane, Crewe, and Churchill) consulted. Elibank and Augustine Birrell learned of the plan only because of their role as intermediaries.[50] Even from these the chancellor had already wrung an extraordinary degree of acquiescence to what was, in effect, a repudiation of the bulk of the Liberal Party platform of previous years, since by far the greater part of the plan was an open concession to the Opposition, especially to the Tariff Reformers. In its latest version, the plan did include clauses on Welsh Disestablishment (by referendum) and an endorsement of the Birrell Bill on education—"the Non-Conformists could not come in on any other terms," according to Lloyd George.[51] These two additions were apparently made by him after consulting his colleagues, but they were the only two points which could be described as clear defenses of Liberal positions of principle.

It was obviously not an arrangement which could be frankly proposed to the Liberal Party as a whole; nor was it likely, as the chancellor realized, to win the instant endorsement of a Unionist Party at least equally charged up and divided internally. Indeed, the introduction of the chancellor's new departure at a point when the conference was ready to dissolve proved an unwelcome embarrassment to the Unionist chief. He was already caught between pressures from Halsbury and Wyndham (the core of what became the "Die-Hard" resistance to the Parliament Bill in 1911) to quit the conference on the one hand and from the proconference group

[50] Elibank and Birrell were the main contact between Lloyd George and Balfour and Austen Chamberlain during the week of 14 October. Elibank to Lloyd George (18 Oct. 1910), *L.G.P.*, C/6/5/3. Lloyd George thought his defense proposals alone would stand little chance of getting through the Cabinet. McKenna, he noted specifically to Masterman, was the likely source of trouble. Masterman, *C. F. G. Masterman*, pp. 170-172.

[51] Lloyd George to Crewe (19 Oct. 1910), *L.G.P.*, C/4/1/1.

spoken for by Garvin and Oliver on the other. When Balfour set about exploring opinion in the party on the new conditions, the division naturally followed along similar lines, with the Die-Hards, who had all along opposed any compromise on the veto, reacting violently even to the most guarded hints at conciliation.[52]

On the other side, however, the chancellor's offer called up an enthusiasm equally spirited in favor of the plan. Balfour's personal secretary, Alfred Lyttleton, had made a "diligent inquiry" during the week the memo appeared and he reported that he had found "very great sympathy among the . . . younger intellectuals" with the proposed settlement of Home Rule by local federation and the method designed to achieve it. He mentioned F. S. Oliver, Brand, Kerr, Amery, "Milner's Kindergarten," Milner himself, and Garvin as those whom the proposal most interested. Balfour had already been made aware of the sentiments in this quarter through Garvin's articles and at a meeting held immediately after the coalition plan was received in which Oliver had delivered a strong endorsement not only of the federal solution for Ireland but also of the proposed "non-party" principle of handling other urgent national business. It was, he argued in the Milner style, the "natural safety valve of popular government," especially in a situation so distracted by "party tactics" and endless debates that constructive legislation was impossible. Moreover, the domestic Parliament in a federal system, being relieved of its excessive responsibilities, would tend more towards expertise and practicality and, therefore, less towards "phrase-mongering" and Socialism.[53] More "*réchauffé*" of Mr. Webb, Campbell-Bannerman might have said.

Unlike Asquith, Balfour was already too conscious of his vulnerability to look upon this restless faction with "detached amusement." In the week following the appearance of the memo, the younger intellectuals and the Milner circle added their voices to

[52] The *Morning Post* spoke for the Die-Hard position throughout the constitutional crisis. They strongly attacked Balfour for faintly hinting at a joint party solution in his Edinburgh speech. *Morning Post*, 16 Oct. 1910, cited in Malcolm Thompson, *David Lloyd George: The Official Biography* (London, 1948), p. 195. Almeric Fitzroy, *Memoirs* (London, 1925), II, 242; A. Chamberlain to Balfour (23 Sept. 1910), *B.P.*, 49736-787B.

[53] Lyttleton to Balfour (16 Oct. 1910), *B.P.*, 49736-787B; Spender and Asquith, *Life of Lord Oxford and Asquith*, p. 77; "Private Memo—F. S. Oliver in Conference" (11 Oct. 1910), *B.P.*, 49861; Sandars to Short (24 Oct. 1910), *B.P.*, 49767-787B.

Oliver's and had momentarily succeeded in winning Balfour to federalism. Garvin assured the Unionist leader, in another wild prognosis, that on the Irish question "the old passions had passed away." Moreover, employing an argument which as we have seen had previously occurred to Lloyd George and to Milner, he asked, would not even a semiautonomous Ireland be less dangerous to the empire than the "antinaval, antimilitarist, and Socialist factions in England itself?"[54]

Balfour could not have been pleased to see the outburst of enthusiasm which the plan had induced in the Milner circle—they were poor party men, a volatile group, and they possessed independent resources in the press and in the extraparliamentary leagues. Nevertheless, he seems to have been genuinely impressed by the case thus put to him, even to believing for a time the editor's assurance that Home Rule could be compromised without an upheaval comparable to that of 1886. He was prepared at this point, as he admitted to Garvin, to recognize the necessity of prolonging the conference for lack of an alternative and in view of the undue power of "Radical Extremists and Irish Nationalists." Moreover, he more or less committed himself to seek the federal solution in order to bring this about.[55]

Even at this, Balfour had not yet recognized the full implications of the proposal. The almost exclusive emphasis laid upon the issue of federation and the Irish question in this stage of the discussion was due to a certain ambiguity in the coalition plan. Like the Liberal leaders who had endorsed the plan, even Garvin and Oliver apparently conceived at this point that the coalition was to be somehow a direct extension of the conference, sitting as a kind of ad hoc super-Cabinet to guide the passage of an agreed plan of legislation. The immediate problem as they saw it was therefore to keep the conference in being by settling the deadlocked Home Rule issue by federation, thus sidestepping the question of the Lords' veto, before passing on to the other projects set forth in the chancellor's memo. This initial impression was, in fact, strangely ingenuous for a group of men who were soon to demonstrate an uncommon penchant for intrigue; for, while it promised an easy

[54] Milner to Balfour (17 April 1910), *M.P.*, A.III; Garvin to Balfour (17 Oct. 1910), *B.P.*, 49795.

[55] Balfour to Sandars (18 Oct. 1910), *B.P.*, 49767-787C; Balfour to Garvin (22 Oct. 1910), *B.P.*, 49795.

method of shackling the Irish and Socialists, it altogether passed over the obvious difficulty posed by unsympathetic and still uninformed members within the two parties themselves. And as the pressure against the conference had already indicated, there were likely to be enough of these to raise a formidable obstacle.

Some of the confusion was no doubt due to the fact that in the first instance the chancellor's scheme had been transmitted verbally and, perhaps intentionally, in an incomplete form which stressed the Irish settlement as the point on which all the rest turned. As the negotiations developed during the following weeks, however, it became evident that the subtle Welshman had not made the same oversight of the likely internal opposition to the plan. He was aware, as we have seen, that a considerable shake-up in Liberal personnel was liable to be necessary in order to gain acceptance of his proposals. In the memo, he had not been overly obscure about the predominance of the "duffers" in both parties, clearly implying that a weeding out on the ministerial level was a necessary prerequisite to his project. He therefore approached the Unionists with the same selectivity he had used in revealing his intentions to the Liberal Cabinet, carefully choosing those whom he felt to be independent, unorthodox, or frightened enough to sacrifice party loyalties to stability at home and a restored sense of national security.[56]

As the terms of the memo rather clearly indicate, Lloyd George felt his most responsive communicants to be the dynamic but politically frustrated group of Tariff Reformers who had so earnestly supported the conference and the truce. Consequently, F. E. Smith, a rising Tariff Reform M.P. and a very close associate of the Chamberlains, was with Garvin the first of the Opposition to whom Lloyd George revealed the entire plan. Like the editor, Smith was immediately won over by the "big thing" the chancellor offered, including now the frank proposal to "shed the Duffers" in both camps. His efforts on behalf of the coalition idea were devoted to personal persuasion among his wide circle of political acquaintance, making use on the whole of Garvin's arguments that this was the way to uphold the Osborne Judgment and insure a degree of

---

[56] The evidence indicates that Lloyd George presented the remarks which appear in appendix B only after a favorable response had been received to the substantive terms of the memo. The version heard by Balfour on 11 October, therefore, would be essentially that appearing in Masterman, *C. F. G. Masterman*, pp. 170-172.

internal security. "A great sigh of relief would go up over the whole of business England," he wrote to Austen Chamberlain, "if a strong and stable Government were formed."[57]

Smith argued the virtues of the plan most forcefully to the beleaguered Balfour as well: how could the leadership reject a federal scheme which both the party and the Unionist constituency overwhelmingly favored? If the "bigger thing," as he described the coalition plan, succeeded it would mean, he said, "a National Party and a well directed power for ten years." And even if it should fail he felt that the Unionists could only gain by it—Lloyd George and Churchill would be ruined and the Unionists might well have ten years of power on their own. Like the author of the plan, Smith's agile mind thus swung between sincere enthusiasm and opportunism. As he argued the case to Bonar Law in October, it swayed toward the former:

> Never in English history has there been a time when there was greater general weariness of the ordinary party ties and I believe that a cry of relief would go up all over the country if both parties would *do things* instead of discussing constitutions.[58]

In an obvious effort to further sweeten the bait for the protectionists, Lloyd George (in a speech before the Liberal Christian League) composed in the same week a public eulogy of Chamberlain and the "historic agitation" of which he had been the author. Without attempting to clothe his meaning, he endorsed in order all the major points of the Tariff Reform platform, including fiscal reform. Noting the "great unrest amongst the people" and warning of the "period of tempests" to come, he called for a bold departure.

> The time has come [he said] for a thorough overhauling of our national and imperial conditions. That time comes in every enterprise —commercial, national and religious; and woe be to the generation that lacks the courage to undertake the task.
> My counsel to the people would be this—let them enlarge the pur-

---

[57] Sandars to Short (n.d., 1910), *B.P.*, 49767-787C. (This memo reporting Smith's meeting with Lloyd George and the terms of the coalition can be dated approximately between 11 October and 20 October). *F. E. Smith, First Earl of Birkenhead*, by the Second Earl of Birkenhead (London, 1933), p. 157.

[58] F. E. Smith to Bonar Law (19 Oct. 1910), *B.L.P.*, 18/6/126

pose of their politics and, having done so, let them adhere to that purpose with unswerving resolve through all difficulties and discouragements until their redemption is accomplished.[59]

Lloyd George's eloquence was obviously more effective in generating passion over grand crusades than over constitutional niceties. He was winding himself up for a venture more daring and a departure more permanent than a mere extension of the conference. He had now made these plans clear to Garvin and Smith, although the eyes of Asquith and Balfour were still kept on the conference. Smith recognized the direction of the chancellor's thoughts when he assured Chamberlain, who favored the idea but was suspicious of Lloyd George, that if the Welshman proved "turbulent" after "a year or two" his position would be much more precarious than theirs, having "sold the pass" and broken his party. (Smith obviously had a clearer sight of the future than did the oracular Garvin.) Moreover, Lloyd George's discussions with Smith had apparently gone quite far into the political substance of the plan, since they had already spoken, according to Smith, of the "fair share of appointments" for the two parties in the projected coalition—a subject the chancellor tactfully avoided when conferring with his Liberal colleagues.[60]

If Asquith was, as he forever maintained, fully cognizant of the profound departure which Lloyd George was constructing with the Tariff Reformers, he must indeed have thought himself in a desperate position, for it would certainly have split his party quite as deeply as it did six years later. But he was clearly not fully informed; if he were, his behavior is inexplicable. It would seem more probable that he and the chancellor were engaged against each other in a rather risky contest of mutual deception, having already lost what trust and regard they may once have had for one another. Asquith tolerated, even playfully encouraged, an intrigue of which he was imperfectly informed in order to gain the time he needed to frustrate it by suddenly producing the royal guarantees. This was to be his ace-in-the-hole. He confidently expected the King's word at any moment (and did receive the guarantees in November), but

[59] Lloyd George speech to the Liberal Christian League, 17 Oct. 1910; cited in du Parcq, *Lloyd George*, pp. 766-774.
[60] Smith to Chamberlain (n.d.), cited in *Birkenhead*, I, 205; Jenkins, *Balfour's Poodle*, p. 114; Sandars to Short (n.d., 1910), B.P., 49767-787C.

had kept his chancellor in the dark about his contacts with the Crown. Lloyd George, on the other hand, played a shell game with at least two differing versions of his plan. Having won the approval of his colleagues to negotiate a limited scheme of specified terms based on the conference, he apparently hoped to draw at least some of them into the "bigger thing" which he had put to Smith and Garvin. His strategy became evident when, on 21 October, the conference unexpectedly broke down due to the chancellor's own blunt refusal, coupled with a threat of resignation, to allow any compromise on the question of the two-to-one majority in joint sessions between the lower and upper houses. This effectively removed the alternative to which his perplexed colleagues had so readily adhered in order to escape the constitutional deadlock and marked the opening of the final stage in the coalition's tortuous course.[61]

The private negotiations concerning the coalition were at no time directly alluded to in the conference itself. But during the two weeks of talks on the subject prior to the chancellor's ultimatum, the energetic gossip of Westminster had inevitably publicized a good part of their content. By November, therefore, some final denouement appeared imminent to nearly everyone concerned. With the conference defunct, though it had not yet been publicly announced, pressure from the coalitionists concentrated on Balfour to bring the party to terms with Lloyd George before risking another election. They urged the patriotic logic of a federal concession to Home Rule, despite feelings in Ulster, in return for the tariff, conscription, and the general promise of political stability held out by the plan. Smith and Chamberlain pressed this position in the party, as did Garvin, Oliver, and Milner's young men in the press.

Garvin became more turgidly persuasive than ever and more determined on some dramatic stand by the two parties against the "extremists." If they failed in this now, he threatened in a November article for the *Fortnightly Review*, "the result would be not merely chaos worse confounded but moral anarchy in public life." Garvin had now found his "bogey," the "Red Revolution" threatening to subvert order and law in Britain and all over Europe, and

---

[61] The objection was made over the 80 to 40 joint-sitting majority dispute. In the first version of the October plan a compromise on this issue was to be the prerequisite of a larger settlement. Lloyd George, however, issued the flat statement, "Anything over 40 I resign." Masterman, *C. F. G. Masterman*, p. 175.

The Lloyd George Plan

the increasingly militant language of the Syndicalists and their growing impatience with parliamentary methods played conveniently into his strategy.[62] A new urgency entered his tone in this latest drive: "Which of us who has given even casual study to the state of unrest in Europe and beyond—to the new audacity and definition of subversive aims—can call with a light heart for conflict in the spirit let loose before the death of King Edward." In the same article he pointed to the "Portuguese revolution, the danger in Spain, the French railway strike, the Moabit riots in Berlin, the vast movement of popular unrest . . . surging even in the United States" as oracles of the revolutionary threat at home.[63]

Milner's Compatriots, some of whom were recruited into Lloyd George's later coalition, added their voice to this coalition campaign in the first printing of the *Round Table* in November. Their quarterly was nominally devoted to a severely "detached," non-partisan exposition of imperial news and issues, but from the very first number it threw its weight openly into domestic politics by becoming an instrument of the coalition insurgency. The November issue denounced the inadequacy of "the System" with the patriotic fervor of the proconsul: ". . . the methods of yesterday will not serve in the competition of tomorrow. . . . National Institutions like the National Safety are not to be lightly handled by temporary majorities embittered and blinded by the excesses of party conflict." The party system, it argued, had become outdated, inadequate to shoulder the "too multifarious and too burdensome" duties of a modern empire. A "non-party" government was therefore needed—a "strong, responsible and non-party second Chamber" and Cabinet—to discharge imperial functions.[64]

The decision now lay with Balfour, whose counsels were naturally confused by the desire to hold his party together, especially since Asquith remained rather an unknown quantity on the coali-

---

[62] For the changing attitudes in the labor movement towards constitutional means see the excellent recent summary by Standish Meacham, "'The Sense of an Impending Clash': English Working-Class Unrest before the First World War," *American Historical Review*, 77/5 (Dec. 1972), 1343-64; and Henry Pelling, *Popular Politics and Society*, pp. 147-164.

[63] Garvin, "Review of Events," *Fortnightly Review*, 94 (Nov. 1910), p. 767.

[64] *Round Table* (Nov. 1910),, n. 1, pp. 3, 62, 68-69, 157; J. R. M. Butler, *Lord Lothian* (New York, 1960), p. 43. Lothian (Philip Kerr) was editor of *Round Table* from 1910 to 1916 when he joined Lloyd George's coalition government.

tion idea and might at any time face him with an election. When he had learned the full intent of the chancellor's device, therefore, he immediately began to drag his feet on the coalition, offering instead to discuss a temporary scheme to keep the Liberal government in power against the will of the Irish and Labour.[65] Balfour was most reluctant to go even this far; it was a major concession to the Tariff Reformers made from a position of weakness. Yet, despite his distaste for the more radical venture, he could do little but witness idly the industrious campaigning and intriguing of Garvin and Smith, who were presently joined by his successor-to-be, Bonar Law. Ironically, his main hope of keeping his party together now appeared to be in Asquith's hands, in the dissolution and an election which would bring the royal guarantees into play and end the historic Tory stronghold in the House of Lords.

On the Liberal side, Asquith was content to maintain a similar aloofness towards the activities of the coalitionists which occupied the first days of November. Feeling reinforced by the expectation of the guarantees, Asquith also found himself in an anomalous situation, that of upholding his "pledges" to the Irish and Labour against the opposition of his own radical section. One of the effects of the Lloyd George plan would of course have been to void those pledges to the Irish and Labour. Claiming throughout his dealings with the Unionists that he had been empowered by the Prime Minister, or at least that he was acting with his knowledge, Lloyd George had quickly gone beyond whatever half-informed concurrence he may have had.[66] Indeed, as he later reported, in the final arrangement which he put to Balfour in early November, he not only granted all the original concessions sanctioned by Asquith three weeks before (set off by a favorable deal on the Welsh church and the Birrell Bill), but had magnanimously proposed that in the coalition government Balfour himself might lead the House of

---

[65] Balfour to A. Chamberlain (24 Oct. 1910), *B.P.*, 49736-787B.

[66] Lloyd George informed Balfour during the final discussions that while Asquith preferred to remain apart for the moment, "he wished me to say that all I did was with his concurrence." Lloyd George to Balfour (2 Nov. 1910), *B.P.*, 49692-786A. Lloyd George maintained the same version ever after and succeeded in persuading Sir John Marriott in 1934 (while he was writing his *England since Waterloo*) that "Asquith was the first to be consulted, and my proposals were submitted to Balfour with his full approval." Frances J. Stevenson to Marriott (9 June 1934), *L.G.P.*, 9/35/1/18; see also his summary of the 1910 events, Lloyd George to Marriott (2 June 1934), *L.G.P.*, 9/35/1/10.

The Lloyd George Plan

Commons while the present Prime Minister could "go to the Lords."[67] It is difficult to imagine how he might have framed such a proposal; couched even in the gentlest words it could not have reassured Balfour about the temper of the coalitionist agitation.

There was no indication at the time that Asquith was content to suffer this premature and humiliating retirement any more than he was in December 1916. The suggestion as put to Balfour had apparently evolved out of the series of midnight trysts of the 2nd and 3rd of November attended by Lloyd George, Churchill, and the Smith-Garvin group—more of the activity which Asquith had looked upon as an amused spectator. Balfour, too, had imprudently, almost disastrously, allowed the "seekers after new things" to whip up a good deal of enthusiasm in their influential circle over the chancellor's creation, with Milner already speaking of "turning the revolutionary current into safe channels" and Garvin of a splendid and powerful "Nationalist revival." Consequently, when it fell upon him to give a decision, he was faced not only with a proposition far more radical than that which he had originally entertained —one which he could not accept in the first place without violent division in the party—but with the prospect of suffering, if he rejected the idea, the frustrated resentment of those who now so earnestly advocated it.[68]

On 8 November, three days before the Constitutional Conference was officially dissolved, Balfour rejected the plan in an interview with Lloyd George at 11 Downing Street. "I cannot become another Robert Peel in my Party," he explained to the chancellor with the conscious insincerity of high drama. It was not the only piece of flummery practiced between these two oddly contrasting men: Lloyd George always seemed a little in awe of Balfour's poise and calm, but felt also that he could be manipulated with flattery, while Balfour supposed that the other would be flattered just to be taken seriously. It is probable that Balfour never really considered accepting the coalition idea once it had ceased to be represented as a temporary expedient to get over the constitutional crisis. The ultimate political crime in his mind was to divide the Conservative Party, as his constant soundings of party opinion at every turn

[67] Reported by Lloyd George to J. W. Hills, a diary entry quoted in Blanche Dugdale, *Arthur James Balfour* (London, 1936), pp. 75-76.

[68] Milner to Balfour (5 Nov. 1910), *M.P.*, Letters, A.III. Garvin to Balfour (25 Oct. 1910), *B.P.*, 49794.

would indicate. Moreover, he made still another survey of this nature through the former Conservative whip, Akers Douglas, and had used its results to justify his rejection to the chancellor, who thereafter chose illogically to place the blame for his failure with the former whip rather than accept Balfour's rejection as the cause. "It very nearly came off. It was not rejected by the real leaders of the party," Lloyd George later insisted, adding a little bitterly, "there are times when the Party system stands seriously in the way of the highest national interests. . . . I shall always regard the rejection of the proposals for cooperation in 1910 as a supreme example of this kind of damage."[69]

The rejection of the plan put a sudden end to the six-month "Truce of God" inaugurated at Edward's death. But the lessons of the summer and fall of that year were not entirely lost. Balfour's decision to end his deference to the stubborn pressures of the Tariff Reformers, both in rejecting the coalition and subsequently in jettisoning Protection from the December platform, rebounded severely upon him in the insurgency of 1911. The absence of that "note of meaning business" had diminished his authority among the "Zany" men in the party, as Amery described his fellow militants. We are "absolutely paralyzed from above," Amery complained to Milner a day after Balfour's rejection; "the general 'malaise' of the last year or two is rapidly developing into open muttering and dissension—more than ever these last few days."[70]

The sequel was somewhat longer delayed in the Liberal Party, which emerged from the December elections without any greater mandate but strengthened by the debacle in the Unionist camp over the fall of Balfour. The impatience with Liberal doctrine, the blunt contempt not only of party loyalties but of the historic constitutional balance they upheld, as well as the unorthodox dynamism which Lloyd George displayed in this first attempt at coalition, were sufficiently submerged during the "Tory Rebellion" of the next few years to maintain the semblance of unity in the Liberal Party. But when six years later he sought to reconstruct his scheme, he drew again on the same resources, the same long-standing discontents, the same conspiratorial tactics, even the same rehearsed conspirators.

[69] Lloyd George, *War Memoirs*, I, 23.
[70] Amery to Milner (9 Nov. 1910), *M.P.*, Letters, A.III.

VIII

The Coalition Plan in the Prewar Crisis

Sharing a hymnbook with Balfour at the investiture of the Prince of Wales after the collapse of his 1910 coalition plan, Lloyd George imparted a last confidence to the harassed Unionist leader: "... looking into the future," he whispered, "I know that our glorified grocers will be more hostile to social reform than your backwoodsmen."[1] The two men, opposites in birth, education, and temperament, had never established a rapport either privately or politically. Their acquaintance was one of mixed admiration and puzzled exasperation with one another. At the time of the investiture, the chancellor had not yet admitted that his proffered coalition had been scotched by the Opposition leader himself. In fact, he seemed persuaded that he was speaking to a potential comrade, one who like himself had been held from joining the great national front only by the inertia of the antiquated party hacks.

Balfour had done little overtly to disenchant either Lloyd George or the Tory adherents of the plan. Indeed, he was at pains to place the responsibility on the Tory rank and file. From the beginning, he refused to grasp the full scope of the chancellor's proposals, failing to comprehend either the motives of the author or the disturbing excitement of his advanced colleagues for such an exotic innovation. Recalling the incident some years later, he betrayed his bewilderment:

> Exactly! Now isn't that like Lloyd George. Principles mean nothing to him—never have. His mind doesn't work that way. It's both his strength and his weakness. He says to himself at a given moment: "Come on now—we've all been squabbling too long, let's

[1] Cited in Lucy Masterman, "Recollections of David Lloyd George," *History Today*, IX (March-April 1959), 168.

find a reasonable way out of the difficulties"—but such solutions are quite impossible for people who don't share his outlook on political principles—the great things.[2]

The gulf separating Balfour from Lloyd George was as much one of generation as of principle or of party. As the Tory chief was painfully to learn before the year was out, the wholesale scrapping of historic institutions and principles was quite as palatable an event to many younger Tories as to the erratic chancellor. As Amery's critical letter of November indicated, the "malaise" among the Tariff Reformers regarding the old leadership had progressed by the end of 1910 to the breaking point. They had beseeched Balfour to set the party firmly against the "Red Budget" of 1909 on their dynamic program of Social-Imperialism, but with no success. Once again, when the coalition was proposed shortly thereafter, they were its warmest supporters, shepherding the reluctant Balfour through back doors to meet the chancellor. Failing again to elicit a spirited cause from him, the protectionists, spearheaded by Garvin, Smith, and the Milner circle, dismissed their bewildered party chief (by means similar to those employed on Asquith later) and brought their party to a peak of revolutionary intransigence unprecedented in recent history.[3]

The loss of three consecutive elections to the Liberals was sufficient cause in itself for unrest within the Unionist ranks. On top of this, Balfour's resistance to the demands of the Tariff Reformers, by far the strongest and most vocal section of the party, made the revolt of 1911 inescapable. What part Balfour's rejection of the coalition, which had so inspired the insurgents, played in his overthrow is not precisely measurable. It did at least help to confirm his reputation for inaction and give force to Amery's charge of "paralysis from above." After being deposed, Balfour himself looked back upon his rejection as "a loss of opportunity incalculable in its consequences." It was an opinion emphatically shared by Lloyd George and, judging from their behavior following the refusal, also by the militant Tory rebels.[4]

[2] Cited in Dugdale, *Arthur James Balfour*, p. 77.

[3] Peter Fraser, "The Unionist Debacle of 1911," pp. 335-337. A more general revolt in the Unionist Party was in progress, exacerbated by the failure of Balfour to act upon the proposed coalition, than that described by Fraser as the cause of Balfour's resignation.

[4] Dugdale, *Arthur James Balfour*, p. 72. "The great lost opportunities of the war constantly brought back to my mind the 'Great Refusal' of 1910." Lloyd George, *War Memoirs*, II, 157.

Amery, still acting as Milner's voice in the party, thought the rejection "a great opportunity tragically thrown away." F. S. Oliver, one of the earliest advocates of the plan among the Unionists, wondered if Balfour was "enough of the human even to understand it."[5] Despite his later regrets, Balfour had not originally taken the proposal with complete seriousness. Moreover, he opposed in principle the idea of abandoning the traditional party system as a peacetime measure.[6] The Garvin-Smith group had no such reservation. They had been attracted by the coalition idea because it appeared to be a strong position from which to deal with the Irish question, the threat from Germany and, probably most important, the rise of social disorder at home. These conditions were present in much more radical form in the years between the conference and the war and, though an occasion as promising as that of 1910 did not arise again, the precedent set by the chancellor was by no means forgotten.

The lines of communication between Lloyd George and the advanced Unionists were discreetly reopened during 1911 on the occasion of the introduction of his National Insurance Bill. As we have seen in previous chapters, the Tariff Reformers had, with expert prodding from the Webbs, incorporated various measures of social reform into their propaganda and given this aspect an emphasis second only to the tariff itself. Reform in housing, unemployment, and health were also prominent ingredients in the 1910 plan to which they had given their assent. As with problems concerning the nation and the empire, they had always put the question of social reform "above parties," in that critical category with which the conventional muddle of party politics was said to be incapable of dealing efficiently. This was the cornerstone of all forms of Social-Imperialist agitation. Consistent with this policy, the Young Tories under the guidance of F. E. Smith established a "private sub-committee" of the party in 1910, calling it the Unionist Social Reform Committee. Its purpose, as stated by one of the charter members, was "to give reasonable support to measures of social reform promoted by the Government and also to counter the efforts of the reactionary and old-fashioned elements in the Party [i.e., the Unionist Party] who wanted to fight such measures."[7]

[5] L. S. Amery, *My Political Life*, I, 526; F. S. Oliver to Milner (9 Nov. 1910), *M.P.*, Letters, A.III.

[6] Dugdale, *Arthur James Balfour*, p. 4.

[7] Edward Turnour (Lord Winterton), *Orders of the Day* (London, 1953), p. 60.

At its inception the U.S.R.C. was merely the latest of the many attempts made by the Tariff Reform League to impart a socially progressive, working-class aura to the movement. Its first enterprise was modest, to sponsor an excursion of "non-party" British working men to protectionist Germany in order to counter the impression given by Radicals that, as Lloyd George once put it, protected industry meant a diet of "black bread and horseflesh for the masses." Since then the Radical leader had himself developed a strong interest in German methods of social policy similar to that of the U.S.R.C. and had pointedly alluded to German models in the Criccieth Memorandum. Indeed, it was partly his own excursion to Germany in the previous year which revealed to him the possibilities of linking the tariff with his expensive program of social reform. That connection had all along been the central tenet of the Tariff Reform League's version of Social-Imperialism; its inclusion in the coalition plan had been one of the main inducements for their otherwise surprising support of their long-time enemy. Bismarckian methods of social planning and control had attracted attention among British imperialists for many years. Such small projects as the excursion of twenty-odd working men to Germany was merely the latest of a number of efforts to point up the advantages of imperialist over Socialist methods of social and economic reform and modernization. The other Unionist "labour organizations" like the U.S.R.C. had had no measurable impact on the labor movement thus far. As we saw in a previous chapter, they were generally pressed halfheartedly, with much rhetoric about the patriotic working man but with scarce funds or enthusiasm. Nor had this aspect of Tariff Reform activity intruded noticeably into politics in Westminster. But the attractions of Lloyd George's plan in the fall of 1910, and his subsequent introduction of the great Insurance Bill, transformed the subcommittee from another temporary organ of counterpropaganda to something like a standing lobby within the Unionist ranks for the promotion of cooperation between the parties on issues critical to the nation's welfare and security.[8]

[8] Most of the twenty-odd workmen on the excursion were members of the small Trade Unionist Tariff Reform League headed by Amery and J. W. Hills, an independent M.P., Milner's chief agent for Labour, and organizer of the Unionist Labour Party in 1912. *Reports on Labour and Social Condition in Germany*, vols. I-III (1910), a U.S.R.C. publication.

The first issue deemed to fall under this heading was the national insurance plan. It is probably of some importance that Lloyd George composed the first draft of the Insurance Bill during the same few weeks late in the summer of 1910 in which he drew up his coalition plan. It was to be the magnum opus of his chancellorship. Learning from his happy experiences with businessmen while at the Board of Trade, he conducted the difficult negotiations with the Friendly Societies, the doctors, and the labor unions confidentially for the most part, trying always to keep an atmosphere of cooperation and nonpartisanship. He diplomatically enlisted the aid of spokesmen from the groups involved and, working mainly through independent "experts" such as Masterman, Beveridge, Braithwaite, and Dr. Addison (and at one point the Webbs), he succeeded in enacting the most revolutionary advance in the history of British social reform almost miraculously free from opposition.[9]

The relatively easy success of the chancellor's Insurance Bill was due less to the parliamentary strength of his own party, which was not unanimously sympathetic anyway, than to sources of support he was able to tap outside. The Webbs, now on better terms with the Labour Party, were willing to speak for the bill in those quarters despite some reservations and a jealous annoyance at what they considered a rather cross-eyed plagiarism of their old "National Minimum" plan. But by far the most important of his allies in securing the easy passage of the scheme were his Unionist confederates of the previous fall.[10]

As before, his active support from the other side was led by F. E. Smith as chairman of the Unionist Social Reform Committee and by J. L. Garvin in the *Observer*. The introduction of the bill was greeted by the *Observer*, on 7 May 1911, with Garvin's characteristic effusiveness:

[9] J. W. Braithwaite's *Lloyd George's Ambulance Wagon*, the fuller Typescript and notes of which are used in this chapter, is an account of the two-year evolution of the National Health Insurance Bill; cf. Typescript of *Lloyd George's Ambulance Wagon*, Br. P., II. The book, edited by Henry Bunbury, was published posthumously.

[10] The Webbs were consulted in February and March 1911, by both Llewellyn Smith, the Permanent Under-Secretary, and by Lloyd George himself, following which they made recommendation to the Labour Party and contributed further support through various Fabian M.P.'s; B. Webb, "Diary" (10 Feb. 1911, 6 March 1911), *P.P.*

'Above Party'
National Insurance
'Do it Together'
Mr. Lloyd George's Appeal
Unionist Response

There is not the slightest doubt as to the attitude that ought to be and will be adopted by the Unionist Party towards the greatest scheme of social reconstruction ever yet attempted by a single effort of legislation. It opens a new epoch of political thought and action. In spirit it transcends all partisanship. It adopts and extends the creative principles of State Insurance founded just thirty years ago by Bismarck. It develops the constructive example set by Mr. Chamberlain. It fulfills the idea of social order and progress foreshadowed by Lord Beaconsfield. . . .

. . . To the Chancellor himself belongs the high and imperishable credit for the personal energy, determination, and resource—and, above all, for the final touch of conciliatory genius—which have at last carried the nation, in this epoch-making matter, from dreaming to doing. . . . The vast work proposed by the C. of E. was not advocated in a party spirit. It never can be accomplished by Party means. But it may—and we believe it will—afford an opportunity for the first piece of constructive cooperation between parties that has yet been known in democratic politics.

. . . Do the audience of that speech, or even its author, realise how completely it marked the definite hour of transition from one national epoch to another? When Mr. Lloyd George sat down on Thursday, the spirit of laissez-faire—still lingering up till then, though in the article of death—was definitely and forever extinguished, and a new age of national organization was as definitely opened. We have organised, more or less, Government, defence, education, production, transport. At last we are setting ourselves deliberately to organise the health and strength, the economic security and the vital efficiency of the mass of the nation.[11]

It had been just one day short of a year since another of Garvin's articles had helped to stir Westminster to a reflective and anxious mood, the mood which had produced the futile Constitutional Conference, the false spirit of conciliation, and eventually the great national plan which he was now striving to resurrect. The editor had clearly not let the incident slip from his mind, nor did he wish the "great thing" to be forgotten by his Unionist readers. His linking of Lloyd George in the line of succession of Bismarck and

[11] *Observer*, 7 May 1911, in response to Lloyd George's speech in the House of Commons, 4 May 1911.

Chamberlain was an exercise in king-making; it was what the Tariff Reformers and Milnerites had been seeking since the demise of the great Joseph—a Muhammed, a war leader, a visionary who would make things plain and restore lost certainties through the gospel of efficiency, social order, and political solidarity. To Garvin's mind, Lloyd George had frequently shown signs of possessing the vision and independence to rise above the detested "System" and the coalition plan of the previous year showed that he also had conceived the means of doing so. Though the Insurance Bill now took the place of the constitutional question as the occasion for a coalition of parties, in neither case was the device to be limited to dealing with these particular and passing issues alone. Indeed, at least for the chancellor and Garvin, the coalition had become something of an end in itself, an idea whose potency grew with each mounting crisis—a solution to a host of real and imagined problems ranging from the intraparty struggle for leadership to the commonly felt threat of economic and social chaos.

Months before the Insurance Bill came up for reading, Garvin had been plying among his readers and the Unionist leaders both the virtues of the chancellor's plan and of its author. Severely disappointed in Balfour over the Canadian-American Reciprocity Agreement of January, the editor's admiration for Lloyd George soared.[12] "He is the only member of the Government," he said in his March article, "with that incalculable element of genius which quickens and vitalises in a mysterious way every human combination of which it forms a part." He admitted that the chancellor's "hypnotic gift of emotional eloquence" (words never lavished on Balfour) captured the imagination. Many Tariff Reformers would remember his admirable record at the Board of Trade and during the conference, where, Garvin reminded them, "Mr. Lloyd George showed glimpses of possibilities far bigger than the role of destructive and vituperative demagogue."[13]

The direction of Garvin's thinking in connection with the chancellor and his plan was rather clearly indicated by the presence, in the adjoining column of the same issue, of his article entitled "The

---

[12] Gollin, *The Observer*, p. 323. The same issue resulted in the sale of the *Observer* to Waldorf Astor in February.

[13] "The Fine Tradition," Garvin's article on Lloyd George (*Observer*, 5 March 1911), coincided with the break from Balfour on Garvin's part. Cf. *Observer* of the same date, "The Crisis in Unionism: The Demand for a Plain Policy."

Crisis in Unionism: The Demand for a Plain Policy." It was his first sweeping censure of the party's leadership and played a major role in setting off the "Balfour Must Go" movement which toppled the party chief a few months later.[14] Following an extended harangue of "Moderates" on both sides, he declared, "We prefer Mr. Lloyd George and Mr. Churchill at their worst to the decorous men who make themselves stalking horses in the abstract for all they deprecate in theory."[15]

The juxtaposition of the two articles carried a warning which the old men of both parties had cause to fear. It was not merely a question of injecting new blood into the existing party machines dominated by old caucus hacks and antiquated manners, but of revolutionizing the party system itself, root and branch. "England," Garvin argued, "in spite of the proverb, has sometimes loved Coalitions when formed of the best men of both sides, created for supreme public ends and aiming in national emergencies at the constitution of a real *national party*." Past coalitions, like that of Fox and North, failed in the long run not because of a mistaken principle but in their failure to extend the union in Parliament down to the level of the constituencies.[16]

It would seem, therefore, that when Garvin pleaded for a non-partisan treatment of the Insurance Bill, his purpose was not merely to further a measure of constructive legislation, but to exploit the occasion for cooperation the bill provided to advance the more momentous project of forming the National Coalition. Pursuing that end, he again arranged a meeting with Elibank, the man who had been the chancellor's emissary on a similar occasion the year before. Two days before the introduction of the bill for its first reading (on Thursday, 4 May), Elibank informed Garvin of the chancellor's desire to avoid partisan attitudes in the treatment of his scheme; it was too vital to be sacrificed to politics. Having received what must have been the expected response from Garvin, Elibank scheduled a rendezvous with Lloyd George for Friday, after the chancellor's introductory speech in the House. It was at

---

[14] Leo Maxse, the author of the "Balfour Must Go" slogan and its leading protagonist, seems to have taken the inspiration from the *Observer* article of 5 March. Cf. Maxse to Garvin, 6 March 1910; cited in Gollin, *The Observer*, p. 325.

[15] *Observer*, 5 March 1911.

[16] *Observer*, 2 April 1911. My italics.

this meeting that the outlines of the *Observer's* Sunday editorial were worked out.[17]

The same forces as had crystallized around the coalition plan in the preceding fall began to array themselves for a second time. Immediately after his meeting with Lloyd George, Garvin saw to it that the revived project was communicated to the Unionist leader in the most favorable terms—Balfour had good reason by now to be wary of the restless maneuvers of this section of the party. Being on somewhat strained relations with Balfour, the editor chose to describe the new situation through Jack Sandars, the confidential secretary:

Private and Confidential

Lloyd George is very anxious to make rapid progress with this bill and talks of the possibility of finishing it in August.

He is afraid that if too much of an interval is allowed, the workmen will grow restive over their contribution of 4d. *That is the quarter from which he anticipates danger.*

He is most anxious that we should pool our interests with his: that we should become partners in the undertaking—credit and blame being exactly distributed. He assured Garvin that he honestly desired no party capital out of it, and obviously he is in his mood of last December. He spoke with but little admiration of his own side: *He sees danger [to] to the State which he says can only be met by the cooperation of the best men of both parties.* . . .[18]

Sandars' account of the 5 May meeting indicates that the chancellor was, indeed, "in his mood of last December." The intent of his proposition, though apparently offered in more general terms now, was essentially unchanged. A coalition of "the best men of both parties" once again was advanced as the most effective device not only, or even primarily, to carry a controversial measure of reform but also to protect against the restiveness of labor and whatever other "danger to the State" he imagined might arise out of factious opposition from the extreme Left or Right, or from his "own side."

As before, the chancellor immediately responded to the flattering distinction made by Garvin between himself and his "more dec-

---

[17] Elibank to Garvin, 3 May 1911; cited in Gollin, *The Observer*, p. 330.
[18] Sandars to Balfour, 6 May 1911, *B.P.*, 49767-787C. My italics.

orous" but less dynamic colleagues. Questioned by the editor at their meeting about the old-age pensions section of the bill, Lloyd George agreeably conceded that it was the weakest aspect of the scheme, but "that it was all Asquith's fault: that Asquith had committed the Government to it without sufficient consideration...."[19]

The confession was not only indiscreet but curiously inaccurate. In the first place, the pensions clauses of the bill, which he seemed so ready to alter, were of his own authorship. Moreover, less than a week before the Garvin conversation he had declared that he would rather withdraw the entire insurance plan than compromise on that particular aspect.[20]

The incident offers a valuable insight into the dense obscurity of Lloyd George's reasoning during this period. His "glorified grocers" caricature of the Liberal establishment and his private denunciations of Asquith to the Opposition reflect mainly the uneasiness he felt in the lukewarm company of his older colleagues more than the relatively small substantive opposition offered by them to his reform policies. On the other hand, there existed across the party fence the vocal group of Social-Imperialists who not only endorsed much of his effort with open enthusiasm and public praise but to a large extent shared his own antipathy to the party establishments. The special attraction between himself and Garvin perhaps lay even deeper. Both members of the "Celtic Fringe," talented risers from obscure petit bourgeois origins, they displayed a notable contempt not only for the conventional ethics and style of politics at Westminster but equally for the hallowed institutions through which the system operated. Party loyalty, traditional principles, and genteel restraint within constitutional bounds all represented a "System," as Milnerism branded it, of which they were never an integrated part, either socially or ideologically. To a lesser extent the rank and file of the parties since the 1906 elections were themselves unabsorbed by the social uniformity of the old political clubs. Returned in a majority in 1910, the Liberal Parliament sitting in 1911 was relatively a new breed—as one disapproving observer remarked, "the most heterogeneous collection of cranks, faddists, killjoys, careerists and Little Englanders ever assembled under a single party flag."[21]

[19] Ibid.

[20] Braithwaite, Typescript, *Br. P.*, II, 145.

[21] Victor Wallace Germains, *The Tragedy of Winston Churchill* (London, 1931), p. 313.

Tariff Reform, under the guidance of Chamberlain, Milner, and Garvin, similarly transformed the stylized Toryism of the party of Disraeli and the Cecils. The coalition idea, coinciding with the revolt against the discredited Unionist leadership, manifested the breakdown of the Victorian homogeneity of the two parties and at the same time offered an escape route for the new men from their archaic hold. The peculiar usefulness of the coalition plan was in providing a *modus operandi* for a coordinated revolt in both parties, one which would leave the existing leaders at the head of the party organizations but, by transferring the basis of political loyalty from the party to "the nation"—to national rather than party leaders—thus remove party control over policy and Parliament. Asking Balfour to accede to any such plan was tantamount to asking his resignation. It is no mere coincidence, then, that his second refusal in May of 1911 was quickly followed by just that demand on the part of those Conservatives who had favored the coalition.

Despite the repeated urging of the *Observer*, reinforced by Northcliffe's powerful *Daily Mail*, Balfour declined the offer to carry national insurance jointly, ignoring pointedly the larger implications of the chancellor's proposal.[22] What followed was an early indication of Balfour's weakening control of his followers. Not only did the bill receive considerable verbal support in the House from the Unionist side, but through the U.S.R.C. it even enlisted the eager participation of the Tariff Reformers in the actual planning of the bill and its passage. While the larger program had been blocked by Balfour, according to Lloyd George's special assistant on insurance, the idea "lived on in some vague promises by an evidently disappointed Lloyd George to help any Committee working on the other side."[23] Amery and Worthington-Evans of the U.S.R.C., with the full support of Austen Chamberlain, Garvin, and the *Daily Mail*, set up such a committee to work with Lloyd George soon after Balfour's refusal.[24] Waldorf Astor, a most welcome recent recruit of the Milner-Garvin circle and the new owner of the *Observer*, was one of those Unionists who offered their ser-

---

[22] *Daily Mail*, 5 May 1911: ". . . a memorable measure, a great step forward in social reform." Northcliffe, however, had qualifications regarding the cost of the Insurance Bill. Balfour declined Lloyd George's offer, according to Braithwaite, a day after it was made; Braithwaite, Typescript, *Br. P.*, III, 6 (n.d. May 1911).

[23] Braithwaite, Typescript, *Br. P.*, III, 6.

[24] Colin Cross, *Liberals in Power* (London, 1963), p. 150.

vices to the bill, eventually even accepting an appointment as one of the commissioners—this was arranged through Garvin's influence.[25]

Braithwaite admitted that until "politics came in, these people really tried to play the game. . . ."[26] The measure of bipartisan cooperation achieved on the Insurance Bill fell far short of that envisioned in the coalition plans; yet it was a first modest realization of the principle discussed since the Rosebery revolt, that great measures of national reconstruction would fare better in the hands of enlightened cross-party combinations than in those of the reactionary party hacks. Furthermore, an ideological wedge which the Tariff Reformers had been hammering at for a decade had been driven into the widening split in the Unionist Party. Balfour's two-time refusal to cooperate on nonparty measures of social reform was equated with hostility toward the principle in general, and therefore toward the essence of the entire Social-Imperialist position. Refined and filled out over a decade, that ideology was more compelling to the Unionist insurgents in 1911 than ever before. To hinder or oppose it was tantamount to treason, since, as we have seen, it had been designed mainly in answer to the threats against national security and social order sensed by its authors. It was this fear that responded to the Lloyd George plan of 1910 and again the following May when considerably more substance could be given to it by the new boldness of labor, the imminence of Home Rule, and the crisis brewing in Morocco. The fear of a war with Germany over Morocco had been present despite the Algeciras Agreements of 1906 and 1909. The fact that the full extent of Britain's commitment to France was not generally known did nothing to quieten the anxiety regarding German aggressiveness in North Africa.

Lloyd George's proposals on both occasions in October and May spoke directly to this existing body of ideas, to which he had had frequent personal exposure, while Garvin translated for his Unionist audience. Applauding the work of the U.S.R.C. in one of his series of insurance articles, entitled "Imperialism and Social Reform," he wrote:

> As the Socialistic tendency is strengthening at a formidable rate, the Real Antidote—Social Reform regarded as an indispensable part

[25] Braithwaite, Typescript, *Br. P.*, III, 22.
[26] Ibid.

of every political programme aiming at increased *national efficiency and full national security*—must be applied in stronger doses (i.e. National Insurance . . .). The difficulty of *breeding an Imperial race in the foul deeps of the town slums* raises a problem for immediate attention. . . .[27]

The article outlined a broad policy on "the Imperial Race," the slums, the birth rate, the Poor Law, and military training which accumulated the work of the Fabians, the Roseberites, the National Service League, the Coefficients, and the Tariff Reform League under the title, "Social and Imperial Patriotism." Into this program, national insurance, and the coalition as the means of implementation, fit snugly. For, as the editor had come to believe, coalitions or national governments were the only practical and modern devices capable of working such far-reaching changes under the political circumstances.[28]

Sitting stubbornly in the way of such a grand solution of the nation's ills was the inertia of the old parties embodied in men like Balfour and Lansdowne. Their reluctance to adopt the protectionists' social and defense program for the last election, it was felt, proved not only their blindness to the interests of the party but of the nation. The young Unionists had become convinced, F. E. Smith assured Garvin, that in the immediate future "national defense will matter more and more and all others [issues] except social reform less and less."[29] Their opposition to the chancellor's proposals proved the older men's insensitivity to both. Hewins, the scholarly ideologue of Tariff Reform, was disgusted with the Front Bench and contemptuous of Balfour. He would, he promised the Webbs, write a book propounding "the real conservative social programme, and that would, in fact, be adopted by the younger men of the party and be imposed on the Front Bench."[30]

Thus there had developed in the Unionist Party a serious ideological cleavage over social reform, always linked with national security by the Social-Imperialists, prior to the famous "Die-Hard" revolt led by the Earl of Halsbury against a compromise on the Parliament Bill in the summer of 1911.[31] Only after Balfour's re-

[27] *Observer*, 9 April 1911.
[28] *Observer*, 9 April 1911; Gollin, *The Observer*, p. 331.
[29] Smith to Garvin, 3 Jan. 1911; cited in Gollin, *The Observer*, p. 278.
[30] B. Webb, "Diary" (6 March 1911), *P.P.*
[31] The adhesion of the Tariff Reformers to the Halsbury club was probably more due to their concern over Ireland and the Osborne Judgment

fusal of May did the Unionist insurgents begin to drift into the kind of extremism which culminated in the "Last-Ditch" revolt of July and August. To a man the Social-Imperialists joined the attack on Balfour and Lansdowne. Garvin, Smith, Amery, Chamberlain, Astor, and Winterton were among the leaders of the Halsbury club and were joined publicly for the first time by the spectral Milner.[32] This association of the Tariff Reformers with the Die-Hards was a temporary one, as we shall see; they were thrown together mainly by their frustration with Balfour whom the Halsbury reactionaries found too conciliatory and the Tariff Reformers too obstinate.

In thus binding themselves to the elements represented by Halsbury, whom they had castigated as reactionaries in the past, they betrayed obvious panic and previewed somewhat the darker nihilism of the years to come. "They were ready," attested a close observer, "for actual armed resistance, or rather, they would like that."[33] Their panic was not so much concerned with the Parliament Bill, and Home Rule which loomed behind it, as it was for Halsbury's backwoodsmen; they had been prepared to negotiate with Lloyd George on that score. Enlisting in the Die-Hard revolt was an alternative to the coalition, though a poor one, and through it they hoped to solve the same problems: namely, the menace of Socialism at home and German power abroad.

In July, as territorial troops were violently silencing the organized dock workers of London and Liverpool, the imperial gunboat *Panther* approached Agadir symbolizing the threat that the Pax Britannica might be nearing its end. Here was that conjunction of threats, long anticipated by Social-Imperialists and accurately foreseen by the Lloyd George plan. It was precisely the kind of crisis needed to dramatize the peculiar virtues of the National Coalition. Unfortunately, Garvin had despaired of the hope, for the moment, apparently convinced that it was futile while Balfour retained the final veto. He was presently engaged in an effort to remedy just that condition. The resourceful chancellor, on the other hand, immediately returned to the idea and repeated his offer to Balfour in July, but without any greater success.[34] As we have seen, Lloyd George

---

than to the historic powers of the upper house, which they had been willing to "reform" along the lines of the "Rosebery Plan" of the previous year. Fraser, "The Unionist Debacle," p. 364.

[32] *Observer*, 15 Oct. 1911.

[33] W. S. Blunt, *My Diaries*, pp. 770-771; Jenkins, *Balfour's Poodle*, pp. 160-161.

[34] Braithwaite, Typescript, *Br. P.*, III, 44.

had never accepted the fact that Balfour looked upon his plan as absurd and had only made a show of considering it in 1910 in order to gain time. He was to bring it up periodically in his dealings with Balfour as though reminiscing about an old mutual sweetheart—"Ah, if we had only brought it off!" One of the most formidable personalities of his era, Lloyd George always looked a little ridiculous courting Balfour.

His unsuccessful proposals of May had been followed once again by a temporary loss of contact between himself and the Garvin group, which had rather gamely returned to the old taunt of the Liberal Cabinet being "wagged by the Labour and Irish tail." The bridge was rapidly repaired, however, during the dramatic developments of July and August, in particular as a result of Lloyd George's famous Mansion House speech. A day following the announcement in the *Times* (20 July) of Germany's demands in Africa, he took up publicly for the first time the role of national patriot, one which he surely knew would recapture the distracted affections of his Unionist admirers. The German terms demanded, he announced, a surrender of vital national interests, of the "great and beneficent position Britain . . . [had] won by centuries of heroism and achievement . . . peace at that price could be a humiliation, intolerable for a great country . . . to endure. National honour," he concluded predictably, "is no party question."[35]

The exact motive of Lloyd George's quick and unorthodox response to the Moroccan crisis is rather obscure, and remains a subject of dispute. His was certainly no sudden conversion from pacifist to nationalist; a change of heart was evident at least as early as August 1910, as we have seen. His increased "Imperial responsibility," as the Tariff Reformers called it, had impressed them even in 1907, and it had grown with the cares of office. Garvin, who appears to have been more sympathetically comprehending of the chancellor's erratic spirit than any other man in politics, likened his transformation to the protagonist's in Wells' *New Machiavelli*, which he admiringly reviewed in January's *Observer*:

> He begins rather a Socialistic Liberal, and after a long period of hesitation he becomes an Imperialist. Neither side completely satisfies him. But he finds in Imperialism a constructive vigour that he has failed to find among his Liberal associates. . . .[36]

[35] Lloyd George, speech at the Mansion House (21 July 1911).
[36] *Observer*, 15 Jan. 1911.

Lloyd George had himself read Wells' book in February, possibly on Garvin's high recommendation, and seems to have been greatly impressed. "He is the only writer whose opinions on politics interest me in the least," he confessed to a close friend. Wells' indictment of the obscurantism of party politics, his talk of a new visionary aristocracy, of a "great intellectual movement," outside the world of traditional politics, were very much suited to the mood of the chancellor's recently assumed crusade of "national regeneration." The Mansion House speech, building on his coalition and insurance plans, added weight to his stature as a national leader, above politics, that image of which the young Unionists seemed so enamored.[37]

Were part of his intention to rekindle the receded attentions of those patriots by highlighting, and somewhat exacerbating, the foreign crisis in his speech, he succeeded immediately. Garvin, soft-pedaling the Die-Hard revolt for the moment, returned to the nonparty line again in the issue following Lloyd George's speech:

> We confess that we have read these noble words with a lifting of heart, and with some sense of glimpsing a greater future through the clouds of the moment. . . . He [L. G.] has infinite courage as well as endless resource, and, like all men who possess these characteristics, he is growing every day. We make these remarks from no party point of view. . . . If Mr. Lloyd George is ever driven to apply his courage and resource and animating genius to foreign policy in a crisis more serious than the present, Herr Diderlen-Wachter and his school may experience a very memorable surprise.[38]

Lloyd George's speech of July was his debut in the field of diplomacy. In making it, he went outside the conventional domain of his office, speaking neither as chancellor nor as the official mouthpiece of the government or party but as a voice of the people. It is doubtful that either the chancellor or even the Foreign Office, which gave its endorsement to the speech, had premeditated the full effect it had on German opinion or on the negotiations going on at the time. Indeed, from Lloyd George's point of view, that side of the issue would seem to have been almost incidental to the impact

---

[37] "Braithwaite Diary," 5 Feb. 1911, Misc. Mss., M623, *Br. P.*; Ibid., 28 Feb. 1911; Lucy Masterman, "Recollections of David Lloyd George," p. 174.

[38] *Observer*, 23 July 1911.

his words made on the critical situation in which he was involved at home.[39]

George Askwith, the ubiquitous industrial troubleshooter for the Board of Trade, working closely with the chancellor at the time, suspected the war scare brought on by the speech to be a ploy designed to head off the general strike threatened by the transportation workers.[40] Lloyd George had also injected himself into the labor dispute, which by July had reached a completely unprecedented peak of size and violence, at the very time he was composing his speech on the danger of war. Nor did he neglect to draw the connection in his appeal to the strikers. Invoking the national interest while war threatened, he succeeded in establishing a temporary halt of the planned railroad strike in mid-August, at the height of the crisis with Germany.[41]

Coming on the heels of his Mansion House speech, which somewhat restored his credit with the Grey-Asquith wing of the government, his intervention in the industrial unrest fully renewed his image among the young Unionist rebels. Even if it had not been his sole intention, he had deftly brought off the successful second reading of his Insurance Bill as a "non-party" enterprise in the midst of the bitterest party strife in the Parliament's history, during the final vote on the Parliament Bill. His great work of reform was exempted from the depredations of the conflict, as well as from a possible Socialist veto, largely through the efforts of Garvin and the U.S.R.C. in Parliament. The strike settlement was, in Garvin's overflowing praise, another triumph for Mr. Lloyd George, Patriot and Reformer. The *Observer* had called during the labor crisis for an "Iron Hand But an Open Mind"—stern repression of Syndicalist terrorism but "social amelioration along non-revolutionary lines." This was the policy of the Tariff Reformer; it had also been that of the chancellor and Churchill, who had first ordered out the troops against the strikers.[42]

---

[39] The Mansion House speech, though its intent is disputed, transformed the Agadir situation from a relatively minor incident into a "matter of honor" for all sides: cf. Dugdale, *German Diplomatic Documents, 1871-1914* (London, 1931), IV, 14-17.

[40] Henry Askwith, *Industrial Problems and Disputes*, p. 166.

[41] On 18 August the House passed without debate both second and third readings of an Official Secrets Act for the event of war. The same day Lloyd George spoke to the railwaymen on the danger of the war. House of Commons, 18 August 1914; Halévy, *History*, VI, 431, 454.

[42] *Observer*, 20 Aug., 27 Aug. 1911.

By the time Parliament was prorogued in August all the forebodings of the previous year had been realized: the German menace and the Syndicalist revolt coming upon the division and strife of parties. For the Die-Hards, the picture was further darkened by their failure to block the passage of the Parliament Act, which passed into law in August with the aid of thirty-seven Unionist peers. Bitterly frustrated, Garvin, Amery, Smith, and Maxse quickly began to transform the Die-Hard clique into a movement to dethrone Balfour and Lansdowne. Their argument against Balfour was somewhat paradoxical. On the one hand, Maxse attacked him for "collusion with the Liberals," while on the other Garvin seemed equally incensed by his refusal to rise above narrow partisanship, for example, on the question of supporting the Insurance Bill.[43]

From Balfour's point of view, the latter attack was the more dangerous, since behind it was the long-harnessed discontent of the Tariff Reformers, now the backbone and the future of the party. Halsbury and the reactionary backwoodsmen, whose argument Maxse had expressed, represented a small challenge by comparison. The Tariff Reform criticism was couched mainly in ideological terms, concentrating on the party's resistance to an advanced social policy. Referring to the party's defense of the employers, the doctors, and the Friendly Societies in the insurance debates, Garvin deplored the "growing habit among many members of the party of confining their sympathies to the commercial, professional, and property-owning classes." Such a policy played into the hands of the revolution and the events of the summer hinted that little time and patience could be spared in persuading the reluctant.[44]

Austen Chamberlain, a member of the ginger group but a good party man more hesitant than Garvin to split the party, made a last effort to win Balfour over to their position. When Parliament reconvened in October, Chamberlain presented him with a memo issued by the chancellor on possible "amendments" to the final draft of the Insurance Bill which might make cooperation more palatable.[45] Although there is no record, Chamberlain's possession of the insurance memo suggests that during the fall recess, as in the previ-

---

[43] The vote on the Parliament Bill in the last reading in the Lords was 131 to 114 in favor, 37 Unionist peers and 13 prelates going into the government lobby, House of Lords, 10 Aug. 1912; *National Review* (Sept. 1911), cited in Fraser, "The Unionist Debacle," p. 360.

[44] *Observer*, 27 Aug. 1911.

[45] A. Chamberlain to Balfour, (16 October), 1911, B.P., 49736-787B.

ous year, some private discussion between the chancellor and the Tariff Reform group on the subject of political cooperation had again taken place. It is evident, also, that their conversations were not strictly limited to insurance. For at least by November, a "Plan of amalgamation" was again under negotiation between the chancellor and the Unionists. Though the terminology had been altered since 1910, the "Liberal-Conservative-Unionist amalgamation" (Bonar Law's expression) alluded to in the unfortunately elusive correspondence could hardly have been much different from the "coalition" proposed on two former occasions by Lloyd George.[46]

Although Balfour had finally been forced to resign his leadership of the Unionist Party in November, an attempt was made, apparently at Lloyd George's urging, to draw him into the "amalgamation" discussions which continued for at least a month longer. One is tempted to ascribe complicated tactical reasons for Lloyd George's stubborn pursuit of Balfour throughout the coalition discussions; possible emotional factors also suggest themselves—Balfour's personal presence obviously intimidated him, perhaps sufficiently to fill the role of the patron, mentor, and "father" whom Lloyd George had always lacked in his political career and perhaps still sought before he felt ready to assume the leader's place in politics himself. Asquith was neither desirous nor capable of playing that part and never won his personal loyalty, yet Lloyd George repeatedly offered greater intimacy to Balfour, from which the latter always recoiled. That unwanted closeness was certainly one of the reasons why Balfour never gave serious thought to the idea of "amalgamation." Ironically, now that he no longer held the deciding voice, his attitude toward the coalition was more positive than before. That voice now belonged to Bonar Law, the new Unionist chief, a protectionist, an imperialist, and less shy than Balfour of unconventional causes.

Bonar Law had been drawn into the conversations with Lloyd George immediately upon succeeding Balfour, whose opinion on the "amalgamation" he solicited in December.[47] His part in the discussion, conducted more discreetly than before, is not exactly documented, yet it seems safe to assume that he would be hesitant to inaugurate his tenure as party leader with such a controversial innovation. Furthermore, one of the major stumbling blocks to the

[46] Bonar Law to Balfour (13 Dec. 1911); Balfour to Lloyd George, (19 Dec. 1911), *B.P.*, 49693-786A.
[47] Bonar Law to Balfour (13 Dec. 1911), *B.P.*, 49693-786A.

coalition discussions of the previous year, Irish Home Rule, was a question on which Bonar Law was more dogmatic than was Balfour; he also had closer ties with the Ulster Unionists. The young Tariff Reformers, as we have seen, were open to a compromise on Ireland in the form of "devolution all round," as suggested by F. S. Oliver. Their flexibility had made the plan at least feasible. The Irish question, then, with the introduction of a Home Rule Bill imminent, stood once more in the way of what had been called the "larger settlement." By early 1912, with the "amalgamation" deadlocked, the Garvin-Smith circle found themselves little more satisfied with the new party than with the old. "Even the 'social reform' Unionists," one of their Fabian friends (Clifford Sharp) observed, "with whom I have been in close touch and who (under F. E. Smith's leadership) were the strongest anti-Balfourists are now admitting that Bonar Law will have to go."[48] Like Lloyd George, they were highly leader-conscious and even more fickle.

Bonar Law had announced what he rightly expected would be a popular policy in the present mood of the rank-and-file Unionists: intransigent resistance to a dictated Home Rule settlement. In the Garvin group, though also opposed to Home Rule, that policy was considered foolhardy because it ignored a more urgent danger: that a civil war in Ireland would have the "almost inevitable reflex result of Labour Anarchy in Great Britain."[49] To meet both ends of the dilemma, and to keep a watch also on the additional threat from abroad, Garvin argued that "ordinary parliamentary methods will no longer serve." The appearance of organized Socialism as a formidable force had by itself already "destroyed the old two-party system." Syndicalism had thrived on the frustrations of a decade of national decline which the most elegant parliamentary oratory was powerless to reverse. Only in the context of a broader solution to such deep political and social problems could the Irish question be satisfactorily treated.[50]

Garvin was still looking hopefully toward Lloyd George for the "broader solution" in the spring of 1912, despite the apparent lapse in their discussions. Needed was a "sane democrat" such as Briand and Clemenceau, he wrote, "to bridge with a strong hand the criminal egotism *on every side*." He did all he could to publicize and aggravate the split between Asquith and the chancellor, damning

[48] Clifford Sharp to S. Webb (22 March 1912), *W.G.C., P.P.*
[49] *Observer*, 4, 18 Feb. 1912.
[50] Ibid., 10 March, 6 June 1912.

one while inviting the other to action before the introduction of the Home Rule Bill.[51] With Smith's U.S.R.C. he offered nonpartisan assistance on urgent measures of social reform as the great coal strike of February and March developed, warning of the greater anarchy to come in the summer. Just as they had aided the passage of Lloyd George's Insurance Bill, they joined in writing the Liberal Housing Bill of March and even drew up, with the Webbs' help, a compromise on the much-disputed subject of Poor Law reform.[52] They were, as Sharp assured Sidney Webb, "prepared to do anything in reason that may tend to prevent the coming of the nightmare of 'Syndicalism' "; even to support a National Minimum wage, an increase in the supertax, "even the nationalization of a staple industry or so would be a cheap price to pay for getting rid of that fear."[53] Not much consolation to the Webbs; all this sounded too much like the amateurish "political" solutions to the poverty question with which Lloyd George as well as some of the Marxists had countered their cherished *Minority Report*. Having spent so many earnest hours tutoring the Tariff Reformers over the past ten years, it seems to have been a great exasperation for the Webbs to see so much of their work sacrificed, as they thought, to partisan fads.

Right up until the introduction of the long-awaited Home Rule Bill of 1912, then, the advanced Unionists were still looking for such an alternative to all-out political war as the chancellor had three times proposed. Largely out of a fear of offending certain party factions—Free Trade Unionists, Die-Hards, or Ulstermen—Balfour and then Bonar Law had hedged first on full support of Tariff Reform and then flinched at a larger settlement. One result was to give to the Garvin-Smith men a strong contempt for "party politics," one which Milner's persistent grumbling about "the System" encouraged. Another was that the Chancellor's coalition idea, incorporating as it did a certain freedom from party hacks and a social and defense policy closely attuned to the Tariff Reform ideology, assumed the dimensions of a panacea whose desirability increased with each deepening crisis. Moreover, though none of the attempts between 1910 and 1912 had come to fruition, they were

[51] *Observer*, 4, 28 Feb., 6 June 1912.
[52] Garvin featured an article by Grey on the coal strike as a gesture towards cooperation. *Observer*, 18 Feb. 1912; Sharp to S. Webb (22 March 1912), *W.G.C., P.P.*
[53] Sharp to S. Webb (10, 12 April 1912), *W.G.C., P.P.*

nonetheless important in distilling the arguments for a national government and even in merely introducing what began as a rather exotic idea into the range of possible political alternatives. Most of all, it became the platform from which to attack incumbents of any party. This much at least had been accomplished by 1912, for in the climactic crises which followed—over Ireland, at the outbreak of war, during the shell crisis and the disasters of 1916—"the coalition" was consistently the first resort of both the distraught and insurgent politicians.

Reluctantly, but with hardly a sound of shifting gears, both Tariff Reformers and Lloyd George were drawn into the stubbornly emotional confrontation of parties inaugurated by the first reading of the Government of Ireland Bill in the spring session of 1912. In the Irish dispute, which was to bring the country to the brink of civil war by 1914, the still-present fears of Syndicalism and German power receded to second place in the verbal attentions of the press and most political leaders. In the atmosphere of frantic vilification between Liberal and Unionist which attended the hatreds of Ireland, discreet communication across party lines became a more hazardous enterprise. Nevertheless, "the policy of Conference," as the nonpartisanship of 1910-1911 was most often described, had by no means passed out of mind. In July, after the lines in Ireland had already hardened, Lloyd George still spoke of the plan, not to Garvin now, but to Churchill:

> Some time ago I thought the entire matter out [i.e., interparty cooperation]. . . . I have two alternatives to propose—the first to form a coalition, settle the old outstanding questions, including Home Rule, and govern the country on middle lines acceptable to both parties but providing measures of moderate social reform. The other, to formulate and carry through an advanced land and social reform policy.

Churchill was enthusiastically for the first, Lloyd George recalled: "I shall never forget the incident. We were playing golf at Criccieth [Lloyd George's Welsh home where the original plan had been drafted]. Winston forgot all about the game and has never forgotten our conversation."[54]

[54] Lord Riddell, *More Pages from My Diary, 1908-1914* (London, 1934), p. 77, related in a conversation between Lloyd George and Riddell on 2 July 1912.

Again in the fall of 1912, with continuing industrial unrest and the Balkan crisis on his mind, he returned to his rejected coalition plan as possibly the only political method capable of carrying conscription. No party alone could handle it "except in some great national emergency," he explained to a group of friends, recalling the main points of the plan. "That [i.e., conscription] was one of them. But, as you know, the whole thing fell through. Some day the facts will be published."[55] That national emergency, he confided soon after to Geoffrey Dawson, might then have been at hand. He talked, Dawson reported, "quite complacently about the rousing of the English national spirit for a war about the Balkans."[56] Lloyd George was obviously aware of the incompatibility of the two courses he outlined to Churchill on the golf links; he was possibly aware as well that a truly perilous "national emergency" held the potential either to make or break the chances for both the coalition and radical social reform. The passage of his insurance scheme marked a major crossroads in his career—the old Radical pro-Boer, the Limehouse firebrand, was now all but dead; no great new social scheme enlivened his day-to-day work; the great question which dominated the remaining years of peace, Ireland, he did not understand and never would.

With the Ulster Covenant signed (28 September) and the House still ringing from the bedlam of the first and second readings of the Ireland Bill, the Chancellor's plan by necessity remained a subject of private conversation only. The gloomy denouement of the dispute appeared to be in sight in July 1913, when 150,000 enlistments for Carson's army, the Ulster volunteers, marched in the streets of Craigavon, near Belfast. It was at this point, with Parliament in long recess and the fear of a bloody incident touching off conflagration at its height, that the "policy of Conference" was implored openly once again.

The initiation of talks on the Irish question in 1913 has generally been credited to a letter of Lord Loreburn to the *Times* of 11 September to the effect "that there should be a Conference or direct communication between the leaders" to prevent civil war.[57] Though

[55] Ibid., pp. 94-95, in a Lloyd George conversation with Masterman and Seely.
[56] Present at the conversation of November 1912 besides Dawson were Churchill, Seely, and Repington. Evelyn Wrench, *Geoffrey Dawson and Our Times* (London, 1955), p. 89.
[57] *Times*, 11 Sept. 1913; cf. also Halévy, *History*, VI, 553.

the letter seems to have been the first public gesture in that direction, Lloyd George had just four days before addressed a group of visitors (including Kennedy Jones) at Criccieth regarding a similar but more ambitious proposal. It was virtually identical to his memo of August 1910. He outlined five points "for reconstruction by Coalition or agreement," including as before education, housing and land, liquor, transport, and defense. He argued to his guests that the political differences of the time were "unreal," especially Home Rule. The latter was to be treated as subsidiary to defense, being but a small part of the larger imperial question, including the "German menace." Everything was to be done on a very bold scale. All this was "practical politics" if the Conservatives would come in, and it was apparently on this score that he hoped to win Northcliffe's help through Kennedy Jones.[58]

Whether the coincidence of dates was accidental or some connection existed between the meeting at Criccieth and Loreburn's letter to the *Times* is uncertain. In either case, the immediate response to the proposal from many quarters testifies to the continuing attraction of the coalition idea. Not unexpectedly, the *Observer* was first to reopen the campaign, three days after Loreburn's letter of the 11th:

> The Last Opportunity
>
> In the due hour, we are convinced, the method and the policy of Conference will be revived. It is less than three years since the *Observer* wrote that parting comment on a chapter of political history whose interest and promise were not obscured by its final disappointment. England was not fated in 1910 to escape from the chains of that mechanical party warfare which has since made her public life an increasing stranger to realities. But the vision has not been forgotten, and in our present crisis it revives to find a wider circle of serious men resting their hopes upon its fundamental truth. Lord Loreburn's letter of last week has profoundly altered the face of politics. Its manner of grappling with the verities has given the ordinary talk of Parliament and platform an air of mere cant and jargon. . . . He has made it infinitely more difficult for a vicious deadlock of constitutional elements to drag a paralysed nation to disaster.
>
> The Conference Plan, then, is alive again, and with new factors

---

[58] From a conversation of 7 September recorded by Braithwaite. Lloyd George was very probably reading directly from a copy of his 1910 memo, referred to by Braithwaite as a "letter," in describing the conversation. Typescript, *Br. P.*, III, 65.

upon its side which were wanting when these columns were first devoted to its advocacy. . . . The typical Englishman has come to entertain little faith in the virtue of what passes for politics, however tightly habit and organization may bind him to the revolution of the rolling wheels. . . .[59]

Garvin, who obviously had in mind something more dramatic than the mere exchange of views suggested by Loreburn, was running again far ahead of his colleagues. He was bound to be disappointed with the cautious response of his party to the new situation. Bonar Law met Churchill, who now acted as liaison for the government, in the King's presence a day after the *Observer* pronouncement. Their talks, as Loreburn had intended, were limited to discussing the possibilities of the "devolution all round" compromise as a way out of the Irish dilemma. Far short of a general "reconstruction" of politics, they proceeded with great trepidation even on the question of opening informal discussions on Ireland, a subject which both Garvin and the chancellor but few others continued to view as a secondary issue in the larger crisis. Nevertheless, they came away from the royal audience prepared to recommend, on the King's urging, an "informal" exchange of views between government and Opposition leaders on the model of the Constitutional Conference.[60]

With Parliament out of session, a full month of soundings among various party factions passed before Asquith was prepared to begin the meetings. In the meantime, lines of opinion on the Loreburn proposal became fairly clearly drawn. Balfour, the Garvin circle, and Bonar Law, braving the probable taunt of betrayal from Carson's Ulstermen, were in favor on the Unionist side; while among the Liberals Churchill, Grey, and Asquith were most vocal in support of discussions.[61] The conspicuous absence of the chancellor's voice in the proceedings and the angry opposition offered by Carson in the press were not discouraging to the advocates of the proposal, who wished to give the talks a "centrist" and moderate tone.

[59] *Observer*, 14 Sept. 1913.
[60] Bonar Law to Balfour (16 Sept. 1913), *B.P.*, 49693-786A, p. 32.
[61] Grey had written a supporting letter to the *Times* (12 Sept. 1913). Churchill conferred with Bonar Law during the three weeks prior to Asquith's assent (11 Oct.) and was the one responsible for getting his approval. Bonar Law to Balfour (16 Sept. 1913); Bonar Law to Stamfordham (4 Oct. 1913); Asquith to Bonar Law (11 Oct. 1913), *B.P.*, 49693-786A, pp. 30, 60, 81-82.

Garvin reiterated his former criticism of the extreme Ulstermen in reporting Carson's rejection of negotiations, warning again of the danger in setting an "example of violence . . . to every subversive movement of the future." Hewins, still high in Tariff Reform circles, also deplored the dangerous influence of "reactionary Carsonism" on the explosive situation in the nation.[62]

Lloyd George's continued silence during the slow-moving developments from September to November (the informal talks only began in mid-October) was a frustrating mystery to Garvin, for he had obviously been looking in that direction for the major initiative which would again advance the discussion from conference to coalition. However, expectantly covering the chancellor's speech at Bedford (10 October), he could only report "profound disappointment."

> His audience [Garvin wrote] wanted not his rhetoric, but his proposals. Strange to relate, amid a huge formless mass of general verbiage, he has no proposals—none in the sense of serious statesmanship. . . .
>
> This then is the oration expected with more interest than any platform event since Mr. Chamberlain's tariff speech at Glasgow ten years ago.[63]

Garvin's impatience was understandable, even justifiable. He naturally assumed that Churchill was the chancellor's stalking-horse in the meetings with Bonar Law (as indeed he was). What puzzled him was Lloyd George's failure to resume personal contact as before, that is, to employ the editor again as a private liaison with the sympathetic Unionists. His confidential contact with Lloyd George since 1910 had increased his usefulness and standing both as a journalist and as a political kibitzer; he did not have quite that relationship with Churchill and certainly not with Asquith, the two Liberals who now led the discussions with Bonar Law. With the bulk of the press, Garvin had not been kind to Lloyd George during the Marconi affair earlier in the year and this alone may have ac-

---

[62] *Observer*, 14, 21 Sept. 1913; Hewins, *Apologia*, I, 304; in a conversation with the Webbs.

[63] Lloyd George, speech at Bedford (10 Oct. 1913) on the subject of land reform. Though it made no reference to the conference, it was conciliatory towards traditional Tariff Reform land policies. *Observer*, 12 Oct. 1913.

counted for the chancellor's apparent aloofness.[64] For, contrary to Garvin's impression, the chancellor was very much interested still in cooperating across party lines and was closely informed of the discussions by Churchill and by F. E. Smith, who now replaced Garvin as his main link with the Tariff Reform section. As we have seen, Smith was one of the younger Unionists who had been excited by the coalition idea before and he now became the principal mover on the Tory side of a conference on Ireland.

Circumstances within the two parties had not changed much since the removal of Balfour, or so Smith thought when he bruited the question of a new conference to Lloyd George early in September. Having already spoken with Churchill and with the King, he suggested that a conference based on the exclusion of Ulster with some Unionist concessions in the south might head off the extremists and even develop into something "bigger":

F. E. Smith to Lloyd George, 26 September, 1913
Secret and Confidential

... [the] conference should be summoned by the King. ... Our extremists would hate a conference—they think they have you beat—so would yours—but neither of them could hold out against the question—'would you have us refuse the King when he asks us to confer?'

In the most strict confidence I inform you that I received this morning a letter from Steel-Maitland suggesting to me that if a conference was held on Home Rule it might and ought to be extended to cover the House of Lords reform and the Land.

From such a conference anything might follow. ... Under these circumstances while fully *making your* case at Bedford could you not do it in a restrained way and without unfriendliness to landlords as a class? If things fail you can return at any time to a war basis. I think a 'statesmanlike' speech (odious phrase) might produce some remarkable consequences.[65]

The Bedford speech was the occasion on which Garvin had been so disappointed, obviously unaware of Smith's overture and conse-

[64] Northcliffe, Garvin's publisher, apparently made an attempt to "play down" the Marconi scandal for Isaacs and Lloyd George if, as he cryptically suggested to Churchill, it could be "stage-managed" properly. Churchill to Lloyd George (March 1913), *L.G.P.*, C/3/15/20.

[65] F. E. Smith to Lloyd George (9 Sept. 1913), *L.G.P.*, C/3/7/1. Lloyd George's Bedford speech was scheduled two weeks later (10 Oct. 1913).

quently misunderstanding the kind of "statesmanship" at which Lloyd George was aiming in the speech. Garvin was not exactly being snubbed either by Lloyd George or by Smith—both were playing an extremely cautious hand at this stage, both having already aroused the suspicions of important conservative sections of their respective parties for their previous breaches of loyalty. Garvin's trumpeting voice and wide network of political leaks, although invaluable at other times, was not felt to be needed yet. He would not learn the full account of this episode in the coalition maneuvers until the end of the year, while in the meantime he was allowed to run the risk of looking a little ridiculous in his persistent and generally irrelevant wanderings about the talks on Ireland and in particular about the puzzling inaction of the chancellor. "We have been told," he wrote either to soften his own disappointment or to stir some response, "that Mr. Lloyd George could not speak 'unmuzzled' unless he quitted the Cabinet. . . ."[66] Sulking under the cloud of scandal, nothing was further from the chancellor's mind at this moment—he would not have borne the fate of Ishmael as well as Milner.

It was a rather ironic reversal of roles that the main proponents of cooperation should now be those who had dragged their feet on the earlier occasions. Balfour now worked assiduously with Bonar Law for the conference. The latter, repenting his encouragement of Carson's militant excesses, now dwelt on the "terrible position" in which the parties would be placed without a compromise. "The idea of a conference," he implored Churchill, "ought not lightly to be thrown aside."[67] Balfour, whose opinion the new leader now solicited at every turn, listed the possible advantages of going even further on nonparty lines than the Home Rule question, very much the same tack Smith had taken with Lloyd George. The rejected proposals of the chancellor could hardly have been far from his mind when he suggested to his colleague during the discussions that with Home Rule and the Welsh church out of the way, "putting Tariff Reform aside," it was more a question of method than of policy blocking the cooperation of the two parties.[68]

[66] *Observer*, 12 Oct. 1913. Garvin was undoubtedly right that Lloyd George was informed of developments, surely by Churchill, who made the major public initiatives in his speech at Dundee (25 Oct. 1913); cf. also Asquith's speech at Ladybank (25 Oct. 1913). Both were favorably reported by Garvin. *Observer*, 12 and 26 Oct. 1913.

[67] Bonar Law to Balfour (16 Sept. 1913), *B.P.*, 49693-786A, p. 30.

[68] Balfour to Bonar Law (8 Nov. 1913), *B.P.*, 49693-786A, p. 30.

It may well have been with some amusement that Lloyd George viewed the nervous drift of the conferees towards just the kind of arrangement he had thrice presented and which they had rejected as many times. For the direction the talks were taking was widely known. Hewins, on "authentic information as distinct from views and opinions," had it that a "sort of Whig Coalition" was in the making, based on a compromise for Ireland, exclusion of Tariff Reform, and the "outing" of Lloyd George.[69] Hewins' information, moreover, seems largely substantiated in Balfour's advice to Bonar Law. The new Unionist leader, though he was interested in a combination, could not have been completely comfortable with the idea of joining an exclusive company of "Whigs." Yet, as Garvin warned him, "How compromise without *combination*?" If a deal was made in Ulster, he would surely have to keep Asquith in office (the fools' mate which Balfour had offered in 1910). Conceding that "*combination* would be in some respects easier now than three years ago," Bonar Law wondered on the other hand what would be the alternative if Lloyd George opposed the idea now as strongly as he had supported it before?[70]

Whatever the fortunes of the Lloyd George plan were eventually to be, he was obviously reaping dividends already from the 1910 investment—whenever "non-party" cooperation was sought, his attitude would be considered critical. He had merely to listen now while others came inquiring to him. It was a position not to be underestimated (as Asquith eventually did); and as we shall see, it was a factor which helps somewhat to explain his enigmatic silences in the early crises of the war when many looked to him for initiative and were disappointed. Few Unionists who played significant parts in the wartime administration expected inspiration from Asquith.

While Lloyd George thus remained in the background, Churchill functioned as the main link between the Prime Minister and the leader of the Opposition in the discussions about a conference on Ireland during September and October. Smith and Steel-Maitland served a similar purpose on the Unionist side. The relations between Lloyd George and Smith had blossomed in the past year or two into something of a mutual understanding. Smith apparently saw in the Radical chancellor what Garvin had seen before him, an enemy closer to his own mind than most of his friends. Nursed

[69] Hewins, *Apologia*, I, 303; from a diary entry of 26 Sept. 1913.
[70] Garvin to Bonar Law, and return (Oct. 1913); cited in Gollin, *The Observer*, p. 410.

by similar real and imagined grievances, the feeling was shared on Lloyd George's part as well. The correspondence between them, full of oblique complaints about the "decorous old men," reflected that attraction. When Smith was pushing for an all-out conference on Ireland in the past two months he had met with the same partisan sluggishness and suspicion that Lloyd George experienced three years earlier—in Smith's case, Lansdowne and Stamfordham played the role of obstructionists.[71] Nevertheless, Smith and Lloyd George met several times in October and November about a possible compromise on Ireland. Their discussions were entirely separate from the talks still in progress between Asquith and Bonar Law (although with Churchill in attendance at a number of meetings on either side, Lloyd George was well informed of the difficulties the leaders were having). Smith and the chancellor established very quick rapport and seemed able to reach general agreement on virtually any issue—Balfour might have said that was because neither had any understanding of "principles, the important things." There was certainly some truth in the charge, for neither was much involved in the kind of team loyalties which sanctified party policy, nor did either have personal commitments to the opposing militants of the Home Rule battle. More or less excluded from the intimate friendships which fueled the inner circles of both parties, men like Smith and Lloyd George and numerous other "new men" had been slowly sensing the existence and enjoying the clandestine camaraderie of a potential countergroup in the political society of Westminster, based more as yet on frustrations and ambition than on loyalty and patronage.

Initiating the meetings with Smith in a letter of October, Lloyd George complained of the treatment he had received at the hands of the Young Tories over the Marconi business in the press and in their speeches. The personal character of many of the attacks upon him was most distressing since, he wrote to Smith, "You know how anxious I've been for years to work with you and a few others on your side. I have always realized that our differences have been very artificial and do not reach the 'realities.' "[72] Whatever the "realities" were, the two found few obstacles in the way of agreement on Ireland. Few of these men cared much about the prospect

---

[71] Memos summarizing F. E. Smith's actions and proposals on Home Rule settlement based on Ulster exclusion (26 to 30 Sept. 1913), *B.L.P.*, 30/2/28, 29, 37.

[72] Lloyd George to F. E. Smith (6 Oct. 1913), *L.G.P.*, C/3/7/2.

of mutual slaughter in Ireland—it was a small chip on the imperial board to them. After Smith had apologized to the chancellor for the personal attacks in Tory speeches (particularly for Maxse's "scurrility" in a speech at Bedford), and promised to stifle mention of Marconi as much as possible, the two began to map out a formula based on the exclusion of Ulster from the Irish Bill (Smith's well-known "compromise" position) with a proviso added by Lloyd George that after an indeterminate time to be established by negotiation (his own suggestion was five years) the six northern counties would automatically be incorporated into a Dublin Parliament.[73] Like so many of the chancellor's "agreements" with the Young Tories, this was little more than a mere statement of the two opposing positions simultaneously, as though that magically removed the conflict. These were meetings of spirit and personality and not of substance.

Lloyd George finally broke his silence on the Irish talks on 25 November. He proposed the "5 Year Plan" about which he and Smith had spoken, receiving wide coverage in the press and immediately throwing the talks still going on between Asquith and Bonar Law (occasionally joined by Carson) into a turmoil.[74] Asquith's task was formidable enough, acting as prism and arbiter of at least three bitterly divided factions on Ireland, without such unexpected bombshells as his chancellor was wont to hurl from time to time. As they were obviously designed to do, his impossible terms immediately confounded the conciliations of Asquith and Bonar Law. The latter's fear of the chancellor's hostility to a combination, it seemed, had been borne out. In early December, the meetings inaugurated by Loreburn's letter came to an end without result.[75]

Almost at the same moment as his intervention in the compromise talks, Lloyd George personally presented what amounted to an ultimatum to Redmond, informing him that unless he was prepared to offer terms to Ulster, Grey, Haldane, and Churchill (and by implication himself as well) were ready to resign. The resulting damage to the chances of the Home Rule Bill was obvious. Thus, in two strokes, he had laid the way to severing commitments to the

[73] F. E. Smith to Lloyd George (9 Oct. 1913), *L.G.P.*, C/3/7/3.

[74] The "5 Year Plan" was proposed two days after Garvin's last appeal in the *Observer*, 23 Nov. 1913. Gollin, *The Observer*, p. 410.

[75] F. E. Smith to Bonar Law (30 Oct. 1913), *B.L.P.*, 30/3/75; "Memos" (24 Dec. 1913), *B.L.P.*, 31/1/55, 67.

rival Irish factions on Home Rule.[76] The possible direction the actions of Smith and Lloyd George were going to take became somewhat clearer when, shortly after, he injected once again his plan for a coalition of the moderates "to make a national settlement of some of the great issues of the day." Significantly, the approach was made this time not to Balfour or Bonar Law, but to Austen Chamberlain, the recognized parliamentary leader of the Tariff Reformers and one whose relations were reasonably good with the Tory old guard.[77]

By New Year 1914, the method being discussed to deal with the crisis had once again come round to the now familiar formula of the chancellor. Furthermore, the political base for the coalition was still to be the alliance of the Tariff Reform forces and those of Lloyd George, still an unknown quantity as far as Parliament was concerned. With the discussion again in this context, Lloyd George was willing to go much further than in the fall towards settling the Ulster problem; that is, further than the mere five-year reprieve. While Asquith was vainly offering a complicated solution by plebiscite for the Ulster question, he took up what had become the favored scheme of Tariff Reformers: "Federalism," a method of general imperial devolution warmly expounded by F. S. Oliver in the *Round Table* and for many years the cherished doctrine of the Tariff Reform League.

By February of 1914, preliminary agreement on the federal formula had apparently been approached in private conversations between Lloyd George, Churchill, Garvin, Astor, and Oliver. (Garvin and Lloyd George had just made up their brief quarrel, as we shall see). The chancellor insisted that an advance commitment must be made by the Opposition not only to endorse the federal plan if it were introduced by the government but also "to help the Cabinet carry it through" against what might be a sizable defection in the Liberal rank and file. This agreed, they would then "practically scrap" the present bill in favor of an agreed-upon federal solution. An "important section of the Cabinet," he continued, was prepared to face the revolt on the Liberal side if the Unionists, whose leader differed with Chamberlain over federalism, could mount the

---

[76] See also Lloyd George's account of his interview with Dillon at 11 Downing Street (18 Nov. 1913), in *L.G.P.*, C/20/2/4.

[77] Cited in Lewis Broad, *Winston Churchill* (London, 1931), p. 161; a proposal made through Churchill, dated only "late in 1913," most probably late in December.

The Prewar Crisis

necessary support from theirs.[78] Lloyd George's previous claim about Grey and Haldane resigning cannot be supported, though it probably suggests an only slightly exaggerated reading by him of the extent of Liberal disaffection from the Nationalists.

The chances of this, the fourth plan for a political combination, rested upon the ability of the Tariff Reformers to bring over the weight of the party leader to the venture. This was felt to be a prerequisite, first, because without him there was no assurance that the "National Coalition" would ever command a sufficient majority to control the House and, equally important, because their rather inconstant admiration for Lloyd George and his scheme never went far enough to warrant joining him in a condition of one-sided dependency. But perhaps the most critical factor of all regarding the success or failure of the coalition plan was in the timing. A parliamentary recess, the scheduled reading of a controversial bill, the cycles of labor unrest, as well as developments abroad had all affected its fortunes on previous occasions. Thus, the test of the Tariff Reformers' strength over a harassed party leader was averted in March 1914 by the calamitous decision of the army at the Curragh to defy whatever decision the government in London might hand down regarding a settlement for Ireland.

In as short a time as the news passed over St. George's Channel, the would-be partners in the coalition were back at the head of their respective factions, none the less happily equipped with righteous threats and militant slogans. His rising hopes for a "national settlement" blasted, and having just completed drafting plans for a fratricidal war in Ireland, Churchill was found by a friend in a gloomy House of Commons singing tunelessly to himself in the lavatory behind the Speaker's chair. It was his habit, he said, "to confront difficult situations with an outward serenity of aspect."[79]

Amid the memos, the letters, the sporadic bits of conversation and the journalistic rhetoric through which the National Coalition plan had emerged and receded four times in as many years before the outbreak of war, the continuing impulse behind its persistence is largely obscured. Perhaps the best clue to what it was, besides personal ambitions and animosities, that drew those like Lloyd George and Garvin repeatedly into contact is Garvin's first re-

---

[78] W. Astor to Garvin (mid-Feb. 1914), describing a talk with Lloyd George; cited in Gollin, *The Observer*, pp. 416-417.

[79] Diary note of Cecil Harmsworth (25 March 1914), in George Harmsworth and Reginald Pound, *Northcliffe*, p. 454.

sponse to the Insurance Bill in 1911. He spoke with conviction of the "transition from one national epoch to another," the death of laissez-faire, a "new age of national organization" in government, defense, education, production, and transport—the deliberate organization of "the economic security and the vital efficiency" of the nation. Lloyd George's great bill, Garvin sensed, inaugurated a profound revolution which reached both government and people, carrying both into a pattern of conduct that belonged to the future.[80]

The personal magnetism felt between Garvin, Lloyd George, Smith, Churchill, and the rest is unmistakable. Between the first two it had become particularly strong since 1910. The coolness which ensued from the *Observer*'s treatment of the Marconi affair was keenly felt by both and, as we saw, had some influence on the course of the Irish negotiations in the previous fall. Like Smith, the editor came to regret the severity of the assault on Lloyd George and took the initiative in patching up the friendship in a warm and admiring letter on the last day of the year. Lloyd George's immediate response contained equal warmth and a frankness he rarely allowed himself. Referring to the scandal, he wrote,

> I have always been utterly indifferent to attacks made upon me by my enemies and I have never taken the slightest notice of them except when I have thought it suited my purpose to do so. I can assure you this is not a mere affectation of unconcern on my part—it represents my real feelings. But I am extremely sensitive to all criticisms emanating from my friends, and I felt hurt when I saw you joining—and joining with apparent gusto—in the dart slinging. I thought we were friends. F. E. behaved with a personal loyalty that has given me a higher conception altogether of his character.[81]

There is a little of the schoolboy on both sides in the emotional play of these men—Lloyd George, resentful, wishing to induce a sure consciousness of guilt, but even more anxious to restore the lost friendship.

> ... I realize fully your attitude. You honestly considered my personality a distinct peril to the realisation of ideals to which you are attached. In forming that opinion I think you were wrong. I can see no man on your side who is more likely or indeed as likely to

[80] Gollin, *The Observer*, p. 327.
[81] Lloyd George to Garvin (31 Dec. 1913), *L.G.P.*, C/4/13/1.

advance those great aims as I am. But that is immaterial—you entertained that fear and you acted accordingly. That is now over. Whatever fault I have committed I have paid fourfold the penalty of. I have no bitterness in my mind as a result of it. I blame no one except myself and I can now heartily reciprocate your good wishes for the New Year without a trace of ill will or resentment. I wish the New Year would ensure a cooperation for common ends. Essentially yours are mine and mine are yours. Our quarrel is about methods and it is the fault of your leaders that those are not identical. *You know the story of their great refusal.*[82]

Garvin's answer to Lloyd George's "manly and generous response," as he put it, launched their revived friendship in the coming critical year with the assurance that he was "not a less deep friend" than Smith. He also alluded to their adventure of 1910 which had become a kind of bond between them like a onetime mutual sweetheart who still eluded them both: ". . . if parties had come together three years ago when you attempted the larger settlement with the nerve and insight of genius, neither progress nor patriotism would have lost anything by companionship between you and me. Was there not, is there not, some touch of incommunicable understanding between two Celts? You are Merlin and follow the gleam. You must pursue it again, though it seemed quenched altogether for a time and is faint enough now."[83]

Youth, class, religion, and temperament all inclined Garvin and, to a less ardent degree, his imperialist circle toward identification with the fiery Welshman, who like most of them had inherited neither a political career nor a reverence for historic institutions and principles. The inspired rhetoric of a "new age" of organization and efficiency was equally a challenge to the long-ensconced men of the establishment and to their antiquated shibboleths, for there remained as much unconscious attachment to the spirit of the Manchester School among the patricians of one party as of the other. Both partners in the coalition adorned their cause with the language of the new age and drew heavily upon the catalogue of organization and efficiency, social reform and national revival, prepared over a decade by the Social-Imperialists. This ideology was their primary means not only of distinguishing their policies from the old individualism lingering in both parties, but also of telling friend from foe over the spectrum of political factions.

[82] Ibid.
[83] Garvin to Lloyd George (1 Jan. 1914), *L.G.P.*, C/4/13/2.

Thus the coalition plan, by breaking down the traditional hold of parliamentary discipline and enabling a new coalescence to form more strictly on the basis of ideology, was the natural product and a genuine application of the Social-Imperialist doctrine. Eclectically expounded over the previous decade by Roseberites, Fabians, Coefficients, and protectionists, that doctrine had always contained a strong antiparliamentary undertone, clothed transparently in constant abuse of the "party system" in a plentiful literature. Not only did the coalitionists of 1910 to 1914 share that distaste but they also benefited greatly from the continued outpouring of Social-Imperialist literature during the period.

In a *Daily Mail* "Enquiry," published under the title "Labour Unrest: What the Worker Wants" (1912), Wells, William Ashley, Hugh Cecil, Philip Snowden, George Barnes, and Normal Angell (among others) presented a broad sweep of opinion on social and political problems which testifies, if not to the success of Social-Imperialist propaganda, at least to the widespread sympathy for its case against "the System." Wells, a former Coefficient and a favorite of Lloyd George, characterized Parliament as the "House of Lawyers" indifferent to any constructive impulse and blind to great and urgent social needs.

> Now [wrote Wells] for that great multitude of prosperous people who find themselves at once deeply concerned in our present social and economic crisis, and either helplessly entangled in party organisation or helplessly outside politics, the elimination and cure of this disease of statecraft, the professional politician, has become a very urgent matter. To destroy him, to get him back to his law courts and keep him there, it is necessary to destroy the machinery of the party system that sustains him....[84]

A "National Conference" and a "National Plan of Social Reconstruction ... to take 'politics' out of national life" was the solution recommended by Wells in the year of Lloyd George's third coalition proposal.

Norman Angell, who had had no personal association with the various Social-Imperialist groups, thought Wells' suggestion sound but inadequate to solve the problem:

---

[84] Norman Angell, Introduction, *What the Worker Wants: a Daily Mail Enquiry* (London, 1912), p. 14.

There is a revolution [he argued] because of a 'New Fact' . . . The failure of parliamentary government as we know it. . . .

This is the biggest fact in the whole situation. It marks probably a turning point in the political structure of European society. . . .

Parliamentary government . . . is breaking down probably because it has played its role; its function has become feeble because it is no longer an urgent one in the social organism . . . (i.e.) to balance the political power of the privileged class. . . .

The enormously complex problems of today have rendered the voter 'incompetent'—election is now a device perfectly well-fitted to a village green in choosing the village elders, but a rank absurdity when applied to a complex society like ours.[85]

The other contributors wrote largely in the same vein: G. Drage, a Poor Law administrator, asked ". . . how can we reconcile democracy and liberty with authority and organisation in the social and industrial sphere?" The Labour men, Barnes and Snowden, spoke of "lawyer-made entanglements" as the cause of the social chaos and "disciplined democracy" as its cure.[86] The consensus of the enquiry commissioned by Northcliffe, deliberately to include the widest political range, was that the present system could not sustain its burden. The *Daily Mail* repeated the message to its readers for most of the year 1912, needless to say, with the added support of the *Observer* and numerous other imperialist, Fabian, protectionist, and general periodicals.[87]

The Fabians, too, believed that the anarchy of the period raised questions not merely as to the efficacy of a particular policy or party but concerning "the validity of democratic government." Their tracts as well repeated the complaint of the "barrenness of the Parliamentary machine."[88] The Fabians had helped to author a good part of Tariff Reform doctrine in the past and their influ-

[85] Ibid., pp. 75-78.

[86] George N. Barnes, "The Disillusioned Working Man," *What the Worker Wants*, p. 36.

[87] The articles in the series began in the *Daily Mail* of 13 May 1912, continuing into September before being published together. The other contributors were Sidney Low, H. M. Hyndman, Hugh Cecil, Hamilton Fyfe, John Galsworthy, Seebohm Rowntree, W. Runciman, and A. Conan Doyle.

[88] B. Webb, "Diary" (8 Dec. 1913); C. Sharp, "The Case of the Referendum," *Fabian Tract* no. 155 (April 1911), p. 6; S. Webb, "The Necessary Basis of Society," *Fabian Tract* no. 159 (July 1911), p. 6.

ence was still considerable in that section of the Unionist Party represented by such organizations as the Tariff Reform League and the U.S.R.C. Not only their distaste for the "crude democracy," with which a number of the young Unionists became acquainted in the Coefficients Club, but their jargon of "Efficiency–Organization–Expertise" had been incorporated into the vocabulary of Tariff Reform—most noticeably in the *Observer* and the pamphlets of Smith's U.S.R.C.[89]

Considering the peculiar reverence in which Milner was held by nearly all the leaders of the Tariff Reform movement, perhaps his was the strongest influence in focusing their attitudes on the social and political crisis, and thus also on the coalition, shifting the eclectic body of ideas about "efficiency" from a generalized social analysis to a political doctrine. At the height of the crisis in 1913, in the preface to a well-known collection of his speeches (*The Nation and the Empire*), he wrote:

> The truth is . . . that there is no object of supreme national importance at the present time which can be attained by the method of party conflict. Imperial Union certainly cannot be, but no more can a sound system of National Defence, or the solution of the Irish problem, or the repair of the mutilated constitution. . . . And if this is the case in the purely political field, it is surely no less true of the economic and social problems, of which all thoughtful men recognise the urgency. In none of these directions is there much hope from the competition of rival bands of politicians in devising superficially attractive panaceas. . . .
>
> But on the whole I am inclined to think that there is a sufficiently widespread and increasing weariness of the partisan treatment of every great national question to give the exponents of a different method a chance.[90]

When Milner wrote, there was already in existence a wide consensus among the Social-Imperialists as to the faults of the system and on a general policy for the treatment of the main social and

---

[89] The U.S.R.C. reports and pamphlets were widely reprinted in the Unionist press, especially by the *National Review*, the *19th Century and After*, and the *Times*, from 1912 to 1914. They were published in collected form under the titles *Industrial Unrest* (1914) and *Unionist Policy and Other Essays* (1913); cf. in the latter, Smith's "State Toryism and Social Reform," pp. 20-46.

[90] Lord Alfred Milner, *The Nation and the Empire* (London, 1913), p. 2.

economic problems. But until Lloyd George's coalition plan, that "different method" to which Milner alluded had been lacking. Moreover, since Rosebery, Social-Imperialism had always been premised on the existence of a crisis—an imminent threat either to the nation, to the empire, to the economy, or to social order. Yet its major tenets had not been conceived as temporary expedients or mere emergency measures. They had the permanence of ideological truth. So were the various coalition plans explained as an extraordinary but necessary measure to meet the present crisis. But at no time was a term put to their efficacy by the exponents. For in addition to the four attempted coalitions before the war, there were to be three wartime attempts and at least two more after the peace, the last in 1922. And the response evoked from the various political factions on the first occasion presaged to a remarkable degree the attitude they were to take up twelve years later.

IX

The Rise and Fall of the First Coalition

The only successful effort to implement the Lloyd George plan came after two years of war, six years from the conception of the plan, with the formation of the National Coalition government in December of 1916. It was constructed in three progressive stages through a complicated process of Cabinet reconstructions, resignations, press campaigns, and intrigues. Yet it has been suggested by one who played an important part in the process, that amid the shifting policies and conflicting personalities of the war the "idea of Coalition" provided the clue to much that otherwise would be mysterious or even incomprehensible.[1]

The first move toward a wartime coalition was made by Churchill on the last day of July 1914, five days before the formal declaration of war. Churchill informed Smith and Bonar Law in a private meeting at the home of Sir Edward Goulding that the Cabinet was facing a crisis over the question of intervention. There was no real threat to the government's majority posed by the defections of those who opposed the mobilization orders, yet they would render the government dependent again upon the Nationalists and Labour for the duration, a situation dreaded as much by the Opposition as by the Cabinet. Churchill's proposal, warmly endorsed by Smith, was apparently to arrange the coalition by the simple expedient of filling the Cabinet posts expected to be vacated by the pacifists with friendly Unionists, with perhaps some reshuffling of offices.[2]

---

[1] Lord Beaverbrook, *Politicians and the War* (London, 1928), p. 19.

[2] Burns, Beauchamp, and Morley resigned over the mobilization order and Simon, originally doing the same, withdrew his resignation temporarily, after Crewe (2 Aug.) persuaded the Cabinet to postpone a declaration. S. W. Churchill, *The World Crisis*, 2 vols. (London, 1923-1931), I, 174; Beaverbrook, *Politicians*, pp. 17-23.

Smith, Beaverbrook suggests, could have obtained "plenty of support" for the step to create a two-party war government free of dependence on the factions had he pursued it. Bonar Law, however, though he had no abstract objection to the idea—indeed, he had sought it once before and was to do the same again—declined to go any further now than to offer the party's support for any decision the government might make in the event of a violation of Belgian neutrality.[3] This would of course give the interventionists in the Cabinet a freer hand over both the pacifists and the Irish-Labour minority in case a declaration of war became necessary. But it also reserved the right of the Opposition to challenge the government elsewhere, especially on the Home Rule and Welsh Disestablishment Bills which were due to be read into the statute book without amendment in August. Rejection was Bonar Law's only choice, considering the intensity of feeling on the part of Carson and most of the Back Benchers. Thus, Ireland again seemed to bar the path to a coalition—it was to remain one of the decisive stumbling blocks to a full coalition until the crisis of 1916.[4]

Although Lloyd George played no direct part in the short-lived discussions of July and August, his attitude was of central concern to the participants. It must be assumed that he was informed by Churchill, but he remained silent on the question of coalition as he had the previous fall. Indeed, there was some fear for a time that his erstwhile pacifist convictions would revive and incline him to lead the movement against intervention, in which case the Liberal Cabinet could not have gone to war without the active support of the Bonar Law–Lansdowne Conservatives. The attack in Belgium, it was thought, removed whatever doubt may have been in his mind. Though it is tempting to imagine the difference his defection must have made in the course of the war, there could have been little cause for this fear, for as we have already seen, the youthful pro-Boer and critic of the Big Navy had shed the weightier part of his pacifism some years earlier—sufficiently at least to have thought of "rousing . . . the English national spirit for a war about the Balkans" in 1912.

It was reasonable to assume, on the basis of his behavior over the past few years, that Lloyd George would come out forcefully

---

[3] Churchill, *World Crisis*, I, 174.

[4] Beaverbrook, *Politicians*, p. 52. The Government of Ireland Bill was finally passed into law, with postponed enforcement, on 15 September. The Unionists walked out of the House in a body in protest.

behind intervention; it would have surprised everyone, not least of all himself, to find him in the company of those who held out against the Cabinet decision to intervene—Morley, Burns, Simon —who had been his bitterest critics of late. His friends certainly did not expect it. Garvin wrote expectantly to him immediately after the critical Cabinet meeting of Sunday, 3 August: "This crisis so *sweeps* the old things aside that all is possible. . . ." He ended imploring melodramatically, "Oh Agadir, Agadir, and your courage then!"[5]

Lloyd George's reasons for standing aloof from Churchill's proposal were most likely similar to Bonar Law's—simply that the plan could not succeed given the state of sentiment in both parties concerning Ireland. It is impossible to tell whether his silence during the Cabinet crisis of August and for the first month of the war was spent more in soul-searching or merely in awaiting a clearer picture to develop from the confusion (his personal correspondence is scanty for these weeks and his later recollections are simply not trustworthy). By early September he had at least made his mind up, as he wrote to Chamberlain, that ". . . this war is a righteous war."[6] There is no doubt about the genuineness of this conviction and when combined with the proper opportunity it would become as irresistible as the righteous simplicity of Calvin. He made his first belligerent speech of the war a few days later (15 September), the day on which the Government of Ireland Bill was read into law, beating the drum already for sterner measures, an end of peacetime partisanship, and greater efficiency in the hour of trial.[7] The spirit and logic of the coalition plan was now unchallengeable, the peril now visible to all.

The inevitable chaos of the first few months of war did serious damage to a government largely unprepared and, in large part disinclined, to meet the awesome demands of mobilizing and reorganizing the resources of a nation at war. Despite the self-imposed restraint of the political press, private criticism of the Asquith government's conduct of the war appeared immediately and mounted rapidly, concentrating upon the apparent determination of the Cabinet Free Traders to hold the line as much as possible on a free economy and peacetime liberties. "Democracy," wrote F. S. Oliver in December, "is not going to win this war or any other—if we win

[5] Garvin to Lloyd George ("Sunday," August 1914), *L.G.P.*, C/4/13/3.
[6] Lloyd George to Chamberlain (2 Sept. 1914), *L.G.P.*, C/3/14/3.
[7] Lloyd George, speech at Queen's Hall (15 Sept. 1914).

it will be because the spirit of the small remnant who hate and despise democracy and all its works will save the country in spite of its democratic government. . . . It is democracy which has nearly betrayed France. . . . Democracy has already in five month's war proved its utter incapacity both to prepare for war and to conduct war."[8]

A majority of the Free Traders in the Liberal Cabinet (though not the Free Traders alone) had opposed entry into the war before the violation of Belgian neutrality. Yet, even after accepting the necessity to intervene, they clung immovably and vocally to the doctrine of laissez-faire. Almost with gaiety, the Tariff Reform Unionists recognized early that the war would put the sternest possible test to the contemptible dogma and its adherents in both parties. As open criticism of the government emerged, the argument was put in terms polished for the purpose in the years of opposition: Organization, Efficiency, Discipline, National Reconstruction —the well-learned catechism of Social-Imperialism. Along with it, as before, came the call for a coalition in the first two months of 1915. In a move again initiated by Churchill, Bonar Law and Lansdowne were invited to a meeting of the War Council to discuss a suggestion to promise Constantinople, should it be captured, to Russia as a means of strengthening the alliance. Such a binding pledge could not well be made by a party that might be out of office at any time. Expecting the Tories to demand access to full information before assuming responsibility, Churchill thought it would not be difficult to "draw them on one step further—namely, that they should share power if they were asked to share responsibility."[9]

Since his memorable conversation with the chancellor on the golf course, Churchill had pressed for the coalition at every opportunity without success. In every case initiated by him, Lloyd George had remained aloof, probably realizing that from the Tory point of view no emissary could be more ill-chosen for the task than the traitor who had crossed the floor over Chamberlain's tariff speech. Suspicious of Churchill and coolly received by Asquith at the meeting, the Unionists left without any commitment.[10]

A more successful initiative was taken by Lloyd George himself a few weeks later in discussions with Smith and the Unionist leader over a plan to bring the government into the purchase and control

---

[8] F. S. Oliver to Milner (26 Dec. 1914), *M.P.*, Letters–1914.
[9] Beaverbrook, *Politicians*, p. 53.
[10] Ibid., p. 54.

of liquor in order to promote war efficiency ("Drink" had a way of turning up in most of the Welshman's package agreements—it had also been one of the main headings of the 1910 plan). Although his hopes of drawing them into the drafting of a Liquor Bill were frustrated by a premature press leak, his frank consultation on an issue of national importance had successfully broken through the lingering cloud left by the last reading of the Home Rule Bill. Moreover, he had reopened a personal channel of communication with the Opposition in time to coincide with his first great accomplishment of the war, the Treasury Agreement with Labour, and with the beginning of open attacks on Asquith in the press leading up to the disastrous shell scandal of May. After months of relative quiescence, the chancellor had entered his first burst of wartime activities which, by mixed calculation and instinct, led to the Ministry of Munitions and eventually raised him above Asquith as the obvious choice for war leader.[11]

The crisis which produced the first coalition of May 1915 arose out of the concurrence of three almost simultaneous incidents. The first was the introduction on 13 May of a motion against the government on the shell shortage put down by the Unionist Business Committee, a rebellious group of Tories of which Carson and Hewins were members (they had let it be known already that they favored replacing Asquith with Lloyd George).[12] It was followed the next day by a further revelation in the *Times*, inspired by Sir John French, of the government's deficiency in the supply of shells. On the same day, Admiral Lord Fisher resigned as First Sea Lord in protest of Churchill's Dardenelles campaign.[13]

The timing of the three, any one of which might have brought Asquith down, is suggestive of some degree of coordination, though no firm evidence of it has been put forward in the numerous descriptions of this most confused crisis of the war. Nevertheless, all three militated towards the formation of the coalition. The Unionist Business Committee's motion was accompanied by a call for a "Coalition Cabinet." Lloyd George, with Balfour and Bonar Law,

[11] Ibid., pp. 65-68. In the Treasury Agreement Lloyd George promised profit controls and a union voice in directing "dilution"—the mixing of women and unskilled workers into union shops—to head off a brewing crisis caused by voluntary enlistment of workers.
[12] Gollin, *Proconsul in Politics*, p. 260.
[13] "Need for Shells: British Attack Checked: Limited Supply the Cause," *Times*, 14 May 1913; Lloyd George, *War Memoirs*, I, 119-120. On the U.B.C. motion, see Hewins, *Apologia*, II, 21.

had been notified in advance of the *Times*'s article. But, possibly without design, they neglected to warn either the Cabinet or any members of the War Council which was to meet on the 14th, for the first time since mid-April. None of them could have been unaware of the likelihood that the attacks would force a crisis in the government, a situation all publicly professed a desire to avoid. Yet, the coalition discussions had been reopened not two weeks before. Moreover, Garvin, the assiduous servant of the plan, had suddenly revived the coalition campaign in the *Observer* the Sunday just before the crisis, calling for "A Government of Public Safety" with a Cabinet drawn from both parties.[14]

The actual reconstruction of the government ensued quickly after threats of resignation from Lloyd George and of an open debate in the House from Bonar Law. The result was not the full coalition of parties envisioned in the Lloyd George plan, but a "Front Bench Coalition," sufficient only to stifle criticism from the back benches of either side—a short rather than long step towards the complete emasculation of Parliament which followed later. With Bonar Law at the Admiralty, replacing Churchill, Carson as Attorney General and Lansdowne as Minister Without Portfolio, a token observance of national unity was made and an election averted. Lloyd George, however, had won his immediate objective, possibly his primary purpose in encouraging the crisis: That a new Ministry of Munitions under himself would supersede the authority of Kitchener and the War Council in domestic wartime controls. Apart from the new ministry, the arrangement was widely looked upon as a fragile and temporary affair, likely to be replaced in due course by a solider instrument.[15]

Northcliffe's *Daily Mail*, which had ardently supported the coalition plan when first announced with headlines of "Good-bye to Party," now decried the failure to construct a truly "National Government," giving the rickety solution now in force six months' expectancy of life.[16] Amery also expected the half-measure accomplished so far to break under renewed crises. "The Real Crisis," he

[14] Lloyd George, *War Memoirs*, I, 119, 138; *Observer*, 9 May 1915; House of Commons, 13 May 1915.

[15] Some, like Lord Newton, held their civilian positions open when asked to serve in the new government, expecting soon again to be idle. Cf. Newton to Milner (8 June 1915), *M.P.*, Private Letters–1915; Churchill, *World Crisis*, I, 365.

[16] *Daily Mail*, 18, 19, 22, 24 May 1915.

wrote to Milner, "when you'll be wanted hasn't come yet and will not come until the Autumn or Winter. . . . It may come through military failure. . . ." That prospect Amery anticipated with a curious equanimity for such a vocal patriot, revealing an only slightly submerged aspect of the Social-Imperialist's view of the war.

> . . . there is nothing [he explained to Milner] inherently impossible in the German Army's being in Paris, Milan and Warsaw by the end of the year. And I am not sure it wouldn't be the best thing for us. We want to have our backs to the wall and have such thwacks as will make us see the world clearly as it is. . . . An easy victory for the Allies now might be a disaster for us, the triumph of Blather enthroned, a false version of all this great event—dominant and fatally influencing all our future policy, till some real day of reckoning comes.
>
> But even if we do have this easy victory then all the more need for a crisis and complete change of Government. . . . All this harping on Prussian militarism as something that must be rooted out . . . is wholly mischievous. It all tends to drag us into a false little England position . . . we shall have to fight the people who will be prepared to sell every Imperial gain the war may have brought us in order to secure what they think the proper frontier between certain foreign nations in Europe, or who after the peace will be hypnotised for years by the emotions and claptrap of the war
>
> . . . One way or another, whether the crisis comes over the sudden recognition that the war is not being waged as it should be, or over a heated discussion of the possible terms of peace, or after peace has been made, I expect it will come within the next year.[17]

Amery's first estimate of the new coalition was unfavorable mainly because it gave him the impression, as it did to many of the back benchers, that the party was merely propping up the discredited Liberal government without a true share of power. It even hinted mildly to some of a feeble conspiracy of those "decorous men" of the old establishment. For one so often given to political fantasies, in his prognosis of wartime politics Amery was ahead of his colleagues and more farsighted than Lloyd George. Within the coming year it would in fact become impossible to separate the dispute over how the war was to be waged and the long-range ideological conflict over the way in which the peacetime society was to

---

[17] Amery to Milner (25 May 1915), *M.P.*, Private Letters–1915.

The First Coalition

be ordered. From this perspective, Amery was quite right, then, in looking upon the coalition of May 1915 as a futile arrangement.

Garvin, often oversanguine, saw greater possibilities in the new alignment. Attempting to stifle possible hostility to the new regime, he insisted darkly that the choice was either "Coalition—Chaos—or Dictatorship." The state would, he said, "eliminate without compunction every influence whatever which in its effect, no matter its intention, weakens and discredits the nation." Inadvertently unveiling the stern intolerance which he had always attached to the coalition formula, Garvin decreed editorially that "The authority of the Coalition was of a very different species from that of any predecessor . . . and those who try to put spokes in its wheels come under a very different category from those of the ordinary political game." To deny its total power and authority would be to "take up the moral ground of rebellion and anarchy."[18] This, he said, was the "Constructive Revolution" growing out of a long-term effort:

> Ever since the Constitutional Conference of 1910 it has been seen —clear to some thinkers on both sides who never quite lost touch with each other . . . that in certain emergencies of the future Coalition would be the only constitutional safeguard left to the country.
> . . . All this created, even before the war, in a quiet, gradual and very British manner, a certain atmosphere of precaution. . . . When the war broke out the question of whether a *National Ministry* should be formed was raised in circumstances that cannot yet be related. If certain Ministerial resignations had then occurred a Coalition Cabinet would have been formed in the first week of last August. We were amongst those who wanted it at the time.[19]

With his usual hyperbole, Garvin was of course referring to the Cabinet crisis in which Burns, Morley, Beauchamp and Simon had resigned. As we have seen, however, Chamberlain and Lloyd George had not in fact come as close to creating the coalition Cabinet as Garvin wished to imply—although he was correct in saying that the thought was undoubtedly present and the possibility existed.

Garvin was soon disenchanted of his hope that the work of years had been crowned in an austere and efficient national government.

[18] *Observer*, 23 May 1915.
[19] *Observer*, 6 June 1915; 23 May 1915.

But with others who shared the memory of 1910 Lloyd George's Ministry of Munitions salvaged some of the hope for an end of the reigning "voluntarism"—the epithet usually applied to any of the government's measures at all which were thought to be insufficiently stern. Garvin frankly regarded Lloyd George's getting the Ministry of Munitions as the "chief object" of the new coalition. The newly created post was, in his words, "the head of the table."[20] Amery agreed. With effective independence from Cabinet and parliamentary control (despite the titular claims of the War Office), Lloyd George industriously set about transforming the British economy and bringing the state into control of the work, the welfare, and even the morals of the nation on a level of intimacy thought fantastic by all but a few, including Wells and the Fabians, before the war.[21]

In his one-year tenure, Lloyd George built a nationwide organization around his ministry which eventually employed a staff of more than 65,000, directly ordered the labor of 3 million workers and dispensed resources totaling more than £2,000 million from ministry funds—more than twelve times the famous "Red Budget" of 1909. "From first to last a business man organisation," in his own words, the Ministry of Munitions entered the fields of profit and wage fixing, plant planning and retooling, research and quality control, movement of labor, training and employment of women, and a host of other areas of regulation and planning, achieving the effect if not the legality of general industrial conscription. Here, in a single independent ministry, was a lion's share of the "National Reconstruction" of the coalition plan, of the Fabian's "National Minimum" and the "Organisation of the Labour Market" spelled out by Masterman and Beveridge to the chancellor of 1909. It was with sound foresight, then, that Garvin thought the creation of the Ministry of Munitions alone was sufficient, if temporary, justification for a faulty National Coalition.[22]

Garvin had by now become Merlin's familiar—an avid volunteer rather than an unwilling victim of the master's spell. All his

---

[20] Garvin to Lloyd George (26 May 1915), *L.G.P.*, D/16/16/1.

[21] Amery to Milner (2 June 1915), *M.P.*, Private Letters–1915. The Cabinet set up a committee to supervise the Ministry of Munitions but it met only once and then dispersed. "Ministry of Munitions Memo" (June 1915), *Bev. P.*, M672, no. 6.

[22] S. J. Hurwitz, *State Intervention in Great Britain*, pp. 34, 109. A. J. P. Taylor, *English History, 1914-45* (Oxford, 1965), p. 34.

efforts were to be bent towards building the Ministry of Munitions into a springboard for the creation of a "real National Ministry" with Lloyd George at its head and Austen Chamberlain at the Treasury. With the new coalition only a month old he was already impatient for the "great stroke." Lloyd George was in a circumspect mood and characteristically throwing all his great energy into the organization and rapid expansion of his new post; it is easy to imagine him a little distracted at this point by Garvin's well-intentioned antics on the sidelines. This was the first work worthy of his powers to come to his hand in the past three years and fully occupied him for the time being. Garvin persisted: "After all you are practically my leader now," he wrote in July. "I can't help wishing that Winston were your right hand man as in the great Conference days of 1910 and that you had him (with all that brain and stomach and physical vigour) in something better than a sinecure. Likewise I wish you had Haldane back in the Min. of Science, and that Milner, a big statesman with all his crochets, were in the War Council. . . ."[23] Garvin's audacity may well have been the wiser judgment in the summer of 1915 than Lloyd George's mere industriousness—the general outline of his scenario for the National Ministry was not too far off from what developed only after another unhappy and costly year or more of the half-breed first coalition.

The life of the 1915 coalition, despite the almost universal complaints about its makeup, lasted beyond the first estimates of its critics. And from the point of view of those who favored the more radical reconstruction, it served a vital function preparatory to the final establishment of a National Coalition. In its eighteen-month duration it bore the onus of the failures of the first two years of war, inevitably a period of frustration and groping inprovisation in which any ministry would look unprepared and indecisive. Moreover, Asquith's apparently astute shunting of the leading Unionist members into the more peripheral departments largely absolved them of the worst criticism for the direction of the war. They had reversed Churchill's strategy and enjoyed a degree of power without real responsibility. Just as important, the months of the Front Bench coalition, in which the basic issues of voluntarism versus compulsion and noninterference versus state control had to be tested, allowed for a regrouping of personal alliances which could later take the offensive on the basis of principle (winning

[23] Garvin to Lloyd George (28 May, 22 June, 5 July 1915), *L.G.P.*, D/16/16/3, 5, 6.

the war) as against party. Thus achieved was the long-time goal of the coalitionists to isolate the "reactionaries" of both parties in the mind of the public as dangerously complacent old men tied to the past and obsolete doctrines. As Amery had predicted, the Prussians were likely to become their trustiest allies against the last strongholds of Victorian Liberalism.

Asquith, Beaverbrook noted in the same vein, seemed to make a particular appeal to the "older and more feudal elements in Toryism" represented by Lansdowne, Curzon, Long, and Cecil. Ironically mimicking the style of his enemies, Asquith began more and more to consult officially within the circle thus formed rather than with the increasingly estranged group clustering around his former Chancellor of the Exchequer. This became especially true in matters such as conscription upon which he could expect more harmony of principle with the Tory Right than with the ardent interventionists.[24] Such action inevitably accelerated the process of disintegrating party lines already under way and to a great extent released Lloyd George and his Tory supporters from the stigma of conspiracy. The coalition formed ostensibly to outflank potential attacks against the government from the rank and file and from outside had thereby opened the way for a far more lethal challenge from within the government itself.

In the conflict which ensued, at first privately but more overtly as the early restraints wore off, the faction led by Asquith, McKenna, Montagu, and Runciman on one side, and Lansdowne, Cecil, and (intermittently) Curzon on the other, had small chance of survival.[25] For, to the vast advantage of the insurgents, the dispute over military and industrial conscription, executive centralization, war aims, and peace terms could now be portrayed as a question of a "soft" versus an "all-out" conduct of the war. As one after another of the "all-out" men defected from it, the first coalition was fast becoming a straw man, at the mercy of its would-be successors whether or not it could command a majority in Parliament. The "Mandarins," the "Whigs," the "reactionaries," as the Asquith cir-

[24] Asquith ignored Bonar Law in consulting the Unionists on the Cabinet Committee for Compulsion, going instead to Curzon and Balfour. Cf. Beaverbrook, *Politicians*, p. 142; Asquith to Balfour (18 Sept. 1915), *A.P.*, Dep. 28.

[25] Probably the sharpest estrangement was that between Lloyd George and McKenna—the "fatal dissension" of the first coalition. The central Asquith group in the Cabinet included McKenna, Runciman, Crewe, Simon and, for a time, Montagu.

cle came increasingly to be called, were no match for the insurgents. Behind the latter there was not only a great majority of strong sentiment in the House and in the nation, but more importantly, also a formidable alliance of the best political talent, the press, and the military. The not yet coordinated assault of that alliance began to take on a recognizable shape within a few weeks after the formation of the May coalition. Its already familiar outline was dimly visible to Beatrice Webb in July:

> From all we hear Lloyd George is going the way of Chamberlain —exchanging the leadership of the Radicals for the leadership of an Imperialist Nationalist Party. He is said to be gradually discarding his old followers and accreting a circle of admiring Tories. The Temptation to become the P.M. to a go-ahead Tory-Democratic-Imperial-Federation Party will be irresistible—he, certainly, is not the man to resist it.[26]

Beatrice Webb's assessment was no doubt colored by her own disappointment, for she had toiled long in the same field and knew very well the potential vitality of that "go-ahead" Tory-Democratic weed. However, the minister's accretion of admirers was not yet sufficient to give him exclusive claim to the Imperialist-Nationalist movement. Milner, as always remembered by the Kindergarten diaspora, was regularly implored to take charge. Amery, suggesting Lloyd George, Carson, and Chamberlain as his "lieutenants," urged the Proconsul in August to assemble an "effective band of conspirators" for the inevitable blow-up. So that they may know where to turn when the moment for "getting rid of Asquith and Co. comes," a "Milner or National Policy" must be prepared on national service, munitions, finance, and the empire.[27]

Whether led by Lloyd George or Milner, the target of any new coalition movement would be much the same. Asquith's image as war leader had been irreparably damaged by the press even now, with the gleeful connivance of both old friends and old enemies. His only chance, and his party's only chance, of survival had been the short, victorious war which Amery dreaded. It is remarkable that it took the insurgents as long as it did to undermine the first coalition, considering the feeble resistance and irresolution of its leaders; it might be explained by the overabundance and mutual

---

[26] B. Webb, "Diary" (8 July 1915), *P.P.*
[27] Amery to Milner (2 Aug. 1915), *M.P.*, Private Letters–1915.

suspicion of leaders on the other side. Except for Balfour, whom Lloyd George continued to treat with deference, the marked victims of the campaign were to be the elements of that once-imagined Whiggish coalition: Asquith, McKenna, Montagu, Runciman and Long, Lansdowne, Curzon (Milner would include Balfour)—"an extraordinary combination of fanatical Cobdenism and dunderheaded Toryism."[28] Here were Lloyd George's "backwoodsmen and glorified grocers" now penned up finally between the waiting axmen.

With the same ultimate object in mind, Milner and Lloyd George employed means that differed primarily because the former was outside and the latter a member of the government. Perhaps pursuing the course suggested by Amery in August, Milner entered into a lengthy effort to organize an "Imperial-Socialist" movement in the country out of an alliance of his own circle and the militant patriotic elements of the Labour and Socialist movements. By December of 1915 a planning "directorate" was established of Milner, Amery, and representatives from the *Clarion*, the National Service League, and the Colonial Institute, many of them familiar faces in the Compatriots Clubs, the Tariff Reform League and the other spin-off imperial organizations in the country.[29] A merger of the groups was discussed but later discarded. Instead, under the guidance of Victor Fisher, one of the wayward progeny of Hyndman's British Socialist Party discovered by Milner in 1915, two new organizations were chartered: the Socialist National Defence Committee, for the electoral support of parliamentary candidates; and the British Workers National League.[30] The purpose of the league was more ambitious than the electoral committee. Its apparent de-

[28] Milner to Philip Gell (20 Aug. 1915); Selbourne to Milner (30 Oct. 1915), *M.P., Private Letters–1915*.

[29] Alex M. Thompson of the *Clarion*, MacIlwaine and G. B. Tydd of the National Service League. F. S. Oliver to Milner (10 Aug. 1915); Thompson to Milner (5 Dec. 1915); Tydd to Milner (5 Dec. 1915); Milner to Tydd (6 Dec. 1915), *M.P., Private Letters–1915*.

[30] P. A. Lockwood, "Milner's Entry into the War Cabinet: Dec. 1916," *Historical Journal*, VII, 1 (1964), 121; Chushichi Tsuzuki, *H. M. Hyndman and British Socialism* (Oxford, 1961), pp. 225-232; C. Turnour to Milner (22 Sept. 1915), *M.P., Private Letters—1915*.

sign was to be the forerunner of a new "National Party" with a wide base among the patriotic working classes (that elusive butterfly of the imperialists) and a platform of "Imperialism and Social Reform." Its purpose, Milner professed, was to "knock out the Independent Labour Party" in an election to be forced by the House of Lords "sometime after next August" (1916). An Imperial Fund was created to finance the work of the league with Waldorf Astor, one of Garvin's employers, the primary contributor.[31]

It is easy to take Milner lightly, a man who held to the trail of a few childishly simple ideas with almost comic single-mindedness. But it is a mistake to do so in this critical year of the war. To speak of "knocking out" the I.L.P. in an election "forced" by the House of Lords seems merely another of his cloudy fantasies, completely out of touch as always with the realities and tolerances of English politics. But the war opened paths which could not be traveled in peacetime and broke down conventions which even as late as 1914 could still end careers if too grievously violated. Milner knew best what the "System" could do to an individual and was the natural focus of all those who harbored grievances against it. As we shall see, the war dramatically increased their numbers and their intensity, some of them highly placed and willing to use Milner as a battering ram against the shaky walls of the party system.

By the spring of 1916 the British Workers National League and its committee were prepared and sufficiently financed to begin their work. The beginning was more encouraging than any but the Proconsul seriously expected; in the seat (Tydvil Boroughs) vacated by Keir Hardie's death in September, an independent miner put up by the committee contested, in violation of the political truce, and won over an I.L.P. candidate. Milner also succeeded very quickly in enlisting in the executive of the league an impressive list of influential names. Working with the founding members by April were Carson, Oliver, Robinson of the *Times*, Leo Maxse, and H. G. Wells, as well as a group of fifteen Labour M.P.'s, including Will Crooks and John Hodge who remained the most active Labour

[31] "Memo" (12 March 1916); Milner to Lady Roberts (28 Feb. 1916), *M.P.*, Private Letters–1916; cited in Lockwood, "Milner's Entry," p. 123. Arrangements were made with Astor in January to open the "Imperial Fund" account in the names of Amery and Milner at the latter's bank. Fisher was contracted for three years of "full-time" service—salary £660; £1000 annual expenses. Cf. Astor to Milner (2 Jan., 12 Jan.); Milner to Astor (12 Jan. 1916), *M.P.*, Great War–1916.

M.P. in Milner's camp. Shortly afterwards, these were joined by Havelock Wilson and Leo Chiozza Money and a further accretion of Labour men, totaling about thirty by the end of the summer. Its manifesto of March, published in the *Clarion*, declared the goal to be the "national control of vital industries under the joint management of administrative and manual workers in the interests of the whole Nation." Public ownership, as well as controls, must in the case of "certain vital industries" be necessary in order for the state to guarantee a "universal living wage." All this would naturally necessitate the determined maintenance of a great empire.[32]

Although the "Socialist" side of the familiar program was far more prominent and adventurous than it had been before the war, the manifesto contained the essence of the Social-Imperialist doctrine which Milner and others had expounded a decade before. On the political side as well, he attached his well-known *doléances* against the party system. Indeed, he was embarrassed, he said, for the resemblance his movement bore to the old system. He thought it "ironical that the only way to get rid of the Incubus (the present Government), the curse of which is due more than anything else to the Party System . . . should be the formation of a New Party." It was, however, a party aiming at nothing more than "energy and forethought" in the conduct of the war, "forethought also for the quite immediate THEREAFTER, so that the end of the war may not land us in absolute chaos."[33]

The irony of Milner as head of a popular party is sharpened when contrasted with Lloyd George's chosen method of attack on the government. On the one hand, here was the autocrat become demagogue, whose public career had been permanently darkened by a mesh of censure and intrigue; while Lloyd George, the man of the people, edged into office through a stealthy manipulation of back doors. However, what may have set out as a rivalry of the two methods in 1915 began to develop a look of purpose and coordination early in the following year. Although his personal indecision about Asquith confused his behavior in 1916, Lloyd George's celebrated deviousness at the time was largely due to the fact that he lacked the kind of organization in his own party necessary for a

---

[32] (3 April, 5 June 1916), *M.P.*, Diary; *British Citizen and Empire Worker* (B.W.N.L. paper), 25 Aug. 1916; Lockwood, "Milner's Entry," p. 124. The league paper, above, published from August 1916 to the breakup of the league in 1921. For the manifesto, cf. the *Clarion*, 17 March 1916.

[33] "Memo" (12 March 1916), *M.P.*, Private Letters–1916.

frontal attack. A party apparatus or the kind of potential coordinated strength possessed by the B.W.N.L., with its allies, the Tariff Reform League, the National Service League, the Unionist "ginger groups" in the House, and their integrated network of personal ties, was a perfect complement to his strength in the press and the nation. Milner, on the other hand, bore a serious handicap in this regard. Like Haldane, but more justly, he bore a disfiguring taint of Prussianism in the eyes of some and, indeed, he had never achieved the full trust of any but his closest circle, much less a popular following.[34]

It was perhaps with this in mind that the two met (18 March), on the day after the publication of the B.W.N.L. manifesto, at Milner's house in Great College Street and again two weeks later in regard to the Tydvil Boroughs election.[35] It was not yet the start of the "Monday Night Cabals" of November from which emerged the menacing "Triumvirate," but it served the purpose of bringing Lloyd George back into personal contact with his former school of admirers, all of them well drilled by now in his distinctive political style and preferences.[36]

There were thorny problems in the way of concerting the strengths of Lloyd George with the diverse cadres of Tory insurgents. The Minister of Munitions was not a popular man in the parliamentary Liberal Party and was losing strength among the Radicals. Moreover, some of the Unionist leaders were naturally ambivalent about his obvious appeal to their own *enragés*—it was never far from Bonar Law's mind or from Chamberlain's that, no matter how abhorrent Asquith's muddling, Lloyd George as leader might satisfy the desire for toughness and action, but otherwise was likely to prove unpredictably dangerous. He disturbed any of them who held an ordered view of the future, any who looked forward to a resumption of the old politics after the war. On the other hand, he was unmistakably becoming the most visible man in government

---

[34] The charge of "Prussianism" was repeatedly leveled at Milner by his inveterate critic, Alfred Gardiner of the *Daily News*. See *Daily News*, 29 March 1913, for example.

[35] Wrench, *Geoffrey Dawson and Our Times*, p. 123; Riddell, *War Diary* (28 Nov. 1915), 139. Riddell reports the two men as "jubilant" over the I.L.P. defeat.

[36] (19 March 1916), *M.P.*, Diary; Lockwood, "Milner's Entry," p. 125. The meeting produced only the nomination of William Hughes of Australia as colonial representative on the War Council. Hughes had been a member of the Australian chapter of the Compatriots.

and the one most likely at the moment to unify the country behind all-out war. His support in the country and in the press, everyone felt, was impressive and growing. Neither party, nor Labour, had anyone to meet this essential prerequisite; no one but Amery took Milner seriously in that role.

It seems unlikely that, as has been suggested, the Milner organization was being especially prepared from the beginning to receive Lloyd George as its strong man to topple the Asquith government.[37] Nevertheless, by the time their meetings took place in March, the government was in a state of almost continuous crisis, had been since the issue of general conscription began to loom in the previous October, and seemed to many ready to give way to a determined shove at any moment. The mere resignation of Lloyd George in these months would have had sufficient impact to do it; he was constantly prodded to take that step by Garvin, Smith, Amery, Churchill, Milner and others and came close to doing so in the spring only to be held back by the resurrected specter of rebellion in Ireland. Restless and sulking, Churchill urged him at Christmas not to miss his opportunity—"the time has come."[38] Every real or rumored crisis in the Cabinet or War Council brought invitations to meet, offers of support, urgings to bring matters to a head. Until the spring, however, none clearly laid out a mature plan of campaign or a plausible method of safely reconstructing a government under the guns of the enemy, as it were. That would take careful planning and consultation, especially on the question of personnel; although Milner was prepared, even eager, to risk a general election, most confined the question to another Front Bench reconstruction. Either method presented grave difficulties and dangers. A reconstruction around Lloyd George would reveal his main weakness if analyzed (as Edmund Talbot did for Bonar Law in October): "Lloyd George would head the H. of C. Tories and a *few* Radicals and nobody else. . . . [It] would mean a general election, strong and bitter opposition and labour strikes."[39] This was essentially the argument which Bonar Law maintained for most of the next year. It underestimated Lloyd George's parliamentary strength, but not by much, and had behind it the lurking suspicion (which Bonar Law shared with Balfour) of a too great affection between the Radical and those "H. of C. Tories."

[37] Lockwood, "Milner's Entry," p. 127.
[38] Winston Churchill to Lloyd George (27 Dec. 1915), *L.G.P.*, D/16/8/2.
[39] Edmund Talbot to Bonar Law (16 Oct. 1915), *B.L.P.*, 51/4/16.

The matter of labor strikes, taken as an indication of the mood in which a possible general election might be run, was particularly sensitive in the fall of 1915 when the slow maneuvers for a second coalition began. The first autumn wave of industrial disputes came on the heels of the Munitions of War Act and immediately embroiled the Minister of Munitions, whose duty it was to invoke the controversial second clause of the act which prohibited strikes for the duration. Like all such instruments, the clause was almost impossible to enforce without creating just the situation it was designed to prevent, in which official force would be needed to keep the men at work. Since the "tribunals" which were to supervise the enforcement of the act were not yet operating effectively (they never did where clause 2 was at issue), the minister was brought personally into the disputes. Appropriately, the first such case for Lloyd George brought him to Cardiff in late summer to face the miners of South Wales who had ignored his back-to-work orders. It was a novel and vulnerable situation for him which he escaped by simply giving in to the miners on almost every point.[40] The miners were quickly followed by increasingly militant strikers through the fall and early winter, at the Thorneycrofts Boilermakers and the Fairfield Shipyards on the Clyde, foreshadowing the growth of the radical shop steward wildcats during the next three years.

This was the first serious test of the underlying issue of "compulsion," the central point around which all the politics of the war would revolve hereafter, and it revealed the relative weakness of executive power in the most critical area of mobilization. The easy success of the Treasury Agreement had been illusory; the fall of 1915 removed any conceit in Lloyd George's mind that his magic would keep working men in line, that they would be awed by ministerial order or overcome by mere hortatory patriotism—those who were merely became inactive or drifted towards right-wing labor groups like the B.W.N.L. It was around this time that Lloyd George finally gave up his wilting democratic ghost. From now on he would want to face recalcitrant workers only from a position of irresistible strength. Wars had many times taken the heart out of greater democrats than he had once been.

The meeting of the Trades Union Congress at Bristol in September quickly advanced Lloyd George's education on labor, particularly about labor's attitudes regarding industrial conscription. Not

[40] (21 July 1915), *Bev. Papers*, M672, no. 6.

yet having entered the Stockholm period, the congress largely ignored the question of war aims and negotiated peace, was ambivalent on compulsory military service, but came down heavily on the general question of industrial conscription—the context in which they particularly condemned the hated "leaving certificate" of the Munitions Act. This was enough for H. A. Gwynne, whom Lloyd George had asked to report on the meeting to him, to deduce that the Trades Union Congress had been taken over by "pacifists." Asquith, who was both encouraged and disturbed by the Bristol congress, took the occasion to try to persuade Balfour (apparently he did not expect much understanding from Bonar Law) that the action of the Trades Union Congress put the whole question of compulsion to rest, hopefully for good. Quoting Shackleton, his own confidential reporter at the meeting, he argued that "either military or industrial" compulsion would encounter the practically united and vehement opposition of organized labor—"Believe me," still quoting Shackleton, "it would mean revolt, if not revolution."[41] He added that a majority of the Liberal Party, as well as the Irish Nationalists, found the "Conscription delusion" repugnant and could be persuaded to swallow their objection, "with wry faces and sore hearts," only by him.[42]

Asquith's analysis of the situation, leaving out his own rather too mighty role, was shared by many of those who wished to dislodge him over the question of compulsion, including Bonar Law and Chamberlain at the moment. Talbot's guess about the probable resistance to a Lloyd George government drew much the same picture—an alliance of Labour, Liberals, and Irish, forced towards the Left by the mixture and capable of developing a majority. It was the parent of the "Red spectre" of two years hence and the child of Garvin's "bogey" revolution of 1909-1910. The reality of that particular specter was always open to doubt, however, no matter how real it was in the minds of some of those who either feared or fostered it. The strength of such a union, if it could ever be consummated, would pose a formidable Opposition indeed to any coalition depending on Lloyd George and his "admiring Tories" in the House of Commons alone; that is, if the coalition were dependent on party and parliamentary majorities against a united Liberal-

---

[41] H. A. Gwynne to Lloyd George (13 Sept. 1915), *L.G.P.*, D/16/19/5; Asquith to Balfour (18 Sept. 1915), *A.P.*, Dep. 28.

[42] Asquith to Balfour (18 Sept. 1915), *A.P.*, Dep. 28.

Labour-Irish resurrection. But neither condition was present: no one but Milner contemplated a general election to create the new National Ministry and the Lib-Lab union of 1905 was moribund—and quite another kind of Easter miracle was in store for the would-be Irish partner. Moreover, as events were to prove, none of the three had usable command over their own houses—more than one hundred Liberal M.P.'s would come over to Lloyd George the following year and the Nationalists at Westminster had entirely lost their always tenuous control of the Irish movement. As for organized labor, its pretense at solidarity on the compulsion question could be unraveled by tugging at its numerous hanging threads.

This was more the view eventually taken by Lloyd George and Milner, although their method of exploiting the weakness differed. Beatrice Webb thought she had Lloyd George's tactic deciphered by 2 January:

> The year begins badly for Labour. The Munitions Act and the Defence of the Realm Act, together with the suppression of a free press, has been followed by the Cabinet's decision in favour of compulsory military service. This decision is the last of a series of cleverly devised steps—each step seeming at once harmless and inevitable, even to the Opponents of Compulsion, but, in fact, necessitating the next step forward to a system of military and industrial conscription. The Labour members were swept into the movement by the Derby recruiting campaign, and were cajoled, bribed and flattered into accepting the Asquith pledge. . . . But it is obvious that if the war continues the married men will have to go into the trenches, and directly the Minister of Munitions *dares to do it* industrial conscription will be introduced into the whole of industry. The servile state will have been established.[43]

Beatrice derived her view from Sidney, who had attended a meeting of the Labour Party executive the same morning in which Henderson, speaking for Lloyd George, warned that the alternative to conscription would have to be a general election, one in which (Henderson added) a good many Labour M.P.'s who opposed the measure would probably lose their seats. The key fact in her mind was not so much the behavior of Henderson, which was expected, but the capitulation of the Labour executive, including the I.L.P. and Fabians, to the threat of a general election in spite of their own

[43] B. Webb, "Diary" (2 Jan. 1916), *P.P.*

sense that the rank and file opposed the measure and were becoming increasingly "discontented and revolutionary."[44]

Here was another wide tear in the fabric of the Lib-Lab alliance at which Lloyd George could be expected to pull. Without himself wanting to bring on an election, the threat could be used to numb both Liberal and Labour leaders. The press, which was to play such a decisive part in the debacle of the following December, was even at this point a powerful influence in persuading the Liberal leadership that the country overwhelmingly demanded the sternest war measures; if that were in fact true, so the reasoning went, a general election might sweep both the Labour and Liberal men out. This persuasion was all the more effective in that the all-outers—Lloyd George, the Tory press, the ginger groups—themselves fully believed it was so. And it was this firm conviction that guided their reaction to Labour's "pacifism." In the same report on the Bristol congress which Gwynne delivered to Lloyd George, he confidently pointed out that the "pacifists" were in no way representative of the rank and file, who were "for victory at all costs" and merely wished to be informed of the government's needs. Acting as Lloyd George's liaison with the Unionist ginger groups at this time, Gwynne was eager to apprise him of the opportunity offered by the breakdown between the leadership and the rank and file of the labor movement as well as the sharp division of the leadership itself. That same conviction was of course the premise of Milner's movement. Significantly, Gwynne offered John Hodge, a member of the directorate of Milner's league and (as Gwynne put it) "leader of Labour in the House of Commons," as the prime illustration of his case. At the Bristol conference Hodge was said to have "denounced any man who would even mention peace at the present time as a traitor to his country."[45]

Before his meetings with Milner in March, Lloyd George was being prodded to follow a course parallel and complementary to Milner's. Gwynne, who was being minutely informed by Amery about the development of the B.W.N.L. (headed by Hodge) and the electoral committee (by Fisher), suggested the formation of still another league to Lloyd George. He mentioned some possible titles: "The League of Patriots," "The Patriotic League," "The National League," "The War League." The precise connection this league would have with Milner's, if any, was not spelled out, but

[44] Ibid.
[45] Gwynne to Lloyd George (13 and 17 Sept. 1915), *L.G.P.*, D/16/19/5.

it was clearly not supposed to be a competitor. Its platform would be based on seven principles: (1) the "vigorous prosecution of the war"; (2) "a war to the finish with no peace injurious" to Great Britain, the empire, or the Allies; (3) maintenance of British sea power after the war; (4) "To put into practice the cry of 'Britain for the British!'" (referring mainly to the tariff); (5) "To do everything possible to cut off and utterly destroy the German connections in Trade and Finance, and resolutely to refuse to the Germans in the future all privileges of domicile, naturalisation, trade partnership, etc." (6) compensation for the war disabled; and (7) to work "for the national good and not for party ends."[46] Gwynne's proposed platform reflected the rapidly growing tendency of wartime politics to be viewed in terms of war aims, Milner's "immediate THEREAFTER." Putting into practice the cry of "Britain for the British" was already becoming inseparable from the "war to the finish," as extensive wartime controls, such as the Ministry of Munitions and the B.W.N.L. were demanding, became essential to the planning of the postwar reconstruction. It is in this connection that compulsion, first military and then economic, inevitably became the key struggle in politics during 1916. The main focus of that struggle, as Beatrice Webb had seen quite early, would be the mobilization of labor. As the war lengthened and toughened, putting completely novel strains on the resources of the combatant nations, the most efficient and complete mobilization of the labor force became more and more necessary not only to the prosecution of the war but, especially if the fighting ended inconclusively or worse, essential to postwar order and economic survival. Expecting a "draw" and a postwar Germany more formidable than ever, she predicted (at the end of 1915) a forced reorganization of British society on a "sterner and more disciplined basis." If the war were to drag on much longer she foresaw the growth of many antitrade union movements: "scientific management, welfare schemes, possibly a method of disciplinary mobilisation of labour under the aegis of compulsory military service . . . the good and bad features of the 'Servile State,' not according to the Webbs but according to Kitchener."[47]

Kitchener's attitude on compulsory military service might have surprised Beatrice Webb at the time if she had known anything of it—he was one of its firmest opponents in the government, though

[46] Gwynne to Lloyd George (8 Nov. 1915), *L.G.P.*, D/16/19/9.
[47] B. Webb, "Diary" (28 Dec. 1915 and 19 May 1915), *P.P.*

his reasons had little to do with averting the Servile State. Also with his eye on the immediate postwar, Kitchener feared exhausting the nation's manpower by "peaking" too soon and thus leaving either the Germans or the French in the stronger position to dictate the terms of settlement.[48] On the other hand, Beatrice Webb's scenario corresponds more closely to the line of thinking then developing in Milner's movement and at the Ministry of Munitions. Lloyd George's unwavering attitude on all-out compulsion had already become the decisive element in all the crises and reshufflings of the first coalition. He himself had not had very great success in dealing with labor opposition to compulsion under the Munitions of War Act, yet he berated Asquith constantly for fearing too much the prospect of working-class resistance to it. In this as in so much else, Asquith was seen to be taking the short view—from the strict voluntarism of the first months, to the Munitions Act, to the Derby Commission, and then to the Military Service Act of January 1916 —he had grudgingly backed off from one Liberal foothold after another only after being persuaded that it was necessary to avert immediate disaster. In the process, he progressively withdrew from the day-to-day operations of the departments, losing the confidence of both friends and foes which he had possessed only probationally for some years before. Even in the light of his distracting and time-consuming private habits at the time, his petulant irresolution and diffidence is puzzling. While at one moment complaining of intrigue and faithlessness around him, he fumbled himself in petty deceptions with Kitchener and Balfour which neither strengthened his position nor which, in retrospect, support the picture so long held of him as the high-minded victim of his colleagues' treachery and ambition. Asquith consoled his indecision on compulsion with unchallengeable democratic virtue in a way which could infuriate those who honestly disagreed with him by casting upon them the role of conspirators and tyrants. In the debacle over Carson's resignation in October 1915, for example, he argued against conscription not only on the grounds of its probable inefficiency, a point which could be taken up coolly, but because it would cause a furor of opposition from Labour and the Irish. It thus had "every evil and no advantage." It was essential in his view, he told the Cabinet, "that before any kind of compulsion is resorted to it should have the general consent of all classes and sections of the people." It was

[48] Sir Philip Magnus, *Kitchener* (London, 1958), p. 352; R. S. Churchill, *Lord Derby* (London, 1959), p. 192.

a democratic pose which left room for neither discussion nor action without resort to a general election which none, least of all he, desired.[49]

The impasse over compulsion created by Asquith's and Kitchener's opposition in the Cabinet and the War Office left only the two methods of acquiring the instruments of control necessary for full-scale mobilization and victory: Milner's route, the mass movement, an election of patriots against pacifists and the creation of the "National Government"; and Lloyd George's subtler method of accreting de facto powers of compulsion through gradual extension of the scope of his Ministry of Munitions. They were roads that soon converged.

Had Lloyd George been the mere ruthless usurper he was so often thought to be, the period between Carson's resignation in October and the crisis of the following May might have offered plentiful opportunity to exploit Asquith's position. Carson's resignation and the subsequent crystallization of Unionist "ginger groups" in the House (the Unionist War Committee and the Unionist Business Committee), the emasculation of Kitchener's authority, Lloyd George's increasing support in the press, the Labour leaders' waning resistance to conscription, and the rising dominance of the Ministry of Munitions all worked to his enormous advantage, making him the natural figure around which the various forces for compulsion would gravitate. The "devolution of business to Committees," for which the Webbs had pressed ten years before, was a further influence in the same direction; accelerating inexorably, it diminished the actual control of both Parliament and Cabinet over the operations of government. Moreover, the Munitions Act and its tribunals, the Defense of the Realm Act, and the Military Service Act had already given the departments coercive legal powers nearly tantamount to full compulsion. The Prime Minister's somnolence significantly speeded this process by reducing even further the effective presence of political direction through the Cabinet—this had been Asquith's greatest failure. He never fully appreciated the reality of this process and, as we shall see, still held to the idea of Cabinet primacy at the time of his fall. The misconception naturally led him to blame his misfortune more on personalities than on politics. The Minister of Munitions, however, was never inclined to mistake mere position or title for effective power. Thus, apart from the one moment in 1910 when he

[49] "Notes for Cabinet Use" (15 Oct. 1915), *A.P.*, Dep. 28.

suggested Asquith's removal to the House of Lords, he showed very little active interest in taking Asquith's title upon himself. Indeed, he was uncertain and reluctant about taking on that office until the last resort. Instead, he worked with vast energy through his own ministry to achieve administratively what others, like Milner, sought to bring about through political action. As at the Board of Trade during his tenure, he created the impression that most of the practical business of governing, as opposed to the political business, was being conducted through his office; and, as in 1907, his Tory admirers and the sundry adherents of efficiency found themselves drawn more and more towards him.

On no issue more than on compulsion did Lloyd George strengthen his credentials as a "non-party" man. He had cultivated that image for some years with intermittent success and had built up a reserve of dormant political credit in Parliament, in the press, and to a lesser extent among the Labour men. And there could have been no more effective focus than the kind of full-scale compulsion which he was known to favor to bring this dispersed support into action. His presence in the government as the most effective voice of compulsion colored and guided virtually every strategy directed against Asquith and the first coalition, particularly in the case of Carson's and F. E. Smith's "ginger groups" and Milner's movement. As we have seen, Garvin, Smith, Amery, and Gwynne provided ample and sustained contact between these and Lloyd George and, although he had so far played a mostly passive part in their frequent attempts to join forces, he had become indispensable to any serious effort to change leadership despite the private misgivings and suspicions of his would-be allies regarding his motives. This was forever the mix of feelings with which the Unionists met Lloyd George—he was essential, he was obviously one who would get on with the war, but what were his true principles beyond victory and what exotic paths might he explore in reaching that goal? Such questions about his motives were major hindrances to collaboration for some of the older Unionist regulars who shared Balfour's uneasiness about the man's principles, "the great things." Garvin, Smith, most of the Milner circle, and eventually Carson—the most adamant critics of Asquith—he had largely won over by the end of 1915. Carson believed absolutely in Lloyd George's "disinterestedness and zeal for the war," according to Evelyn Wrench, but found Law and Austen Chamberlain "less keen" at the moment.⁵⁰ As in 1910, Unionist attitudes about Lloyd George tended to break down along the existing lines of division in the Unionist camp itself.

The specter of a Lloyd George–Carson–Milner "Triumvirate," the proposition which Amery had advanced in August and which continued as a subject of private speculation, held equal terrors for the old guard of both parties. It would have been a lethal combination for the opponents of all-out compulsion and unlimited war. Even separately, the three posed formidable and growing dangers to the independent labor movement: Milner's right-wing workers, Carson's anti-Irish and anti-Socialist following in Ulster (soon to be swelled in England by the conscription troubles and the Easter rising) and Lloyd George's restrictive powers under the Munitions Act, constituted if they could be marshaled together a force which might well fulfill F. S. Oliver's grim demand for "beating that dog [organized labor] to a jelly."⁵¹ Following Carson's resignation, the Ministry of Munitions was the one and most important government office through which immediate action could be taken on the labor question, although Carson's ginger groups (composed of more than one hundred M.P.'s) exerted increasing influence in Parliament. Carson's following, apart from the Ulster members, overlapped notably with Milner's and included most of the leadership of the prewar Unionist Social Reform Committee and the leadership of the Tariff Reform League—Amery, Smith, Oliver, Garvin, as well as a number of Milner's old Kindergarten both in Parliament and in the press. The same active young men were also to be found among the leaders of Milner's B.W.N.L. and the electoral committee, and increasingly in the plethora of committees spawned by the wartime bureaucracy. The highly absorbent Ministry of Munitions included a growing number of these men. Although Lloyd George had not yet launched the wholesale recruitment of Social-Imperialists and Fabians which was to fill the Ministry of Reconstruction during the following year, he was already beginning to draw upon their collective expertise particularly in regard to the ministry's "organization of labour." A highly fruitful means of recruiting such advice from outside the ministry, and outside of Parliament before the habit of formally enlisting private "experts" had fully devel-

⁵⁰ Evelyn Wrench, *Alfred Lord Milner* (London, 1958), pp. 121-122.
⁵¹ Gollin, *Proconsul*, p. 540.

oped, was merely to invite suggestions on a given subject at his informal meetings with Carson and Milner or to employ his gregarious friends in the press for the same purpose; his circle of private consultation at the time more or less excluded any input of ideas from the regular Liberal side by this route.

One such product of this informal method of "brain-trusting" was a series of detailed memos received from the onetime member of the Fabian Society executive who now held a similar post in Milner's B.W.N.L., Leo Chiozza Money. Like many an acquaintance struck up at this time, Money was to reappear as *fonctionnaire* in the Lloyd George government, as Parliamentary Secretary to the Shipping Controller. Characteristically, Lloyd George anticipated the eventual granting of powers for general conscription as early as October 1915, and had asked Money privately to draw up an outline of the administrative preparations and the long-term planning necessary. The two had previously consulted over an idea which Lloyd George had presented to the Cabinet, and which McKenna opposed, to levy a special progressive war tax on incomes to be deducted at the source by the employer. It was one of his highly creative tamperings with other departments which demonstrated his own incomparable political imagination as well as his genius for making dedicated enemies—in this case McKenna. A few weeks after their discussion on the tax scheme, two months before the passage of the first Military Service Act, Money responded with a memo "for the Establishment of a Department for the General Organisation of Labour during the War for all Purposes, with Reference also to the position which will obtain at the close of Hostilities." The emphasis of the memo was put less upon the problems of military recruitment from the war industries, a question which had come to a head in the fall, but upon methods of distributing labor as much as possible in the export industries with a view to preparing for postwar economic recovery. The memo is interesting as an example of the tendency of major wartime decisions to "overflow" into policies for the postwar, particularly when they applied to labor and industry. Money suggested an immediate extension of the functions of the Reserved Occupations Committee into a new and independent department "under one head," to include the "general organisation of male and female labour throughout the country. . . ." Working with the records of the National Register and "special reports" from the Labour Exchanges, such a department would seek "to *draft* into export businesses throughout the country, whatever labour is now available, and *to enlist and to train new supplies of labour* from the men, women and young persons of all classes of the community. . . ." The essential feature of any plan for the export industries in general was control of its mobility and training—the power to "draft" into munitions work and to "bring labour to the place where it is wanted." The same powers and planning needed for the efficient direction of labor during the war would be even more necessary "to help the nation reorganise itself for the purpose of peace," Money argued.[52]

The kind of sweeping controls implicitly assumed in such projects were not yet in the government's possession, not legally, although the leaving certificate, the "badges," the Munitions tribunals, and the Reserved Occupations Committee were major steps in that direction. If it were possible to acquire the necessary powers on a compulsory basis by working through existing agencies like the Labour Exchanges, the R.O.C., and the tribunals, it would probably have suited Lloyd George's mood at this point, though not that of those Unionists who were eager to bring on the big public smash-up with Asquith. (It is noteworthy that a significant number of bellicose Liberals might be included in this group by the spring of 1916.) Lloyd George still hoped to avoid that chancy political crisis and still thought the necessary powers could be acquired by the process of administrative "accretion"; it is easy enough to understand how the unprecedented growth of the Ministry of Munitions thus far might easily have left its head with the feeling that nearly anything could be accomplished by independent executive action without resort to the unpredictable whims of Parliament and the parties. This was much the same attitude, derived through experience, as Rosebery and the Webbs had expounded in principle long before the war, seemingly a simple and efficient method of circumventing divisive political questions. There was a persuasive logic in this, especially in the midst of war, when the "non-party" method could generally pass as an especially enlightened and selfless form of patriotism. However, there were obstacles looming in the way of this method of running the wartime government which emerged only in the spring and summer of 1916, fundamental political and personal questions both old and new which refused to be ignored. There was the question, as Money's memo

[52] "Memos Private and Confidential," Leo Chiozza Money to Lloyd George (24 Nov. 1915), *L.G.P.*, C/11/1/11. My italics.

had put it, of putting the organization of labor "under one head," implying the creation of a new Department of Labour with extraordinary powers or at least a new ministerial appointment in that area, either of which would inevitably raise contentious issues of party and personnel despite all the protestations of nonpartisanship. In much the same way, there were inherent limits to the further expansion of the giant Ministry of Munitions which, in spite of its minister's earnest disclaimers, was becoming more and more evidently a political and highly partisan force—though of a novel kind—with an emergent policy and personnel of its own quite distinct from the balance of forces in the parties. Each wave of expansion tended to encroach upon the purview of other departments and produced frequent personal and ideological clashes—with the War Office, the Treasury, the trade unions and, ultimately and unavoidably, with the Prime Minister. At the root of all was the unresolved issue of compulsion, the total conscription of resources for a total war effort, the principle now embodied in the Ministry of Munitions and its head. That issue was no longer, by 1916, a mere technical question as Asquith insisted on treating it—how many more fighting men could be raised or how much productivity might be improved—but a moral imperative, a criterion by which the patriots could distinguish themselves from the "hesitant Warriors."

As early as the winter of 1915 the needs of full mobilization can be seen to influence the development of war aims policy and to intrude upon the discussion then beginning to take place on peace terms. Perhaps even more important was the intrusion into this process of various postwar "scenarios" and plans of reconstruction. Beaverbrook's description of the coalition idea might apply equally to this preoccupation with reconstruction among the coalitionists, that it provides the clue to much which would otherwise be mysterious or even incomprehensible in the politics of the war. Under the more or less voluntary system as it still operated in 1915, an indefinitely prolonged and inconclusive war remained conceivable, even likely. But the closer the combatants came to total military and industrial mobilization and compulsion, with the progressive depletion of manpower, machinery, and foreign exchange that these entailed, the more necessary a radical plan of reconstruction became and hence the more urgent the "knockout blow," unconditional victory, and mammoth reparations. Consequently, the counterpoint between domestic politics and war aims began to transform the conflict over compulsion from an essentially strategic-administrative one into a more or less open ideological dispute over the shape of postwar society, that is to say, over reconstruction. Full powers of compulsion were felt to be needed by men like Lloyd George, Milner, Carson, and their followers not only to defeat Germany (they had always been the most confident of that anyway) but also to prepare in advance the instruments which would be needed to implement their dissonant visions of the "immediate THEREAFTER." It is in this sense most of all that the movement towards a coalition of these forces should be seen; the coalition, armed with full powers of compulsion, draped in the mantle of patriotism and efficiency, would replace traditional Liberalism and Conservatism as a more effective prophylactic against postwar Socialism.

X

Lloyd George's Estrangement

Of all the peculiar mixtures of men thrown together by political accident, one of the oddest of this century was surely the unstable tandem of Lloyd George and Winston Churchill. Between the two it would seem that the imagined pool of British political genius was nearly drained before the century was half finished. While it is easy to account for their resemblance as leaders in the two great wars, with all the atavistic magic that role attaches to a man, or as the two most sensational failures of the century as peacetime politicians, the similarities distort the profound contrasts in their careers and personalities. Men of the same generation, more or less, their political peaks were separated by yet another generation; Churchill's in an heroic crescendo towards the end after years in and out of limbo, and Lloyd George's growing steadily brighter from youth to middle age, more substantial and promising, then almost perversely burning itself out, flickering only a little for the next twenty years. Of the two, it is Lloyd George's failure which needs the more explaining. Most of that explanation lies in the decisions he made in 1916.

Some have thought that the aberration in the pattern of his political rise began when he accepted responsibility for Munitions in May 1915—". . . the man who does so is going to certain death and some dishonour with the present generation," Hewins thought at the time.[1] From the point of view of public affection, he was undoubtedly right. Lloyd George bound some men to jobs and wages they didn't want and uprooted others from a way of life they wished to keep while Kitchener sent thousands to mostly wasted deaths in Flanders. Yet it was the latter for whom the survivors named their sons, to their lifelong embarrassment.

[1] Hewins, *Apologia*, II, 33.

The decision which created the Ministry of Munitions, saved Kitchener, and delayed the entry of Bonar Law into a key Cabinet post was a momentous one for the course of the war as well as for the relations between Lloyd George and Asquith. Lloyd George's loyalty on that occasion—a "lightning streak of nobility" as Asquith himself called it—was his last tribute to Asquith's waning authority as Liberal leader.[2] Although he remained at Number 11, Munitions took him increasingly further from Asquith's company and personal influence, always the only effective way of keeping his sense of political fealty awake. With all the conflicting views put forth over the past fifty years about Lloyd George's breach with Asquith, it seems odd that his frequent, often melodramatic, professions of personal loyalty should be seen as so inconsistent with his behavior, that is, in conflict with his collusion with Asquith's enemies. It is usually described as deliberate hypocrisy and uncontrollable personal ambition. But if mere private ambition, regardless of personal trusts and party obligations, were his only motive, he had had many opportunities to foster it before overthrowing Asquith in December 1916, not least of all during the crisis and reconstruction which shunted him, without much prospect of acclaim or advancement, into Munitions and again in accepting the War Office a year later. It was Asquith who then acted more out of expediency, fearful of facing a debacle over Kitchener and of raising Bonar Law, than out of concern for his subordinate or for the public interest. It had been more often for private convenience than on questions of great principle that Asquith required demonstrations of loyalty and had received them more often than not. The two most important occasions when Lloyd George's loyalty clearly failed, in 1910 and in 1916, were instances when he obviously believed, mistakenly or not, that party and personal duties profoundly conflicted with the highest national interest. His year at the Ministry of Munitions, working more or less apart from day-to-day Cabinet politics, both reduced the personal factor in his relations with most of the Liberal ministers and eventually estranged him on the most important current question of policy, compulsion, which for him was a question of national survival.

The former president of the Board of Trade and Chancellor of the Exchequer and now Minister of Munitions had already established himself as the most productive and talented Liberal minis-

[2] Asquith to Lloyd George (25 May 1915), *War Memoirs*, I, 235.

ter; in normal times one could have said that he had established his claim to succession in the Liberal Party. But his move to Munitions, followed by Churchill's downfall, upset the pattern of the previous ten years. When he finally took over the War Office after Kitchener's drowning, his relations with Asquith and the party could not be taken up where they had left off a year before. Much the same year-long estrangement had occurred after the budget fight in 1909; the attitude of Asquith and the Liberal ministers towards him had again become defensive and cliquish and as before he had established his own administrative fief and an alternate company of political friends, many of them again of the more forthcoming younger Unionists and the press. If the Asquith Liberals held no affection for him, they were also disturbed to see him wooed by the enemy.

By the time of the Second Military Service Act, the fragile first coalition had already ceased to be an effective source of power, surviving only because its opponents of the Left and Right remained unable to organize an alternative. Losing the democratic-reformist aura once provided by Lloyd George and Churchill by failing to hold off conscription, then alienating its conservative support by attempting to resist it, the remains of the Asquithean party was in no condition to face the strains of the coming year. Under the circumstances, it is more remarkable that it survived so many months than that it came to ruin in the end. This can be attributed about equally to Lloyd George, the Germans, the Clydeside shop stewards, and the Irish. It was on his decision, it might be said on the strength of his ambition, that the fate of the first coalition depended and Asquith with it. No one has attempted to deny the ambition, as strong as Churchill's probably but infinitely less assured and arrogant. Nervously conscious of the suspicion with which his rise was regarded even by close colleagues, he went to great lengths at times to restrain it, as in accepting Munitions and again in taking on the War Office after Kitchener's death. Both were apparent acts of loyalty to Asquith, but not to have done so would inevitably have been condemned as proof of disloyalty and ambition. His relations with Asquith seem always to have been touched with something of this guilty self-denial. Some such emotion as this also attracted him again and again to the idea of coalition and later to the idea of the Triumvirate. It was more impersonal than the leadership of a party and if it were created to insure national survival there could be no charge of mere private ambition. Even so, it is worth noting that in his various allusions to the coalition since 1910, his own place in it was always conspicuously vague—he had even offered, ingenuously, to be left out in 1910, as we have seen.

Lloyd George was offered the crown more than three times before finally accepting it in December. Although most of the entreaties which reached him urging him to take the lead—like one in April suggesting that he do so by "carrying the fiery cross through the great industrial centres"[3]—offered more in the way of fan-club enthusiasm than usable political support, the makings of that support did begin to appear during the spring of 1916, partly as a result of his move and the more public breach with Asquith over conscription and partly in anticipation of a military crisis in the coming summer. Indeed, at several points in the spring these two problems brought him very close to setting off the "big smash-up" so many of his supporters craved. At no point in the first six months of the year was the prospect allowed to pass from his mind. Apart from the ever more strident anti-Asquith press, the Tariff Reformers were always the most impatient, both in private and in their "Monthly Notes," the "War Notes," and several other publications in which they had an interest.[4] It was increasingly from this quarter that allies would have to be recruited if the break were finally to take place, particularly from the circle represented by the Unionist Business Committee in Parliament and the imperialist organizations outside. Although it could not be said that he wooed their support as he had in 1910—that was unnecessary anyway—he quite willingly allowed himself to become a public focus of expectations for these most vociferous anti-Labour and anti-Liberal forces and engaged in a close, though for a long time inconclusive, collaboration with them. These contacts were not, as has sometimes been suggested, part of an unbroken process of alienation from the Liberal Party originating in the 1910 crisis, but part of a particular relationship with the leaders of the Tariff Reform movement which blew hot and cold very much in rhythm with the ups and downs of his own political career. As we have seen, they began after his first

---

[3] Arthur Lee to Lloyd George (2 April 1916), *L.G.P.*, D/1/1/13.

[4] "Monthly Notes" and "War Notes" were the main T.R.L. periodicals during the war years, but the Tariff Reformers, through Amery and Oliver in particular, strongly influenced the line taken by a number of other strongly proconscription and procoalition sheets, like the "Occasional Notes" (the National Service League pamphlet) and the *British Citizen and Empire Worker*, the weekly of Milner's B.W.N.L.

productive year at the Board of Trade and were renewed immediately following the budget, the Insurance Bill and, now again, after his generally acknowledged success in Munitions. Talk of the great coalition accompanied the revival of this liaison in each case, clearly not as a temporary device to get the measures through Parliament, but more to exploit an opportunity for marshaling new political power in approbation of what he had done. It is as though he was able to screw up enough assurance to claim a leadership role only when still flushed with the pride of accomplishment, while the laurels were still fresh. The spring of 1916 was such a time; he had both won the applause of the Tariff Reformers and again incurred suspicion and coolness among his Liberal colleagues as Minister of Munitions in one of his periodic floods of energy. In this instance, however, when coalition was again raised, in his meetings with Milner, Carson, and Smith in February and March, his way back to the Liberal fold would be more difficult than before and his dependence upon Unionist support so much the greater.

The issue upon which the chances of the coalition and the future of the Liberal Party hung in early 1916 was compulsion. Restricted merely to military conscription, there is no doubt that remaining Liberal-Labour resistance would have been overwhelmed by events on the battlefield that summer. Asquith's last effort to delay full conscription, a makeshift arrangement to give direct enlistment one more try, was made in the Secret Session on the day following the uprising in Dublin.[5] Even if military conscription had been the only point in question, Asquith's position on such occasions was hopelessly out of touch with the domestic political whirl of 1916 and with the kind of war which had now developed. It was still a limited war and the traditional kind of peace, envisioning something like a return to normal, to which his thinking doggedly clung, as did that of so many other traditional statesmen who fell during the following tumultuous year. The compulsion issue also subsumed the positions of the Minister of Munitions and the Tariff Reformers on the war and reconstruction; any coalition formed of these forces would be built on the joint principle of unconditional victory and what they regarded as a radical, anti-Socialist reconstruction pol-

---

[5] *A.P.*, Dep. 30 (25 April 1916), "Draft Proposal": clause no. 3— "That if at the end of 4 weeks ending May 27th, 50,000 men have not been secured by direct enlistment, the Government will forthwith ask Parliament for Compulsory Powers." Remaining clauses to the same effect pledged compulsory powers if quotas were not met on a weekly basis.

icy. That policy became refined and fixed in Tariff Reform propaganda and in the thinking of the Ministry of Munitions early in the year. Needless to say, there remained profound differences in the ultimate intent of the Milnerites and Lloyd George, as there were in 1910, but these were not yet regarded as insuperable, not until the actual forming of the coalition put them to the test.

What the Ministry of Munitions and the ginger groups of the Right wanted under the heading of compulsion was more or less unqualified powers of mobilization, both military and industrial. While incensed by Asquith's continued foot-dragging on compulsory military service, they were confident of eventually winning that point before the parliamentary struggle even began in March. In a sense, all parties were agreed that that was not the main issue. The Labour Party annual conference at Bristol in January had endorsed the Miners' resolution against "Conscription *in any form*" after being fraternally warned by the visiting French Socialist Deputies against "being called to the colours when a strike was likely to take place."[6] That continental practice, employed in both France and Germany in the prewar, had been frequently admired by Tariff Reform groups, the Unionist Social Reform Committee, and the National Service League in particular. This was a crude and dangerous method at best and of very limited usefulness for the kind of economic mobilization the "all-outers" had in mind. Direct powers of industrial conscription, as put forth in Chiozza Money's memo, to "draft" labor directly into the desired sectors of production was preferred. Money's proposal for the creation of a Department for the General Organization of Labour reflected the thinking of the Tariff Reform section at the time, with the emphasis on strengthening the export industries for the postwar through the "rationalization" of war production. The mounting opposition from labor after the Bristol conference, which brought the Ministry of Munitions into head-on confrontation with the union leaders over strikes in February, seems to have finally convinced Lloyd George of the need for full powers of compulsion. That ingenuous distinc-

[6] *A.P.*, Dep. 26 (27 Jan. 1916). Asquith made special note of the incident at the Bristol conference and of the overwhelming vote against conscription (1,796,000 to 215,000), no doubt for future use in pointing out the danger from labour should conscription go through. M. Languet was accompanied to Bristol by Pierre Renandel, the editor of *L'Humanité* and a Deputy, who also addressed the Conference just before the vote was taken on conscription. *Report of the 15th Annual Conference of the Labor Party* (Bristol, 1916), pp. 114-124.

tion which he had maintained since taking over Munitions, that he was against conscription but merely wanted to be able "to place men where they were most needed," was impossible to uphold after he had sought the legal prosecution of the strike leaders.[7] For him, the attitude of labor was not only damaging to the war effort but an intolerable hindrance to the successful operation of the ministry. His struggle with the unions in February was the low point in his already degenerating relations with the labor movement and inevitably drove him closer to the openly antilabor forces of the Right; these were just now preparing to launch their first determined effort to bring down the first coalition.

Lloyd George's problems with labor bore out Hewins' prediction that the man in charge of Munitions was bound to lose popularity. He no doubt looked upon the debacle as a failure, first, of his own once great powers of persuasion and, second, a failure of the government to provide him either with sufficient powers of coercion or with moral support. Demands for those powers as well as offers of strong support were now being renewed by his Unionist friends. As we have already noted, his meetings with Milner, Carson, Smith, and other representatives of that section resumed at about the time of the publication of the manifesto of the British Workers National League in March, and coincided with their resumption of the attack on the government. Carson had resigned the previous fall but was only now concentrating his energy, through the Unionist Business Committee, on parliamentary agitation for conscription. By March, this ginger group was meeting every Monday evening together with Milner's people (Amery, Oliver, Robinson, and Waldorf Astor) to devise a method to "somehow or other secure a change of Government."[8] Whether Lloyd George's mind had consciously turned to the same idea this early is not clear, but there is no doubt that it was an unspoken assumption of his conversations with the ginger group throughout the spring. His inclusion in virtually every proposition put forth by them for a new regime, whether the Triumvirate or the coalition, indicates how essential they felt him to be; his own mind in early 1916 was not yet so definite that they were indispensable to him. His talks with them went sufficiently well at least to encourage Smith and Amery to keep him informed of the tactical plans of the Milner and Carson groups during the agitation of March and April.

[7] Cited in G. D. H. Cole, *Labour in Wartime* (London, 1915), p. 213.
[8] Amery, *My Political Life*, II, 81-82.

In the absence of reliable first-hand information about Lloyd George's private state of mind during the few months preceding his move to the War Office it is difficult to gauge his reaction to the friendly overtures from the Milner circle. None of these—Amery, Oliver, Gwynne, nor even Smith—had ever established anything like the casual, personal tie with him that Garvin had. Although the editor still frequently praised the work of the Ministry of Munitions in the *Observer*, the once close personal connection between the two men had cooled since the previous fall (the only correspondence between them during the year was a note of condolence for the loss of Garvin's son in July and a formal acknowledgment).[9] The absence of Garvin, whose role as intermediary Beaverbrook was to fill more fruitfully a little later, probably meant that the meetings with Milner in his Great College Street house remained rather formal and guarded. Two such men could not have found candid conversation easy under any circumstances; and for Lloyd George these meetings must have been touched with some sensation of guilt, if not towards Asquith or the party, perhaps towards his own better instincts. While they could find much in common at the moment on questions like conscription and unconditional victory, Milner's humorless authoritarianism could hardly help but jar even the more dormant democratic senses of his guest. If we can judge from what followed, each was assured of the other's sympathy; Milner was encouraged that the government was vulnerable, and Lloyd George was encouraging but noncommittal.

The sudden heightening of activity on the part of the B.W.N.L. and the Unionist ginger group in Parliament after the meetings with Lloyd George and the publication of the manifesto reflected a rising hope that the first coalition was opening at the seams. Smith expected a crisis at any moment and, on 20 March, asked Lloyd George to confer with the ginger group about a resolution they wished to present in Parliament the next day attacking the government on conscription.[10] The time was still premature for an open break, but though he didn't meet with the Smith-Carson group on this occasion, the offer appears to have been one result of his meeting with Milner three days before. Milner bore a similar attitude about the growing alienation of many Unionist, Liberal, and Labour M.P.'s, including ministers, from the coalition. In an article being prepared for the *Quarterly Review* in the first week of April,

[9] Garvin to Lloyd George (31 July 1916), *L.G.P.*, E/2/12/1.
[10] F. E. Smith to Lloyd George (20 March 1916), *L.G.P.*, D/16/4/2.

Milner noted the earlier resignation of Carson and that of Walter Long a day before as evidence of the breakdown; Lloyd George was mentioned as "uncomfortably quarantined in the Cabinet." The implication was clear: there were, he wrote, "a small section of Liberals, a relatively larger section of Labour men, and a majority of Unionists" who were falling out with the coalition leadership over the conscription issue. Though there was as yet "no political organisation or acknowledged leader," Milner strongly implied that once these were acquired the dissident fragments of the three parties would join to form the effective Opposition—the long-sought "Democratic-Imperialist Party" would have come into being.[11] This was the line of argument he would have used on Lloyd George, garnished very possibly with some milder samples of the anti-Asquith invective he received daily from the military. To quote in full his most frenetic correspondent, Sir Henry Wilson, would have been indelicate; but that unstable giant was an apt caricature of his own thinking at the time. In the same week as Milner's article, he wrote to him from France:

> It seems to me that, if things are properly managed, he (Squiff) can be cornered. I want to see a foundation of Yourself, *L.G.*, and Carson with one Labour man added and possibly one other as our Cabinet. . . . There will be an absolute howl and yell of delight throughout the whole Army the day Squiff falls, and an amazing warmth and belief in those I have mentioned when they take over and *Govern* [Wilson always underlined in red in case the nuances of his meaning be missed].[12]

Despite deep misgivings about the political generals, Lloyd George was liable to be consoled in his "quarantine" by assurances from this quarter, even if Wilson could hardly pass as a popular spokesman for the army. Moreover, the attitude of the army, or at least his reading of it, was one of the vital factors he had to consider shortly after when he replaced Kitchener, a move he agreed to make only after again receiving such assurances from the Unionists.

Asquith's opposition to the Military Service Bill of January and his subsequent holding action against conscription throughout the spring infuriated the General Staff and those in the coalition, like Walter Long, who wished to give the generals a more or less free

---

[11] "The Recruiting Crisis," marked "First Proof" (5 April 1916), *M.P.*, Great War.

[12] Wilson to Milner (4 April 1916), *M.P.*, Letters–1916.

hand. It was at this time that the "Squiff" epithet came into common usage among the military and their more bellicose supporters in the press. If a point were to be chosen where it might be said that the British faced the psychological crisis of modern war, as full of the emotional uncertainties, recrimination, and desperation as that which accompanies revolutions, it would be sometime during this spring. It was Asquith's misfortune to represent all that was seen as inadequate and mistaken in the past, all the supposed indulgence and indiscipline of British life which was now thought to be the root cause of their failure and an intolerable handicap in fighting the German "war machine." Indeed, the increasingly violent fulminations against him in 1916 bear a suggestion of sacrificial regicide, the propitiation all the more devoutly offered when the king was unpopular.

Long's angry resignation in April brought these sentiments to a peak. He accused the coalition of lacking the "will to conquer." There was no "sacred fire." Reactions were immediate and impassioned; led by the Northcliffe press, the protest fastened on the idea of a "Saviour," a man on horseback—the figures most frequently attached being Lloyd George, Carson, or "a General," and in some private conversations even Northcliffe himself. Writing to Lloyd George in this vein after the resignation, Arthur Lee noted the "static neurasthenia," the "sexless apathy" of the current leadership. "The people are yearning for a leader—witness the pathetic quest for 'The Man'. . . ."[13] As might be expected, Wilson was in the forefront of the most extreme reaction, as in a letter to Milner:

> If ever a man deserved to be tried and shot that man is the P.M. There is a volume of feeling vs. him and his miserable crowd, rising out here amongst the soldiers of all ranks which delights me. . . . We hope that you and Carson and L.G. have at last got him by the throat.
> *No mercy please.*[14]

Accompanying the tirades there was most often a demand for some sort of government of "National Unity," the makeup of which varied according to the source, but virtually all suggesting a leadership which included Lloyd George and Carson—mixed, as in Ar-

---

[13] Arthur Lee to Lloyd George (2 April 1916), *L.G.P.*, D/1/1/13, reporting and endorsing Long's reasons for resigning.
[14] Henry Wilson to Milner (20 April 1916), *M.P.*, Letters–1916.

thur Lee's proposition, with "a strong leaven of non-politicians, to which all parties would give loyal support. . . ."[15] All this was, of course, according to Milner's well-known text. As recently as March, when the B.W.N.L. was officially launched, Milner thought the only way of getting rid of the "Incubus," whose continued life was due entirely to the old party system, was a general election which he was convinced would radically alter the character of the House of Commons. For this, he had reluctantly begun what he called his "ad hoc Party." A general election he admitted was an incalculable risk, and might well not reflect the "Spirit of the Army and the battlefront of the Nation," as he hoped. Indeed, the government was capable of delaying election indefinitely and controlled, he thought, the "decaying and discredited but still formidable Party machines."[16] Worse still, the whole plan rested on the shaky premise that the House of Lords could force the election. Under the circumstances, even Milner could recognize the advantages of another "reconstruction" among the collaborators. If the strength of Carson and Lloyd George could be added to his own, the combination of "fanatical Cobdenism and dunderheaded Toryism" which made up the coalition could be broken up and the way opened to his long-sought "non-party" government.

The key figure in any plan to replace the coalition either by general election or reconstruction was always assumed to be the Minister of Munitions. This was so not only for Milner, the military, and the ginger group, who recognized their relative weakness without him (Milner estimated his own faction's basic strength at between forty and sixty Unionist M.P.'s), but also for Bonar Law's body of regulars when Beaverbrook began his industrious campaign a little later in the year. Needless to say, he was considered even more essential by those who wished to preserve the coalition. The attitude of the two sides towards him was remarkably similar. He had no strong personal following among the disgruntled Unionists and had weakened his always lukewarm friendships among the Liberal leaders—both Garvin and Churchill were out of the picture for the time being. Since there was at the time no way of knowing precisely what degree of support Lloyd George commanded in the House (even Addison's later straw poll estimate was speculative), the

[15] Arthur Lee to Lloyd George (2 April 1916), *L.G.P.*, D/1/1/13.
[16] "Some Notes on the present war situation" (12 March 1916), *M.P.*, Letters–1916.

importance which all attached to him would seem to be a great tribute to his personal stature. It is undeniable that, as was demonstrated on numerous occasions, he had the power to make sudden conversions among his detractors in face-to-face interviews. But with a few exceptions, these were generally short-lived; virtually none of his contemporaries proved totally immune from the suspicion which clung to his name. His most influential and steadfast admirers during the war years were of course the Tory papers, both owners and editors, especially those of Northcliffe, Astor, and Beaverbrook. Journalists like Garvin, Gwynne, Oliver, and Robinson were the most vocal in their support, but since they were all involved to one degree or another in the Milner–Tariff Reform agitation, their reasons for boosting Lloyd George were naturally much the same as those of the movement's leaders; that is, they did not so much *shape* right-wing opinion on Lloyd George as *reflect* it. Moreover, as the heavy attacks mounted by the *Daily News* and the *Manchester Guardian* in April and the mounting hostility of journalists of the Left demonstrated, the Minister of Munitions was by no means universally acknowledged as "The Man" to save the situation.

The ambiguity of Lloyd George's situation in the spring of 1916 is perhaps the best gauge of how the traditional political alignment was breaking down during the war; it was also strongly suggestive of the pattern which was in process of replacing it. Since the 1910 crisis, the dominant consideration among the Tariff Reformers in regard to Lloyd George, though not their only one, had been the possibility of preempting the Socialists through him; as we have already seen, that had also been the basis of their interest in the Fabians and the premise of all their rather barren experiments with a social reform program of their own. Their thinking had thus developed at a time when the combinations which made up the two parties were still dominated by their older traditional factions. Within those combinations they saw themselves, the Lloyd George Radicals and the Labour Party as the restless junior partners who would quite soon replace the "Mandarins"; and in that new troika the Lloyd George faction was bound to hold the balance between Left and Right. The main effect on their script of the first eighteen months of the war had been to more or less freeze that expected process in the *union sacrée*. When the edges of the first coalition began to thaw in 1916, the situation revealed in the disarray of both parties and the hardening resistance of the Socialists appeared to follow the Tariff Reform scenario. There were to be some surprises, however.

"One must have friends," Lloyd George is reported to have said to Sir George Riddell after a particularly sharp attack upon him was made in the *Daily News* in April. As radical criticism of him mounted during the labor troubles and the conscription debate, he spoke more often of the support he received from Conservatives and the general coldness of his Liberal colleagues.[17] According to Addison, who was one of his very few intimates at the time, he felt that he had been cut off from his colleagues and that things were "getting to a desperate pass in the Cabinet."[18] This was not a completely new sensation for him, after the 1909 budget dispute, the Insurance Bill, and Marconi, but his sense of having been treated unjustly, of having been left in the lurch, was possibly greater. He was well aware that his taking up Munitions had saved Asquith from a major crisis, making the first coalition possible, and that the present hostility arose directly out of his work in that post. As on those occasions in the past, his success in an assigned post brought him into a period of conflict with his colleagues and into cooperation with the Opposition. In his mind, however, the success of his design for the Ministry of Munitions could not be fully achieved without the compulsory powers of conscription. It was on this point that his relations with the government had now become stuck because Asquith had chosen to uphold labor's contention that it was a matter of fundamental democratic principle. Partly to evade just such a conflict, he generally preferred to treat it merely as an administrative and military necessity, consequently not a question of philosophy or party. For the time being at least, that position inevitably put him on the side of the Conservative Right.

In the middle of the compulsion debate, just after his meeting with Milner, Lloyd George revealed to Addison the "movement among certain Conservatives" to try to get him to take a strong line against the coalition. They were prepared, he said, "to go to the length of recognising him as P.M."[19] It is far from clear what was meant by the word "recognising" in Addison's record of the conversation, but there is no doubt that general allusions were made in

[17] Sir George Riddell, *War Diary* (28 April 1916), p. 179.

[18] Addison Diary (17 March 1916). Dr. Christopher Addison, *Four and a Half Years*, 2 vols. (London, 1934), II, 86-87.

[19] Addison, *Four and a Half Years* (17 March 1916).

his contacts with the Tariff Reformers in March and April to his heading a successor regime. None of the many formulas for the "National Government" discussed by the Tariff Reformers, in private and in the press, ruled out that possibility in principle. As Addison realized instantly, however, it was one thing to ruminate with Milner about a national government created of all those who wished "to get on with the war" and another to acquire the necessary support to uphold it. Both Lloyd George and Milner were strangely muddled and inconsistent in their thinking about the latter. Milner's still embryonic organization in the country, heartening as its beginning was to him, was very far from rivaling any of the regular constituency machines and even further from "knocking out" the I.L.P. And while Lloyd George undoubtedly had a large patriotic following, it was amorphous and still incalculable in terms of parliamentary strength. Addison was quick to point this out to Lloyd George, warning him that no satisfactory result could come from breaking with the "democratic party"—he would, Addison said, be courting failure and division to rely on the backing of the young Conservatives alone.[20]

Such pledges of confidence as the Unionist ginger groups may have given him perhaps assumed more importance in Lloyd George's mind than their actual worth during his period of isolation. He is reported (by Riddell) to have been thinking of forming a "new party." "If I went out," he said to Riddell a bit later, "I should at once form a great party organisation. I have promises of all the money necessary."[21] These reported moods possibly reflect suggestions made in his talks with Milner, Smith, or Amery, but it is still unlikely that he took very seriously any proposal to act as the front man for the fledgling organization founded by Milner and financed by Waldorf Astor, as has sometimes been suggested. Even at the modest height it reached about a year later, the B.W.N.L. was a totally insufficient foundation on which to build a "new party," even though the acquisition of Lloyd George would have greatly increased its strength.[22] Nevertheless, Lloyd George was

[20] Addison, *Four and a Half Years* (5 April 1916).
[21] Riddell, *War Diary* (11 June 1916), p. 189.
[22] The peak of the B.W.N.L. was reached, according to its official organ, the *British Citizen and Empire Worker*, in December 1917, when it claimed 188 branches around the country. No figures exist for the total membership. Lockwood points out that the main period of its expansion occurred after the formation of the Lloyd George government in December 1916.

contemplating the possible consequences of a break with Asquith as their relations continued to worsen. He recognized the obvious sense in Addison's advice and, despite continual prodding from Amery and Smith, decided that the time for him to act had not yet come. But it was likely to come, he told Addison, "late in the summer" after opinion in the party had consolidated in favor of "a more determined action against incompetency."[23]

The Unionist ginger groups in Parliament were hoping for an earlier climax over the conscription dispute. From their point of view, the lines were already clearly drawn between those for and those against general conscription, with the balance decidedly in their favor. Smith and Carson in the Unionist Business Committee had already put hostile resolutions forward in Parliament, challenging Bonar Law as well as Asquith, but had as yet been unable to muster majorities. But they were convinced anyway that there was an overwhelming consensus in the electorate on their side. Quoting a statement made in the *Daily Express* by John Hodge (the leading M.P. in the B.W.N.L.) that 90 percent of the vote would go for full-scale compulsion, Amery tried to persuade Lloyd George to come out boldly. The break between the "all-outers" and the "hesitant warriors" was now inevitable, he argued. The coalition provided no rational unity; it was allowing the patriotism of the country to go sour.[24] The logic of their case pointed clearly to a general election and their prodding of Lloyd George to come out was a means of bringing about an election, a more realistic means than Milner's design for the House of Lords. As we have seen, Lloyd George had given some thought to the same idea when he spoke of forming "a great party organisation" if he were to resign. But that was in the second week of June, after two completely unforeseen events had drastically altered the situation: on one hand the uprising in Dublin on Easter Monday complicated his budding entente with the Ulster Unionists, while on the other Kitchener's death in the North Sea appeared to reopen his way back into the Cabinet with a more or less clean slate, if he chose to accept the War Office.

Contrary to what might have been expected, the violent resurrection of the Irish issue which had been so hastily buried in the swell of unity at the outbreak of the war brought more calm than

---

[23] Lockwood, "*Milner's Entry*," pp. 126-127.
[24] Amery to Lloyd George (13 April and 20 April 1916), *L.G.P.*, D/16/2/4, D/16/2/8.

upheaval to the beleaguered Asquith government, at least for a time. It also meant respite for Bonar Law from the intensifying agitation of the Carson group, whose attentions were naturally distracted for a time from the war to the rebellion. Indeed, the long process of civil strife signaled by the Easter uprising had the effect of permanently parochializing the Ulster Unionists, bringing a corresponding ebb in the overall strength of the Tariff Reform movement of which they made up a large and aggressive part. Carson's growing stature as a national and political figure was immediately diminished; he was too deeply committed to what could now only be regarded as a sectional cause. His name was noticeably less prominent after April in discussions about a "truly National Government."

Although Ireland was not yet seen in the context of the international social upheaval which was about to rock the old regimes all over Europe, it greatly intensified existing anxieties about unseen consequences in the social order arising from the long war. Even before the Easter uprising, violent Irish resistance to recruiting, registration, and "attesting" was feared by some as a possible example for the radical opponents of conscription in other parts of the kingdom, as for example the No Conscription Fellowship, which consciously modeled its methods on Sinn Fein.[25] Much the same connection was made as in 1913–1914, when Nationalist militancy on one side was followed by Socialist militancy on the other. Naturally, that mixture was most conscious in the minds of the Irish Unionists, who never clearly distinguished between the two forces. Protestant Conservatism in Ireland had often displayed a special kind of severity and had produced some of Britain's most adamant autocrats and imperialists, but it had once been balanced by a strong Liberal and Radical tradition, especially in the north. Home Rule agitation had eroded that counterforce over the years, but from this moment onward the Ulster contingent in Westminster became a force of almost unrelieved reaction, its leaders forever tainted with the fanaticism which most of the English attached to the whole island.

The disconcerting effect which the events in Ireland had on the activities of the Unionist insurgents meant at least a temporary reprieve for Bonar Law's leadership in the party. For Asquith, the

[25] J. W. Graham, *Conscription and Conscience* (London, 1922), pp. 172-176; cited in Arthur Marwick, *The Deluge: British Society and the First World War*, Pelican Books (London, 1967), p. 84.

renewal of the Irish question in such disastrous form at a time already filled with danger for the coalition could have brought immediate ruin, and nearly did. After the first days of perplexed reaction to the pitched battle in Dublin, a period outwardly calm compared to the preceding weeks, the rising tide of impatience with Asquith which had built up during the long conscription conflict returned with new vehemence. He was the natural butt of both the war-weary and the bellicose and in this the press of both Left and Right probably reflected public opinion fairly in their attacks of late April and early June. It is difficult to imagine how the "Asquith Must Go" campaign which mounted between Easter and the first stunning reports of the Somme casualties might have been resisted were it not for the odd new twist introduced by Kitchener's death. That most visible and impervious face proved to be more useful to the coalition buried at sea than in the War Office, for the vacancy created both an opportunity and an excuse for a shifting of government posts and what at first seemed to be a major concession to its hard-line critics. During the week following Kitchener's accident on 5 June, the discussion about his replacement brought Bonar Law and Lloyd George together as the coalition's rescuers much in the way they had come together to create it a year before, this time through the industrious fiddling of Beaverbrook.

On the same day (11 June) that Lloyd George was speculating with Riddell about "promises of all the money necessary" to found a new party organization, he met with Bonar Law and Beaverbrook at Cherkley. According to a recent description of their meeting, Bonar Law resisted Beaverbrook's pressure to demand the War Office himself and instead agreed to recommend Lloyd George in return for the leadership of the House. In this, as in the crisis of the previous May, Bonar Law is pictured, probably fairly, as reluctant to press his own claims to commanding posts in the coalition or to put excessive pressures on Asquith. His failure to demand either the Treasury or House leadership on the earlier occasion, though conceived by him to be a prudent way of exculpating both himself and the party from the coalition's mistakes, was seen by many Unionists as mere lack of force. Even such a close admirer as Beaverbrook found the advancement of Bonar Law a frustrating labor. A much less confident man than Balfour, he was even more nervously aware of the lack of consensus or enthusiasm his leadership inspired in the party, especially among the very leader-conscious

Tariff Reformers. Again in making up his mind about the War Office, his first concerns were to avoid any course which might either arouse the Unionist factions or endanger the existence of the coalition so long as the Unionist Party remained unable to form a government itself. He was inclined from the beginning to view the coalition in the narrow sense, merely an arrangement to maintain the Liberal government in power for the duration of a relatively short war, not a full sharing of power and key posts beyond what was necessary for the war effort. Most of the party regulars had shared this view in the beginning, but growing discontent with the direction of the war combined with either a reluctance or an inability to force a change had confused opinion all around. The behavior of Bonar Law in June reflected that confusion; he was willing neither to commit himself wholeheartedly to the coalition by demanding the War Office as the right of a full partner, nor to lead the Opposition against it. Thus his reluctance to put himself forward for the War Office, which Asquith must have granted under pressure or even welcomed, was wholly consistent with his original conception of the Unionist role in the coalition, if not with Beaverbrook's.

The Tariff Reformers and Ulster Unionists were not the only dissident factions which Bonar Law had to consider in the meeting of 11 June. There was a potentially strong body of opinion in the party and in the press which wanted the army to play a greater role in making policy which affected the battlefield; a few indeed felt that since all major Cabinet decisions had to be made in light of the military situation, a general should head the Cabinet. Inevitably, the vacating of the War Office stimulated those who held such views. Generals Robertson and Whigham had immediately begun to press the Unionist leaders to have Walter Long in the post. Considering the views which Long had made well known by the time he resigned a few weeks before, he was considered a cat's-paw of the generals and his appointment would have amounted to putting Robertson in the War Office. While Kitchener's aloofness had made him more or less politically innocuous, generals like Robertson or Wilson were a potential incubus in the Unionist Party which would be nourished by Long's appointment. At the same time, if he were to take the post himself, he would be trapped by the conscription question, having to stand between Asquith and the militants. To appease the Unionist "all-outers" he would have to challenge Asquith and probably destroy the coalition by resigning; to uphold

Asquith would inevitably provoke rebellion in the party against him. That had been the situation he meant to avoid from the beginning by remaining in but not of the coalition government. Under the circumstances, his preference for Lloyd George to move to the War Office was understandable. The latter's reasons for agreeing to the move are less clear.

Lloyd George's relations with Asquith had reached their lowest point in mid-April. After head-to-head confrontations with Asquith over compulsion, he was on the point of resigning several times, changing his mind and mood from day to day according to the course of the Cabinet meetings and the tone of the daily press. He was under continuous pressure from two sides: Smith, Churchill, and Robertson urged resignation and a showdown before the summer offensives; the Cabinet Unionists (except for Smith) vacillated between a hard and soft line but, like Bonar Law, still hoped to avert the general melee which resignations would cause. Into this highly liquid situation Lloyd George introduced a conciliatory proposal (on 18 April) which went far towards meeting the position of Asquith and Henderson, or at least would allow them to escape from their position unobtrusively. Adopting figures supplied by Robertson and the Army Council, he proposed that if 60,000 men could not be raised in the first month and 15,000 *per week* afterward, general compulsion would be applied by resolution in Parliament with the support of the whole Cabinet. It was tacitly understood to be a dignified coup de grace for the voluntary system, but the voluntarists in the Cabinet (excepting McKenna) were at first disposed to accept it, both as a face-saving device and as a tolerable method of prolonging the life of the coalition. Lloyd George described it as the "American system," thinking that Asquith would be comforted to have a "precedent."[26] He had come to the opinion that compulsion could not yet be carried in the House of Commons without Asquith and consequently that Cabinet resignations, even if they included Bonar Law, Smith, and Robertson, would not necessarily marshal enough strength to achieve the desired policy for conducting the war; indeed they might have the negative effect of consolidating the growing sentiment for a negotiated peace if the coalition could neither rule nor be replaced.

[26] A. J. P. Taylor (ed.), *Lloyd George: A Diary by Frances Stevenson* (London, 1971), (18 April 1916), p. 106. Asquith's favorable response to the plan (with minor alterations) was made to a secret session of Parliament a week later, the day after the Dublin fighting.

Circumstances had placed Lloyd George in what appeared to be the decisive role; he was perhaps excessively conscious of the impact his resignation would have on the coalition, the Liberal Party, and on the course of the war. Had he resigned in April, as many expected and some hoped he would, the commotion would have been great and the ultimate consequences for the war and the parties incalculable. But it is unlikely that the coalition would have broken up immediately, perhaps not at all. With a great deal of pressure focused on him from all sides, his decision to attempt a compromise on conscription was remarkably cool-headed, taking into account both his own political weaknesses and the dubious negotiability of the sundry promises and exhortations he had received. Moreover, even if the latest conscription plan were adopted and failed to meet the contingencies (it was defeated as the second Conscription Bill in the Secret Session of 25 April), the full compulsory powers at which it was aimed would still not be available without another prolonged struggle. Thus, nothing substantial could be achieved merely by resigning, not yet, and much could be lost. In particular, Lloyd George was not anxious to leave the Ministry of Munitions before the goals he had set for it were reached; although the giant ministry was functioning well internally, there was a host of unsettled labor problems (including prosecutions of strikers) and reorganized factories still below full production. Were he to resign now, or even move to another department, it could be seen as a retreat from increasingly bitter conflict with the Clydeside workers; it might also mean, as he confided to Miss Stevenson, that another man would receive the credit for achieving optimum munitions production, which he expected to reach in five or six weeks' time, that is, some time in June. He had suggested to Addison and Riddell as well that the time for him to act, when opinion in the parties would harden against the present coalition, would not come until summer, presumably if the planned summer offensive failed to achieve the great things that were promised.[27]

Before events in France could intervene to simplify political choices in London, the failure of the Conscription Bill, the Irish uprising, and Kitchener's death suddenly made some immediate action necessary. However, at the time of their meeting of 11 June, the general inclinations of Bonar Law and Lloyd George had not

---

[27] Ibid., p. 107; Addison, *Four and a Half Years*, p. 157.

altered: the first still preferred to remain in the background and Lloyd George was not yet ready to hand over his ministry. Again it was Asquith and Bonar Law who prevailed and Lloyd George who again acquiesced after a few weeks of persuasion. It is difficult to see him at this point other than as a scapegoat, whether or not those who set him up for that role did so consciously or not. In the period between the Easter uprising and his move to the War Office (4 July), he was persuaded to stick his arm into the Irish mangle, to suspend his drive for conscription, to abandon Munitions, and to accept a post he wished to avoid, under conditions which none of the major leaders would have tolerated. Both his tactical compromise on conscription and the careful prospectus for his own future action were abandoned when he accepted the commission to seek a solution to the labyrinthine Irish question. In the latter case, he momentarily reverted back to the old Liberal mind on Ireland by guaranteeing to Redmond immediate Home Rule for twenty-six counties. He had a poorly informed understanding of the dreadful complexities of Irish politics; his consequent assumption that the question could be quickly put out of the way through a personal arrangement between Redmond, Carson, and himself was absurdly naive and foolhardy—not an unusual state for men with a reputation for political ruthlessness. Despite an impressive display of personal charm, he could not make a success of the negotiations, which were doomed to fail anyway so long as Redmond and Carson were still recognized as the leaders of Irish opinion and Westminster the arbiter of the internal future of Ireland. The same few weeks in which Lloyd George floundered in the Irish troubles produced in him an irritable impatience with regard to Ireland (with disastrous consequences for that country) and the final, inevitable breach of trust with Asquith. Having agreed to the conscription plan, Asquith retreated when opposition to it appeared; having pledged to uphold Lloyd George in the difficult Irish negotiations, he again backed down and left him the choice of resigning (as Lloyd George had pledged to Redmond if Home Rule for the twenty-six counties were rejected) or violating his own agreements with the Irish.

Lloyd George had thus come to Asquith's aid twice in the week of the Easter uprising and now in June he was under pressure to do so again; this time to suit Bonar Law's convenience as much as Asquith's, as we have seen. However, Asquith preferred the Unionist leader for the War Office; he tried to persuade him to accept it in a meeting on 12 June and finally agreed to offer it to Lloyd George only after Bonar Law refused. It is not known exactly what arguments were used by Bonar Law and Beaverbrook to bring the reluctant minister to accept the appointment. It is clear, however, that he was still reluctant to move, for the reasons already described, and even drafted a resignation and a refusal of the War Office on the 17th.[28] He would not become Secretary of State for War, he told Asquith, under the "humiliating conditions to which poor Kitchener had been reduced. . . ." Unless the Secretary of State controlled the patronage of the office he would be treated with "supreme contempt" by his own department and by the army. Despite his good relations with Robertson during the conscription dispute he was aware of the preference of the military for an agreeable cipher in the top civilian post—that was the part they wished Long to play. The soldiers feared to promote brilliant men, he thought, out of an "unconscious" fear of rivalry. Thus, it was all the more important that a civilian heading the War Office be armed with the fullest possible authority.[29] There was little that could be done by this time to strengthen the office, since the secretary had been divested of his staff function and Robertson was Chief of the Imperial General Staff. There was also the question of the soldiers' franchise: the opportunity, as he put it to Asquith, of their choosing the Parliament and policy on which their lives depended. This too he made an implicit condition of his accepting the office, not at all expecting either to be granted.[30]

Lloyd George's apparently firm and repeated resolve not to move to the War Office weakened under the pressures of persuasion and the distractions of the Irish negotiations. The two alternatives available, to resign or to remain in the Ministry of Munitions, both had the possible drawback of removing him from the center stage of events. As he had predicted, the Ministry of Munitions had passed out of its most dynamic stage and was beginning to operate near capacity by June; hereafter, its business would become more routine and parochial while political attention shifted to the wider range of strategy in Europe. In most important respects, the World War had only just begun—what went before had been preparation. The Irish negotiations had already moved him somewhat towards

[28] "Draft Resignation," Lloyd George to Asquith (17 June 1916), *L.G.P.*, D/18/2/19.
[29] Ibid.
[30] Ibid.; Lloyd George to Asquith (17 June 1916), *A.P.*, Dep. 30.

that wider sphere. German guns in Ireland and alleged foreign interference on the Clyde had also suggested to him new ramifications of the war which could not be confronted from the point of view of Munitions, no matter how broad its scope. To stay where he was, therefore, was to court increasing obscurity. Resignation might have the same result. He feared that it would be possible for Asquith to form a reconstructed Cabinet without him, and one which might well be able to pursue indefinitely the same timorous policy if Bonar Law and the older Unionists continued their support; if, for example, Bonar Law again reversed himself and chose to take the War Office rather than let the coalition go down. Bonar Law's irresolution made him unpredictable but such a preference for the course of least resistance was entirely in character.

These two courses held only the most unpromising possibilities both for his own political future and for affecting the conduct of the war, though it is interesting to speculate what his released energy could have made of that glimmering alliance with the Milner-Carson forces had he resigned at this point. That avenue was cluttered for the moment with the question of partition but, while it had temporarily patched some of the rents in the Unionist Party, it also showed up the serious weaknesses in the coalition, with the moderate Unionists like Lansdowne imposing strong objections to the settlement and many patriotic Liberals feeling that Asquith's continued deference to the Nationalists was self-indulgent and dangerous at a time of such national and international crises. Like Lloyd George, many more loyal Liberals felt betrayed by the Irish "stab in the back" and considered the deferred Home Rule agreement to have been abused. Their resentment as well as the Nationalists' inevitably rubbed off on Asquith when he withdrew his support for Lloyd George's proposals, which many of them believed to be viable. The onus for prolonging that nagging irritation fell upon Asquith and, with the help of a wide section of the press, heightened the image of squeamish lethargy attaching to his government.

Even before the reshuffling of Cabinet posts brought about by Kitchener's death, the Irish problem had prompted the demand for a reconstruction. The *Times* departed from its previously soft line in May and urged an immediate reorganization of the coalition. The same argument was echoed in editorials for the rest of the month. In June the new vacancy at the War Office provided a convenient occasion for Asquith to mollify criticism and allowed both Bonar Law and Lloyd George to nourish the impression that something was being done by moving the strongest man into a prominent, though anomalous, position without inciting the crisis for which neither was prepared. When Lloyd George finally relented and accepted the change of office, the Somme offensive had just begun (on 1 July) and the time for an election or a basic change in the government had passed, thanks primarily to the Irish diversion. If the campaign succeeded to the extent that the General Staff assured the government it would, assuming a sufficient supply of men (Robertson's obvious hedge), Asquith's position would be largely restored; otherwise, military failure would inevitably open up new opportunities for replacing him.

The move to the War Office thus temporarily neutralized Lloyd George as an immediate threat to the vulnerable coalition. Civilian ministers ran a particular risk of becoming entangled in its intricate prejudices. Despite the salutary effects of prewar reforms, the War Office had still not fully emerged from its "tropical jungle of festooned obstructiveness," as Lytton Strachey described it two years later. Most would still agree with his Miss Nightingale, who had found it "a very slow office, an enormously expensive office, and one in which the Minister's intentions can be entirely negatived by all his sub-departments, and those of each of the sub-departments by every other." The Kitchener-Robertson arrangement did nothing to clarify the proper relation of the minister to the C.I.G.S. nor to forestall a clash between the military and such an active minister as now occupied the civilian post. Even after basing his original refusal to Asquith on the absence of civilian control and of effective ministerial authority (as to patronage, for example), Lloyd George either forgot his objections or assumed that he could overcome Kitchener's handicaps when he accepted a month later. Inevitably, he soon found himself at odds with the generals, accused of exceeding his authority, of meddling in the military preserve on the matter of transport in France and the opening of a front in eastern Europe. The constraints under which he worked at the War Office, imposed by the terms he accepted in July, became a prime stimulus a few months later in his campaign for an executive War Council. Thus the ultimate dispute which led to his resignation and the fall of Asquith started as an effort to overrule Robertson on the question of civilian control at the War Office. Here was one ambition which could be held with a clear conscience amid the suspicion and intrigue to come and a principle not to be forgotten in the framing of future War Ministries.

The prospects for trouble at the War Office were not borne out immediately. In the first flush, Lloyd George immersed himself with his usual vigor in the seductive illusions of the office: grand strategy, tours of the front amid the flattering rigmarole of military jargon and protocol—narcotics that few neophyte ministers were able to resist. The new experience was a stimulating release from the increasingly pedestrian business of Munitions and the ungrateful labors of the Irish talks. It was, according to Miss Stevenson (who naturally moved with him), "like children going to a new school."[31]

Lloyd George's five months as Secretary of State for War made up the least distinguished period of his administrative career. He left no such imprint on the office as he had left on his other ministries, only partly because its diminished powers left him so little scope for energy and innovation. He was appointed by a Prime Minister whose confidence he did not enjoy, in the full knowledge that he was completely out of sympathy with the running of the war, and to a post in which his sympathies could not help but bring him into conflict with his subordinates, with the military, and ultimately with the government. The appointment served only the short-term comfort of the harassed leadership and could not have been made if the office carried the powers which he originally stipulated; if Asquith had granted those powers he would in effect have been renouncing his own stated policy of the limited war and a whole range of domestic and international positions which derived from it. Like Lloyd George's contentious scheme for the War Council in November, Asquith's appointment of him to the War Office had relatively little to do with improving the machinery for making war. Both were political gambits aimed at cloaking deeper rifts in the Liberal view of the war and the society which neither yet fully understood or desired to recognize as permanent.

Lloyd George had now entered on a new stage in his career and a critical phase in the development of his overall political outlook. The period between July and December was a last apprenticeship in his transformation from a parochial, sectarian, then national figure into a European politician. We see him after each step in his

---

[31] A. J. P. Taylor (ed.), *Lloyd George: A Diary* (26 July 1916), p. 109.

progress from the Board of Trade to the premiership being drawn closer to one and then another section of the forces of order: to the industrial managers and the Fabians, whose catechism of efficiency promised both progress and social justice through order and discipline; to the Tariff Reformers who preached the same simple and just cause on the imperial scale; and, finally, to the patro-bureaucracy of managers and intellectuals advanced by the war who could see opposition to their guidance only as treasonous, anarchist, or simpleminded. Ten years before 1916 a "businessmen government," Fabian social engineering, and even Tariff Reform Social-Imperialism could pass as radical ideas in a political milieu dominated by landed interests and laissez-faire Liberalism. They offered new instruments of social change to that generation of reformist politicians who found the traditional parliamentary route slow and frustrating and, more often than not, futile. The war opened new uses and demands for such methods. But frequently, when the prewar reformers found themselves thrust onto the international stage, they also found the once wanted instruments of domestic progress to be most adaptable to defending the status quo.

XI

"Advocates of Another Method"

Any judgment on the Lloyd George coalition must depend primarily on the successes and failures of its first two years. It was first of all a war government, deriving its sanction and most of the public support for its extraordinary executive powers from the commitment to an all-out war effort and unconditional victory. Judged solely on that commitment, the Lloyd George government of 1917-1918 was undisputably a success—the grosser blunders of the previous two years were generally avoided, the executive war machinery was streamlined and, though the "knockout blow" was never delivered, an unconditional surrender was won. While it is not impossible that much the same would have been accomplished by the Asquith government had it survived, perhaps even a similar peace settlement, it still remains that Lloyd George presided at the victory. When he took office in December 1916 the basic problems of wartime organization, production, and manpower which had mortified the Liberal government were largely under control; wartime methods were at least understood if not yet fully accepted. The issue which brought about the fall of Asquith turned on how and by whom the already existing machinery was to be directed and to what eventual end the mobilized strength of the nation was to be devoted. Well before the prospect of victory had become assured, concern for the postwar had begun to influence and sometimes dominate political and military plans.

Just as prewar prejudices such as those surrounding Irish Home Rule tended to distract the politics of the first two years of war, preoccupations about the postwar heavily influenced thinking within the new coalition. Despite great differences in their political and social outlook, few Europeans had been made cynical enough even yet to accept the horrible waste of men and resources without ascribing some future purpose to it, whether a vision of the "land fit for heroes" or new and greater empires. Those who had been worried about social disorder and the decay of discipline and old virtues before the war often hoped to gain something from the war by carrying over the wartime militarization of politics and society into the peace; on the other hand, many of the prewar reformers who had been frustrated by the obstinacy of the old men and institutions dreaded handing over their new powers, dismantling their efficiently operating agencies and commissions to return to the weary mill of parliamentary committees and party compromises. The Lloyd George coalition drew from both these sources; indeed, in some of its leading men the two inclinations were felt simultaneously and produced an odd authoritarian and progressive mix in the coalition's policies.

In a prospectus on "The Labour Exchanges After the War" written at the Board of Trade during the summer of 1916, William Beveridge laid out a plan which fairly accurately reflects the ambiguous tendencies which went into the coalition. Extending Leo Chiozza Money's earlier suggestion to employ the Labour Exchanges as the instrument of mobilizing labor for war production, Beveridge proposed using the exchanges not merely to guide the flow of labor back into civilian work during the process of demobilization, but to organize labor after the war "for the purpose of National recuperation." The latter role could be by far the more important, he said, since the exchanges would be serving both as a clearinghouse between the wartime and peacetime economy and as the central input for the revitalization of the old industrial system. Thus the key to the operations of such agencies as the Labour Exchanges during the war would be in their use of the wartime powers in preparing the way for social and economic reconstruction. The work of mobilizing labor for the purpose of "National recuperation," he argued, "should occupy the Exchanges, not merely after the process of demobilisation had been completed, but during that period, and . . . of the two processes the former is the more important: in fact . . . demobilisation should itself be but an incident of mobilisation."[1]

For many of the non-Socialist and nonpacifist intellectuals who found themselves recruited into the wartime bureaucracies, here was a potential means of fulfilling some of the frustrated promises of prewar reform ideals. Reconstruction along lines such as those

[1] William Beveridge, "The Labour Exchanges After the War" (summer 1916), *Bev. P.*, M672, no. 7.

suggested in Beveridge's plan, and later embodied in the Ministry of Reconstruction, was to be a last chance to test those ideals against postwar reaction and radicalism—a last assertion of the Victorian faith in Improvement and the Edwardian science of Efficiency.

It was widely thought that two years of war had brought the principles of efficiency—organization, expertise, and planning—further into the actual functioning of government than had the previous decade, despite the effusive lip service paid to those principles before the war. It would be an intolerable waste of the massive sacrifices it took to achieve this if all the wartime controls and agencies were to be dismantled with the coming of peace. The decisive moment, Beveridge pointed out, would occur during the period of demobilization and in that period labor was bound to be one of the most critical areas in which the conflicting visions of the postwar would be tested. The guiding principle of the Labour Exchanges as well as the other planning agencies in preparing for that moment, he argued, should be "Organisation":

> Perhaps no word denoting a general principle is so frequently used today as 'Organisation.' Rightly or wrongly organisation is said to have been conspicuously lacking in the past; . . . it has an unpleasant and disturbing sound, if it means anything. It suggests unwelcome visions of the curtailing of liberty and the transformation of the individual into a unit. The fact remains, however, that it represents a necessity forced upon us by circumstances from which there is no escape. There is talk of organising everything after the war; possibly there may be some form of general military service; there are rumours that a definite attempt is to be made to organise trade; even the Churches are thinking about some general scheme of unification. It will be the duty of the Labour Exchanges so to organise Labour that waste is eliminated and the best possible value obtained from every source.
>
> We have double reason for doing so. In the first place, such organisation is necessary in the national interest. The reasons are too well known and have been too often stated to need repetition.[2]

Beveridge was the most experienced man in government on the operations of the Labour Exchanges, having been recruited by Churchill to the Board of Trade (on Beatrice Webb's recommendation) to assist in drawing up the bill which had created them seven

[2] Ibid.

years earlier. By the same token, he had a particular interest in seeing their functions expanded to what he felt was their full potential —indeed, his suggestions for expansion were nothing less than revolutionary. His basic proposal was to make the engagement of all labor through the Labour Exchanges *compulsory* in the six critical national industries: munitions, docks, railroads, shipping, mining, and agriculture. By an order in Council or an act of Parliament, the exchanges would be invested with "sole and complete control" of the supply and movement of labor in those categories. Beveridge was conscious only to a limited degree of the opposition his proposals would encounter. He put forth several rather blunt methods by which opposition might be overcome if the government were sufficiently determined. First, in certain industries where management was likely to be hostile to the controls, compliance "could probably be effected by a threat to have the work performed in Government establishments, and if necessary this threat could be carried out"—as an afterthought, he also suggested that in the long run it would probably be cheaper "to erect and equip National factories and save intermediate profits. . . ." Private firms would then be given the choice between cooperating in bearing a fair share of the cost of supplying their labor or facing "competition by nationalisation." Without referring directly to the problem of overcoming the inevitable outrage of organized labor, he also made several unconvincing but imaginative suggestions to soften opposition from that side:

> In the first place, habit is a strong thing. The war measures have already engendered a certain sense of custom in this respect, and the opposition would not be as strong as it would have been had such a thing never been attempted before. Secondly, the proposal can be put forward as, in the first instance, a temporary measure, to hold good for a certain period after the close of the war. By a series of gradual extensions, backed by a reference to the good results occurring, it can be made permanent.
>
> Thirdly, there is not the least reason why arguments which have been effectively used during the war should not be equally effectively used after it. We should undertake a strenuous and unrelenting campaign in the press and on the platform, showing the national need for the measures we propose.
>
> We can back up our efforts by an appeal to interest and to sentiment. . . .
>
> A further measure, which would appeal both to interest and to

sentiment, would be to reorganise and strengthen the Advisory Trade Committees with a view both to letting employers and workmen feel that they had a real living share in the administration of affairs instead of being subject to an irksome bureaucratic control. . . .

I think we might go even further in our efforts to mobilise an army for the work of the trades we are considering. Sentiment is an extremely useful handle, and *I suggest that we should regard the men who answered our appeal as a special industrial force, and treat them on quasi-military lines.* We should supply them with enrollment forms and attractive badges and have an annual holiday and review on the anniversary of the date upon which peace is signed. After the experience of the present war, it scarcely seems necessary to excuse the apparent childishness of such methods by pointing out, childish or not, they really do appeal to an existing instinct, the gratification of which it would be mere folly to decline if something useful is to be gained by it. . . .

The opportunity is unique, and it is wisdom to strike while the iron is hot. . . . *It seems well worth while, profiting by the lesson of the war, to do all that is possible to turn the present favorable state of public opinion to good account by organising Labour on a sound basis and making the organisation permanent.*[3]

Needless to say, Beveridge's grandiose scheme was not the routine stuff of committee meetings at the Board of Trade. In fact, the Labour Exchanges report seems to have been circulated only privately and not always in complete form; the only officials who appear to have seen the whole document in 1916 were Vaughan Nash (Beveridge's immediate superior), Llewellyn Smith, and Lloyd George, for whose eyes it was originally intended. One section, proposing that workers and employers participating in the Labour Exchanges plan be granted special concessions under the National Insurance Act, was presented by Vaughan Nash to the Webbs who were then engaged in drafting a report on the control of industry for the Board of Trade. Another excerpt, also bearing a strong resemblance to the B.W.N.L. "industrial pyramid" plan, reached Beatrice Webb from the same source in the form of a memorandum describing a great profit-sharing scheme to be set up between the unions and management of the six industries. The Webbs saw the project as a sign that the permanent officials of the Board of Trade were intent, as they also thought Lloyd George's ministry to be, on undermining the strength of the trades unions.[4]

[3] Ibid. My italics.
[4] Beatrice Webb, "Diary" (8 June 1916), *P.P.*

310

Both the stimulus and the circulation of such brainstorms as the Labour Exchanges plan often ran obliquely across the usual departmental and party lines, as well as between government agencies and private groups such as the Round Table, the Fabian Society, and the B.W.N.L. The war had greatly raised the bureaucratic metabolism, producing a disorderly profusion of advisory boards and special commissions whose exact purpose was not always remembered or recognized when they were ready to report. The surplus energies of amateur recruits, the breakdown of party patronage, sudden shifts among the coalition ministers, and the intrusion of whole new ministries not only brought the inevitable cross-purposes and jurisdictional confusion, but tended to further weaken central coordination and the chain of command within and below the Cabinet level. The process necessarily had the effect of further eroding party discipline and party leadership while it enhanced the influence of permanent officials and private members, especially those affiliated with the various leagues and pressure groups which enjoyed a relatively greater cohesion as party deterioriated.

Since Lloyd George's own Ministry of Munitions had been one of the main causes and principal beneficiaries of this fraying in the bureaucratic web, it is perhaps not surprising that one of the first acts of the Lloyd George coalition government was to set up the Machinery of Government Committee under Haldane to bring the burgeoning departments under control. What had happened in Parliament and the parties was also in progress in the permanent bureaucracy—the traditional divisions and discipline were apparently giving way to freewheeling ginger groups and private circles orbiting around insurgent leaders like Lloyd George, Milner, and Carson. As always, the Webbs' numerous protégés kept them well informed. Beatrice Webb noted the "intellectual ferment" stirring in the departments during the spring and summer of 1916, led mainly by their own "Fabian Research young men" along with the Round Table and Lloyd George troops. Over the whole bureaucracy there was breeding a "spirit of secrecy and suspicion—Government Departments, refusing to publish the Reports of their Advisory Committees, employers concerting in private, rival groups of reformers and rebels scheming this way and that." There were definite potential dangers in all this, given examples like Beveridge's plan, but possible benefits as well, the Webbs thought: ". . . in spite of all this muddle and cross purpose there is a steady drift towards Government control and responsibility, on the one hand, and on the other towards the full recognition of the producer's organisations as junior partners in the control."[5]

That steady drift was apparent outside as well as inside the government offices. On the question of controls, especially when it came to controls in labor and industry, a definite but as yet uncoordinated movement of opinion was emerging in the country made up of a combination of the longtime proponents of massive state intervention, such as the Milnerites, the Fabians, and the Lloyd George reformers on the one hand, and on the other patriotic hardliners of all political descriptions, including a growing percentage of the trades union movement and the Liberal Party. The concerns of the two were not always the same, or even compatible; in the popular press and patriotic trades union circles the demand for increasingly sterner controls was stimulated mainly by the twin bogeys of "shirking" and profiteering. This was part of the "sentiment" which Beveridge urged the government to reach in order to gain popular approval of the permanent controls.

While Beveridge, like the host of Edwardian reformers who operated somewhere between Fabian collectivism and the Radical wing of the Liberal Party, undoubtedly looked upon himself as a democrat, his position had now become hardly distinguishable from that of the Milnerites. The mingling of the two forces had been foreshadowed at various points before the war in what we have called the Social-Imperialist movement, but never before had there existed such a harmony of views on a range of specific issues as now developed in 1916. It had always been characterized by a mutual faith in the efficacy of state interference in the social and economic process through a more or less independent bureaucracy of "experts"—the reverse side of that concept naturally involved some degree of contempt for the democratic institutions, including the parliamentary and party system whose most useful purpose, Beatrice Webb had once observed, was as a "Foolometer" for the expert. Lloyd George's "glorified grocers and Tory backwoodsmen" and Milner's "Mandarins" had come in for a great deal more such abuse during the war from much the same sources and that abuse could now be focused sharply on the leadership of the first coalition. It was also more plausible now to project that elusive combination of conservative working men and enlightened bureaucrats which Chamberlain, Rosebery, Milner, the Fabians, and Lloyd George had more or less vainly sought before and which

[5] Ibid. (27 July 1916).

Beveridge envisioned as a possible political basis for the postwar reconstruction. Here also was something of Haldane's once-imagined "Centre," what Beatrice Webb had interpreted to mean the "non-political voter . . . the moderate politician: the capitalist or proletarian man who desires little social change and the Empire maintained."

The two wings of the movement had been divided in the past by a basic mutual mistrust dating back at least to the Boer War—the one side doubting the imperialists' interest in social progress and the other doubting the reformers' commitment to social order. Since then the imperialists had spent their main energy in developing a social program, mostly borrowed from the Fabians, while the bulk of the Fabian and Radical reformers showed a markedly greater interest in restraining the restless forces to their Left. Milner's once hazy affectations of "semi-Socialism" also became more substantial (if not much more Socialist): by the summer of 1916, his British Workers National League had adopted a program which included a standard minimum wage for industrial and agricultural workers as well as "National or Municipal Control of the Natural Monopolies and Vital Industries."[6] It need hardly be said that the Milner movement remained as stridently imperialist as ever (the same B.W.N.L. program also demanded expropriation of enemy holdings in the empire and a permanent system of national service), but its tone and understanding about working-class Socialism had become more sophisticated, if it had not otherwise changed, since the mock experiments with the Conservative Working Men's Association ten years before. Now, accompanying the shrill attacks on Socialist leaders and insipid appeals to old yeoman virtue were more tangible counterproposals like the minimum wage and public controls; at one point, for example, following a tirade against Mac-Donald for promoting pacifism and class strife, the league's official organ suggested a scheme similar to Beveridge's in which a vast network of labor-management cooperatives would "pyramid" into a National Council of Industry to regulate the economy with the aid of "expert State officials."[7]

What had once been a movement of atavistic imperial ideals, but still more or less frankly devoted to the middle class and property,

[6] *British Citizen and Empire Worker*, I, 1 (25 Aug. 1916).
[7] Ibid., I, 3 (8 Sept. 1916). The *B.C.E.W.* proposal for a National Council of Industry was directed explicitly at the Trades Union Congress about to meet, where John Hodge expected to move the plan formally.

streamlined during the war into a form of corporate Socialism more familiar to the twentieth than to the nineteenth century, one which is as hostile to traditional bourgeois and capitalist values as to revolutionary Socialism. Though the tendency was always there in Social-Imperialist thought and in the personalities of men like Milner, the war helped to sharpen both its edges. In its very first lead article, "What We Think," the B.W.N.L. weekly of August 1916 argued that the war had changed all the old divisions in class and politics:

> Unprepared, untaught, every tradition and every prejudice exploited, mainly by middle-class treason-mongers, the manual workers have risen with splendid virility to the full heights of their responsibilities. . . . They have done this while party politicians have flirted with treason or used their positions for self-aggrandisement, and while a minority of the employing class has been, to our utter shame, tolerated in the dirty business of making huge profits while their fellows were dying on the battlefield.[8]

The minds of the Milnerites and the other Tory insurgent groups in the summer and fall of 1916 were also fastened on the postwar. As we have seen, the B.W.N.L. had been founded with the "immediate THEREAFTER" primarily in view, to prevent the reopening of the "dreary record of class struggle when the *international* war comes to an end," as the league's weekly put it. Like Beveridge and the Fabians, Milner's organizations made it clear that the various projects they were putting forth were meant to extend beyond the war—indeed, that whatever advantages they contained for the war effort were secondary to their longer-range purpose. Similarly, the urgency for administering the coup de grace to the first coalition and the old parties was argued from the long-range perspective. Milner expounded this side of the argument in the *Times* just two days before the surprise Nigerian division of 8 November: the mistake being made by many of the coalition's critics (obviously referring to Lloyd George as well as to some of the Tariff Reformers) was "in thinking that the principles of GO AS YOU PLEASE and the General Scramble, which may have been necessary and even appropriate during the inevitable break-up of the Old Order, could possibly be the permanent foundations of the New."[9]

The coalition's critics from the Right were thus in agreement

[8] Ibid., I, 1 (25 Aug. 1916).   [9] *Times*, 6 Nov. 1916.

with the bureaucrat-reformers that, whatever new order was to replace it, the regular Liberal and Unionist forces combined in the present regime were incapable of providing either progress or order for the future, were perhaps even incapable or unwilling to achieve a decisive victory in the war. Unmistakable also in both their private reports and propaganda by the summer of 1916 was the confident assumption, first, that the breakup of the so-called old order was imminent and inevitable and, second, that whatever measures they proposed to hasten that end and prepare for the aftermath were ordained and justified by *necessity*. Here was one of the descendants of the Social-Imperialist dialectic born in the Boer War —for them efficiency was ordained by sheer survival in a world they had divided into order versus chaos, success versus failure, and all else must be sacrificed to it. So had Shaw defended his imperialism: "The world is to the great and powerful of necessity." The appeal to fated necessity, as most of Europe was soon to discover, could be as persuasive a weapon in the hands of bureaucrats as in those of revolutionaries.

The most significant and telling aspect of the agitation against the first coalition was the year-long debate over military and industrial compulsion. By early 1916, the issue had ceased to be primarily a question of supplying military manpower and had begun to focus, as we have seen, on the far more volatile subject of "general" compulsion. The Ministry of Munitions was the natural locus of the dispute, since its assigned function inevitably brought it up against the profound ambiguities of wartime democratic controls. Once voluntarism, along with the hope of a short and limited war, had been discarded as a method of supplying soldiers, the pressure to shift to a compulsory system for supplying industrial manpower as well became almost irresistible. Even before the Second Military Service Act, the advocates of universal conscription had taken it for granted that voluntary recruitment was doomed. The same assumption was made by the advocates of general compulsion—that Asquith's pledges against industrial conscription must inevitably be abandoned, either by progressive "accretion" of powers to the Ministry of Munitions and other control agencies or, as some would have preferred, by a simple *ukase* of a new war government. It was out of this confident assumption that plans such as Chiozza Money's, Beveridge's, and the Milnerites' for the organization of labor and industry were made months before the Asquith government's demise. The Beveridge plan, for example, originated in a private memo for the Minister of Munitions sometime in the spring before Lloyd George had left for the War Office. The original memo, titled "Heads of a Scheme for the Compulsory Transference of Men from Unessential Work to Work of National Importance," was a straightforward method of conscripting any men who refused work assigned by the ministry and was explicitly made contingent on obtaining release from Asquith's pledges to labor.[10]

Chiozza Money's plan to "draft" labor into the export industries, with the same contingency, had appeared the previous November.

Perhaps most indicative of the momentum the expectation of general compulsion had built up by the time of the Military Service Acts was the pessimistic fatalism of many of its principal opponents. Asquith, irretrievably tethered to the pledges, and the Liberal voluntarists were irresolutely fighting a rearguard action in the debates of March and April. The Labour Party conference and executive, once having formally protested military conscription at Bristol, soon became more concerned with losing control of the northern shop stewards after failing to hold out against the January act and failing to prevent the prosecution of the strikers in February. Henderson, according to Sidney Webb, had succeeded in cowing the Labour Party executive by warnings that the alternative to extending conscription would be a general election in which every Labour seat might be lost.[11] Indeed, the increasing resort to unauthorized action by the rank-and-file workers on the Clyde, one of the more powerful stimulants in moving opinion towards industrial compulsion, might itself be seen as a loss of faith in the ability or intention of the government to resist it. Just as McKenna had allowed the great Free Trade dike to be breached by protectionist pressures in the 1915 budget, a large part of the labor movement acquiesced in the extension of industrial compulsion partly out of the feeling that controls over labor would be paralleled by controls over profits and partly because the argument for some degree of wartime controls seemed unanswerable. Even the severest labor critics of industrial compulsion seemed convinced that Asquith was bound to renege on the pledges anyway. Walter Runciman, whose name was synonymous with the staunchest defense of laissez-faire principles, had to admit (as president of the Board of Trade), "We

[10] Memo, "Industrial Compulsion and Conscription," *Bev. P.*, M672, no. 3 (n.d.).

[11] B. Webb, "Diary" (2 Jan. 1916), *P.P.*; quoting Sidney Webb's description of a meeting of the executive committee of the Labour Party.

have been driven bit by bit, against our will to suspend the easy flow of purely voluntary action." What else could be done to control the supply of food but to appoint a Food Controller?[12]

In practically every wartime department and agency having anything to do with the supply and exchange of goods, manpower, or capital, Runciman's experience was duplicated, almost regardless of the former ideological bent of its chief official. If there were significant exceptions, they were more likley to be found in cases like the Ministry of Munitions or Milner's Committee on Agriculture where the inclination was more in the direction of making controls complete than towards restraining them. It is true that before the formation of the Lloyd George government, most of the government departments and the Cabinet were still headed by voluntarists of one sort or another, but their position was defensive and was being progressively undermined not only by the necessities of war but by their subordinates in the bureaucracy, by the encroachments of the larger ministries and by mounting agitation in the press for government action. Thus, the view that the wartime controls did not grow according to an overall plan but accumulated "regulation upon regulation" in response to specific needs accurately describes the process which occurred in most government departments. This has been the prevailing view of economic historians and corresponds closely with the official histories published after the war, such as the *History of the Ministry of Munitions* (a large part of which was based on materials and commentary supplied by Beveridge).[13] However, such a description takes no account of the massive accumulated influx of committee reports, memorandums, speeches, pamphlets, editorials, and private opinion which pressed heavily upon the Asquith government by 1916 to institute sweeping and systematic controls over the nation's resources and manpower. Whether that pressure was communicated through traditional opponents of state intervention like the *Daily News*, the

[12] House of Commons, 15 Nov. 1916; see Arthur Marwick's excellent chapter, "The Challenge to Laissez-Faire," in *The Deluge*, pp. 178-192.

[13] Marwick, *The Deluge*. Marwick describes a broad spectrum of "informed public opinion" in 1916 which favored general state action towards a controlled economy. Based also on scattered but persistent trends within the Civil Service in 1915, his evidence suggests that the "theories" which guided the Lloyd George government in the matter of controls were "fully hatched by the Autumn of 1915." Cf. *Official History of the Ministry of Munitions*, 8 vols. (1918-1922), vol. VII, pt. I, pp. 6-9; vol. VIII, pt. I, pp. 29-35.

Manchester Guardian, and the *Economist* (and ministers like Runciman) who conceded the need for controls for the sake of wartime efficiency or to restrain profiteering and strikes, or whether it came from more expected sources like the Fabians and the Tariff Reformers, the weight of most influential opinion in the country militated towards a deliberate shift in the basic policies of the government.

The fundamental difference between the two schools of thought on questions like general compulsion was no longer the relatively simple matter of how much was necessary to mobilize the nation for war but also of how far the wartime precedents and powers might survive afterward, to create either the "Servile State" or the "land fit for heroes." That question would have to be confronted in 1916 unless the war were to come to a quick end either on the battlefield or through negotiation. Efforts were made in the year to achieve both, but failing that improbable reprieve, all the methods and attitudes predicated on a limited war were doomed by the time the Somme offensive opened in July. The "advocates of another method" had won their point and the public mind by then—all that remained was to find the political will and opportunity to put it into action.

The Political Crisis of November–December 1916

The final assault against the first coalition was mounted only after the staggering cost of the Somme had become known at home— more than 400,000 casualties by the time it finally halted in the October mud and, even more incredibly, no strategical gains. None of the prewar European governments had been prepared ideologically for a struggle of this magnitude and none survived this phase of the fighting intact. But the same shock which visibly paralyzed the morale of the established leadership provided new stimulus for insurgent forces in all the belligerent nations and elsewhere in the world. Under the circumstances, the collapse of the ten-year-old Liberal government in England is less remarkable than its tenacity in the final throes.

The immediate series of events which culminated in the new coalition of December was initiated, as several coalition attempts had been before, by an uprising of the Unionist right wing, spearheaded by the Tariff Reform section. This time the agitation arose over the seemingly trivial issue of whether enemy property in Nigeria should be sold at open auction, with no distinction or advantage made for British bidders. This was the government's policy. Organized by Carson and the Unionist Business Committee, which included the most vocal members of the Tariff Reform League, the revolt of 8 November came close to marshaling a majority of the Unionist Party in Parliament for the vote against the government. Since the government motion was put by Bonar Law's Under-Secretary at the Colonial Office, Steel-Maitland, the division represented a serious challenge to the leadership of the Unionist Party as well as to its participation in the coalition.[14]

The debate was rightly taken by the Unionist leadership to be a challenge for control of the parliamentary party, but it is a mistake commonly made to view the Nigerian Properties issue as a mere pretext for Carson's revolt, without important substance in itself. Its connection with the sequence of events leading to the fall of Asquith was not and could not have been planned by Carson and the insurgents since that result depended on the rather subtle and unforeseeable change in Bonar Law's mind over the next few weeks and by the intervention of Lloyd George and Beaverbrook. Although the Tariff Reformers did not mourn the fall of Asquith and the breakup of the Liberal Party later on, the Carson revolt in November was directed primarily against the Unionist leadership—the Nigerian issue was chosen to demonstrate the strength of the Tariff Reform section on a question which had divided the Unionist Party since Chamberlain, the same issue which had expelled Balfour in 1911. The cluster of ideas with which the Tariff Reformers had surrounded the basic principle of Imperial Protection inevitably helped to divide the Unionist Party on policies to be followed during the war, not only on big domestic questions like conscription and controls but on a whole range of world issues in which they felt their concept of a modern anti-Socialist empire was at stake. The Lansdowne letter on negotiated peace and Balfour's memorandum on Palestine were to be only the most obvious examples of the profound difference in outlook which increasingly separated the two sections of the Unionist Party as the war progressed.

With his eyes focused steadfastly at his own feet, Bonar Law was always to be found plodding along in that gap. His approval of the

[14] Although the Steel-Maitland motion passed by more than 100 votes in the House, Carson managed to raise 117 against, 24 short of a majority of the Unionist section.

government motion was based on an honest application of the spirit of the resolutions of the recent Paris conference in which the Allies promised to abandon such economic restrictions for the duration in the name of cooperation against Germany. The Tariff Reform League, in fact, had enthusiastically endorsed the resolutions up to the time of the debate and even during the revolt showed little personal animosity toward Bonar Law.[15] It was Bonar Law himself who escalated the debate to a question of confidence in his own leadership when he rose to defend the government against the increasingly fierce attacks from the ginger group late on the evening of 8 November. Only after he had done so did Carson take the opportunity to shift the focus of the attack to the Unionist leadership. Noting the absence of the Liberal Front Bench, "every one of them," he turned to the Tory side: "I wish the Prime Minister was here. I dare say he has very good reasons for being away, because I always notice that whenever I and my Friends get up on this side of the House, and whenever I and my Friends come into collision with the Government, it is always left to the Unionist Members of the Government to reply. That is a pretty tactical manoeuvre but I do not think my honourable and right honourable Friends opposite ought to lend themselves to it. I tell them this, however, that the country thinks so also."[16] Obviously upset and unprepared, Bonar Law acted hastily, first, by bringing up the matter of confidence in the government while it was still possible to avoid it and then foolishly ignoring the fact that he was the senior representative of the government present in the House.[17]

Poorly considered as Bonar Law's move was, it had unexpectedly favorable consequences for him. If Carson's uprising was meant as a demonstration of the insurgent Unionists' strength or as a serious challenge to the government, it had been very sloppily prepared, though improvisation was not one of Carson's usual faults. The vote in fact split the strength of the Tariff Reformers by forcing moderate leaders like Chamberlain and Smith into the government lobby and underexposed the power of antigovernment sentiment in Parliament by making the issue so sectarian on protectionism that relatively few disaffected Liberals could cross over. With a large segment of their support registered by the Irish, who impressed no one at this stage by voting against the government, and

[15] "War Notes," *T.R.L.*, II, 29 (1 Nov. 1916), 65.
[16] House of Commons, 8 Nov. 1916.
[17] Ibid.

"Advocates of Another Method"

by Liberal mavericks like Churchill and Alfred Mond, it was not a plausible threat to either the Unionist or the Liberal leaders. Yet, it had quite another impact on decisions made by those leaders over the next few weeks. The division momentarily dampened the hopes of the Tariff Reform vanguard of withdrawing the party from the coalition while it opened up a greater freedom of action for Bonar Law who was now relieved of the fear that the long-held protectionist majority in the party could be used to force his hand. With all Beaverbrook's persuasion, it is difficult to imagine Bonar Law acting as he did without that assurance. Perhaps more important still, the temporary check to the Unionist ginger group's campaign substituted Bonar Law for the far more radical Carson or Milner as the main collaborator with Lloyd George in creating the new coalition of December and as his main partner in the reconstruction. This was one change in the pattern of the previous year which was to have a profound effect on Lloyd George's behavior and on the character of the second coalition.

The Nigerian vote was not needed to heighten the importance of Lloyd George to all parties in the political crisis; without a private constituency comparable to either Carson's or Milner's and lacking even the ordinary influence among the leaders of his own party, it is one of the remarkable proofs of his personal force and reputation that he alone was considered essential to any plan either to overturn or to preserve the government. The division of 8 November was for him a mock battle which he felt free to observe with relative detachment. On the night of the debate, when the Liberal whips sought him out, they were informed that he was "dining with Carson." In fact, as near as can now be gathered (mainly from Beaverbrook's account), he spent the early evening dining at the house of Arthur Lee, his Military Secretary at the War Office, with both Carson and Milner—their conversation is said to have concerned the general situation and the "possibilities of cooperation" without the Nigerian question even arising.[18] It is well known that the rumor of his seeing Carson just before the debate caused many to think that he was in some way behind the uprising in the House a few hours later. But there was no indication in the debate or the division of the incident having been organized between them. Addison indicated the attitude of the Lloyd George men: he stayed out of the debate and voted with the government. Only Churchill's

[18] Beaverbrook, *Politicians and the War*, p. 301.

largely unnoticed defection and Mond's hyperbolic attack on the government policy gave any clue to sympathy between the Lloyd George and Carson factions. Mond, who was not yet so closely identified with Lloyd George as he was later to be, outdid both Carson and Hewins in assailing the Free Trade principle of the Colonial Office motion: the policy suggested for Nigeria not only would set a precedent for allowing foreign interests into the empire but if followed after the war might permit those interests, especially the Americans, to penetrate the English home market by an indirect route. Thus, as he put it, ". . . not a German but an American capitalist is to come here and we are to work for him and slave for him and the profits are to go over to the United States." Some sense of the disarray of the Tariff Reform attack may be gotten from the fact that Halford Mackinder, the leading theorist of the Tariff Reform League, found himself defending the government motion against Mond.[19]

Though Lloyd George had long been closer ideologically and temperamentally to the Tariff Reformers than to the "glorified grocers" of his own party, it had always been a tacit condition of their cooperation that, as during the constitutional crisis and the passage of the Insurance Bill, each side could deliver tangible strength. Carson is more likely to have grasped the opportunity of the Nigerian debate merely to demonstrate that strength for the future than to have volunteered as Lloyd George's pawn in what must otherwise be regarded as a rather clumsy gambit.

Over the weeks preceding the November crisis, periodic meetings between Lloyd George, Carson, and Milner had been taking place at Arthur Lee's Great College Street residence, a few doors from Milner's.[20] The "Triumvirate" (a name first given to them by Amery) focused the hopes of the most vehement "Asquith Must Go" sentiment, combining among them a diverse but potentially powerful alignment of the insurgent forces against the patricians of both parties over the previous decade—an alliance of Lloyd George Radicals, protectionists, and Ulstermen. It is impossible to give precise demarcations to the popular base of the three factions during the war years, yet there was an evident convergence in what

[19] House of Commons, 8 Nov. 1916.
[20] Evelyn Wrench, *Alfred Lord Milner*, p. 307. Wrench adds Lee's name to the list of Lloyd George's "go-betweens" of 1916. Lee, who followed Lloyd George from Munitions to the War Office, is described by Wrench as the "main link" with Milner.

the three leaders *felt* to be their "moral" constituency into something resembling Haldane's erstwhile "Centre": "the capitalist or proletarian man who desired little social change and the Empire maintained."

Within that supposed constituency there was obviously room for a wide variation of class and ideology, but by 1916 there was just as clearly no room for Socialists of the shop steward, I.L.P., or academic variety or for pacifists, Irishmen, Free Traders, or internationalists. On top of their shared dislikes, we have also seen a substantial basis of agreement being built among the three on the old party system, on the permanent expansion of state controls, on unconditional victory, and on a general approach to postwar reconstruction. At the moment, the public image of the "Triumvirate" was distinctly that of the "all-outers" and in the demoralized atmosphere produced by the Somme any effective combination of the three would contain a potent, perhaps irresistible, force in the political balance, whether or not they were able to muster parliamentary majorities.

It was the fear of this body of opinion that Henderson had appealed to when persuading the Labour Party executive to accept military conscription despite the resistance of the party conference, warning that the wave of warlike opinion might sweep every Labour seat before it in a general election.[21] Milner shared Henderson's view all along and pressed futilely for election during 1916. Though he was probably overconfident in the strength and influence of the B.W.N.L. and the various other right-wing leagues and organizations, an election any time after July might well have resulted in a defensive drift toward the Right in all parties and a consequent weakening in the moderate coalition leadership. This was Milner's hope at all times and, rightly or wrongly, not only the Labour Party executive and the I.L.P. but Asquith and Bonar Law dreaded the prospects of a "Coupon Election" in that atmosphere even if the coupons were theirs to dispense. It is well to bear that fear in mind also when trying to understand Asquith's puzzling moments of timidity during the coming crisis.

Milner's position, as always, was more radical than his collaborators'. The overwhelming weight of opinion on the question of a general election was against him on all sides and he had no means of forcing an election as yet (his idea of the Lords bringing one

---

[21] B. Webb, "Diary" (2 Jan. 1916), *P.P.*

about was one of his more simpleminded projects). His cherished prospect of a "big Smash-up," a "Constructive Revolution," depended on Lloyd George and Carson; his hope was for them to act from the inside to bring about a break between the two party leaders, thus opening the way for a sweeping reconstruction of the government or an election. What he dreaded would come from their agitation was a "patch-up," merely another reshuffling of offices to placate the critics, with no basic change of policy and personnel. He was quite right in looking upon the present coalition as a device for shielding the detested party structures and leaders from below; the arrangement of May 1915 was certainly not the "above-party" National Coalition for which he and the imperialists had argued so long and upon which their periodic interest in Lloyd George was based. Any risk, including the inevitable chaos and disunity of a wartime election, was justified in his mind in preference to keeping the "truckload of Mandarins" of both parties in the government, even under a new head.

Milner and his *enragés*, and practically no one else, welcomed such a perilous showdown with "the System." Thus it was probably inevitable that Lloyd George and Carson would disappoint him in the course they chose to follow over the next few weeks. Neither held such optimistic (or fatalistic) prospects about a general election as he did. Lloyd George in particular did not stand to gain anything from an election at this point; indeed, he had to be extremely careful in his dealings with Asquith not to leave him without an alternative to dissolution. For, up until the early days of December, when Bonar Law had decided to abandon the coalition, Asquith was still in a position to appeal to the country against the dissidents with every probability of destroying them, at least for the short run. Backed by Bonar Law (as Asquith would have been before December) as well as the Conservative ministers and Labour, the coalition would have looked formidable indeed. Strong and spirited as the insurgents' support was in some quarters, they had very little to set against the Liberal, Labour, and Conservative electoral organizations if they could be made to work together to elect a slate of candidates loyal to the government.

Barring a general election, then, the situation brought about by the Nigerian debate appeared to be a standoff between the government and the antiministerial forces. Asquith's hand was especially strong now if he had had the will to use it, stronger objectively than it had been for some years: the Conservative Party looked to be on the verge of shattering between the Curzon, Bonar Law, and Tariff Reform factions; Labour, though also sorely divided internally, was formally committed to the government and, in fact, had been weaned away from its former sympathies with the Lloyd George–Churchill section during the compulsion fight. Like Labour, the Irish in Parliament were more firmly wedded to Asquith than ever, suspended as they were between a hostile English Parliament and public opinion and the radicals in Ireland. There was opportunity now for Asquith to repair much of the erosion of his position which had taken place over the past year either by resolving some of the sorest grievances of his rivals, like Lloyd George's complaints about the command structure, or by mobilizing the coalition against the dissidents while Bonar Law was still dependent upon him. It might be said that his situation in November was amenable to almost anything but inaction.

One of the most puzzling aspects of the crisis which finally created the National Coalition of December was the behavior of Asquith. He had been Prime Minister and leader of the party during the most distinguished and productive decade of Liberalism in England. Historically, one might also have expected him to have the place of the *prima persona* in Liberalism's closing scene. Yet he hardly appears to have been on stage at the climax of his own career and that of the tradition which he represented as faithfully as ever Gladstone did.

His own recollections and most of the later apologies picture him surrounded by treacheries and intrigues spun between friends and enemies, Lloyd George's ruthless ambition on one side and the foes of traditional freedoms on the other, making impossible demands, hamstringing him, leaving him no allies and no loyalties. It is a picture made plausible only by hindsight, however, when one already has in mind the postwar wreck of the Liberal Party rather than the formidable combination of forces which Asquith had at his disposal before his fall. The coming together of Lloyd George and Bonar Law was the crucial preliminary to Asquith's destruction, but that occurred only at the last moment, no more than two weeks before the final breakup. Moreover, even during the last few days of negotiation over the makeup of the new War Committee (from 2 to 5 December), no persuasive evidence has yet appeared to indicate that either of them wished to do any more than remove Asquith from the day-to-day operation of the committee, leaving him as Head of State and in a supervisory relation to the War Committee.

While the proposition made to him would undeniably reduce his influence on the direction of the war and over several of the key departments, by shifting powers from the Cabinet to the War Committee, his position would not have to be regarded as intolerable unless his main concern was to save face, to avoid seeming to be kept on the sufferance of his enemies.

Through the crisis of early December, that point of personal pride seems to have been Asquith's guiding emotion. All who were involved in the negotiations over the proposed new War Committee were acutely aware of his sensitivities, especially where Lloyd George was concerned. The pejorative epithets commonly employed in the press by Northcliffe and F. S. Oliver, "Squiff" or the "Great Exhauster,"[22] inevitably increased that sensitivity and made compromise more difficult; any arrangement which even appeared to raise Lloyd George or to curtail his powers he felt would be a public humiliation, bearing out the caricature projected of him by his enemies in the press. Under the circumstances, his contrary and generally inflexible attitude on the several proposals for the construction of the new War Committee submitted to him by Lloyd George, an attitude which was not at first expected by either his enemies or his supporters, is perhaps understandable. That he first accepted and then flatly rejected the Lloyd George proposals (of 1 and 4 December) which appeared to resolve their most serious differences over the War Committee, leaving Lloyd George no choice but to resign, is the question which requires further explanation.

We have seen already the confused circumstances under which Lloyd George accepted the War Office after Kitchener's death in June. Asquith frankly preferred to have Bonar Law for that post. When he refused, Lloyd George finally consented to become Secretary of State, but only after stating to the Prime Minister that the "humiliating conditions" under which Kitchener had worked must be improved. The situation which had now created the crisis be-

---

[22] F. S. Oliver was by far the most adept in creating such verbal caricatures of Asquith in the press and the clubs. He came to this last epithet through the following historical analysis: "There is the great 'Inspirer' but there is also the great 'Exhauster.' In the first class you have of course the elder Pitt and Cavour, and Jo. In the second class you have Louis XI, Li Hung Chang, Abdul Hamid, a number of Renaissance church statesmen, and Squiff." Oliver to Milner (22 Oct. 1916), *M.P.*, Letters–1916; *Times*, 26 Oct. 1916.

tween Lloyd George and Asquith—that is, the reconstruction of the War Committee—arose mainly because Lloyd George had failed to press for that clarification of his powers at the War Office and his authority vis-à-vis Robertson and the General Staff. In a sense, he was now trying to recoup that mistake through the reconstruction of the War Committee into a small, civilian board with complete authority for all policy and planning concerning the conduct of the war. The two keys to the working of such a committee were that it should have clear authority over the generals and that it should be free of parliamentary or "political" interference. In effect, it was to supersede the Cabinet in the control of the departments while Asquith was to remain as the link with the Cabinet—that is, as the buffer between the War Committee and Parliament. The small War Committee would thus escape its accountability to Parliament and the parties and become something of the "non-party" government for which both Lloyd George and the Social-Imperialists had searched so long.

Lloyd George's basic demands for the reconstruction of the War Committee (which he submitted to Asquith on 1 December) consisted of the following five points:

> That the War Committee consist of three Members, two of which must be the First Lord of the Admiralty and the Secretary of State for War, who should have in their offices deputies capable of attending to and deciding all departmental business—and a third Minister without portfolio. One of these three to be Chairman.
> That the War Committee shall have full power subject to the supreme control of the P.M. to direct all questions connected with the war.
> That the P.M. in his discretion to have the power to refer any question to the Cabinet.
> Unless the Cabinet on reference from the P.M. reverses decision of the War Committee, that decision to be carried out by the Department concerned.
> The War Committee to have the power to invite any Minister and to summon the expert advisors and officers of any Department to its meeting.[23]

[23] Lloyd George to Asquith, "Given to P.M. on Friday morning, 1 Dec.," *A.P.*, Dep. 31 (5 Dec. 1916); the list of demands submitted on 1 December is attached in Asquith's papers on the crisis to Lloyd George's letter of resignation of 5 December.

This was the document to which Asquith referred throughout the discussions of the following four days; it contained all of Lloyd George's essential demands and he never deviated from them. From the first there were two points of conflict over the proposals. The first and fatal one was that the Prime Minister should *not* be a member of the new War Committee. This of course was the issue over which Asquith finally stuck, but only after many hesitations and changes of heart. The second difference between them was far more substantial, although Asquith hardly seemed to be aware of it, at least not until the very end. The clear purport of Lloyd George's demands was that the War Committee of three would become the supreme executive agency in the government, directing "all questions connected with the war," subject only to the veto of the Cabinet. For that control to operate at all, however, the Prime Minister would have to initiate a reversal by the Cabinet (including the three committee members) and, in effect, precipitate just the sort of political crisis which they were now trying to avert. Asquith appreciated the constitutional weakness of such a position, but apparently did not fully realize that the War Committee's powers were to extend to the whole range of war mobilization, including the organization of manpower, labor, industry, shipping, food, and the myriad other areas in which the wartime departments had established a planning role. The intricate and crucial connection between such wartime domestic powers and long-term strategy, which Lloyd George understood very well, were still mostly a mystery to Asquith.

In his reply later that day to Lloyd George's demands, Asquith agreed in general with the complaints raised and the need for streamlining the War Committee: it was too large, there were obstructions and delays in some departments in obeying it, vital information was sometimes withheld by the departments, and it was generally overcharged with duties which could be delegated. He agreed also that the War Committee should exercise authority over the departments subject to appeal to the Cabinet. But he insisted that the Prime Minister must be the committee's chairman— "He can not be relegated to the position of an arbiter in the background or a referee to the Cabinet." The degree to which he misunderstood the intent of the Lloyd George proposals became obvious when he added, wishing to be cooperative in the reconstruction, that the change in the War Committee should be accompanied by the setting up of a Committee of National Organization "to deal with the purely domestic side of war Problems."[24]

The personal relations between Asquith and Lloyd George were at their lowest ebb but if the conflict had been limited to the two men, to an agreement about the powers of the War Committee and the Prime Minister's role, the situation would still have been far from irretrievable by Friday, 1 December. Indeed, by Monday morning Asquith had agreed to the essential points of Lloyd George's proposal, including his own exclusion from the War Committee; an agreement between them was apparently within reach with only the question of personnel (who was to occupy the third and possibly fourth chairs on the War Committee) yet to be determined.[25] The compromise which Asquith had himself introduced in a note to Lloyd George on Monday morning included the following stipulations: that the daily agenda of the committee be submitted to the Prime Minister; that the chairman report to him daily; that the Prime Minister could direct the committee to take up particular topics or proposals; that he retain a personal veto (presumably after consulting the Cabinet); and, finally, that he attend meetings of the War Committee at his discretion.[26] These conditions had a formidable appearance; they seemed to guarantee, as Asquith put it, that the Prime Minister would retain "supreme and effective control of War Policy." In this, as Asquith must have been at least partly aware, he was trading substance for semblance—most of the essential powers of the Cabinet were to be transferred to the War Committee which, with the suspension of parliamentary opposition, would have become the government. Asquith would be isolated, his position resembling that of one of the weaker constitutional monarchs.

The conditions laid down by Asquith were completely acceptable to Lloyd George once the principle of the Prime Minister's ex-

[24] Asquith to Lloyd George (1 Dec. 1916), *A.P.*, Dep. 31. Asquith was arguing at this time for a War Committee of four: the Secretary of State for War, the First Lord, the Minister of Munitions, and the Prime Minister.

[25] Asquith carefully avoided bringing up the "delicate and difficult question of personnel" in his discussions with Lloyd George and Bonar Law about the War Committee, yet he apparently felt that the problem could eventually be solved merely by adding members to "balance" the committee. Asquith to Lloyd George (1 Dec. 1916), *A.P.*, Dep. 31.

[26] Asquith to Lloyd George (4 Dec. 1916), *A.P.*, Dep. 31.

clusion from regular membership was established. That point had been discussed and, it seemed, settled at a meeting of the Prime Minister, Bonar Law, and himself in Downing Street on Sunday afternoon. It is clear that following that meeting the three principal parties to the negotiations expected the crisis would be settled by a reconstruction of the War Committee without the kind of general smash-up that men like Milner and Northcliffe had been working for. Bonar Law and Lloyd George were meeting regularly (mostly in the company of Beaverbrook) before and after speaking with the Prime Minister and up until their meeting at Downing Street they had a coordinated idea of what concessions were required from Asquith in order to establish the small, independent War Committee. While the very difficult question of personnel remained to be worked out, Asquith had been far more yielding than either of them had anticipated; in a sense he had taken them off guard.

The strategy being followed by the two before the concessions was to force a general reconstruction of the coalition through the threat of resignation by its major Conservative members and Lloyd George over the issue of inefficiency in the conduct of the war. Lloyd George had already prepared his letter of resignation (on Saturday, 2 December) and Bonar Law had acquired the permission of Curzon, Cecil, and Chamberlain to threaten their resignation unless a reconstruction was made.[27] The situation expected to arise from such an impasse was not, as Milner and some others hoped, a dissolution and an election but one in which the press and the most vociferous voices in the Paliament, the ginger groups and the patriotic orators, would replace the electorate in deciding the mandate and makeup of the new coalition.

The style and tactic of the campaign which Lloyd George and Bonar Law had planned to wage before the possibility of a negotiated agreement with Asquith offered itself is evident from the resignation which the Secretary of State for War had prepared for publication on 2 December. Addressing himself rhetorically to the

[27] Bonar Law's raising the prospect of general Conservative resignations at the meeting of 3 December must be considered a major factor in Asquith's decision to conciliate. It was probably his first clear evidence of the agreement, or "conspiracy," between Lloyd George and the Conservative Party leader. When the Conservative ministers finally sent in their resignations on 5 December, Bonar Law claimed to be reverting to the "course we urged on Sunday," i.e., either the government resign or the Conservative ministers would. Bonar Law to Asquith (5 Dec. 1916), *A.P.*, Dep. 31.

Prime Minister, he wrote, "... it is my duty to leave the Government in order to inform the people of the real condition of affairs and to give them an opportunity before it is too late to save their native land...."[28] What might seem like antic outrage in many other politicians was in Lloyd George an emotional peak which was many months in the making—a private overture of self-persuasion through which he frequently labored before coming to a decisive act. His resignation was to be offered simultaneously with those of the Conservative ministers on Saturday, in time for full coverage in the Beaverbrook and Northcliffe papers on Monday morning; Lloyd George pointedly stated his intention in the letter to Asquith to publish their correspondence concerning the crisis if the Prime Minister, as expected, remained obdurate.[29]

The first of Asquith's two sudden shifts on the question of the War Committee—his agreement to remain a nonmember—postponed the crisis which was supposed to climax on Monday morning. Though not by design, it also threw the program agreed upon by Bonar Law, Lloyd George, and Beaverbrook out of synchronization. The intentions of the War Secretary and the Conservative ministers had already been leaked to the press before the Downing Street meeting on Saturday. They underwent the inevitable mutations of rumor and speculation over the weekend and finally appeared in a form obviously designed, especially in the Northcliffe papers, to enrage the Prime Minister. It was to the *Times* article on the crisis that he referred on Monday morning in a note to Lloyd George stating the terms under which he would accept exclusion from the War Committee: "Unless the impression is at once corrected that I am being relegated to the position of an irresponsible spectator of the War, I cannot possibly go on."[30] The terms he offered were sufficiently stern, he thought at first, to correct that impression and to leave him in "supreme and effective control." In fact, through mutual mistrust and misunderstanding they had reached what might have formed a workable basis for the reconstruction of the wartime government. With the small "above-party" War Committee in effective control of war strategy and organization, the brunt of public criticism would have been diverted from Asquith, whose function would then have been to insulate the com-

---

[28] Lloyd George to Prime Minister (2 Dec. 1916), "Not sent," *L.G.P.*, E/2/23/11.
[29] Ibid.
[30] Asquith to Lloyd George (4 Dec. 1916), *A.P.*, Dep. 31.

mittee from factious political opposition, particularly Liberal and Labour opposition. It was not a system likely to enjoy a long life but it had the potential of holding off the immediate fracture of the Liberal Party which ensued when Asquith finally rejected it.

Lloyd George received Asquith's terms, along with his remonstrance about the *Times* article, on Monday morning and replied immediately in his most conciliatory manner. Obviously trying to disarm Asquith's well-grounded suspicions about the source of Northcliffe's information, he implored the Prime Minister not to be upset by the "misrepresentations" and "effusions" in the press that morning.

> N. frankly wants a smash. Derby and I do not [he explained]. N. would like to make this and any other arrangement under your Premiership impossible. Derby and I attach great importance to your retaining your present position—effectively. I can not restrain, nor, I fear, influence N.[31]

While Lloyd George spoke only the literal truth about Northcliffe, he was quite sincere in stating that he now wished Asquith to retain his position according to the morning's terms. Had Asquith not done another sudden reversal later the same day, at least the Liberal side of the crisis would have been resolved except for the personnel of the committee—that question was a serious one but still not unanswerable if the two felt the basic compromise worth saving. On the other hand, if Asquith had wished mainly to confound his upstart Secretary for War, he would now have to go back on the general agreements which had already been reached. He chose to do this by sticking on the question of personnel.

By Monday afternoon, Asquith's objection to the agreement about the War Committee had become the exclusion of Balfour and the inclusion of Carson: he would not be a party to "any suggestion that Mr. Balfour should be displaced," he informed Lloyd George; and he was "against Carson as a feasible choice."[32] This last turn-

---

[31] Lloyd George to Prime Minister (4 Dec. 1916), *L.G.P.*, E/2/23/13, in two typescript copies; a third which was sent to Asquith appears in *A.P.*, Dep. 31, Lloyd George to Asquith (4 Dec. 1916). Anticipating the "smash-up" and a dispute in the press over the reasons, Lloyd George began to make copies of his correspondence from 4 December to the end of the crisis.

[32] Asquith to Lloyd George (4 Dec. 1916), *A.P.*, Dep. 31 (second letter to Lloyd George on 4 December).

about could not have been due alone to Northcliffe's article, since he had already seen it before writing to Lloyd George the same morning. Nor was there anything in Lloyd George's reply to raise any further problems between them. Yet by the afternoon of 4 December he had already received permission from the King to form a new government and notified Lloyd George that he intended to do so,[33] presumably without Carson. It was this last note which precipitated the resignation of Lloyd George on the following morning.

In his letter of resignation on 5 December, Lloyd George made a generally fair summary of Asquith's oscillations on the War Committee (though like his previous resignation this one was also composed for possible publication):

> I received your letter with some surprise. On Friday I made proposals which involved not merely your retention of the Premiership, but the supreme control of the War, whilst the executive functions, subject to that supreme control, were left to others. I thought you received these suggestions favourably. In fact, you yourself proposed that I should be the Chairman of the Executive Committee, although as you know I never put forward that demand.

On Saturday, Asquith had gone back on the latter proposition, insisting that the Prime Minister be chairman of the committee; on Sunday, Lloyd George concluded, "You put new proposals before me—written in your letter on Monday. I wrote accepting them. Today you have gone back on your proposals."[34]

The decision to dissolve the first coalition, the last Liberal government in England, was thus made by Asquith sometime during Monday afternoon. While the personal side of his reasons for resigning rather than remaining within the proposed new War Committee arrangement are still far from clear, the undertone of wounded dignity is constant throughout his behavior during the crisis. As even his warmest apologists conceded, there was an inevitable conflict between his *amour propre* and his patriotic duty. He could retain the premiership and the Liberal Party intact by holding to the previous arrangement—his advancing years and long

---

[33] Asquith to Lloyd George (4 Dec. 1916), *L.G.P.*, E/2/23/14; copy in *A.P.*, Dep. 31 (4 Dec. 1916).

[34] Lloyd George to Asquith (5 Dec. 1916), *A.P.*, Dep. 31. Writing on the evening of 4 December (Monday), Lloyd George is referring to Asquith's second note of the same day.

term in office suggested a fairly short public future anyway. But he could not endure the role of Merovingian king in a house ruled by Lloyd George, even if his duty dictated that he stay on in office for the sake of national unity as nearly all parties to the dispute urged him to do.[35]

Lloyd George was not the only one to be surprised by Asquith's recurrent obstinacy. Edwin Montagu, one of the few men on good terms with both of the Liberal leaders and the most energetic mediator during the crisis, was dismayed and puzzled by the news of Asquith's decision. "What has broken down the arrangement? What has caused your withdrawal of your own proposals?" he asked the Prime Minister on Tuesday. He guessed that the decision was taken on the advice of the McKenna faction in the Cabinet, including Runciman, Grey, and Crewe. If it was so, he warned Asquith, it could only have been due to McKenna's well-known hatred of the War Secretary. McKenna could see only one object to be achieved, he said, "to drive Lloyd George out of the Government, and he takes no view but that."[36]

Montagu rejected any suggestion that Lloyd George was conspiring with Northcliffe, a rumor which had circulated quickly in Liberal circles since the Sunday article. Having just returned from a meeting with Lloyd George, Montagu felt he was in "almost as great a condition of misery and unhappiness as I am myself." He assured Asquith that Lloyd George meant to work loyally within the agreement and in fact "rejoiced in the fact that he was to see you daily."[37]

Whether or not Montagu's defense of Lloyd George's motives can be taken as literally accurate, there was much in his assessment of the general situation which now seems justified. The simultaneous blows of the Unionist resignations (including Balfour's) and the Northcliffe attack on Sunday, added to Asquith's inner cer-

---

[35] Crewe's recollection of the decision not to participate in the reconstructed coalition (written two weeks after the events) is cited by Asquith in his *Memories* as authoritative: ". . . it was felt that while the present break-up might be a national misfortune, it would amount to a serious disaster if later on Mr. Asquith and those Liberals who might join with him felt compelled to bring about another crisis . . . ; and if a new system was to be tried it had best be entrusted to colleagues of the same school of thought as the new Prime Minister." Earl of Oxford and Asquith, *Memories and Reflections*, II, 162.

[36] Edwin Montagu to Asquith (5 Dec. 1916), *A.P.*, Dep. 17.

[37] Ibid.

tainty of being conspired against, would have provoked more self-assured men than Asquith into a show of defensive dignity. Reinforced by the loyal circle of his Liberal ministers, most of them deeply hostile to Lloyd George, the temptation for him to trade the responsibility of powers which increasingly bewildered him for a shady seat as leader of a righteous opposition was irresistible.

The attitude of "detached amusement" which Asquith had affected during the crisis of 1910 was even less defensible now, yet he was clearly looking again for some way of withdrawing to the sidelines—even to win at such a sordid intrigue would be degrading. Even so, once the magnitude of the defection from him became clear, when even his friends urged him to accept office under Lloyd George, Asquith no longer wished to win, to continue in office. Only a small group of his colleagues supported him in this (McKenna, Runciman, Grey, Buckmaster, and McKinnon Wood) and even fewer understood his reasons. Like Montagu, his friends were as puzzled as his opponents. Churchill, the man least likely to comprehend anyone's desire to be "out," instinctively sensed what was missing in Asquith's behavior: "A fierce, resolute Asquith, fighting with all his powers, would have conquered easily. But the whole trouble arose from the fact that there was no fierce, resolute Asquith to win this war or any other."[38]

When Bonar Law saw Asquith on Monday afternoon, probably before the decision to reject the new War Committee plan was finally made, he found him in a "glum and obstinate silence." Their meeting ended any hopes that remained for a reconstruction from within the existing coalition. By refusing the Unionist ministers' ultimatum of Sunday that he resign and reconstitute the government on the lines already agreed, Asquith cut off the last possible route for a new coalition which might include himself, Bonar Law, and Lloyd George together.

[38] Cited in Taylor, *Beaverbrook* (London, 1971), p. 119.

XII

The Coalition Government

The significance of the conflict over the War Committee depends ultimately upon whether we see it mainly as a dispute *within* the Cabinet about the size and personnel of the new committee, and the Prime Minister's relation to it, or whether the labyrinth of memos, meetings, and rumors and the mass of daily correspondence which has given rise to so many conflicting interpretations of the event is not, as Lord Beaverbrook once suggested, merely a narrow circle of light in a darkened room, dominant but diminishing as the main lights go on. The former view tends to make Lloyd George look stubborn, ambitious, and excessive in his demands upon Asquith; the latter, considering the magnitude of the world issues at stake, could make Asquith seem almost criminally blind and irresponsible, intent merely on humiliating Lloyd George and Bonar Law at the possible expense not only of the war effort but of the future of his own party.

At the time of the Buckingham Palace Conference on 6 December, after both Lloyd George's resignation and his own had already been submitted, Asquith was still convinced that neither of his enemies would be able to form a government; he was supported in this view by most of his Liberal ministers as well as by the elder Conservative leaders—that is, by most of those in the narrow circle of light at the top. Asquith's fatal miscalculations were due in large part to his self-imposed isolation from the realities outside the Cabinet circle, realities which he had long ignored because they were both perplexing and unflattering. To a disastrous extent he was denied the use of the general press as a barometer of public and political opinion because he had become increasingly convinced that it was perversely hostile to him personally and, in the cases of Northcliffe and Beaverbrook, even that it was engaged in a Lloyd George-inspired conspiracy to destroy him. The events of the weekend of 3 December only served to strengthen that conviction and make it impossible for him to make any of the basic concessions necessary to preserve the government or to continue in a reconstructed ministry himself. Looking upon Bonar Law as one of the conspirators, he could not accept a post under him as he was asked to do on the evening of the 5th and again during the palace conference the next day. When it was suggested at one point that he serve under a possible Balfour ministry, he again refused, in part, because Balfour too had refused to stay on at the Admiralty after Asquith had defended him against Lloyd George's criticism; Balfour's resignation was therefore also seen as something of a betrayal. His eventual acceptance of the Foreign Office under Lloyd George merely confirmed Asquith's original suspicions.

Thus, by the evening of the 6th, when Lloyd George was finally invited by the King to form a new government, the only remaining alternative for Asquith was to step out altogether. Despite the urging of some of the elder Conservatives of the Cecil-Curzon-Chamberlain circle as well as Montagu, it had now become unthinkable for him to serve under Lloyd George, even after it had been demonstrated that Lloyd George was the only remaining leader with any realistic chance of forming a new government.[1] Asquith had painted himself into this corner during the previous week, first by attempting to satisfy the nearly universal discontent with the present administration by the narrowest possible reconstruction, a mere reshuffling of offices, and second by disdaining the potential strength of his critics in areas outside of the Cabinet.

Balfour, Curzon, Cecil, Chamberlain, and Long, the "elder statesmen" of the Conservative side, were as hostile to Lloyd George as were their Liberal counterparts. They had decided in their Sunday meeting to deliver their resignations more to constrain the restless and rebellious elements of both parties than to overturn Asquith. Like him, they would have preferred a limited reconstruction, enough to allay the strongest criticism from the "all-outers" by including some, like Carson or Milner, in the coalition government. But they realized at the same time that if their opposition to a Lloyd George or Bonar Law ministry were not sufficient to make either one impossible to form then the only way to retain any meaningful influence in their own party and to preserve its remaining unity would be to serve in whatever new coalition was devised. It

[1] Cecil urged Asquith to accept office under Lloyd George on Tuesday, 5 December, for the sake of national unity and added that "every one" of his Unionist colleagues agreed. Robert Cecil to Asquith (5 Dec. 1916), *A.P.*, Dep. 17.

was in large part this difference between Asquith and the elder Conservative leaders that eventually determined the survival of one party and the decline of the other.

Outside the narrow circle of light which encompassed the leadership of the Asquith coalition were forces which almost certainly would have necessitated major changes in both the personnel and the methods of the wartime regime regardless of the personal frictions at the top. In the press, in the army, in Parliament (whose existence tended to be ignored during the crisis but which in the end would be decisive), in the increasingly restive trade union locals, and in the massive wartime bureaucracy, there had developed lines of conflict over the aims and methods of the war which had already spelled the end of the *union sacrée* during the year. Not all of this restlessness acted in Lloyd George's favor; only in the press could it be said that he commanded a definite margin of personal support. But in every way the development of war-weariness, labor recalcitrance, pacifism, and the impatience of the all-outers worked against Asquith, who could not be identified in the public mind either with the ruthless and efficient prosecution of the war or with the effort for negotiated peace.

Carson is probably typical of the opposition to Asquith from the Right and of Lloyd George's support from that side. "No 'patchwork,' " he warned Bonar Law on Monday when the crisis broke. He had been one of the strongest advocates of a Lloyd George reconstruction since the fall and the threat which he represented to Unionist leadership since the Nigerian debate was one of the main incentives for Bonar Law to seek an agreement with Lloyd George. He now demanded of him that Lloyd George be assisted in forming a government, "a very small one," presumably with Asquith out and himself in it:

> If the House won't support it he [Lloyd George] should go to the country. I quite admit that the want of patriotism of many Liberals may raise a good deal of opposition but it will either be overcome or it will lead to ruin and in the latter case we will not be worse off than in the gulf to which we are now heading. If the country is sound then everything will come right—if not (and I think England under the present regime is producing pacifists) we will save further sacrifice.[2]

[2] Carson to Bonar Law (4 Dec. 1916), *B.L.P.*, 117/1/31. Carson met with Derby and Lloyd George the next morning when, he told Bonar Law, he stated the same view.

Carson's views not only represented his immediate following in Parliament, the so-called ginger group, but corresponded exactly with those of Milner and his vocal advocates in the press, Oliver, Garvin, and Gwynne. Those, especially among Milner's and Carson's following, who were most anxious about Liberal determination to prosecute the war all-out had looked to Lloyd George ever since he was at Munitions as the main hope in the government against either defeat or partial victory, against the growing pacifist pressure as Carson saw it. Gwynne had written to Lloyd George in October that he "alone in the Cabinet" realized that the Germans must be "thoroughly beaten." He echoed Carson's concern that the rest of his Liberal colleagues were "already whispering the words 'armistice,' 'peace.' "[3] Bonar Law was hardly less blamed in these circles than Asquith for the lack of purpose in the government. Most of their suggestions about the formation of a new coalition focused on Lloyd George, Carson, and Milner (who in their correspondence and articles had come to be called the "Triumvirate") and excluded Bonar Law as well as the old guard Conservatives.[4]

Caught between the pincers of the older Conservatives and the looming "Triumvirate," Bonar Law was in a position little safer than Asquith's. When Lloyd George informed him of the Prime Minister's refusal to forego the chairmanship of the new War Committee (in Asquith's letter of Friday), he fully expected Bonar Law to smash the coalition and demand a major reconstruction: "The life of the country depends on resolute action by you now . . . ," he wrote to the Unionist chief.[5] Bonar Law's behavior during the next week of crisis and negotiation left Lloyd George far from satisfied that the necessary action would be taken in his support. Indeed, on 6 December, when Asquith had gone to see the King, Bonar Law informed his expectant partner that since the King had agreed to

---

[3] H. A. Gwynne to Lloyd George (11 Oct. 1916), *L.G.P.*, C/2/14/1. According to Gwynne, Leo Maxse agreed and both thought the main thing standing in the way of their closer cooperation was Lloyd George's "tinkering" with the army.

[4] F. S. Oliver, who was Carson's most vociferous advocate in the press, pressed Milner with the necessity of centralizing the supreme direction of the war in a small "committee of public safety" with Lloyd George as Prime Minister, Carson as his chief executive, a "soldier" at the War Office, and a "sailor" as First Lord of the Admiralty, with "all other posts filled by businessmen subordinate to the four."

[5] Lloyd George to Bonar Law (2 Dec. 1916), *B.L.P.*, 117/1/30.

Asquith's making a moderate reconstruction, the two of them had better suspend the plans they had projected under Beaverbrook's stimulus. "I suppose you ought not to see me. I have nothing special to say," were his only words to Lloyd George.[6]

Bonar Law's behavior was as uncertain and indecisive as the Prime Minister's. By Sunday he was repairing his relations with the Conservative Cabinet ministers and had apparently adopted their view that an Asquith ministry, reconstructed with greater dependence on their support, would be most desirable, but that if that were impossible it would be best to participate in whatever new government were formed, more or less regardless of its leadership. Thus neither were they Asquith's resolute friends nor were they enthusiastic about the insurgency against him. At all costs they must remain in the government after the reconstruction or lose control of the party to the hotheads who were adamant for Lloyd George and Carson.

The same consideration weighed in Bonar Law's dealings with Lloyd George along with the general concerns about the effective prosecution of the war effort and in the end decided him first to attempt forming a government with Asquith serving under him (on the evening of the 5th) and then to suggest to the King that he invite Lloyd George to do so with his support. It was only after that decision had been made that his cooperation with the Liberal insurgence became full and open.

In the National Reconstruction announced on 8 December, Milner's name was missing. It had been replaced in the Triumvirate advocated by the Tariff Reform section by Bonar Law's as part of the price of his support. The new Triumvirate of Lloyd George, Bonar Law, and Carson had been advanced in the press by Beaverbrook during the crisis, first as the logical makeup of the new War Council under Asquith's titular leadership and, after Asquith had withdrawn, as the triarchy in a Lloyd George coalition. For Milner, though he was not apparently stung personally by his exclusion, the new coalition fell short of his hopes. He rejoiced at the prospect of Lloyd George and Carson "being left almost alone, with a hostile House of Commons," thus forced to appeal to the country over the heads of the old Mandarins. However, he was not entirely happy with the new structure, as he confessed on the day of its inauguration:

[6] Bonar Law to Lloyd George (6 Dec. 1916), *L.G.P.*, E/2/17/6.

Unfortunately, as I think, the *unexpected firmness* of B.L., while it certainly gave the *coup de grace* to Squiff, has resulted in the return of the old Unionist tail—A.J.B. and all the rest of them—so that the new Government is really the old Unionist hordes, L.G. and *some* new men—I don't know how many. So we have not, after all, completely sloughed off the party skin.[7]

Despite the unhappiness of many of his ardent followers that he was not immediately included in the new coalition Cabinet, his name had come up regularly in the various projections about reconstructing the government which had been made since the Nigerian debate. In fact, as the pressure for a change was mounting towards the end of November, even Asquith was moved (presumably with great reluctance) to invite his severest critic to Downing Street in order to offer him the office of Food Controller—an offer he declined only after a "protracted" conversation with Lloyd George the following day.[8] Again, when Lloyd George finally heard from Addison that at least 126 Liberal M.P.'s were willing to support an administration formed by him, he immediately informed Bonar Law and in the same message asked, "Can I send for Milner and Stanley now?"[9] At least for the two Liberal rivals, then, it would seem that some importance was attached to Milner and the Milner forces. His original exclusion from the coalition Cabinet announced on 8 December was a result of Bonar Law's and the Conservative members' misgivings.

Milner's own reservations, which persisted after his eventual inclusion in the War Cabinet on the 11th, were not primarily that the continuance of party would any longer damage the war effort, for the new executive was virtually free of any parliamentary control for the time being. There was still, as he noted when founding the British Workers National League, the "immediate THEREAFTER" during which a revived party system could be as pernicious to his idea of national interest as he felt it had been before the war.

[7] *Daily Express*, 2 and 5 Dec. 1916; Milner to Lady Cecil (8 Dec. 1916), *M.P.*, Private Letters–1916.

[8] Asquith made the offer on 29 November and received the rejection two days later, according to Milner's account (29 Nov. 1916), *M.P.*, Great War). Milner met with Lloyd George on 30 November; Lockwood, "Milner's Entry," p. 128.

[9] Lloyd George to Bonar Law (n.d., Dec. 1916—probably 7 Dec.), *B.L.P.*, 81/1/21.

The same apprehension motivated a good part of the Milner forces as well and received constant attention in the propaganda of the Tariff Reform League, the National Service League, and the British Workers National League. The Tariff Reform League, remaining a staunch supporter of Lloyd George and the coalition during the war and for a while afterward, warned in its bimonthly "War Notes" that the great political, social, and economic changes of the war could not be reversed in the peace. The old parties were obsolete: "Things can never revert to their previous positions; movements can not be re-started in their old grooves." As the advocates of negotiated peace began to be heard, these orchestrated groups immediately began to preach the danger of "pro-Germanism after the war" in their publications. The "Last War Fallacy," declared a National Service League pamphlet too as early as April, must be exploded:

> ... We may be pretty certain that the anti-militarists are looking forward to doing very extensive propaganda work when the war is over.[10]

Milner's distinctive mark is evident in the antipacifist campaign mounted by the leagues during 1916, as in the "vast co-operative management scheme culminating in a National Council of Industry" proposed by the B.W.N.L. to the Bristol T.U.C. conference. With such a scheme, the B.W.N.L. asked, would it be necessary "to re-open the dreary record of the class struggle when the *international* war comes to an end?"[11] In November, the Tariff Reform League announced what they called the "New Crusade" "to combat organizations which are in opposition to the resolutions of the Paris Conference" where the hard line of Allied economic policy toward Germany after the war was established. The crusade was to expose the "true character" of the propaganda being carried on in the "guise" of such movements as the Free Trade campaign and the Union of Democratic Control; they were, according to the Tariff Reform League, "an organized conspiracy" to oppose the policy unanimously agreed upon by the Allies at the Paris Eco-

---

[10] The Tariff Reform League launched its campaign against postwar "pro-Germanism" and in favor of unconditional surrender and a punitive peace settlement as early as September 1915, and continued it in the "Monthly Notes" throughout 1916; see "War Notes," *T.R.L.*, I, 2 (15 Sept. 1915) through II, 29 (1 Nov. 1916); "Occasional Notes," *N.S.L.*, I, 1 (Feb. 1916).

[11] *British Citizen and Empire Worker*, I, 3 (8 Sept. 1916).

nomic Conference. The league would "fight these anti-patriots wherever they raise their foreign flag."[12]

When the Tariff Reform League's "War Notes" announced the formation of the British Workers National League in the spring of 1916, it listed its main objects in the following three points: (1) the maintenance of "national rights"; (2) the consolidation of all the states in the British Empire into a democratic federation "with a permanent understanding with our present allies"; and (3) "to put an end to the laissez-faire policy which would mean the ruin of England and to bring about a reversal of the Little England Cobdenite doctrines of the Radical Party."[13] As we have already seen, Milner's B.W.N.L. had originally been founded with funds provided by Waldorf Astor with the intent of mobilizing working-class support—or at least to counteract those elements in the labor movement who were becoming vocally disenchanted with the war's progress. It also hoped to advance the idea formulated before 1914 in the Social-Imperialist credo of allying a part of that class with the state and the empire, creating as one persistent critic (Alfred Gardiner) put it, "a drilled and disciplined proletariat . . . against an insurgent democracy."[14]

The Milner forces had now derived from the Social-Imperialist scenario a European policy based on the unconditional defeat of Germany and the liquidation of the German as well as the Turkish empires. A gradual but unmistakable shift was taking place in the propaganda of the leagues towards Germany during 1916. Despite the military frustrations of the summer campaigns, it is very evident in their literature that by the fall their main concern had moved from the problem of defeating the German armies in Europe to the question of what should be done with the spoils of victory—as though the military outcome was no longer in question. The principle of "national rights," as the league projected it, encompassed not only a policy of heavy reparations from Germany to assist in the reconstruction of the Allied economies but also the systematic restriction of postwar imports of foreign manufactured goods and immigrant labor. A strong resolution "to prevent [a] flood of foreign goods from swamping England to further complicate the problem of re-employment of returning and women labour" was passed

[12] "War Notes," *T.R.L.*, II, 29 (1 Nov. 1916); see especially Page-Croft's editorial of 19 Oct. 1916, II, 28, pp. 66-67.
[13] Ibid., I, 19 (1 June 1916).
[14] *Daily News*, 29 March 1913; cited in Gollin, *Proconsul*, p. 170.

at the T.U.C. conference in September based on motions by John Hodge and Page-Croft, the leading labor representatives in the B.W.N.L.[15] Having searched for years for a plausible method of linking labor interests to the protectionist program, the Tariff Reformers now successfully hinged the principle to the question of unconditional surrender and reparations. Where once the menace was German competition, it was now American and Japanese, both of them strengthened in the world market by the war and untouched by its destruction.[16]

The Tariff Reformers and Milnerites were by no means the only ones to see a future menace in the growing influence of the United States and the Allies' increasing dependence on American loans and resources. By the fall of 1916 it had become one of the critical factors in the development of British war aims and reconstruction planning and, consequently, an important influence also in the political crisis. We have already seen that the fear of a flood of American investment capital into the former German colonial territories was one of the principal arguments in the Nigerian debate. Shortly before that, in a report to the Cabinet on "Our Financial Position in America," Reginald McKenna issued the following warning:

> There are two sets of circumstances, and in my opinion two only, which may deprive us of the liberty to fix for ourselves the time and terms of peace. One is the inability of a principal Ally to continue. The other is the power of the United States to dictate to us.
>
> We ought never to be so placed that only a public issue in America within a fortnight stands between us and insolvency. Yet we are quickly drifting in this direction.
>
> If things go on as at present, I venture to say with certainty that by next June or earlier the President of the American Republic will be in a position, if he wishes, to dictate his own terms to us.[17]

McKenna's somber warning was seconded shortly afterward by John Maynard Keynes in a Treasury report to the War Committee.

[15] *Birmingham Post*, 6 Sept. 1916; "War Notes," *T.R.L.*, II, 27 (1 Oct. 1916), p. 34.

[16] For Tariff Reform projections of American and Japanese competition in the postwar see "War Notes," *T.R.L.*, II, 28 (15 Oct. 1916), pp. 53-58.

[17] Reginald McKenna, "Our Financial Position in America," printed for the Cabinet, 24 Oct. 1916; *L.G.P.*, E/9/2/2.

It would be hardly an exaggeration, Keynes argued, to say that in a few months' time the American executive "and the American public" will be in a position to dictate to this country on matters, like peace terms, "that affect us more nearly than them."[18]

Many of the forebodings about the possible influence of America in the determination of the terms, and possibly the timing, of a peace settlement were transmitted to Lloyd George during the fall through Beveridge, Keynes, and the Milner men after Milner entered the War Cabinet on 11 December. He was a logical recipient for these expressions of concern, especially after a much-publicized and criticized interview he gave for the American press late in September in which he advanced the "knockout blow" principle as the only acceptable means of ending the conflict. Grey immediately remonstrated with him for what he felt was a dangerous lack of tact in that remark in light of President Wilson's already well-known views on the war. Keynes also concluded his Treasury report on America with an obvious reference to such outbursts: "that the policy of this country toward the U.S.A. should be so directed as not only to avoid any form of reprisal or active irritation, but also to conciliate and to please."[19]

But there could be two minds about the significance of American influence as the war progressed. Like Keynes and Grey (and possibly McKenna), one could argue that the necessity of placating American feelings required concessions to the principle of limited war aims and possibly eventual concessions on the question of a negotiated settlement. On the other hand, as in the view of both Milner and Lloyd George, the dangers of increasing financial dependence on the United States while the war lasted suggested the need for a "knockout blow," severe reparations, and extensive territorial and trading demands. In short, if the war dragged on, the pressure from the United States for a negotiated peace, reinforcing the pressure from domestic opponents of the war, would increase in proportion to Allied indebtedness—the difficulties of achieving a stable reconstruction naturally would mount likewise. Projecting policies for peace terms and reconstruction were to become enormously complicated within the following year with America's entry into the war and the revolutions in Russia, but even at the close of 1916 considerations of American influence and Russian ability to

[18] J. M. Keynes, "Report for the War Committee—Secret" (6 Nov. 1916), *L.G.P.*, E/9/2/3.
[19] Ibid.

continue the war were already major factors in developing those policies and, consequently, in the political crisis of December as well.

The original coalition idea advocated by Lloyd George in 1910 had been devised largely to cope with a set of anxieties similar to those which arose again at the end of the second year of the war. It was designed, as its author first described it, "to equip us for a state of things with which we have never before been confronted" —the rapid rise of great foreign competitors, internal and external conflict, and "deficiencies in our national system" (see appendix B). With the final realization of the coalition plan in December, the recurrent effort to synchronize the bulk of the Social-Imperialist program with Lloyd George's political formula would be given its most serious test. Into the offices of the new government trooped a host of mostly unfamiliar faces, prominent among them the scattered lieutenants of the Social-Imperialist movement. The Webbs, who found themselves conscripted shortly afterward, were at first a little bewildered by the visage of the creature they had helped to create over the years since the Boer War:

> The L. G. government, announced today, is a brilliant improvisation—reactionary in composition and undemocratic in form. For the first time (since Cromwell) we have a dictatorship by one, or possibly by three, men; for the first time we see called to high office distinguished experts not in Parliament . . . labour leaders in open alliance with Tory Chieftains. . . . A Cabinet has been created, not by a party political organisation or any combination of party organisations, nor by the will of the H. of C., but by a powerful combination of newspaper proprietors. The H. of C. . . . almost disappears as the originator and controller of the Cabinet. All these momentous changes may be War measures, or they may have come to stay. . . . Whatever happens the shake up is bound to lead to more deliberate organisation—either for the purpose of enslavement or for the purpose of enforced equality.[20]

Although the new government was not strictly an improvisation nor was it created primarily by newspaper proprietors, Beatrice Webb was right in calling it a departure from any previous political precedent and right in wondering whether it was, as its creators protested in public, a war measure or whether it had "come to

[20] B. Webb, "Diary" (12 Dec. 1916), *P.P.*

stay." Whether it would ultimately be directed toward "enslavement" or "enforced equality," the intimidating appearance it gave at the moment of its inception was one which should have been familiar to the Webbs—the "Government of National Efficiency" built, with some streamlining and improvisation, on the model of Rosebery's prototype. As in 1910, the improvisation was mostly Lloyd George's. With efficiency as the criterion, "party politics" had always been seen as the obstacle. Two years of war had succeeded in first loosening and then discrediting party ties and principles, including the essential principle of ministerial responsibility to party leadership or to the House of Commons. Where the pre-war fears of unrest and decline had failed, the war had opened gaps in the old system into which the "non-party" men rushed, at least at first, with great eagerness and confidence.

With Milner's inclusion in the War Cabinet on the 11th, the first reservations about "sloughing off the old party skin" began to disappear. The B.W.N.L. paper greeted the new government with hearty approval after the first week. It now contained, the *British Citizen and Empire Worker* proclaimed, some of the most conspicuous figures in government and "patriotic labour," no doubt referring to Milner and John Hodge, the B.W.N.L. vice-president. Its first priority should be to demand "extra-constitutional powers" in order to "lay the foundations of that new industrial and social Britain which will assuredly arise after the war."[21] The Milner forces had sufficient reason to rejoice over the shape the Lloyd George government seemed to be taking in the first few weeks of its life, for among the "distinguished experts not in Parliament" to whom Beatrice Webb referred were more than a fair share from the Kindergarten and the other Milner attachments. The "Brains Trust" assembled to guide and advise the various new projects immediately initiated by the new Prime Minister included Philip Kerr and Lionel Curtis of the Kindergarten and Beveridge, Webb, and Haldane (rescued from exile) at the Ministry of Reconstruction, which was to be the fountainhead for that "new industrial and social Britain" after the war. At the urging of his erstwhile booster, J. L. Garvin, Lloyd George also took on as his Parliamentary Secretary Waldorf Astor, the financial angel of the B.W.N.L.[22] Hodge took a key post as Minister of Labour; Leo Chiozza Money, once a

[21] *British Citizen and Empire Worker*, I, no. 17 (16 Dec. 1916).
[22] J. L. Garvin to Lloyd George (18 Dec. 1916), *L.G.P.*, F/94/1/39.

Fabian and now a vice-president of the B.W.N.L. was recruited as Parliamentary Secretary to the Shipping Controller, and Amery served as Political Secretary to the War Cabinet. These were all posts within the patronage of the ministers and positions which could exert a meaningful influence on the making of government policy if held by energetic men, as nearly all of them proved to be. In a more informal, but not necessarily less influential, connection as advisers to Lloyd George and Milner in the War Cabinet were Hewins, Mackinder, and Oliver.[23]

It is both logical and significant that the bulk of the Milnerite and Fabian "experts" were channeled into the Ministry of Reconstruction, the Ministry of Labour, and the Cabinet. The former administration, as Beatrice Webb noted, in particular Asquith and his closest associates, had been fundamentally hostile to both the principle and practice of state intervention. The new government, she knew, would be "boldly and even brutally interventionist—it will break up all conventions and even control inconvenient vested interests."[24] The three offices into which the new recruits flowed were those which would have the greatest input into the planning of that intervention, particularly in those areas in which Lloyd George and Milner had the greatest common interest and concern, labor and the reconstruction. It is noteworthy, for example, that the best part of their available expert talent, like Beveridge, Kerr, Curtis, and the Webbs, was invested in functions having little or nothing to do with the actual conduct of the war but with longer range projects having to do with the permanent reorganization of the government and the society.

In fact, the new official and unofficial bureaucracy recruited into the Lloyd George government during its first year was an extraordinarily faithful representation of the elements which had contributed to the building of the Social-Imperialist doctrine from its Conservative, Liberal, and Fabian roots. The guiding language and attitudes of that movement—efficiency, expertise, and organization "above party"—abounded in the products of the Brains Trust, and

[23] The list of outside "experts" being enrolled was noted by some of the opposition press with alarm. Even the *New Statesman*, the Fabian mouthpiece, criticized the sudden turn to the Right, until the Webbs' inclusion. See especially "The New Bureaucracy," in the *Nation* (24 Feb. 1917); Lockwood, "Milner's Entry," p. 133. Mackinder was apparently overlooked in the first recruiting and wrote to Milner practically begging to be included; Mackinder to Milner (11 Dec. 1916), *M.P.*, Private Letters–1916.

[24] B. Webb, "Diary" (12 Dec. 1916), *P.P.*

especially in the work of the Ministry of Reconstruction in which their main effort was concentrated. Such slogans as Campbell-Bannerman had once derided as "mere *réchauffé* of Mr. Sidney Webb" were now as common as Kitchener's mustache. They were the obvious necessities of the war effort. But in the minds of the new bureaucracy they related distinctly to the "new industrial and social Britain" which such organs as the Ministry of Reconstruction were to prepare for the peace.

The general direction their planning was likely to take regarding the postwar is evident from the beginning in the choice of personnel to replace the Asquith Reconstruction Committee, which had been a rather casual effort. Lloyd George asked Montagu to reorganize it in the first weeks of 1917. When Montagu suggested merely to carry over himself and two of the secretaries of the Asquith committee, Vaughan Nash and Bonham Carter, the new Prime Minister responded, "This is a mere shadow of Asquith. . . . Bring me a list of persons with ideas." By February a list of fourteen names was submitted (excluding Bonham Carter) and was approved by Lloyd George with two changes: the names of H. G. Wells and George Bernard Shaw were replaced by him with Jack Hills, a progressive Tariff Reform Conservative, and Seebohm Rowntree, a choice which turned out to be fortunate for the work of the committee if not for its color.[25] Overall, the Reconstruction Committee was a cameo of the coalition itself, though the Conservative section was represented more by the Milner than by the Bonar Law section of the party: there were three Fabians (and one former Fabian in Arthur Greenwood, now a "law and order collectivist" of the Round Table circle), four young Conservatives of the Tariff Reform wing led by Philip Kerr, four of Lloyd George's own protégés from the business world (including two "entrepreneurs turned bureaucrat" carried over from the Ministry of Munitions) and three Labour members who, according to Beatrice Webb's account, seldom attended.[26]

The Reconstruction Committee was the Brains Trust of the Min-

[25] Reported by Tom Jones to Beatrice Webb from the meeting at which Lloyd George ordered the restaffing of the Reconstruction Committee; B. Webb, "Diary" (22 Feb. 1917), *P.P.*

[26] Ibid. (3 June 1917). Sir James Stephenson and Sir Arthur Duckham were two knighted businessmen who had established favor with Lloyd George and a reputation as highly competent bureaucrats while at the Ministry of Munitions.

istry of Reconstruction and was supposed to be both the clearinghouse and the fountainhead of ideas. Into it flowed numerous reports and memoranda from the other new ministry committees and from the new Cabinet Secretariat, another stronghold of the Milner faction in the Lloyd George government. The early enthusiasm of the projects which emanated from the new bureaucracy reflected the excited conviction that finally the "advocates of another method" were to have the chance to reshape the nation's habits and institutions along the lines developed by the Social-Imperialist movement over the previous twenty years. Since the Rosebery agitation about National Efficiency, one of the great bogeys of the movement, as we have seen, was the traditional parliamentary and party system. In a report on the "Better Government of the United Kingdom," done for the Ministry of Reconstruction's Committee on the Machinery of Government (chaired by Haldane), Lionel Curtis described the need for a sweeping review of the relationship between the Parliament and the permanent bureaucracy as follows:

> For the last 40 years thoughtful observers have been noting the fact that Parliament was becoming less and less able to meet the demands made upon its time by a population which was growing in size and still more in the intricacy of its organisation. . . .
> The . . . difficulty of passing a measure needed for efficient government is largely responsible for degrading British politics from the plane of real statesmanship to that of the demagogue. . . .
> The naked fact is that the country, the mother of free institutions, was four years ago on the brink of civil war. And if the Germans had not saved us the struggle would have raged not only between Catholic and Protestant Ireland but throughout G. B. between class and class. The Irish difficulty would have been, not the cause, but only the occasion of conflict.[27]

The central argument of the Curtis report was identical to that made more than a decade earlier by Rosebery and Milner, the "devolution" of business to committees. "No deliberative assembly," he argued, "can turn out 318 Acts in 276 days unless it can be dissuaded from debating them." The essential conflict between modern democratic politics and efficiency was that elected and re-

[27] Lionel Curtis, "Better Government of the United Kingdom," Report for the Haldane Committee on the Machinery of Government, Ministry of Reconstruction (n.d., 1917), *Bev. P.*, M672, no. 8.

sponsible ministers were unlikely to favor a measure which could provoke the opposition of vested interests unless there were a wave of public sentiment behind it, but the measures most vital to the public interest, like reform of local taxation, of the Poor Law, or of land title, were usually just those "which do not touch the popular imagination." Thus, Curtis concluded, the real "menace to freedom" was not the tyranny of majorities, as traditional Conservatism held, but the tyranny of minorities. Consequently, the scientific reform of administration which he suggested, by removing such questions as affected the public interest from the daily purview of Parliament to expert and nonpartisan committees, was in effect the best modern defense of the democratic interest.[28]

Curtis's report, reiterating the arguments of Rosebery, the Webbs, and the Coefficients, was answered by the Haldane committee with a recommendation for a permanent staff of administrative experts to "supervise legislative efficiency." Their recommendation to the parent committee advised that "in all such matters of administration progressive efficiency can only be secured by constant attention, and that more systematic arrangements than at present exist should be made for this purpose."[29] In the natural sequence, the Curtis and Haldane recommendations were passed on to the Reconstruction Committee where Beatrice Webb began the arduous task, or at least what must have seemed an arduous task to most others, of drawing up a specific plan of administrative reorganization from the very general principles suggested in the initiating memos. In the plan which she eventually produced by the late spring of 1917, some of the peculiar characteristics and some of the profound shortcomings of the new class of bureaucrats became evident, shortcomings which have since become associated with the general phenomenon of introducing intellectuals into the bureaucracy. In her familiar soporific style, Mrs. Webb produced two lengthy memos on "The Distribution of Business Between Government Departments" and "A Suggested Scheme of Redistribution" in which she argued against the current trend toward "concentration" of authority in autonomous departments each with its own minister in Parliament. While the principle of concentration had the virtue of reducing the number of independent minis-

[28] Ibid.
[29] "Report of the Haldane Committee" (n.d., 1917), *Bev. P.*, M672, no. 8.

ters, an idea which she thought appealed to most of the committee, there remained in it the difficulty which had become increasingly evident during the past year: interferences and overlapping between the departments. There were what she called "rival categories of concentration," as in the Ministry of Munitions, where no clear distinction was made between the "class of persons dealt with" and the "kind of Service rendered." If that distinction were clearly maintained in the creation and allocation of new departments, the necessary principles of "expertise, division of labour, and differentiation of technique" could be respected. Thus, a Ministry of Mines could be created "to take over the administration of health, education, housing and productivity and the establishment of special judicial courts for miners' offences, wages, methods, to take over from the Ministry of Justice." Or a Ministry of Employment which would handle "the ascertainment and regulation of the conditions of employment, especially as regards wages and continuity (arbitration); and (with the Ministry of Health) as regards hours of Labour, condition of sanitation and safety. . . ." Its responsibilities would also be to "regularise and aggregate the demand for labour in the nation as a whole."[30]

The same suggestions were made for areas such as Education (which would be responsible for the "mental environment of the citizen"), Health (for the "physical environment"), Productivity (for the supervision of "Material Production"), Transportation, and so on, according to either the "class of persons dealt with" or the "services rendered" principle. Theoretically, these authorities would not be overlapping but clearly demarked, and in the areas where overlapping or coordination was required separate ministries and boards would be set up to serve that function: a Ministry of Finance replacing the Treasury to control the finances of all other departments; a Ministry of Research for "the maintenance of Efficiency beyond our present knowledge"; a "Prime Minister's Department" under its own minister with a permanent under-secretary and expert staff "charged with the continual increase in Efficiency and Economy of the whole Government machine, with necessary control of the Civil Service"; an Advisory Board of Efficiency and Economy; a Civil Service Commission (for recruitment); and a Standing Consultative Committee for the coordination of depart-

[30] B. Webb, "Memo on the Distribution of Business Between Government Departments" and "Memo on a Suggested Scheme of Redistribution," for the Ministry of Reconstruction (June 1917), *Bev. P.*, M672, no. 8.

mental policy. All this would produce, according to Mrs. Webb, "more departments and less overlapping."[31]

Such grandiose bureaucratic visions as Beatrice Webb's symptomized the unrestrained élan of the new Brains Trust in the maiden months of the new regime. Part of that spirit was due to the sheer momentum of the earlier recruits in the various wartime departments concerned with long-distance planning, some of whom were fresh from the universities, industry, and the junior bureaucracy, unknowing or indifferent about the methods, protocols, and limitations of brainstorms issuing from junior men hoping to reach the ears of those with enough authority to give them life. As we have seen, in munitions, shipping, and conscription, many such propositions did indeed percolate upward in a manner which often contemptuously overlooked the accustomed hierarchies of departments and ministries. The agencies of the new coalition government acted at first as though all the old routines, so long derided by the critics of the "System," were permanently overthrown and replaced by the clubmanship of experts. Given the personnel of such agencies as the Reconstruction Committee and the Secretariat, the new regime appeared to be a kind of haven for many of those who had been drifting for years on the peripheries of power in the leagues, societies, and clubs, venting their frustrated energies and their contempt for the regular hacks. Most of those pastimes had intensified the sense of being among the "outs" but, with their considerable overlapping, they also helped to provide the basis of a sense of common cause.

The most dynamic and significant figures in the new bureaucracy, drawn almost entirely from the three circles of the Fabian Society, the Milner–Tariff Reform group, and Lloyd George's Munitions bureaucracy, were not only familiar with each other personally but had also a fairly clear sense of having been chosen by the Prime Minister *because* they were thought to share something in their outlook. In addressing the Reconstruction Committee at its inauguration in March 1917, Lloyd George appealed forcefully to the crusading, almost messianic, social consciousness which he felt moved most of its members, a consciousness shared by himself, though in a more instinctive than systematic way. The main questions he wished the committee to study, he said, were firstly those "which would arise immediately at the end of the War, and would

[31] Ibid.

require settlement without delay," and secondly "those which looked to laying the foundations of a new order." His emphasis was unmistakably on the latter in what amounted to a kind of pep talk to the first meeting of the committee. The immediate and vexing problems would obviously concern demobilization and the transition from war work which would arise in the very first days of peace; these were critical and difficult questions and work had already begun on them by Beveridge and others. But the committee's work "does not end there," he emphasized:

> ... they have the power to assist in painting a new picture of Britain. It was common ground to everyone that conditions before the War were often impossible and stupid. The Committee must advise the Government what steps could be taken to make a repetition impossible. . . .

Concluding his charge to the committee, Lloyd George added that

> No such opportunity had ever been given to any nation before—not even by the French Revolution. The nation now was in a moulten condition: it was malleable now, and would continue to be so for a short time after the war, but not for long.[32]

There is no reason to question the persuasiveness of Lloyd George's rather inflated rhetoric before the committee. What on other occasions, before other audiences, might have seemed almost laughable trumpery touched directly the shared instincts of this group as he had correctly perceived them. As we have seen, both Beatrice Webb and Beveridge, perhaps the two most able and experienced bureaucrat-intellectuals of the time, had been sufficiently moved by the promise of possible change embodied in Lloyd George's leadership to produce for serious consideration proposals of almost unheard-of extravagance and naiveté, one for the future Machinery of Government and the other for postwar labor relations. Lloyd George had said he wanted "a committee at large to advise about everything."[33] He advised it in its first meeting to "be fearless." Both its initial exuberance and its rapid demoralization were the direct consequence of his own quickly deflated confidence

---

[32] Notes taken from Lloyd George's address to the Reconstruction Committee, marked "Conclusions: First Meeting" (16 March 1917), *L.G.P.*, F/80/2/1.

[33] B. Webb, "Diary" (22 Feb. 1917), *P.P.*

that the painful debacle of December had finally purged the half-hearted and that now all was possible.

The Milner recruits responded with at least equal enthusiasm to the call for founding the "new order." The Kindergarten had also been a kind of hothouse in which plants of only one variety flourished; they were all infused with the master's mystique, his deep sense of grievance against the system, and with his Social-Imperialist doctrine. It was a highly leader-conscious group of men, utterly dependent upon their association with Milner for their identity as a group whether they were acting within organizations such as the Tariff Reform League, the Compatriots, the Round Table, and the recent B.W.N.L. or when placed singly in the various agencies of the new government. They were consciously Milner's men at all times and were recognized as such by those they worked with. They were certainly known by Lloyd George to be of the Kindergarten when he appointed them to the Reconstruction Committee and the Secretariat. Indeed, he heavily favored the Milnerites in making the numerous appointments of "outside experts" in the early months of the new government; in addition to the familiar names of that circle such as Kerr, Curtis, Amery, Astor, Oliver, and Hewins and Hodge and Leo Chiozza Money from Milner's league, there were more obscure graduates of the South African Kindergarten seeded throughout the new bureaucracy. At one point, when considering four new appointments to the Secretariat, Lloyd George chose three who had been with Milner at the Cape while they were in their twenties: Dougal Malcolm, once a secretary to Milner in South Africa following the Boer War, who moved into government through the Ministry of Munitions under Lloyd George; Robert Brand, a Canadian protégé of Milner representing the Canadian Munitions Board at the Ministry of Munitions; and Frederick Perry, a representative of Lazard Bros. of Canada who had also been one of the imperial secretaries in South Africa.[34]

Lloyd George's inclination to bring as many "outsiders" as possible into the new government had both a practical and a philosophical basis. Without a significant organizational base even the original 126 Liberal M.P.'s who came over to him in December constituted only an ad hoc force which could—and did—dissolve over critical issues to come. Had it been arranged to call a general election to accomplish the change in government, as Milner and

---

[34] "List of names considered for the Secretariat," with Lloyd George's notes (n.d., 1917), *L.G.P.*, F/74/5/1.

others had wanted, his situation might have been quite different in 1917 when he went about his reconstruction. As it was, however, his constituency was liquid and nonelectoral, resting primarily on the press (and on public opinion so far as the press reflected it) and on the diverse groups and individuals in the now fairly atomized fabric of the party and bureaucratic structure. As has frequently been noted, the most obvious replacement for traditional party control, with its network of local organizations and loyalties, as a basis for forming a government was the labor movement. There had often been speculation before the war about Lloyd George's hopes of winning that base from the I.L.P. as a personal following. So far as its leadership and the union organizations were concerned, he had demonstrably failed to further those alleged hopes during the war. But as the presence of men like Hills and Hodge in the coalition hierarchy suggested, he was well aware of the diversity of views and ideology dividing labor from top to bottom, a diversity which was becoming increasingly bitter and evident with the lengthening and intensification of the war, especially after the intrusion of the revolutions in Russia as a pivotal factor in domestic wartime politics. That issue began to arise in the early months of the coalition government at about the time that Lloyd George first had to face the problem of finding a more lasting base for the new government, a base sufficiently strong to support it not only through the war but into the founding of that "new order" upon which so much of its mental resources were already being expended.

The task of cultivating an organized mass base for the coalition had most unpromising prospects—in hindsight perhaps no prospects at all. Few national leaders who had been raised up by the war, especially in the victor nations, acquired an organized political base which was able to survive the aftermath. For Lloyd George and the coalition the difficulty was greater than for most. From its inception, the coalition was a house of splinters, held at its crucial points by tangles of personal jealousies and ambitions, younger men's contempt for former superiors, older men's disgust and perplexity with the lack of heroism and conviction of their peers, and the frustrated idealism of a host of men new to politics. Some of their political careers were made by the war, but relatively few. Membership in the coalition government was seldom invoked for future preferment; indeed, even before its demise it had acquired certain disreputable connotations, not all attributable either to the war or to Lloyd George's official improprieties. But in its first months there were few other governments that were able to inspire a comparable sense of opportunity, a *tabula rasa* such as Lloyd George promised upon which to paint "a new picture of Britain." That was the promise that excited the Brains Trusters in the beginning. Translating that purpose into organized mass support would be a more difficult matter, but it was essential that it be done if the ambitious plans for the reconstruction were to have any hope of being fulfilled.

The lack of an organizational base was the outstanding weakness of the coalition until its fall and from the beginning severely limited its leader's ability to set domestic policy. The prosaic question of what sort of postwar parliamentary force would uphold and implement the elaborate and highly controversial reconstruction plans gave these plans a somewhat academic appearance. It was partly in the search of a means of building such a force that Lloyd George drew closer to the Milner faction in the coalition during and after 1917. Not only did that faction contain some of the most promising and useful recruits to the coalition but it was also one which enjoyed a good deal more independence of action with regard to the old parties. Its men and resources were more or less Milner's to dispose at his own inclination, a situation which did not exist, for example, for either Bonar Law or Lloyd George himself. The main organizational resource of the group was the B.W.N.L., not yet comparable in strength or finances to any of the traditional national organizations, but one of the most solidly unified in the prevailing party chaos and one which had obvious potential for expansion with the acquisition of the Prime Minister. At about the time of the December crisis the B.W.N.L. organizations had leveled off at approximately 70 local branches around the country. In the year following the formation of the coalition, however, new expansion added more than 118 additional branches with a corresponding increase in financing and new membership concentrated in the urban and industrial areas.[35]

Lloyd George and Milner had never developed close personal ties in the preceding years. Indeed, their meetings since Milner's return were remarkably few considering the small-town proximities of Westminster social life. Nevertheless, a conscious and mutual

[35] Establishment of new branches is periodically announced in the *British Citizen and Empire Worker*; see summaries in *B.C.E.W.*, 4 Nov. 1916 and 3 Dec. 1917.

empathy developed at a distance and through the agency of many common associates, J. L. Garvin in particular. That empathy, it might be said, was based mostly on shared negative emotions about the political society, its styles and taboos, and especially the rigid and (they felt) stultifying etiquette of the political parties. "Milner and I stand for much the same things," Lloyd George confided to a friend shortly after becoming Prime Minister. "He is a poor man, and so am I. He does not represent the landed or capitalist classes any more than I do. He is keen on social reform, and so am I."[36] He had come back to that intuition of comradeship with the Milnerites in several past crises: in 1910, when they had been the most enthusiastic supporters of the "great opportunity" he had offered; during the struggles for National Insurance and conscription; and finally during the ouster of Asquith. Now he needed partners who were free agents and the Milnerites were again the most forthcoming. For the first time in many months he again heard from his most ardent admirer: Garvin wrote, "Providence keep you twenty years in that title. It's possible."[37] Garvin's was not a wish that would have been seconded by most of his other allies.

As later events were to show, Lloyd George's intuition that the patchwork agreements which had created the coalition would weaken with time and especially with the termination of the war was justified. Much of his political effort in the last two years of the war was directed towards finding a sounder political base for continuing it into the reconstruction. Any method that could be found to achieve this result would be justified in his mind by the importance, as Halévy put it later, of building a new social edifice with the tools forged by the war. The success of that mission, he felt strongly, was the only way of insuring that the great sacrifices made would not be wasted. Victory alone would not be enough, but it was a necessary prerequisite.

Part of the price that might have to be paid for the help of such elements in the new government as the Milnerites and the war-rich entrepreneurs would likely be some restraint on his own democratic instincts, still very much alive, and on the influence of others like the Webbs and Beveridge whose views and temperaments did not always run along the same lines. Basic divergences of view began to appear quite early in the new committees. By March, Tom Jones

---

[36] In a conversation recorded by Lord Riddell, *War Diary* (18 Feb. 1917), p. 243; cited in Lockwood, "Milner's Entry," p. 133.

[37] Garvin to Lloyd George (18 Dec. 1916), *L.G.P.*, F/94/1/39.

The Coalition Government

was warning the Webbs of the Milnerites' sinister influence in the Cabinet Committee on Territorial Terms of Peace, of which Milner was chairman:

> There is a vivid movement, guided by Milner & served by Amery, to prepare for another war, to complete the ruin of Germany & the domination of the British Empire. This gang of Power worshippers are running down the Russian revolution & minimising the entry of the U.S.A. as one of the belligerents. They are bent on maintaining a ruling caste of a ruling race: they fear & despise democracy. Any aspirations towards self-government among British subjects, who do not already possess it, is sedition to be put down by machine guns & plentiful hangings.[38]

Tom Jones had been with Lloyd George since serving on the Welsh Insurance Committee, "a good Welsh radical with a bias toward a well-ordered collectivist state," as Beatrice Webb described him. His main purpose in the committees, she thought, was as "keeper of his [Lloyd George's] democratic conscience."[39] If that were indeed his role, his was both a more difficult and a more important post than many a minister's.

The main elements of Labour and the Fabians who agreed to support or to take office in the new government had done so rather skeptically. Lloyd George had been evasive in a meeting with Labour M.P.'s arranged by Arthur Henderson in December and, according to a recollection of Sidney Webb's, was obvious and cynical in his offers of places in the government. After some dispute, they agreed to accept office by a vote of eighteen to twelve, Webb opposing.[40] Most of the Liberal and Fabian press took a similar view, accepting the need for a change but suspicious of the reactionary incubus of the new regime. In an article for the *New Statesman*, which she also expected to be suppressed, Beatrice Webb expressed the misgivings with which most of the Fabians entered into the new government:

> ... the Lloyd George–Curzon group want to mobilize labour whilst retaining for the ruling class property intact and the control of trade

---

[38] Tom Jones was acting as secretary to the Cabinet Committee on Territorial Terms of Peace when he spoke to Beatrice Webb; B. Webb, "Diary" (18 March 1917), *P.P.*

[39] Ibid. (19 Feb. 1917).

[40] B. Webb, "Diary" (7 Dec. 1916), *P.P.*

and industry. Lloyd George is indifferent rather than hostile to democracy—he wants to win the war and as he finds more effective resistance, to any interference, from the capitalists than he does from the ranks of labour, he limits his demands to the enslavement of the working class. A servile state, as Germany has proved recently, is one efficient instrument for waging war: an equalitarian democratic state might be more efficient but it would entail upsetting the existing social order—at any rate for the period of the war. A Lloyd George–Curzon–Carson administration will not promote an equalitarian regime! . . . it is ruinous to the cause we have at heart: it means death and disease to millions of our fellow citizens, a balking among 4/5 of the population of all impulse towards a free and more responsible life. It means the continual suppression by an Imperialist Government of Ireland and India and other subject races. And it means a continuous [sic], to the bitter end, not only of the present war, but of faith in war as the universal solvent. It means the supremacy of all I think evil and the suppression of all I think good. Lloyd George would represent Mammon, though heaven knows that Asquith & Co. do not represent God. God is unrepresented in the effective political world of today.[41]

This and Sidney Webb's article for the *New Statesman* (both suppressed as expected) were meant to be "unpleasant reading for the new dictator."[42]

With the same thrifty instinct for not wasting opportunities that marred so many episodes of their otherwise distinguished careers, the Webbs nevertheless joined the Lloyd George administration. Within a few months of its creation the Reconstruction Committee had become, according to Beatrice Webb, "a sham organization." By July 1917 the committee, in which for them so much of the constructive possibility of the coalition resided, was reduced to an advisory committee to Addison, the new Minister of Reconstruction. In the same "shake-up" of July, Churchill became the Minister of Munitions, Carson entered the Cabinet, and Geddes went to the Admiralty, all changes which boded ill for the socially progressive side of the Lloyd George promise.

It is fair to say that the first six months of the coalition were the final testing ground for the Social-Imperialist argument, one in which its fatal contradictions were quickly revealed. Almost immediately the misgivings of Jones and the Webbs were borne out by the behavior and the ascendancy of the Milner wing in the vari-

[41] Ibid.   [42] Ibid. (9 Dec. 1916).

ous committees, in the Secretariat, and in the Cabinet. Their greatest influence was exerted, beginning in the spring of 1917, towards developing a counterattack against labor and antiwar agitation—a proposition which they rightly felt Lloyd George was inclined to favor. Milner's contingent, and Milner himself, barraged the Prime Minister and the committees with sensational warnings about the expanding subversions of such organizations as the I.L.P. and the Union of Democratic Control. A report about the "great strides" these groups were making, sent by Milner to Lloyd George in May, is typical of their effort:

> ... their [I.L.P. & U.D.C.] immediate object is to bring about a strike, followed by rioting of such a nature that troops would be obliged to fire and from this they hoped to evolve a general strike which would bring the whole war up with a jerk here, in much the same manner in which the Revolution has stopped all military proceedings in Russia. ...

Their "immense success" was due, the report suggested, to the use of a pool of 100,000 unmarried men who had taken refuge in reserved occupations to avoid service, and to agitation among discharged soldiers harboring grievances.

> The combination between the U.D.C., Quaker money, the I.L.P., the vast number of shirkers, together with the discharged and dissatisfied soldiers is a very ugly one. ...
>
> I have thought for a long time that there is a *master brain* behind both the U.D.C. and the I.L.P. [It was *probably* not MacDonald, the report said] ... I find that it is Morrell (De Ville) [*sic*]. ... In spite of the fact that every body knows he is a German agent, he nearly succeeded last week in bringing about a complete Labour revolt in this country.[43]

Milner conceded that he relied for this information on "a labour man, ... a capable fellow, Victor Fisher ..., not himself a workman, but a middle-class man, of good education, and a lifelong Socialist." Like much else of the intelligence regarding labor which began to reach Lloyd George from these sources, the report on the U.D.C. and I.L.P. agitation emanated from Milner's own league (now known as the British Workers League) of which Fisher was

[43] "Enclosure: Re Industrial Unrest," Milner to Lloyd George (26 May 1917), *L.G.P.*, F/38/2/5. My italics.

secretary and treasurer. Pretending only a casual acquaintance with the league, Milner described it as a "countermining" effort by labor men, recently organized: "This League is not, like some previous organisations of the kind, a bogus thing. It consists of genuine Labour men." Milner concluded by saying that the Prime Minister should meet Fisher, who "with his League, might, with a little encouragement and guidance, do a great deal more useful work than he is already doing."[44]

Tom Jones's early inkling of the "vivid Movement" in the government led by Milner and Amery accurately described the industrious action of the Milner group as the year progressed. Milner's report above (later published in amended form in the *British Citizen and Empire Worker*) was followed up in the succeeding months by memorandums and notes to the same effect, all towards influencing Lloyd George in the direction of a hard, punitive approach to labor unrest, the negotiated peace movement and, later, against Wilson and the international Socialist Conferences. In June, Milner was warning him (through another of Fisher's reports) against what he called the "Follow Russia plot," referring to a planned trip by Henderson and I.L.P. representatives to Russia.[45] He was warned of a "rapidly growing" rank-and-file movement in the country run by the I.W.W., the warning illustrated by maps showing the "correspondence" of their delegates and the occurrence of damaging strikes. These movements were all "avowedly revolutionary and saboteur" and somehow "connected" with Germany.[46] The consistent theme of the arguments directed at the Prime Minister, who admittedly still lacked any reliable organizational base among the working classes, was that he should interest and associate himself with the "countermining" effort of the British Workers League.

A similar and complementary effort was begun by Carson, Oliver, Amery, and Kerr to alert Lloyd George to the growing danger of the peace-by-negotiation movement on both sides of the Atlantic. The increasing currency of the Wilsonian doctrine particularly agitated Carson and Oliver who saw it working in concert with

[44] Ibid.
[45] Milner to Lloyd George (1 June 1917), *L.G.P.*, F/38/2/8.
[46] "Strictly Private and Confidential," unsigned (30 June 1917), *L.G.P.*, F/78/5/-. This report and accompanying maps emanated privately from a member of the Commission of Enquiry into Labour Unrest, noting that it was "not the mind of the whole Commission." (12 June 1917), *L.G.P.*, F/78/6/2.

the international Socialist movement as the ultimate danger both to the final defeat of Germany and to the future of the empire—and it was a danger which would inevitably mount along with the financial dependence on America. As we have seen, the question had already become a subject of concern in the previous year, but the Milnerites gave it a far more alarming implication by linking it with the fears of labor and Socialist agitation throughout the Allied nations. Those fears naturally reached a crescendo later in the year with the Stockholm Conference and the October Revolution, but the attempted indoctrination of Lloyd George began immediately. Carson, who had particularly vehement grievances about American influence because of the Irish connection, pressed his view about Wilson forcefully to Lloyd George. Wilson, "this monster of vanity on the other side of the Atlantic," was becoming the symbol and focal point of all the antiwar agitation and "longing for peace" which was debilitating the war effort among the Allies. Passing on a memo from Oliver, a "clever and clear-minded man," he added,

> Now, old Wilson is a detestable, immoral, cold-blooded, hot-air materialist. In a sense he is an ass as well. . . . But picking a time for pressing his policy to end the war (i.e. at a point where the U.S. will be left financially, industrially, and politically holding the balance of power) he is an exceedingly astute old fox.[47]

The mixing of the long-held fears about American ascendancy with the double-edged threat of domestic unrest and a negotiated peace was deeply inimical to the progressive side of the coalition and the more ambitious hopes for a reformist reconstruction. As we have seen, that element represented by such individuals as Beveridge, Webb, and Jones was quickly depressed and eroded by the ascendancy of the Milner-Amery influence and by the definite shift to the Right in the July shake-up which brought in Carson, Churchill, Addison, and Geddes. The process accelerated thereafter in the international crises of the fall and assisted in the increasing polarization of the forces inside and outside the coalition. Beatrice Webb expected that, as the government became more reactionary (as she thought it could hardly fail to do), the rebel minority in the Labour Party would either force a breakup in the party truce or "become an embittered and revolutionary minority." That would mean, she

---

[47] Carson to Lloyd George (29 Jan. 1917), *L.G.P.*, F/6/2/11; the Oliver memo cited is dated 26 Jan. 1917.

thought, "sedition and the suppression of sedition and a state of chaos out of which anything might emerge."[48] From a different point of view, Philip Kerr made much the same analysis during the debacle over the Lansdowne letter: writing to Lloyd George, he suggested that the obvious loss of purpose for the war, the success of the Bolshevik argument, the demoralization of the Allied armies, and the movement of working-class opinion was due mainly to the gradual defection of the moderate and stalwart men "who normally enlighten and steady public opinion."

> If they become pacific, or even neutral, the pacifists, the revolutionary agitators, the faint-hearted and German agents will soon begin to run away with the mob and strikes and social trouble of every kind will become chronic everywhere to Germany's immense gain. This body of opinion, however, can no longer be dealt with by phrases or fine speeches, or appeals to history, or to the fighting instinct of mankind. It can only be dealt with by convincing the idealists who are the backbone of every country . . . that premature peace would mean another war. . . .[49]

Both analyses were persuasive, given Lloyd George's own deep convictions about the defeat of Germany and his desire to tap the vast body of patriotic sentiment in the labor movement. In fact, the two became basic assumptions of coalition strategy for the remainder of the war and during the peace settlement, because they were thought to contain the antidote to its two most troublesome obstacles—Wilsonian propaganda and the defection of labor sentiment to Wilson and, later, to Lenin. In short, the unconditional surrender of Germany must be seen as one prerequisite of a "war to end war" and labor unity must be the other. In this the strategies of the Milnerites and of Lloyd George were in almost exact unison. Without either a party or any other organized base that strategy was in danger of sudden disintegration, at the mercy of faction and the accidents of war. Moreover, the plan of reconstruction would inevitably suffer whatever fate came to the coalition since it was predicated on the same conditions, as Beveridge had pointed out in his earlier report on the Labour Exchanges after the war. He reiterated the point even more forcefully to the new Reconstruction Committee:

[48] B. Webb, "Diary" (9 Dec. 1916).
[49] Philip Kerr to Lloyd George (5 Dec. 1917), *L.G.P.*, F/89/1/10.

> The War has shown . . . very considerable bitterness of feeling between employers and work people . . . [which] have been to a large extent suppressed during the war by patriotic feelings, though the difficulty with which this has been done in some cases illustrates the strength of the evil. There will be ground for considerable fear as soon as the war pressure is removed, even if the circumstances were then likely to be otherwise normal.
>
> As soon, therefore, as the cessation of war appears to remove the imperious necessity for national unity at all points, there is a possibility that the relations of Capital and Labour may go from bad to worse, producing either open disputes or secret hostilities with disastrous effects upon the economic prosperity of the country; for in fact, though the actual war may have ended, the necessity for national unity and industrial efficiency will remain hardly less than before.[50]

Thus the future survival of the coalition, the resistance to American war aims policy, postwar economic solvency, and the success of a stable reconstruction plan were all made to hinge on the "imperious necessity for national unity at all points" both during and after the war. That thought became the overriding concern of the coalition in its relations with labor and the war opponents on the one side and with Milner's "countermining" effort on the other.

At several points in the previous ten years, the movement embodied in Chamberlain and Milner had been drawn to the idea of "drafting" Lloyd George. Milner served as a unifying symbol of their grievances but since the loss of Chamberlain they had been orphaned of any effective political leader and had been in search of a successor. The primary qualification for that role, as we have seen, was that he be someone outside and critical of "the System." That alone was enough to rule out such logical successors as Austen Chamberlain and to recommend the maverick Welsh Radical despite their apparently profound ideological differences over such questions as the Boer War and the 1909 budget. His behavior since the constitutional crisis more than offset those differences and the overthrow of Asquith seemed to confirm their expectations of him. On his part, Lloyd George had often reciprocated their inter-

---

[50] William Beveridge, "Relations of Capital and Labour after the War," Report to the Reconstruction Committee (n.d., 1917), *Bev. P.*, M672, no. 7. An original draft was made for the previous Reconstruction Committee in the summer of 1916 and resubmitted to its successor during the spring of 1917.

est in him, especially on those occasions like the Insurance Bill, the coalition plan, and the conscription debate when he found most of his own party either lukewarm or openly hostile. The lack of such a personal following and organization as they were apparently prepared to offer was a sore and constricting weakness in those cases and would impose even more galling restraints on his actions as leader of the coalition; to enter the inevitable turmoil of postwar politics without some such following could be (and eventually was) fatal.

In their alliance of 1917, the Milnerites exchanged the resources of the movement for the long-denied opportunities of government office and influence on the making of state policy. Needing support at the ministerial level, in Parliament, and some organizational base in the country as a hedge against any major defections in the coalition, Lloyd George made rather a poor bargain with them. The Milnerites provided a large number of distinguished and energetic men for key positions in the new bureaucracy but, excepting only Milner and Hodge, none at the Cabinet level. It soon became evident as well that they could provide no significant wedge into the main body of Conservatives in Parliament, none at least that would free Lloyd George from dependence on Bonar Law. The offers of support from the B.W.L. attached to most of the "intelligence" coming in from the Milner men were also of questionable political value and in some cases altogether fanciful. For despite its fairly illustrious list of contributors, its vice-presidents, its newspaper, and its 188 local branches, the league was still an embryonic organization with an annual budget of less than £10,000, an irregular and nonpaying membership, and (despite some of Milner's illusions) a completely undemonstrated influence as yet in the labor movement.[51] Milner and Amery nevertheless succeeded in giving a much more formidable appearance to the league and its activities. By the fall, Victor Fisher was casually hobnobbing with the coalition leaders, coasting in these high circles on the inflated promises of the Milner group. Addison was one of the first to be impressed

---

[51] A statement of the financial condition of the B.W.L. appears in a report from an A. MacLeod to Milner (6 March 1917), *M.P.*, Great War, 1917. The sum of £9100 is listed as the total resources of the league at that time, distributed among four accounts. The primary contributors were announced in the 25 August 1916 issue of the *B.C.E.W.* as Sir Frederick Milner, Lord Heresford, Sir Leo Chiozza Money, Cecil Chesterton, Leslie Scott (of the Reconstruction Committee), and Leo Maxse. Astor, the heaviest contributor, is not mentioned.

and was soon extolling the merits of Fisher and Hodge to Lloyd George, passing on Fisher's suggestions about dealing with strikers and finally recommending that he be included in a new Council of Ministers (led by Milner) to report to the Cabinet on reconstruction—a council that would obviously supersede the waning influence of the Reconstruction Committee.[52]

In all the dunning of Lloyd George from this quarter, the theme was "countermining" the supposed activities of the I.L.P. and the U.D.C. in the labor disturbances and the peace movement. In a memo to Lloyd George, Amery argued against allowing British delegates to attend the Stockholm Conference:

> ... even if the Conference did no harm, it would be the beginning of a claim on the part of a sectional organization to be consulted at every step affecting the conclusion of peace, which might end by landing us in an intolerable situation—a second 'Soviet' in fact. ...
> The avowed object of the Conference is to exalt international Socialism at the expense of the Party truce in the different countries.[53]

The several fruitless attempts of the Milner section to found patriotic labor-political organizations in the past had been for the purpose of averting just such a mixture of domestic industrial unrest and international Socialist organization as now seemed to be occurring despite the general conservatism of the Labour Party leadership. The present strategy was to link Lloyd George with their current organization, the B.W.L., as a counterforce now supported by the formidable instruments of wartime government powers like the D.O.R.A. and the Military Service Acts. Milner's suggestion had been to "comb out and call up" all the radical agitators of military age. Much the same policy was also urged upon the Prime Minister by Addison, based again on a suggestion of Fisher's for dealing with shop stewards and strikers in the winter of 1917-1918.[54] Since neither Milner's nor Amery's name was publicly as-

[52] Addison to Lloyd George (17 Jan. and 21 Feb. 1918), *L.G.P.*, F/1/4/8 and F/1/4/9.

[53] Amery to Lloyd George (7 Sept. 1917), *L.G.P.*, F/2/1/5. Memo, "The Stockholm Conference," attached.

[54] Milner to Lloyd George (26 May 1917), *L.G.P.*, F/38/2/5; Addison to Lloyd George (17 Jan. 1918), cited above, n. 52. In his letter recommending that closer attention be given to B.W.L. activity, Addison also passed on Fisher's warning that it would be "unwise to do anything against threatening strikers until *after* the Nottingham conference" which was to be held a week later.

sociated with the B.W.L., the advancement of Hodge and Fisher in the Lloyd George government was a way of enhancing the prestige, and hopefully the meager finances, of the league and thus making more plausible the effort to counteract the influence of the I.L.P. in the labor movement. Meetings arranged by Milner between the Prime Minister and Hodge, Fisher, and other B.W.L. officers, such as the one in January 1918 in which methods of dealing with the I.L.P. and the strikers were discussed, were intended to wed Lloyd George both to their conspiratorial theory of the labor unrest and to their bluntly repressive manner of dealing with it[55]—this was the kind of influence which the "keeper of Lloyd George's democratic conscience" had suspected might develop as the Milner troops entered the coalition.

The Milnerite pressure on Lloyd George became most intense in the critical fall and winter of 1917 but it was only partially successful. As a recent commentator on Milner has put it, "If Lloyd George was surrounded, he was not to be captured."[56] A few years later, when the coalition was at last on the point of breaking up, Lloyd George asked Beaverbrook his opinion of the best options open to him. Beaverbrook's analysis, with which Lloyd George fully agreed, was realistic and moderate; it also suggests the relatively small difference the turmoil of wartime politics had made in Lloyd George's position. There were two options only, Beaverbrook reasoned: the first was "to become absolute head of a 'Fusion Party' leaving out Die-Hards and Wee Frees on each side," in short, a permanent coalition with Bonar Law; the second was to move to the Left in an attempt at a Liberal re-union. Beaverbrook's scenario was predicated on two conditions in the political picture which were as much in force in 1917 as they were five years later: in the first place, the coalition Liberals, always "uncertain, coy and hard to please," would accept office and honors from Lloyd George's hand but they would not sacrifice their permanent Liberal affiliation; on the other hand, the Bonar Law Conservatives were essential to the coalition while the die-hard protectionists were not.[57]

[55] The meeting of 16 January 1918 was arranged by Milner to include Hodge and "other B.W.L. men" but was apparently attended by Addison and Fisher. Milner to Lloyd George (15 Jan. 1918), F/38/3/3.

[56] Eric Stokes, "Milnerism," the *Historical Journal*, v, 1 (1962).

[57] Beaverbrook to Lloyd George (13 March 1922), *L.G.P.*, F/4/6/6; Lloyd George to Beaverbrook (15 March 1922), *L.G.P.*, F/4/6/7.

The essence of the original coalition plan of 1910 and the prospect of permanence for the coalition government was that the effective hold of the parties in Parliament be broken. While Lloyd George mistakenly hoped to accomplish that feat by the skillful manipulation of party factions and by the force of his own personality, eventually becoming a Prime Minister without a party, he remained always a parliamentary politician. Milner's was a far more radical approach in which the power of the parties would be reduced by reducing the power of the Parliament. That had been the portent of the imperialist attack on the party system since Rosebery invoked the model of the Prussian bureaucracy sixteen years before and it continued to be the overriding principle of the numerous veterans of that attack who were now spinning out the great volume of reports from the committees of the Ministry of Reconstruction.[58] The consistent emphasis was again efficiency and expertise in administration—a condition, it was argued, which could only be achieved by a permanent imperial bureaucracy virtually free from party and parliamentary interference. All this was clearly recognizable by now as excerpts from the Social-Imperialist text. After the July shake-up, however, the social reform side which had always accompanied that argument was conspicuously muted, as Hobson had warned years ago that it would be if the imperialists ever achieved the power to put their doctrine into practice. The idea of a "Constructive Revolution" being made out of the necessities of war and reconstruction gave way rather meekly in the first year of the coalition and was eventually buried by the twin specters of financial insolvency and world revolution.

The failure of the Lloyd George coalition to become a more permanent force in English politics cannot be ascribed to any inherent impossibility in the idea or, as it often has been, to some historic national distaste for coalitions. Nor is it entirely plausible to relegate the coalition to the host of wartime innovations which disappeared after their purpose had been served. It had been a prewar idea which came very close to succeeding four years before the out-

[58] A great many reports on the Machinery of Government were produced while Haldane was chairman of the committee of that name in the Ministry of Reconstruction. For some of those which reached Lloyd George, see the "Report of the Machinery of Government Committee" (7 March 1918), *L.G.P.*, F/74/10/5; Amery's memo, "The Future of the Cabinet System" (n.d., 1918), *L.G.P.*, F/74/11/2; and from Haldane's committee, "War and the Machinery of Government" (n.d., 1917), F/74/21/1.

break of war and it reached its greatest success in the two years after the peace. Its failure was more likely due to the deficiencies of its author and leader as a revolutionary. Lloyd George, it has often been noted, "was not a man of plan and system." Bountifully endowed with all the public talents for success, he also lacked the one most admired in public men in his own country, the gift of either giving or inspiring personal loyalty of the kind, for example, that bound the Kindergarten through the years. He seemed to admire that quality in Milner without ever recognizing its source, the unbending fanaticism which magnetized grievances to it, all the frustrated ambition, idealism, and arrogance of a generation born a little too late to enjoy the rule of subject races. They were a brotherhood of exiles in the English democracy where Lloyd George felt more or less at home.

Appendix A

Campaign Literature

Memo, Garvin to Sandars, 29 November–1 December, 1909
—*Balfour Papers*, Additional Manuscripts, 49795-787E

I General character it ought to have

As a simplified argument is always a relief even to educated people, it is everything for democratic purposes. All election literature should be as short and plain and bold as possible. A full use should be made of heavy black type. That is half the force of the ammunition, perhaps more than half. Considering that the mind of the masses is inconceivably crude; that you can't be sure of their understanding any word more than two syllables long; that some of the most common terms of political controversy never carry a clear idea to the majority of voters on either side; and that their attention, wandering easily, must be seized and fixed in spite of themselves—the most important thing of all is to make the effect of every leaflet and picture so prompt and strong, that some impressions must be received and maintained by voters who can be induced to cast a single glance at what is offered to them.

II Poorest Unionist Literature judged by principle first laid down

It has, by comparison with the red-hot, brief, pungent style of Radical compaigning, many defects. For popular purposes ours is largely dead stuff. It is nearly all too abstract, academic and verbose. It is full of long words, and of learned phrases. There is something about "The Justice of Decrement." There is something else about "The Dethronement of the Judicature." There is a vast deal more of that sort of thing which only applies to intellectual people certain to vote for us in any case. Some of the leaflets are four pages long, consisting of sustained argument in solid paragraphs, with nothing whatever in the shape of an introductory or final summary. There is a great deal, in matter good in manner dull, about land; but there is not nearly enough about tariff reform, about unemployment, about the favouring of foreign trade, about the crushing down of home enterprise, about the cigarette and tobacco taxes clapped on to save "the foreigner," about the Empire, the navy and the rest, not forgetting the Conservative and Unionist record on Social reform. An especially important part is the following. It is a most dangerous thing and in my view the greatest folly to adopt and emphasize Mr. Philip Snowden's statement of one of the main fallacies of the Social creed—that the weight of all taxation under the present system must be transferred to the shoulders of the working man; that *he* must bear the whole burden in any case of the money that has to be found; that his employer will lower his wages while his landlord raises his rent. This state of things maddens the working man, fills him with hatred of all that Unionists represent, and enables the Socialists to cry to him: "You see the Tories themselves admit that what we say is true." Every leaflet and sentence framed in that spirit should be struck out. The Budget Protest league are the worst offenders by far in this particular.

Again the British workman must appear in all our pictures as a fine fellow, not the debased and uncouth and grotesque person that he seems in some of our pictures.

Upon the whole the inferiority of our party literature for its campaign purposes is a most serious disadvantage and indeed a very real danger.

III Scrapping necessary

While some leaflets are plain and familiar enough to be retained a good deal ought to be withdrawn altogether.

IV Improvements in Form

    a. Golden rule—*one leaflet one idea.*
    b. Sentences and paragraphs short and strong.
    c. Utmost possible use of big black type.
    d. All figures set out heavily and boldly.
    e. Some main point should be made in two or three lines at top of each leaflet.
    f. Text before sermon—brief summons prefixing long quote or argument.

Appendix A

    g. As far as possible every single argument should be got into one side of the paper.
    h. The ideal leaflet is a single sheet with the printed argument on the front and a picture of some kind on the back. If I were running a campaign department I would use that kind almost exclusively.

V Matter of New Literature

To seize imagination which our present dead stuff can't do, we—like other side, must have two things.

    A. A Dream
    B. A Bogey
        a). Their dream is Socialism and the earthly paradise and their bogey—landlords.
        Our dream—Imperial Strength and Industrial Security based upon Tariff Reform; our bogey must be the freely importing foreigner.
        b). Tariff Reform, instead of playing an insignificant part in our campaign literature, should dominate whole of it.
        c). We have to concentrate upon the ten per cent or so of undecided voters in town and country, and we have to get them at any cost. For this purpose we must work on their *real* feelings.

VI The Real Feelings of the average unfixed voters whose support we may reasonably expect to gain by vigorous effort

    a. They dread dimly an Imperial and Social catastrophe. That dread has got to be developed and defined in their minds. We have got to show them that the Budget does represent the spirit of the Socialistic Revolution; and that the Limehouse Speech is a firebrand's signal for a class war. The argument that the nation is prepared for is that the Radical-Socialist method means revolution, chaos and peril, while the Unionist party stands for power, union and security.
    b. The average Englishman loathes favouring the foreigner and wants him to be taxed, and is very sensible to the absurdity of pulling the empire and society to pieces and plunging into political convulsions without end rather than lay upon foreign imports a farthing of taxation.

c. The country responds strongly to every form of the appeal "Britons hold your own."
d. It wants the fleet to be placed under a footing of unassailable superiority.
e. It wants Imperial Union and Commercial equality.
f. And above all it wants to combine social progress with national security. It is therefore of vital importance to consider what part ought to be played in Unionist campaign-literature by promises of social reform. It would be fatal to leave the devil all the good tunes in this matter. One has the very strongest conviction that a social programme ought to play at least as strong a part in our policy now as in the Unionist Campaign of 1895. This, however, is a suggestion requiring detailed development in another communication.

Appendix B

The Criccieth Memorandum

Lloyd George, 17 August 1910—*Lloyd George Papers*, C/6/5/1

Some of the most urgent problems awaiting settlement, problems which concern intimately the happiness and the efficiency of the inhabitants of these Islands, their strength and influence can only be successfully coped with by the active co-operation of both the great Parties in the State. Parties will always disagree on certain vital issues affecting the government of this country: their respective points of view are essentially different; but it is rather fortunate at the present moment the questions which are of the most vital importance to the well-being of this great community are all questions which are not only capable of being settled by the joint section of the two great Parties without involving any sacrifice of principle on the part of either but which can be better settled by such cooperation than by the normal working of party machinery. This country has gained a good deal from the conflict and rivalry of Parties, and it will gain a good deal more in the future from the same cause; but I cannot help thinking that the time has arrived for a truce, for bringing the resources of the two Parties into joint stock in order to liquidate arrears which, if much longer neglected, may end in national impoverishment, if not insolvency. It must be quite clear to any observer that the rapid raise of great foreign competitors has put us in a position where no time ought to be lost in repairing the deficiencies of our national system and putting our machinery in better order, in order to equip us for a state of things with which we have never before been confronted. For the first time in hundreds of years the Continent has enjoyed a long period of peace and repose and foreign nations have employed the immunity from internal and external conflicts in developing their industrial and commercial equipment to an extent which menaces our supremacy. Under these circumstances, it becomes us to sink our differences and to unite in combined and sustained effort to re-organise the national life of our country in all its branches, so as to put us in a position where we need have no apprehension as to the future of the British Empire whatever the strain may be that shall be put upon its resources. I would summarize the advantages which in my judgment will be gained by attempting a non-Party solution of the great Imperial and National problems to which I have alluded:

(1) None of these great problems can be effectively dealt with without incurring temporary unpopularity.

There is always some essential part of a scheme, sometimes the most useful and far-reaching in its beneficial results, which for the moment has to face a good deal of misapprehension. A large number of people misunderstand it, and it causes an amount of apprehension which experience alone can dispel. If you have a hostile Party with nearly half the nation amongst its organised supporters waiting to take advantage of every slip, no Ministry will be disposed to take unnecessary risks, and often the unpopular section of a project has to be ruthlessly cut out, in order to save the remnant, although that section may be essential to a complete and successful treatment of the subject.

(2) When you come to subjects of this kind, the equality of the Parties in numbers is in itself a source of weakness, for it means that a Government has only to alienate a comparatively small number of the Electorate of the country in order to incur defeat, and an Opposition has only to win the support of the same number in order to oust their opponents from power. Thus, often the least-responsible, the least well-informed and the most selfish amongst the Electorate may have a decisive voice in determining the issues upon which the whole future of the British Empire may depend. If joint action between the Parties could be negotiated, these undesirable elements would sink to their proper insignificance as factors.

(3) This is a corollary of the two preceding propositions. No settlement is possible without exciting a good many ill-informed prejudices, some of them with an historical basis. They cannot be argued with, they cannot always be voted down; but they are extremely pernicious in their influence upon the settlement of a difficult and complex problem. Separate action means that a Party in opposition is driven into enlisting the support of these

Appendix B

prejudices, whether it wishes to do so or not: the more extreme men amongst their own supporters on the platform and in the Press always take advantage of these elements, however enlightened a view the Party leaders may take.

Joint action will enable a Government based on the best of the strength of the two Parties to ignore these prejudices.

(4) Parties are now committed through a long course of controversy to particular methods of dealing with problems, and, however much the more instructed amongst them may feel that there are other and better alternatives which have not yet been put forward, no Party can afford to abandon the position which it has deliberately taken up and long defended in the presence of the enemy. Governments are therefore driven to the second best method of settling a question, because their Party programme and Party pledges make it impossible for them to take the best course.

(5) Extreme partisans supporting the Government often drive it against its better judgment to attempting legislation on lines which are the least useful in dealing with a question. As a rule the advanced sections of a Party, being propagandist, are the most active, the best organised, the most resolute and therefore the most irresistible. Joint action would make it possible to settle these urgent questions without paying undue regard to the formulae and projects of rival faddists.

(6) No Party has a monopoly of able and efficient men, nor has it a monopoly of duffers. No Party commands the services of more than half a dozen first-rate men, and it has to depend for the filling up of all the other posts in the Government upon the services of men of second, and even third-rate capacity.

Inasmuch as some of these posts are of great importance when you come to questions of national organization, under the present system their presence as the heads of these Departments presents an effective barrier to reform. The head of a Department is supreme in that Department; not even the Prime Minister can effectively direct, guide and control his action; and, as for the rest of the Government, they are too concerned in the management of their own Departments to be able to give the necessary attention even if it were possible for them to interfere with a colleague. It is therefore vital to any great scheme of National re-organisation that the best men that the nation provides should be secured as heads during the period of reconstruction. This can only be achieved by drawing upon the resources of both Parties in the State.

What are the questions which call for immediate attention and which could properly and effectively be dealt with by some such combined effort as I indicate? There are first of all the questions which come under the category of Social Reform: they affect the health, the vitality, the efficiency and the happiness of the individuals who constitute the races that dwell in these islands.

Housing

The putting an end to a system which houses millions of the people under conditions which devitalizes their strength, depresses their energies and deprives them of all motive power for putting forth their best.

Drink

The problem of excessive drinking has a most intimate relation to other questions of Social Reform.

There is no doubt that a vast number of people in this country destroy their physical, mental and moral powers owing to their addiction to alcohol. One Party has been for the moment completely captured by a rigid and sterile plan for effecting reform; the other Party's energies are concentrated upon resistance to this scheme. If both Parties put their heads together, they could discover some idea which, whilst treating vested interests fairly and even generously, would advance the cause of national sobriety.

Insurance

Provision against the accidents of life which bring so much undeserved poverty to hundreds of thousands of homes, accidents which are quite inevitable, such as the death of the bread-winner or his premature break-down in health. I have always thought that the poverty which was brought upon families owing to these causes presents a much more urgent demand upon the practical sympathy of the community than even Old Age Pensions. With old age, the suffering is confined to the individual alone; but, in these other cases, it extends to the whole family of the victim of circumstances.

Appendix B

Unemployment

Unemployment might also be put in the same category. Whatever is done towards improving the trade conditions, we shall at any rate for some time to come have to face a percentage of unemployment, especially in certain precarious trades. No country has been able to avoid it, and, with fluctuations in trade, the constant improvements in machinery, the variations in public demands for commodities and many other reasons, men will be thrown out of employment temporarily, and great difficulty will be found in absorbing this surplus labour. Much misery will thereby be caused, misery often culminating in hunger and starvation. Every country ought to provide adequately against such disasters.

This question of Insurance illustrates one of the difficulties that must necessarily be encountered by every Government that attempts to grapple with it without first of all securing the co-operation of its opponents. The hardest case of all is that of the man who dies in the prime of life leaving a widow and young children. She suddenly finds herself without any adequate means, very often with all her means exhausted by medical and funeral expenses, face to face with the task of having not merely to attend to her household duties and the bringing up of the children, but also with that of earning a livelihood for herself and for them. In Germany they contemplate adding provision for widows under these conditions to their ordinary invalidity insurance. It is comparatively easy to set up a system of that kind in Germany; but, here, one would have to encounter the bitter hostility of powerful organisations like the Prudential, the Liver, the Royal Victoria, the Pearl and similar institutions, with an army, numbering scores if not hundreds of thousands, of agents and collectors who make a living out of collecting a few pence a week from millions of households in this country for the purpose of providing death allowances. The expenses of collection and administration come to something like 50 per cent of the total receipts, and these poor widows and children are by this extravagant system robbed of one-half of the benefits which it has cost the workman so much to provide for them. Sometimes these agents and collectors sell their books and sub-let them and make hundreds of pounds out of the transaction, all at the expense of the poorest and most helpless creatures in the land. This system ought to be terminated at the earliest possible moment. The benefits are small, costly and precarious, for, if a man is unable,

Appendix B

owing to ill-health, or lack of employment, to keep up his payments his policy is forfeited. State insurance costs 10 per cent to administer, and, inasmuch as the State and the employer both contribute, either the premium is considerably less, or the benefits are substantially greater than with the Insurance Companies. But, however desirable it may be to substitute State insurance, which does not involve collection and therefore is more economical, any Party that attempted it would instantly incur the relentless hostility of all these agents and collectors.

They visit every house, they are indefatigable, they are often very intelligent, and a Government which attempted to take over their work without first of all securing the co-operation of the other Party would inevitably fail in its undertaking; so that, if a scheme of national insurance is taken in hand by any Party Government, it must be confined to Invalidity, and the most urgent and pitiable case of all must be left out. I may add that compensation on an adequate scale is well-nigh impossible, inasmuch as it would cost something like 20 or 30 millions at the very least to buy off the interest of these collectors, and such a payment would crush the scheme and destroy its usefulness. On the other hand the agents cannot be absorbed in the new system than [*sic*] being as door to door collection contemplated. This is an excellent illustration of the difficulty of dealing with some of these problems except by joint action.

The Poor Law

This requires overhauling and recasting, and I can see nothing in the principles of either Party which are irreconcileable in this matter.

National Re-organisation

There are several questions coming under this head which could be much better dealt with by a Coalition than by a Party Administration.

There is Education. Not merely could the denominational question be thus much more satisfactorily disposed of, inasmuch as the Parties are committed to certain controversial solutions which may not be the very best; but there are questions like the raising of the age limit, which is quite essential if the youth of the country are to

Appendix B

receive a training which will enable them to cope with the workmen of Germany and the United States of America.

The same observation applies to the development of Technical Instruction in this country. The raising of the age limit would excite a good deal of opposition in many quarters and might gain for a Government great unpopularity even amongst sections of its own supporters who benefit now largely by Boy labour. The Unionist Govt of 1886 discovered this, and it is only a Coalition that could, here again, have the strength to face the ignorant and selfish prejudices that will be aroused by any effort to keep the children at School instead of turning them on to make money for their parents.

National Defence

This ought to be thoroughly looked into from the point of view of both efficiency and economy. There are undoubtedly directions in which money can be saved: there are others in which it is imperative that more money should be spent. The whole question of National Defence ought to be boldly faced. I doubt whether we are getting our money's worth in any direction. I am strongly of opinion that even the question of compulsory training should not be shirked. No Party dare touch it, because of the violent prejudices which would be excited even if it were suspected that a Government contemplated the possibility of establishing anything of the kind. For that reason it has never really been looked into by Statesmen in this country. The Swiss Militia system might be considered and those liable to service might be chosen by ballot. We have no such need as continental countries labour under of organising an army of 3 or 4.000.000 for defence but we might aim at raising 500.000 armed militia to supplement our regular army and provide against contingencies.

Local Government

Our whole system of Local Government is on a very unsatisfactory basis. There are too many Boards & there is no system of intelligent direction, such as is provided by the Burgomiasters [sic] on the Continent. Whilst there are too many small Boards and Councils, there are too few large ones, and a good deal of work is cast upon the Imperial Parliament which could be much more efficiently discharged by Local bodies on a large scale.

Trade

The various problems connected with State assistance to Trade and Commerce could be enquired into with some approach to intelligent and judicial impartiality if Party rivalries were eliminated. We have, not merely problems connected with Tariffs, but we have the question of inland transport that ought to be thoroughly overhauled. In Germany the Railway is one of the most important weapons in the armoury of the State for the purpose of promoting the Foreign trade of that country.

The Land

There is no question which would gain more by the elimination of Party strife and bitterness than that of the Land. It is admitted on all hands that the land of this country is capable of much more profitable uses than is now given of [sic] it. Both Parties seem to imagine, for the moment, that the real solution lies in the direction of establishing a system of Small Holdings. I think they have been rather too readily rushed by small but well organised groups of their own supporters into an acceptance of this doctrine. These groups are inspired by men of no marked intelligence and with little knowledge of land cultivation. The Small holdings craze is of very doubtful utility, and I do not think its devotees have sufficiently considered whether farming on a large scale by competent persons with adequate capital is not more likely to be profitable to the community than a system which divides the land amongst a large number of more or less incompetent small holders. After all, farming is a business and it requires just as much capacity to successfully run a 50-acre farm as it would to manage a 50-acre holding. There ought to be the same knowledge of the qualities of the soil, the same gift of buying and selling, the same skill in making the best of the soil in both cases. It is very rarely that men enjoy a combination of all these gifts, and it is far better that the majority of men should work under competent guidance, direction and command, than that they should undertake the responsibilities of management. Few are the men who can if left to themselves put their own labour to the most fruitful use. The alternatives are worthy of much more careful and thorough consideration than has hitherto been given to them. If a mistake is made it will be irreparable for generations. Once a system of small holdings is rooted in this coun-

Appendix B

try, it will be almost impossible for a very long period to substitute for it a system of farming on a large scale with adequate capital, where the State might very well assist, and under intelligent management.

Imperial Problems

Schemes for uniting together the Empire and utilising and concentrating its resources for Defence as well as for Commerce might also to much better advantage be undertaken and put through by a Coalition. They are the most delicate and difficult questions that have to be settled by modern statesmanship. In many respects they are the most urgent. Now is undoubtedly the best time to approach them. After all, there are Parties in the Colonies as well as here: there are Parties in our Colonies whose sympathies are more naturally attracted to the Liberals, and some whose views perhaps bear an affinity to the Conservatives. In one section, Conservative statesmen are viewed with some suspicion; by others, the Liberal Party is regarded with much distrust; but a Govt that represented both Parties would appeal to all sections and would carry infinitely greater weight.*

Foreign Policy

Such a Govt representing as it would not a fragment but the whole nation would undoubtedly enhance the prestige of this country abroad.

* In this connection the settlement of the Irish Question would come up for consideration. The advantages of a non-party treatment of this vexed problem are obvious. Parties might deal with it without being subject to the embarassing [sic] dictation of extreme partisans whether from Nationalist or Orangeman

Supplementary Memorandum

Lloyd George, 29 October 1910

(1) The Constitutional Question to be settled substantially on the terms of the August Memorandum.
(2) A very careful inquiry to be instituted by the Cabinet, aided by the Committee of Defence, into the adequacy of our defensive preparations. All necessary steps to be taken for the defence of the Empire at home and abroad.
(3) Every effort to be made by Diplomatic means to secure an International understanding which will, if not effect a reduction in the cost of Armaments, at least arrest the alarming growth in expenditure on preparation for war.
(4) A settlement of the Irish Question and of the difficulties of congestion in the House of Commons to be attempted on some such lines as were sketched by Mr. Chamberlain in his speech on the First Reading of the Home Rule Bill of 1886. Ireland to be treated as a unit for the purpose of any measure of self-government. This settlement should be of a kind which might form a nucleus for the Federation of the Empire at some future date. The powers delegated to subordinate Assemblies to be such as are set forth in the Memorandum attached hereto.
(5) A full and impartial Enquiry to be instituted into the working and results of our Fiscal System and also of the Systems of our Trade rivals.
(6) Every effort to be made to promote the trade of the United Kingdom at home and abroad. No action on the Tariff Question to be taken until after the result of the Enquiry above-mentioned. A preference, however, to be given to the Colonies on existing Duties where found practicable. No difficulty about Wine.
(7) The Welsh Church Question to be settled on the terms, not of the Welsh Church Bill now before the House, but on the more liberal terms of the Irish Disestablishment Act of 1869, but no factitious vested interests to be created. If, as a preliminary to such a Measure, it is desired to test the opinions of the Welsh people on the Question, a Referendum to be taken in the Principality.

(8) A National Scheme for Insurance against Unemployment, Sickness and Invalidity, and to make provision for Widows and Orphans, to be passed next year. Contributions to be levied from both Employers and Workmen, with a liberal State subsidy. Friendly Societies to be employed as agents, where possible.

(9) The Housing conditions of the Working-Classes, both in Town and Country, to be thoroughly examined, with a view to immediate administrative and legislative action. An effort to be made on a much larger scale than has hitherto been attempted towards improving them. For this purpose State credit to be utilised, the powers of the central authority to be fortified and the compulsory powers given to Local Authorities for purchase of land to be strengthened.

(10) The Poor Law to be remodelled, with a view to striking at the causes of destitution in the light of information and recommendations of the two Reports.

(11) Agriculture and the Rural Industries of the Country to be effectively assisted, by means of Credit Banks, Grants towards Agricultural and Technical Instruction in the Villages, improved facilities for transporting and marketing Agricultural Produce, and by scientific experiments for informing and instructing Agriculturists. In this connection, the question of a further extension of the principles either of State purchase or of State-aid to Purchasers to be impartially inquired into, with a view to ascertaining which of the two systems is the more likely to produce beneficial results having regard to the economic conditions of the United Kingdom. Also, the reclamation, cultivation and afforestation of Waste Lands to be encouraged and assisted.

(12) The Denominational Controversy to be settled substantially on the lines of Mr. Birrell's 1906 Bill. In addition to this, the whole Educational system to be thoroughly overhauled, so as to make it a more efficient agent for training and equipping the children of this Country for the avocations they are expected to pursue. Amongst other things, the age-limit to be raised; and in this and in other respects British Boys and Girls to have an equally thorough training with the children of competing nations, like Germany and America.

(13) Public Expenditure in all Departments to be thoroughly examined, with a view to effecting economies.

(14) The relations of Local and Imperial Finance to be re-adjusted, with a view, if possible, to relieving the burden of the rates on certain classes of the Community who at the present mo-

ment are bearing an undue share of those burdens. No fresh burdens to be placed upon Agricultural land; but men who are now escaping their fair share, or perhaps escaping contribution altogether, to be called upon to contribute according to their means.

(15) Whilst the Osborne Judgment is not to be completely reversed, inasmuch as its effect at the present moment is rather obscure, a Declaratory Bill to be passed, making quite clear what political functions Trade Unions may exercise. Provision also to be made for Payment of Members of Parliament.

(16) A further effort to be made to reduce the number of Public-Houses in districts where they are now too numerous.

Bibliography

Because of the nature of this study, scanning as it does a period which is fairly broad in time and extraordinarily rich in memoirs, tracts, pamphlets, and private papers, it has not been feasible either to exhaust all the materials which might bear on the subject or to offer a definitive bibliography. Moreover, as I conceive the subject of this book, its implications extend to nearly every aspect of British society in the Edwardian and war years; consequently, in the course of my research I have found a great many primary and secondary sources to be useful which only indirectly bear on the central political theme. Where such peripheral material might prove useful to students of the coalition and the related events of the period I have included them in this bibliography in the hope that it might be of some help in their labor.

I have listed below all the private collections I have consulted, although it is far from a complete catalog of all those available. For further information concerning private collections I would refer the reader to the bibliographies and notes of Searle's *Quest for National Efficiency*, Gollin's *Proconsul in Politics* and his *The Observer and J. L. Garvin*, Semmel's *Imperialism and Social Reform*, and Hazlehurst's *Politicians at War*, which are listed below. Since the numerous biographies, autobiographies, and memoirs of the figures which appear in this study are of very irregular quality and usefulness, I have included only those which are indispensable for filling in important details or help to evoke the milieu in which the events took place.

For a discussion of the secondary sources I refer the reader to the introduction where I have attempted to put the major interpretive literature into a general perspective.

Private Manuscripts

H. H. Asquith Papers, Bodleian Library, Oxford.
A. J. Balfour Papers, British Museum, London.

William Beveridge Papers, British Library of Political and Economic Science, London.
A. Bonar Law Papers, Beaverbrook Library, London.
J. W. Braithwaite Papers, British Library of Political and Economic Science, London.
Lloyd George Papers, Beaverbrook Library, London.
Alfred Milner Papers, New College Library, Oxford.
Passfield Papers, British Library of Political and Economic Science, London.

Party and Parliamentary Reports, Registers, Periodicals, and Pamphlets Collections

Listed below are the main publications in which appeared the more important official reports and articles referred to in the text. The notes may be consulted for the titles, dates, and authors of specific items. Those which are not available at the British Museum may be found either at the Newspaper Library at Colindale or at the Public Record Office.

Annual Register.
Board of Trade: *Reports and Memoranda*, 1901-1902.
British Citizen and Empire Worker.
Cabinet Papers, P. R. O.
Clarion.
Contemporary Review.
Daily Chronicle.
Daily Mail.
Daily News.
Daily Telegraph.
Directory of Directors: List of the Directors of the Joint Stock Companies of the United Kingdom, and the Companies in Which They Are Concerned. London, 1907.
Fabian News.
Fabian Tracts.
Foreign Office Papers, P. R. O.
Fortnightly Review.
Globe.
House of Commons. *Constitutional Yearbooks*, 1900-1903.
House of Commons. *The New Parliament*, 1902.
House of Commons. *Parliamentary Debates.*
House of Lords. *Parliamentary Debates.*

Labour Representation Committee. *Reports of the Annual Conferences.*
The Labour Year Book, 1916.
Liberal League Manifesto (May 1902).
Liberal League Publications. Pamphlet and Leaflet series (1902-1905).
Liberal Magazine.
"Monthly Notes on Tariff Reform." *Tariff Reform League Publications* (1902-1908).
Monthly Review.
Morning Post.
Nation.
National Review.
Nineteenth Century and After.
Observer.
"Occasional Notes." *National Service League Wartime Publications* (1915-1917).
Quarterly Review.
Round Table.
Spectator.
Tariff Reform League Publications. Leaflets and Industrial series (1902-1914).
Times (London).
Unionist Social Reform Committee. *Industrial Inertia, A Practical Solution.* London: U.S.R.C., 1914.
Unionist Social Reform Committee. *Industrial Unrest.* London: U.S.R.C., 1914.
Unionist Social Reform Committee. *Reports on Labour and Social Conditions in Germany.* London: U.S.R.C., 1910.
Unionist Social Reform Committee. *Unionist Policy and Other Essays.* London: U.S.R.C., 1913.
Papers of the War Committee, P. R. O.
Papers of the War Council, P. R. O.
"War Notes." *Tariff Reform League Publications* (1915-1917).
World's Work.

Published Contemporary Sources: Memoirs, Articles, Letters, Tracts, etc.

Addison, Christopher. *Politics from Within.* London: H. Jenkins, 1924.
Amery, Leo S. *My Political Life.* London: Hutchinson, 1955.

Amery, Leo S. *The Problem of the Army.* London: Arnold, 1903.
Armstrong, H. E. "The Reign of the Engineer," *Quarterly Review,* vol. 198 (Oct. 1903).
Ashley, W. *The Tariff Problem.* London: King and Son, 1920.
Askwith, Henry. *Industrial Problems and Disputes.* London: J. Murray, 1920.
Asquith, H. H. *Fifty Years of Parliament.* London: Cassell, 1935.
———. *Memories and Reflections, 1852-1927.* London: Cassell, 1928.
Beaverbrook, Lord (William Maxwell Aitken). *Decline and Fall of Lloyd George.* London: Collins, 1963.
———. *Men and Power, 1917-1918.* London: Hutchinson, 1956.
———. *Politicians and the War.* London: Butterworth, 1928.
Belloc, Hilaire, and Cecil Chesterton. *The Party System.* London: Stephen Swift, 1911.
Bentinck, Ruth C. "The Point of Honour. A Correspondence on Aristocracy and Socialism," *Fabian Tract* no. 151 (1910).
Beveridge, William. *Labour Exchanges.* London: privately printed, 1907.
———. *Power and Influence.* London: Hodder and Stoughton, 1953.
———. *Unemployment: A Problem of Industry.* London: Longmans, Green, 1909.
Birchenough, Henry. "Military Training and Industrial Efficiency," *National Service Journal,* I, 5 (March 1904).
Blatchford, Robert. *My Eighty Years.* London: Cassell, 1931.
Blondel, Georges. *La politique protectionniste en Angleterre: un nouveau danger pour la France.* Paris: Libraire Victor Lecoffre, 1904.
Blunt, Wilfred Scawen. *My Diaries.* New York: Knopf, 1923.
Board of Trade. "Memorandum on the Comparative Statistics of Population, Industry and Commerce in the United Kingdom and some Leading Foreign Countries." London: H.M.S.O., 1902.
Bosanquet, Bernard. *The Philosophical Theory of the State.* London: Macmillan, 1899.
Boyd, Charles (ed.). *Mr. Chamberlain's Speeches.* New York: Houghton Mifflin, 1914.
Bryer, James. *Studies in History and Jurisprudence.* London: Aldwych Publications, 1901.
Bunbury, Henry (ed.). *Lloyd George's Ambulance Wagon: Memoirs of J. W. Braithwaite.* London: Methuen, 1957.

Carpenter, Edward (ed.). *Forecasts of the Coming Century by a Decade of Writers.* London: W. Scott, Clarion and Labour Press, 1897.
Chamberlain, Austen. *Down the Years.* London: Cassell, 1935.
———. *Politics from Inside.* New Haven: Yale University Press, 1937.
Chamberlain, Joseph. "The Labour Question," *Nineteenth Century and After* (Nov. 1892).
Chesterton, Cecil. *Party and People.* London: Unwin, 1910.
———. *The Perils of Peace.* London: T. Werner Laurie, 1916.
Chesterton, G. K. *Autobiography.* London: Hutchinson, 1936.
Chiozza Money, Leo. *Riches and Poverty.* London: Methuen, 1911.
Churchill, Winston. "The Untrodden Field in Politics," *Nation* (March 1908).
———. *The World Crisis.* London: Butterworth, 1923-1931.
Coates, T. F. G. *Lord Rosebery, His Life and Speeches.* London: Hutchinson, 1900.
Cole, Margaret (ed.). *Beatrice Webb's Diaries, 1918-24.* London: Longmans, Green, 1952.
Cross, J. W. "British Trade in 1898: A Warning Note," *Nineteenth Century and After* (May 1899).
Cunningham, William. *The Causes of Labour Unrest and the Remedies for It.* London: J. Murray, 1912.
———. "The Failure of Free-Traders to Attain their Ideal," *Economic Review*, vol. 14 (Jan. 1904).
Curzon, Lord of Kedleston. *Subjects of the Day.* New York: Macmillan, 1915.
Daily Mail. *What the Worker Wants: A Daily Mail Enquiry.* London: Daily Mail, 1912.
Davies, A. Emil. *The Collectivist State in the Making.* London: G. Bell and Sons, 1914.
Esher, Viscount. *Journals and Letters.* London: Nicolson and Watson, 1934-1938.
Fitzroy, Almeric. *Memoirs.* London: Hutchinson, 1935.
Flux, A. W. "British Trade and German Competition," *Economic Journal*, vol. VII (1899).
Garvin, James Louis. "The Break-up of the Old Party System," *Fortnightly Review*, no. 73 (1910).
———. *The Life of Joseph Chamberlain.* London: Macmillan, 1932.

Garvin, James Louis. "Review of Events," *Fortnightly Review*, no. 94 (1910).

———. *Tariff or Budget: The Nation and the Crisis.* London: Tariff Reform League, 1910.

Garvin, Katherine. *J. L. Garvin: A Memoir.* London: Heinemann, 1948.

Giffen, Robert. "A Financial Retrospect, 1861-1901," *Journal of the Royal Statistical Society* (31 March 1902).

———. "The Excess of Imports," *Journal of the Royal Statistical Society*, vol. LXII (March 1899).

Grey of Falloden, Lord Edward. *Twenty-Five Years, 1892-1916.* New York: F. A. Stokes Co., 1925.

———. *Falloden Papers.* Boston: Houghton Mifflin, 1926.

Haldane, Richard Burton. *Autobiography.* New York: Doubleday, 1929.

———. *Before the War.* New York: Funk and Wagnalls, 1920.

———. "The Cabinet and the Empire," *British Empire Review*, vol. 5 (July 1903).

———. "The Lesson of the Free Trade Controversy," *World's Work* (London), vol. III (March 1904).

Hankey, Lord. *The Supreme Command*, 2 vols. London: Allen and Unwin, 1961.

Headlam, Cecil (ed.). *The Milner Papers: South Africa, 1899-1905*, II. London: Cassell, 1933.

Headley, F. W. *Darwinism and Modern Socialism.* London: Methuen, 1909.

Hewins, William Albert Samuel. *Apologia of an Imperialist: Forty Years of Empire Policy.* London: Constable, 1929.

Hills, J. W., W. T. Ashley, and M. Woods. *Industrial Inertia, A Practical Solution.* London: Unionist Social Reform Committee, 1914.

Hobhouse, Leonard Trevelyan. *Democracy and Reaction.* London: Unwin, 1904.

———. *Social Evolution and Political Theory.* New York: Columbia University Press, 1911.

Hobson, J. A. *Imperialism: A Study.* London: Allen and Unwin, 1938.

———. *The Industrial System: An Enquiry into Earned and Unearned Income.* London: Longmans, Green, 1909.

———. *The New Protectionism.* New York: Putnam, 1916.

———. *The Psychology of Jingoism.* London: Grant Richards, 1901.

———. "Some Principles of Industrial Organization: The Case for and Against Scientific Management," *Sociological Review*, vol. I (July 1913).

Iwan-Muller, E. B. *Lord Milner and South Africa*. London: Heinemann, 1902.

Kidd, Benjamin. "A National Policy," *Fortnightly Review*, no. 93 (1910).

———. *Individualism and After*. Oxford: Oxford University Press 1908.

———. *Social Evolution*. London: Macmillan, 1894.

Lansbury, George. *Looking Backwards and Forwards*. London: Blackie and Sons, 1935.

Lenin, V. I. *Imperialism: The Highest Stage of Capitalism*, 2nd ed. New York: International Publishers, 1934.

Lloyd George, David. *Slings and Arrows*. New York: Harper, 1929.

———. *War Memoirs*. London: Odhams, 1934.

Long, Walter. *Memoirs*. London: Hutchinson, 1923.

Mackinder, Halford J. "The Geographical Pivot of History," *Geographical Journal*, XXIII (April 1904).

———. "Great Trade Routes," *Journal of the Institute of Bankers* (May 1900).

———. "Man-Power as a Measure of National and Imperial Strength," *National Review* (March 1905).

———. *Money-Power and Man-Power*. London: Simpkin, Hamilton, Marshall, Kent, 1906.

Macnamara, Thomas J. *Tariff Reform and the Working Man*. London: Hodder and Stoughton, 1910.

MacRosty, H. W. "The Growth of Monopoly in English Industry," *Fabian Tract* no. 88 (1899).

———. "The Revival of Agriculture: A National Policy for Great Britain," *Fabian Tract* no. 123 (1905).

Majoribanks, Edward. *Life of Lord Carson*. London: Gollancz, 1923.

Masterman, Charles F. G. *The Condition of England*. London: Grant Richards, 1909.

Maxse, Leopold. *Germany on the Brain: Gleanings from the National Review*. London: National Review, 1915.

Milner, Lord Alfred. *The Nation and the Empire*. London: Constable, 1913.

Milner, Lord Alfred. *Our Imperial Heritage.* London: Tariff Reform League, 1910.

———. "Some Reflections on the Coming Conference," *National Review* (April 1907).

Milner, Viscountess. "Mr. Chamberlain's Letters to Admiral Maxse, 1872-1889," *National Review* (Feb. 1933).

Mosely, Alfred. *Mosely Industrial Commission: Reports of the Delegates.* London: H.M.S.O., 1903.

Murray, Arthur Cecil (Lord Elibank). *Master and Brother.* London: J. Murray, 1945.

Oliver, F. S. *Alternatives to Civil War.* London: Unionist Social Reform Committee, 1913.

Orwell, George. *The Collected Essays, Journalism and Letters.* New York: Harcourt, Brace & World, 1968.

Riddell, Lord George. *More Pages from My Diary, 1908-1914.* London: Country Life, 1934.

Rosebery, Henry Archibald, Earl of. *Miscellanies: Literary and Historical.* London: Hodder and Stoughton, 1921.

Russell, Bertrand. *The Autobiography of Bertrand Russell, 1872-1941.* London: Allen and Unwin, 1967.

———. *Portraits from Memory and Other Essays.* London: Allen and Unwin, 1956.

Shadwell, Arthur. *Industrial Efficiency: A Comparative Study of Industrial Life in England, Germany and America.* London: Longmans, Green, 1906.

Shaw, George Bernard. *Fabianism and the Empire.* London: Grant Richards, 1900.

———. "Fabianism and the Fiscal Question: An Alternative Policy," *Fabian Tract* no. 116 (1904).

———. *Man and Superman.* New York: Penguin Books, 1953.

———. "Socialism and Superior Brains: A Reply to Mr. Mallock," *Fabian Tract* no. 146 (1909).

Smith, F. E., First Earl of Birkenhead. *The First Phase.* London: Butterworth, 1933.

Stead, Alfred. *Great Japan: A Study of National Efficiency.* London: J. Lane, 1905.

Tournour, Edward (Lord Winterton). *Orders of the Day.* London: Cassell, 1953.

Webb, Beatrice. *Our Partnership.* New York: Longmans, Green, 1948.

Webb, Beatrice and Sidney. *The Break-Up of the Poor Law: Part I of the Minority Report of the Poor Law Commission.* London: H.M.S.O., 1909.
———. *The History of Trade Unionism.* London: Longmans, Green, 1920.
Webb, Sidney. *The Basis and Policy of Socialism.* London: A. C. Field, 1908.
———. "Lord Rosebery's Escape from Houndsditch," *Nineteenth Century and After* (Sept. 1901).
———. "War and the Workers: A Handbook of Some Immediate Measures to Prevent Unemployment and Relieve Distress," *Fabian Tract* no. 176 (1914).
———. "When Peace Comes: The Way of Industrial Reconstruction," *Fabian Tract* no. 181 (1917).
Webb, Sidney and Beatrice. *The Problem of Modern Industry.* London: Fabian Publications, 1898.
———. *The Public Organization of the Labour Market.* London: Longmans, Green, 1909.
Wells, H. G. *Experiment in Autobiography.* London: Gollancz, 1934.
———. *A Modern Utopia.* London: Chapman and Hall, 1905.
———. *The New Machiavelli.* London: John Lane, 1911.
White, Arnold. *Efficiency and Empire.* London: Heinemann, 1901.

Secondary Sources

Aldcroft, D. H. (ed.). *The Development of British Industry and Foreign Competition, 1875-1914.* London: Allen and Unwin, 1968.
———. "The Entrepreneur and the British Economy, 1870-1914," *Economic Historical Review*, 17/1 (August 1964).
Amery, Julian, and J. L. Garvin. *The Life of Joseph Chamberlain.* London: Macmillan, 1932-1937.
Anderson, Pauline. *The Background of Anti-British Feeling in Germany, 1890-1902.* Washington: American University Press, 1939.
Annan, Noel G. "The Intellectual Aristocracy," in *Studies in Social History: In Honor of G. M. Trevelyan.* London: Longmans, Green, 1955.

Barlow, Ima C. *The Agadir Crisis.* Chapel Hill: University of North Carolina Press, 1940.

Beales, H. L. *The Making of Social Policy.* London: G. Cumberledge & Oxford University Press, 1946.

Bealey, F. "Les travaillistes et la guerre des Boers," *Le mouvement social*, no. 45 (1963).

Bealey, F., and Henry Pelling. *Labour and Politics, 1900-1906: A History of the Labour Representation Committee.* London: Macmillan, 1958.

Beloff, Max. *Imperial Sunset, I: Britain's Liberal Empire, 1898-1921.* London: Methuen, 1969.

Birkenhead, the Second Earl of. *Life of F. E. Smith, First Earl of Birkenhead.* London: Butterworth, 1933.

Blake, Robert. *The Unknown Prime Minister.* London: Eyre and Spottiswoode, 1955.

Blewett, Neal. *The Peers, the Parties and the People: the British General Elections of 1910.* Toronto: University of Toronto Press, 1972.

―――. "Free Fooders, Balfourites, Whole Hoggers: Factionalism within the Unionist Party, 1906-1910," *Historical Journal*, 11/1 (1968).

Bowley, Arthur L. *Prices and Wages in the United Kingdom, 1914-1920.* Oxford: Clarendon Press, 1921.

Boyle, T. "The Formation of Campbell-Bannerman's Government in December, 1905: A Memo by J. A. Spender," *Bulletin of the Institute of Historical Research* (Nov. 1972).

Broad, Lewis. *Winston Churchill.* London: Hutchinson, 1943.

Brown, Benjamin. *The Tariff Reform Movement in Great Britain.* New York: Columbia University Press, 1943.

Burgess, Joseph. *Will Lloyd George Supplant Ramsay MacDonald?* Ilford: Joseph Burgess Publication Depot, 1926.

Butler, J. R. M. *Lord Lothian* (Philip Kerr). New York: St. Martin's Press, 1960.

Cairncross, A. K. "The English Capital Market before 1914," *Economica*, 25/98 (May 1958).

―――. *Home and Foreign Investment, 1870-1914.* Cambridge: Cambridge University Press, 1953.

Churchill, Randolph. *Winston Churchill: Young Statesman, 1901-1914.* Boston: Houghton Mifflin, 1967.

Clarke, I. F. *Voices Prophesying War, 1763-1984.* London: Oxford University Press, 1966.

Clegg, H. A., Alan Fox, and A. F. Thompson. *A History of British Trade Unions, since 1889*. Oxford: Clarendon Press, 1964.
Coates, T. F. G. *Lord Rosebery, His Life and Speeches*. London: Hutchinson, 1900.
Cole, Margaret. *The Story of Fabian Socialism*. London: Heinemann, 1961.
Cole, Margaret, and R. C. K. Ensor. *The Webbs and Their Work*. London: F. Muller, 1949.
Collier, Basil. *Brasshat: A Biography of Field Marshall Sir Henry Wilson*. London: Secker and Warburg, 1961.
Colvin, Ian. *Lord Carson*. London: Macmillan, 1937.
Cook, George. "Sir Robert Borden, Lloyd George and British Military Policy, 1917-1918," *Historical Journal*, 14/2 (June 1971).
Cornford, James. "The Transformation of Victorian Conservatism," *Victorian Studies*, 7 (Sept. 1963).
Cosgrave, Robert. "Lloyd George's Mansion House Speech," *Historical Journal*, 12/4 (Dec. 1969).
Cotgrove, Stephen. *Technical Education and Social Change*. London: Ruskin House, 1958.
Crankshaw, Edwin. *The Forsaken Idea*. London: Longmans, Green, 1952.
Creighton, D. G. "The Victorians and the Empire," *Canadian Historical Review*, 19 (1938).
Crewe, Marquis of. *Lord Rosebery*. London: Harper, 1931.
Crosby, Gerda R. *Disarmament and Peace in British Politics, 1914-1919*. Cambridge: Harvard University Press, 1957.
Cross, Colin. *The Fall of the British Empire, 1918-1968*. London: Hodder and Stoughton, 1968.
———. *The Liberals in Power, 1905-1914*. London: Barrie and Rockliff, 1963.
Dangerfield, George. *The Strange Death of Liberal England*. New York: Smith and Haas, 1935.
David, Edward. "The Liberal Party Divided," *Historical Journal*. 13/3 (1970).
Davis, Horace B. "Imperialism and Labor: An Analysis of Marxist Views," *Science and Society,* XXVI (Winter, 1962).
Dearle, N. B. *The Labour Cost of the World War to Great Britain, 1914-1922*. London: Oxford University Press, 1940.
Dickson, Lovat. *H. G. Wells: His Turbulent Life and Times*. New York: Atheneum, 1969.

Douglas, Roy. "The Background to the 'Coupon' Election," *English Historical Review*, 86/339 (April 1971).

———. "The National Democratic Party and the British Workers League," *Historical Journal*, 15/3 (Sept. 1972).

Dugdale, Blanche E. C. *Arthur James Balfour*. London: Hutchinson, 1936.

Ehrman, John. *Cabinet Government and War, 1890-1940*. Cambridge: Harvard University Press, 1958.

Fanning, Ronan. "The Unionist Party and Ireland, 1906-1910," *Irish Historical Studies*, xv (1966).

Fergusson, Sir James. *The Curragh Incident*. London: Faber and Faber, 1964.

Fieldhouse, D. K. "Imperialism: An Historiographical Revision," *Economic Historical Review*, 2/14 (Dec. 1961).

Ford, Percy and Grace. *Breviate of Parliamentary Papers, 1900-1916: Foundation of the Welfare State*. London: H.M.S.O., 1957.

Fraser, Peter. *Joseph Chamberlain: Radicalism and Empire, 1868-1914*. London: Cassell, 1966.

———. "Unionism and Tariff Reform: The Crisis of 1906," *Historical Journal*, 5/2 (April 1962).

———. "The Unionist Debacle of 1911," *Journal of Modern History*, 69/4 (Dec. 1963).

Fremantle, Anne. *This Little Band of Prophets*. Boston: Little, Brown, 1957.

Fyfe, Hamilton. *The British Liberal Party*. London: Allen and Unwin, 1928.

Gallagher, Frank. *The Indivisible Island: the History of Partition of Ireland*. London: Gollancz, 1957.

Geiss, Immanuel. "The Outbreak of the First World War and German War Aims," *Journal of Contemporary History*, I (1966).

Giddens, Anthony. "Elites in the British Class Structure," *Sociological Review*, 20/3 (August 1972).

Gilbert, Bentley, *British Social Policy, 1914-1939*. London: B. T. Batsford, 1970.

———. *The Evolution of National Insurance in Great Britain*. London: Joseph, 1966.

Glaser, John. "English Nonconformity and the Decline of Liberalism," *American Historical Review*, 63/2 (April 1958).

Gollin, Alfred M. *Balfour's Burden: Arthur Balfour and Imperial Preference*. London: Anthony Blond, 1965.

———. *The Observer and J. L. Garvin*. London: Oxford University Press, 1960.

———. *Proconsul in Politics*. London: Anthony Blond, 1964.

Gooch, G. P. and H. W. Temperley (eds.). *British Documents on the Origins of the War, 1898-1914*. London: Johnson reprint, 1967.

Gosses, F. *The Management of British Foreign Policy before the First World War*. Trans. from the Dutch by E. C. van der Gaaf. Leiden: A. W. Sitjhoff, 1948.

Graham, J. W. *Conscription and Conscience: A History, 1916-1919*. London: Allen and Unwin, 1922.

Grigg, John. *The Young Lloyd George*. London: Methuen, 1974.

Guinn, Paul. *British Strategy and Politics, 1914-1918*. Oxford: Clarendon Press, 1961.

Guttsman, W. L. *The British Political Elite*. London: Macgibbon and Kee, 1963.

———. "Aristocracy and the Middle Classes in the British Political Elite, 1886-1916," *British Journal of Sociology*, 4 (1954).

———. "The Changing Social Structure of the British Political Elite, 1886-1935," *British Journal of Sociology*, 2 (1951).

Habakkuk, H. J. *American and British Technology in the Nineteenth Century*. Cambridge: Cambridge University Press, 1962.

Hale, O. J. *Germany and the Diplomatic Revolution: A Study of Diplomacy and the Press, 1904-1906*. Philadephia: University of Pennsylvania Press, 1931.

Halévy, Elie. *L'ère des tyrannies: études sur le socialisme et la guerre*. Librairie Gallimard, 1938.

———. *Imperialism and the Rise of Labour* (vol. v of the *History of the English People*). London: Ernest Benn, 1961.

———. *The Rule of Democracy* (vol. vi of the *History of the English People*). London: Ernest Benn, 1961.

———. *The World Crisis of 1914-1918: An Interpretation*. Oxford: Clarendon Press, 1930.

Hammond, Matthew. *British Labour Conditions and Legislation During the War*. New York: Oxford University Press, 1919.

Hanak, H. H. "The Union of Democratic Control during the First World War," *Bulletin of the Institute of Historical Research* (1963).

Hardie, Frank. "The King and the Constitutional Crisis," *History Today* (May 1970).

Harmsworth, George, and Reginald Pound. *Northcliffe*. London: Cassell, 1959.

Harris, José. *Unemployment and Social Policy: A Study in English Social Policy, 1886-1914*. London: Oxford University Press, 1972.

Haussonville, le Comte d'. "Les élections et la situation politique en Angleterre," *Revue des Deux Mondes*, 437 (Feb. 1911).

Hazlehurst, Cameron. *Politicians at War*. New York: Knopf, 1971.

———. "Asquith as Prime Minister," *English Historical Review*, 85/336 (July 1970).

Heyck, T. W. and W. Klecka. "British Radical M.P.'s: New Evidence from Discriminant Analysis," *Albion*, 1 (1972).

Hirst, F. W., and J. E. Allen. *British War Budgets*. London: Oxford University Press, 1926.

Hobsbawm, E. J. *Labouring Men*. London: Weidenfeld and Nicolson, 1964.

———. "General Labour Unionism in Great Britain, 1889-1914," *English Historical Review*, 2nd ser., I (August 1948).

Hoffman, R. J. S. *Great Britain and the German Trade Rivalry, 1875-1914*. London: Oxford University Press, 1933.

Hurwitz, Samuel J. *State-Intervention in Great Britain: A Study of Economic Control and Social Response*. New York: Columbia University Press, 1949.

Hutchison, Keith. *The Decline and Fall of British Capitalism*. New York: Scribner, 1950.

Hyde, H. M. *Carson: The Life of Sir Edward Carson*. London: Heinemann, 1953.

Imlah, Albert H. *Economic Elements in the Pax Britannica*. Cambridge: Harvard University Press, 1958.

James, Robert Rhodes. *Churchill: A Study in Failure, 1900-1939*. New York: World, 1970.

———. *Rosebery: A Biography of Archibald Philip Primrose, 5th Earl of Rosebery*. London: Weidenfeld and Nicolson, 1963.

Jarausch, Konrad. "World Power or Tragic Fate? The Kriegschuldfrage as Historical Neurosis," *Central European History*, 5/1 (1972).

Jenkins, Roy. *Asquith*. London: Collins, 1964.

———. *Mr. Balfour's Poodle*. London: Heinemann, 1954.

Johnson, P. B. *A Land Fit for Heroes*. Chicago: University of Chicago Press, 1968.

Kendle, John E. *The Colonial and Imperial Conferences, 1887-1911.* London: Longmans, Green, 1967.
———. "The Round Table Movement and 'Home Rule All Round,' " *Historical Journal,* 2/2 (April 1968).
Kindleberger, Charles. *Economic Growth in France and Britain.* Cambridge: Harvard University Press, 1964.
Kirkcaldy, A. W. (ed.). *British Finance During and After the War, 1914-1921.* London: Pitman, 1921.
Koebner, R. "The Concept of Economic Imperialism," *Economic Historical Review,* 2/1 (1949).
Koebner, R., and H. D. Schmidt. *Imperialism: The Story and Significance of a Political Word.* Cambridge: Cambridge University Press, 1964.
Koss, Stephen. *Lord Haldane: Scapegoat for Liberalism.* New York: Columbia University Press, 1969.
Krieger, Leonard. "The Idea of the Welfare State in Britain and the United States," *Journal of the History of Ideas,* 23 (1963).
Kruger, D. H. "Hobson, Lenin and Schumpeter on Imperialism," *Journal of the History of Ideas,* 16 (1955).
Kruger, Rayne. *Goodbye Dolly Gray: the Story of the Boer War.* London: Cassell, 1959.
Lammers, Donald. "Arno Mayer and the British Decision for War: 1914," *Journal of British Studies,* 11/2 (May 1973).
Langer, William. *The Diplomacy of Imperialism, 1890-1902.* New York: Knopf, 1935.
Lewis, W. R. *Great Britain and Germany's Lost Colonies, 1914-1919.* London: Oxford University Press, 1967.
Lilly, W. S. "The Collapse of England," *Fortnightly Review,* 61 (May 1902).
Lipson, Leslie. "Party Systems in the United Kingdom and the Older Commonwealth: Causes, Resemblances and Variations," *Political Studies* (Oxford), 7 (1959).
Lockwood, P. A. "Milner's Entry into the War Cabinet: December 1916," *Historical Journal,* 7/1 (1964).
Loewenberg, Peter. "Arno Mayer's 'Internal Causes and Purposes of War in Europe, 1870-1956'—An Inadequate Model of Human Behavior, National Conflict and Historical Change," *Journal of Modern History,* 42/4 (1970).
Low, D. A. *Lion Rampant: Essays in the Study of British Imperialism.* London: Frank Cass, 1973.

Lowe, C. J. *The Reluctant Imperialists: I, British Foreign Policy, 1878-1902*. Routledge & Kegan Paul, 1967.

Lowenstein, F. E. "The Shaw-Wells Controversy of 1906-1908," *Fabian Quarterly*, no. 41 (1944).

Lyons, F. S. L. *The Irish Parliamentary Party, 1890-1910*. London: Faber and Faber, 1951.

McBriar, A. M. *Fabian Socialism and English Politics*. Cambridge: Cambridge University Press, 1962.

McCarran, Sister M. P. *Fabianism in the Political Life of Britain*. Washington: Catholic University Press, 1952.

Maccoby, Simon. *English Radicalism, 1886-1914*. London: Allen and Unwin, 1953.

McCormick, Donald. *The Mask of Merlin*. London: MacDonald, 1963.

McDowell, Richard. *British Conservatism, 1832-1914*. London: Faber and Faber, 1959.

McEwen, John M. "The Liberal Party and the Irish Question During the First World War," *Journal of British Studies*, 11/1 (Nov. 1972).

———. "Campaign Election of 1918 and Unionist Members in Parliament," *Journal of Modern History*, 34/3 (Sept. 1962).

McGill, Barry. "Lloyd George's Timing of the 1918 Election," *Journal of British Studies*, 14/1 (1974).

MacKenzie, W. J. M. "Technocracy and the Role of Experts in Government: United Kingdom," *International Political Science Association* (Paris: Sept. 1961).

Magnus, Philip. *King Edward the Seventh*. New York: Dutton, 1964.

———. *Kitchener: Portrait of an Imperialist*. London: J. Murray, 1958.

Mansergh, Nicholas. *The Irish Question, 1840-1921*. London: Allen and Unwin, 1965.

Marder, A. J. *The Anatomy of British Sea Power, A History of British Naval Policy, 1880-1905*. New York: Knopf, 1940.

Marwick, Arthur. *The Deluge: British Society and the First World War*. Boston: Little, Brown, 1965.

———. "The Labour Party and the Welfare State in Britain, 1900-1948," *American Historical Review*, 72/5 (Dec. 1967).

———. "The Impact of the First World War on Britain," *Journal of Contemporary History*, I (Jan. 1968).

Masterman, Lucy. *C. F. G. Masterman: A Biography.* London: Nicholson, 1939.

———. "Recollections of David Lloyd George," *History Today,* 9 (April 1959).

Matthew, H. C. G. *The Liberal Imperialists.* London: Oxford University Press, 1973.

Mayer, Arno. *The Dynamics of Counter-revolution in Europe, 1870-1956: An Analytic Framework.* New York: Harper & Row, 1971.

———. "Internal Causes and Purposes of War in Europe, 1870-1956: A Research Assignment," *Journal of Modern History,* 41/3 (1969).

Meacham, Standish. "The Sense of an Impending Clash: English Working-Class Unrest before the First World War," *American Historical Review,* 77/5 (Dec. 1972).

Monger, G. W. *The End of Isolation: British Foreign Policy, 1900-1907.* London: Nelson, 1963.

Morgan, Kenneth O. *The Age of Lloyd George.* New York: Barnes and Noble, 1971.

———. "Lloyd George's Premiership," *Historical Journal,* 13/1 (1970).

Morris, A. J. Anthony. "Haldane's Army Reforms, 1906-1908: the Deception of the Radicals," *History,* 56/186 (1971).

Muggeridge, Kitty, and Ruth Adam. *Beatrice Webb: A Life.* London: Secker and Warburg, 1967.

Nimocks, Walter. *Milner's Young Men: The 'Kindergarten' in Edwardian Imperial Affairs.* Durham, N.C.: Duke University Press, 1968.

Nowell-Smith, Simon (ed.). *Edwardian England, 1901-1914.* London: Oxford University Press, 1964.

Parkin, Frank. "Working-Class Conservatives: A Theory of Political Deviance," *British Journal of Sociology,* 4 (Sept. 1967).

Pearson, Hesketh. *G.B.S.* New York: Garden City, 1942.

Pease, Edward R. *The History of the Fabian Society.* London: Allen and Unwin, 1925.

Pelling, Henry. *America and the British Left.* London: Adam and Charles Black, 1956.

———. *Popular Politics and Society in Late Victorian Britain.* London: Macmillan, 1968.

———. *Winston Churchill.* New York: E. P. Dutton, 1974.

Pelling, Henry. "Working-Class Conservatives: a review article," *Historical Journal*, 13/2 (1970).
Phelps Brown, E. H. *The Growth of British Industrial Relations*. London: J. Murray, 1965.
Playne, Caroline. *The Pre-War Mind in Britain*. London: Allen and Unwin, 1928.
Pope-Hennessy, James. *Lord Crewe, 1858-1945*. London: Cassell, 1955.
Potter, Bernard. *Critics of Empire: British Radical Attitudes to Colonisation in Africa, 1895-1914*. New York: St. Martin's, 1968.
Pribicevik, B. *The Shop-Steward's Movement and Workers' Control, 1910-1922*. Oxford: Blackwell, 1959.
Pumphrey, R. E. "The Introduction of Industrialists into the British Peerage: A Study in the Adaptation of a Social Institution," *American Historical Review*, 65/3 (Oct. 1959).
Raymond, E. T. *The Life of Arthur James Balfour*. Boston: Little, Brown, 1920.
———. *The Man of Promise: Lord Rosebery*. London: Unwin, 1923.
Rempel, Richard. *Unionists Divided: Balfour, Chamberlain and the Unionists Free Traders*. New York: Archon, 1972.
Roach, John. "Liberalism and the Victorian Intelligentsia," *Cambridge Historical Journal*, 13/1 (1957).
Roberts, Benjamin C. *The Trades Union Congress, 1868-1921*. London: Allen and Unwin, 1958.
Robinson, Ronald, and John Gallagher. *Africa and the Victorians*. London: Macmillan, 1961.
———. "The Imperialism of Free Trade," *Economic Historical Review*, 6/1 (1953).
Robson, W. A. *The Civil Service in Britain and France*. London: Hogarth, 1956.
Rostow, W. W. *The British Economy of the Nineteenth Century*. Oxford: Oxford University Press, 1948.
Rowland, Peter. *The Last Liberal Governments: the Promised Land, 1910-1914*. New York: Macmillan, 1969.
Ryan, Alfred P. *Mutiny at the Curragh*. London: Macmillan, 1956.
Savage, David. "The Parnell of Wales has become the Chamberlain of England; Lloyd George and the Irish Question," *Journal of British Studies*, 12/1 (Nov. 1972).

Sayers, R. S. "The Springs of Technical Progress in Britain," *Economic Journal*, 60/238 (June 1950).

Schumpeter, Joseph. *Imperialism and Social Classes*. Oxford: Blackwell, 1951.

Schurman, D. M. *The Education of a Navy: the Development of British Naval Strategic Thought, 1867-1914*. London: Cassell, 1965.

Searle, G. R. *The Quest for National Efficiency: A Study in British Politics and British Political Thought, 1899-1914*. Oxford: Blackwell, 1971.

Semmel, Bernard. *Imperialism and Social Reform: English Social-Imperial Thought, 1895-1914*. Cambridge: Harvard University Press, 1960.

Spender, J. A. *The Life of the Rt. Honorable Sir Henry Campbell-Bannerman*. London: Hodder and Stoughton, 1923.

Spender, J. A. and Cyril Asquith. *The Life of H. H. Asquith, Lord Oxford and Asquith*. London: Hutchinson, 1932.

Stansky, Peter. *Ambitions and Strategies*. Oxford: Clarendon, 1964.

———. "The Diminishing Post-Edwardians, or Private Lives and Public Process: Biographical Evidence," *Journal of Interdisciplinary History*. (Summer 1972).

Steiner, Zara. *The Foreign Office and Foreign Policy, 1898-1914*. Cambridge: Cambridge University Press, 1969.

Stenning, H. J. (ed.). *The Causes of War*. New York: The Telegraph Press, 1935.

Stokes, Eric. "Milnerism," *Historical Journal*, 5/1 (1962).

Strauss, E. *Irish Nationalism and British Democracy*. London: Methuen, 1951.

Stubbs, J. O. "Lord Milner and Patriotic Labour, 1914-1918," *English Historical Review*, 87/345 (Oct. 1972).

Swartz, Marvin. *The Union of Democratic Control in British Politics During the First World War*. Oxford: Clarendon Press, 1971.

Taylor, A. J. P. *Beaverbrook*. London: Hamish Hamilton, 1972.

———. *Lloyd George: Rise and Fall*. London: Cambridge University Press, 1961.

———. *Politics in Wartime*. London: Hamish Hamilton, 1964.

———. "Politics in the First World War," *Proceedings of the British Academy* (1959).

Taylor, A. J. P. (ed). *Lloyd George: A Diary by Frances Stevenson.* London, 1971.

———. (ed). *Lloyd George: Twelve Essays.* London: Hamish Hamilton, 1971.

Terraine, John. "Lloyd George's Dilemma," *History Today,* 11/5 (May 1961).

Thomas J. A. *The House of Commons, 1832-1901; A Study of its Economic and Functional Character.* Cardiff: University of Wales, 1939.

———. *The House of Commons, 1906-1911; An Analysis of its Economic and Social Character.* Cardiff: University of Wales, 1958.

Thompson, J. A. *The Collapse of the British Liberal Party.* Lexington, Mass.: Heath, 1969.

Thompson, Paul. "Fabian Socialism," *Past and Present,* 25 (July 1963).

Thomson, Malcolm, and Frances Lloyd George. *David Lloyd George: The Official Biography.* London: Hutchinson, 1948.

Thornton, A. P. *Doctrines of Imperialism.* New York: Wiley, 1965.

———. *For the File on Empire.* London: Macmillan, 1968.

———. *The Imperial Idea and its Enemies.* London: Macmillan, 1959.

Titmuss, Richard H. *Essays on the Welfare State.* New Haven: Yale University Press, 1959.

Tucker, A. "The Issue of Army Reform in the Unionist Government, 1903-1905," *Historical Journal,* 9/1 (1966).

Tyler, J. E. *The Struggle for Imperial Unity.* London: Longmans, Green, 1938.

Ullman, R. H. *Intervention and the War: Anglo-Soviet Relations, 1917-1921.* Princeton: Princeton University Press, 1961.

Watt, D. C. *Personalities and Policies.* London: Longmans, Green, 1965.

Weintraub, Stanley. *Shaw: An Autobiography.* London: Weybright and Talley, 1973.

West, Geoffrey. *H. G. Wells.* New York: Norton, 1930.

Weston, C. C. "The Liberal Leadership and the Lords' Veto, 1907-1910," *Historical Journal,* 11/3 (1968).

Whyte, Frederic. *The Life of W. T. Stead.* London: Jonathan Cape, 1925.

Williamson, Samuel R. *The Politics of Grand Strategy: Britain and France Prepare for War, 1904-1914*. Cambridge: Harvard University Press, 1969.

Wilson, Keith. "The Agadir Crisis, the Mansion House Speech and the Double-Edgedness of Agreements," *Historical Journal*, 15/3 (1972).

Wilson, Trevor. *The Downfall of the Liberal Party*. London: Collins, 1966.

———. "The Coupon and the British General Election of 1918," *Journal of Modern History*, 36/1 (March 1964).

Wingfield-Stratford, Esmé. *The Victorian Aftermath*. London: Routledge and Sons, 1933.

Winkler, Henry. *The League of Nations Movement in Great Britain, 1914-1919*. New Brunswick: Rutgers University Press, 1952.

Winslow, E. M. *The Pattern of Imperialism: A Study in the Theories of Power*. New York: Columbia University Press, 1948.

Wootton, Graham. *The Politics of Influence: British ex-Servicemen, Cabinet Decisions and Cultural Change*. London: Routledge and Kegan Paul, 1963.

Wrench, J. Evelyn. *Alfred Lord Milner*. London: Eyre and Spottiswoode, 1958.

———. *Geoffrey Dawson and Our Times*. London: Hutchinson, 1955.

Index

Addison, Dr. Christopher, 292–293, 321; and British Worker's League, 367n; as Minister of Reconstruction, 360; and National Insurance Bill, 215, 215n; poll of Liberal M.P.'s, 341
Akers-Douglas, William, 210
Amery, Leo S., 78, 201, 213, 228; constitutional crisis of 1910, 159; and Coefficients, 75–76, 79ff; and Compatriots, 110–112, 114; defense planning, 127ff; Imperial "Zollverein," 87; in Lloyd George Government, 348; National Service League, 136; and Unionist Social Reform Committee, 221; on the war, 255–257
Angell, Norman, 246–247
Ashley, William, 24; and Compatriots, 115, 115n, 246
Askwith, George, 227; growing labor unrest, 174–175, 174n
Asquith, Herbert Henry, 13; and the army, 288–289; "Asquith Must Go" movement, 296; and Balfour in War Committee, 332; and compulsion, 268; and conscription, 284, 284n; and Constitutional Conference, 161, 180ff; and crisis of August, 1914, 18; and decision for war, 15; at the Exchequer, 137; on Free Trade, 137–138; Irish Question, 181, 208, 235, 240; last Liberal Government, 333; Liberal support for, 335; Lawson resolution, 32; and Lloyd George, 298, 304, 325ff; and Lloyd George Plan, 6, 197–199, 205–206, 208–209, 209n; Lords' Veto, 154–155, 155n; loss of control, 272ff; National Insurance Bill, 220; outside opposition to, 338; and the press, 261, 326, 326n, 336; position in 1916, 324–325; royal guarantees, 181; and Tariff Reformers, 137; and old Tories, 260; War Committee, 327ff
Astor, Waldorf, 224; and British Worker's National League, 263, 263n; owner of *Observer*, 221–222; Parliamentary Secretary, 347

Balfour, Arthur James, 13, 70; arbitration on Lords' Veto, 160; "Balfour Must Go" movement, 218, 218n; Constitutional Conference, 181ff; fall of, 221; insurgency against, 210; and Irish Unionists, 185; and Lloyd George, 211–212; and Lloyd George Plan, 208–210; and National Insurance Bill, 221, 221n; reform of House of Lords, 177; on social reform, 98; and Tariff Reformers, 114, 212, 212n, 228; and Unionist defeat of 1905, 124; and Unionist factions, 231
Barnes, George, 246–247
Beaverbrook, Lord (Max Aitken), 278, 287, 290, 296, 321, 330, 368
Bellairs, Carlyon, and Coefficients, 79ff
Belloc, Hilaire, 11
Beveridge, William, 9, 139, 315, 316; *History of the Ministry of Munitions*, 317; Labour and Capital after the war, 364–365,

Beveridge, William (*cont.*)
365n; "The Labour Exchanges After the War," 307–313; and National Insurance Bill, 215, 215n
Birchenough, Henry, and Coefficients, 94
Birrell, Augustine, 200; in Constitutional Conference, 182
Blatchford, Robert, 43, 101
Bonar Law, Andrew, 208; at Admiralty, 255; "amalgamation" of parties, 229–230; abandons Asquith, 324; conference on Ireland, 238; and Irish Unionists, 230; and the Triumvirate, 339; and Unionist insurgents, 296–298
Braithwaite, J. W., 222; and National Insurance Bill, 215, 215n
British Workers League, *see* British Workers National League
British Workers National League, 99, 99n, 262–263, 286, 287, 293n; finances of British Workers (National) League, 366n; the Manifesto, 265; a National Council of Industry, 313–314, 313n; and Tariff Reform League, 343
Buchan, John, and Compatriots, 114
Buckingham Palace Conference (6 December, 1916), 336–337
Burns, John, 200

Cabinet System, imperialist critics of, 8
Campbell-Bannerman, Henry, 56, 61; on Lawson resolution, 32n; and Liberal-Imperialism, 33
Carson, Edward, 16; as Attorney General, 255; decline after Easter uprising, 295; supports Lloyd George, 338; and Milner circle, 286; Nigerian properties debate, 319–320; and Ulster Volunteers, 233; Unionist Business Committee, 254, 273, 286, 294

Cecil, Hugh, 246; Conservative meeting of 3 December, 1916, 330, 330n
Chalmers, Robert, 196
Chamberlain, Austen, 228; in Constitutional Conference, 182; on Labour, 160; and Lloyd George's second proposal, 242; on Socialism, 123; and Tariff Reform, 124; and Unionist Social Reform Committee, 221
Chamberlain, Joseph, 73, 89; Conservative meeting of 3 December 1916, 330, 330n; Liberal reaction to tariff reform, 89; and Lloyd George Plan, 206; and Social-Imperialism, 7; and tariff reform campaign, 80n; and Tariff Reform League, 21
Chesterton, Cecil, 11; on imperial decline, 174
Chiozza-Money, Leo, and British Workers National League, 264; General Organization of Labour, 276–277, 285; and Labour Exchanges, 307; Labour plan, 316; in Lloyd George Government, 347–348
Churchill, Winston, 9; leaves Admiralty, 255; and coalition plan, 1910, 232; and coalition plan, 1914, 250–251, 253; and Coefficients, 94; and Curragh Mutiny, 243; Dardanelles campaign, 254; and reform of House of Lords, 169; conference on Ireland, 239; and Labour Exchanges, 191, 191n; and labor unrest, 227; and Lloyd George, 280; and Lloyd George Plan, 197–198
Coefficients, 13, 110, 246; Coefficients Club, 9, 73ff, founding of, 75, 78, 248; and Compatriots, 110; and Rosebery, 79; split over tariff reform, 89–91, 89n
Compatriots, 13, 110, 110ff; Compatriots Club: as Brains Trust

410

Index

of Tariff Reform, 118–119, and Conservative leadership, 114–115, financing of, 111n, founding of, 110–111; and Lloyd George Plan, 207, 207n; and the press, 120–121; and the Tariff Reform League, 110; and Unionist defeat of 1905, 123–124
Compulsion, 278-279, 285; and First Coalition, 315
Confederates, 110. *See also* Compatriots
Constitutional Conference (1910), 181ff; failure of, 206, 206n, 209
Corbett, Julian, and Coefficients, 94
Crewe, Marquess of, 13; and the crisis of August, 1918, 18; in Constitutional Conference, 182; and Lloyd George Coalition, 334n; and Lloyd George Plan, 198
Cricceith Memorandum, 214, 234, 234n. *See* Appendix A
Curragh Mutiny, 243
Curtis, Lionel, 158, 347; on bureaucracy, 350–351, 350n
Curzon of Kedleston, Earl, 13, 175; Conservative meeting of 3 December, 1916, 330, 330n

Dawkins, Clinton, and Coefficients Club, 79ff, 79n; and National Service League, 136
Dawson, Geoffrey, 158, 233
Defense of the Realm Act, 273

Edward VII, King, in constitutional crisis, 166–168; his death, 172ff
The Empire and the Century, Compatriots Club publication, 120ff

Fabian Society, 11, 190; split over Boer War, 36n, 39–40, 39n; and Independent Labour Party, 40; and labor anarchy, 247–248; and Liberal-Imperialists, 38; and Ministry of Reconstruction, 275;

"National Minimum," 258; "permeation," 76
First Coalition, 255, 259–260; and compulsion, 315; fall of, 282ff, 291; reconstruction of, 266
Fisher, John, dispute with Lloyd George, 151
Fisher, Victor, and British Workers National League, 361, 366
Fowler, Henry, and Liberal League, 61

Garvin, James Louis, 16; anti-Socialist propaganda, 149ff; and Balfour, 148; budget debacle of 1909, 147ff; on Carson, 236; on coalition, 218; proposes coalition with Asquith, 157–158; on wartime coalitions, 256; and Coefficients, 94; and Compatriots Club, 114; Constitutional Conference Plan, 172ff; "Doctrine of Development," 117–118; Government of Public Safety, 255; on potential of Irish antiSocialism, 164; on Liberal factions, 186; on "detaching" Liberal Leaguers, 168; and Loreburn Letter, 234–235; and Lloyd George, 165, 217, 226, 258; and Lloyd George Plan, 195–196, 213; policy of "National Combination," 143–144; and National Insurance Bill, 215–219, 222–223; and Northcliffe, 149, 199; and "red Crusade," 147–148; as Tariff Reform propagandist, 100, 115–116, 116n
Goldman, C. S., and Compatriots Club, 114
Grey, Edward, and Coefficients Club, 79ff; and the crisis of August, 1918, 18; as Foreign Secretary, 135; on Irish and Labour, 156; on Lawson resolution, 32; return to Liberal Party, 91–92; and Lloyd George Plan, 198; and Rosebery, 58; and the decision for war, 15

411

Gwynne, H. A., and Compatriots, 115, 268; League of Patriots, 270–271; Lloyd George's liaison, 270

Haldane, Richard Burton, on a "Cabinet of Empire," 121–122; and Coefficients Club, 79ff; on Lawson resolution, 32; return to Liberal Party, 91–92; and Lloyd George Plan, 198; Machinery of Government Committee, 311, 350; and Rosebery, 32; and Territorial Army, 135; at War Office, 135–136
Halevy, Elie, 34; and post-war reconstruction, 3–4
Hewins, W.A.S., 24, 35, 79, 79n, 223; on "Carsonism," 236; and Coefficients Club, 79ff; and Compatriots Club, 110, 114; on the expert in government, 126; on Imperial "Zollverein," 87; in Lloyd George Government, 348; and Tariff Reform League, 103, 103n; and Unionist Business Committee, 254; a "Whig Coalition," 239
Hobson, J. A., 45–47; on imperialism and nationalism, 30
Hodge, John, 270, 294, 344; and British Workers National League, 263–264; as Minister of Labour, 347
Holland, Bernard, 122
House of Lords, imperialist critics of, 8; veto of Lloyd George Budget, 151, 151n. *See also* Constitutional Conference

Imperial Preference, 87
Industrial decline, debate on 1901–1902, 64–66, 64n. *See also* Mosely Industrial Commission
Irish Question, 251; Easter uprising, 294–295; Irish Home Rule, 59, 154–155, deadlock in 1910, 166; Home Rule Bill, 231–233, 251, 251n
Irish Unionists, 295
Isaacs, Rufus, and Liberal League, 62

Jones, Tom, on danger of Milnerites in Lloyd George Government, 358–359

Kerr, Phillip (Lord Lothian), 158, 201, 347
Keynes, John Maynard, American influence, 344–345
Kidd, Benjamin, 8

Labour Exchanges Act, 191, 191n
Labour Party, Bristol Conference, 285, 285n, 316; on conscription, 269–270; Arthur Henderson and conscription, 323; industrial compulsion, 316; and National Insurance Bill, 215, 215n; and decision for war, 20
Labour Representation Committee, 98
Labour Unrest, 207, 207n, 230–231, 231n, 233, 267–268, 362n; *Daily Mail* Enquiry, 246–247
Lansdowne, Marquess of, 19, 223; in Constitutional Conference, 182; in First Coalition, 255ff; Lansdowne letter, 319; conciliation on Lords' Veto, 160
Lawson, Wilfred, resolution to censure Unionist Government, 31–32
Liberal Cabinet, crisis of August, 1914, 250n, 251
Liberal Free Traders, and the war, 252–253
Liberal-Imperialism, 11, 18, 73; and Milner's censure, 134–135; and modernization, 66–67; origins of, 29n; and Tariff Reform compared, 97; and the Webbs, 35–36
Liberal League, 6, 10; and pro-Boers, 112; collapse of, 70–71; founding of, 34, 59ff; and indus-

412

Index

trial crisis, 65–66; Leeds by-election, 60n; "Manifesto," 67; membership, 62–63, 62n; on Tariff Reform, 66n
Liberal Party, break-up of 1916, 332; and compulsion, 284; critics of, 68; and Irish rebellion, 302; "new breed" of 1910, 220; and Social-Imperialism, 93
Lloyd George, and Addison's poll of Liberal M.P.'s, 341; and Asquith, 254, 281ff; and Balfour, 196, 209–211, 225, 229; Bedford speech, 236–238; at Board of Trade, 139ff; budget of 1909, 144ff; a "businessmen" government, 170, 170n; and British Workers National League, 357; and Churchill, 232, 280; Coalition Plan of 1910, 188ff; and Coefficients, 94; 141–142; and compulsion, 274; and conscription, 298, 298n; and older Conservatives, 330–331; and Constitutional Conference, 186, 187, 187n; and constitutional crisis, 176; the Criccieth Memo, 187–188; and Garvin, 165, 220, 243–245; and Germany, 193–194, 214; and House of Lords, 151, 151n; and Irish Question, 165–166, 169, 188, 194–195, 195n, 241–243, 300; and labor unrest, 227, 227n, 267–268, 286; and the Left, 11; and Lloyd George Government, 306ff; Mansion House Speech, 225–227; and Marconi affair, 236–237, 240–241; and Milner, 264–265, 357–358; and Ministry of Munitions, 255ff, 265, 281; and Minority Report, 193; and National Coalition, 5; a "new party," 292; Nigerian property debate, 321; and Patents and Design Bill, 140; and Poor Law, 190–191; and the press, 291; and protection, 204–205; and Reconstruction Committee, 353–355; and Redmond, 241; resignation, 333; and F. E. Smith, 239–240; and Social-Imperialism, 7; and Tariff Reformers, 193, 203, 217, 245–246, 283–284; and the Treasury Agreement, 254, 254n; the Triumvirate, 275, 322; Unionist overtures, 292; and decision for war, 251–252; War Committee, 327ff; War Office, 282, 300ff
Lloyd George Plan, and Asquith, 6, 197–199, 205–206, 208–209, 208n; and Balfour, 208–210; and Churchill, 197–198; and Compatriots, 207, 207n; and Crewe, 198; and Garvin, 195–196, 213; and Grey, 198; and Haldane, 198. See also Criccieth Memorandum
Lyttleton, Alfred, and Compatriots Club, 114

McKenna, Reginald, 200; American debt, 344; and Lloyd George, 334; progressive war tax, 276
MacDonald, J. Ramsay, 18
Mackinder, Halford J., 35, 322; and Compatriots Club, 79n, 79ff, 110, 114; in Lloyd George Government, 348; and Tariff Reform League, 103–104, 104n
Marconi Affair, 244
Masterman, C.F.G., 139, 196; and Coefficients, 94, 141–142; and National Insurance Bill, 142, 142n, 215, 215n
Maxse, Leo, 57, 228; "Balfour Must Go" movement, 184; and British Workers National League, 263; and Coefficients, 79ff; and Compatriots, 110; and National Service League, 136
Milner, Alfred Lord, 4, 6, 209, 261; "big Smash-up," 323–324; and British Workers National League, 262; succeeds Chamberlain, 100–101; and Coefficients, 94; and Compatriots, 110; and constitutional crisis of 1910, 158–159;

413

Milner, Alfred Lord (*cont.*) and the Left, 11; and Liberal Government of 1906, 135; and Liberal Imperialists, 74–75, 74n; and Lloyd George, 262, 266, 287; on the National Coalition, 340–341; and National Service League, 136; "The Nation and the Empire," 248–249; the "nobler Socialism," 101–102; and Social-Imperialism, 7, 105–106; on "the System," 107–108, 159; and Tariff Reform League, 103n; on "Unionist Labour M.P.'s," 163, 163n; on Union of Democratic Control and subversives, 360–362; in War Cabinet, 341; and Webbs, 106

Military Service Act, 272–273

Milner's "Kindergarten," 106, 110, 158–159; critics of Balfour, 202, 275; in Lloyd George Government, 347; and Lloyd George Plan of 1910; 201–202; and Reconstruction Committee, 355

Ministry of Munitions, 277–278, 311; and conscription, 315; and labor, 275

Mond, Alfred, and Lloyd George, 170; Nigerian properties debate, 322

Moneypenny, W. F., and Coefficients, 94

Montagu, Edwin, 334; and Liberal League, 62

Morel, E. D., 14

Moroccan Crisis, 222, 224–225

Mosely Industrial Commission, 65, 65n. *See also* Industrial Decline

Mosley, Oswald, and Social-Imperialism, 9

Munitions of War Act, 267

Murray of Elibank, Lord, and constitutional conference, 161–162; on "detaching" Labour, 162–163; as liaison between parties, 176ff, 218

Nash, Vaughan, 310, 349

National Coalition, of 1916, 250; social basis of, 26–27

National Efficiency, 4n, 10, 11, 71, 190; and Anglo-German rivalry, 22; doctrine of, 69–70; and Social-Imperialism, 22

National Free Labour Association, 99, 99n

National Insurance Bill, 186–188, 188n, 213, 215, 215n; bipartisan support for, 179, 179n; first reading, 217; Unionist support for, 228

National Service League, 81, 81n, 97, 130, 136; the "Last War Fallacy," 342, 342n

Northcliffe, Lord (Alfred Harmsworth), 18; *Daily Mail* Enquiry, 246–247, 247n

Observer, 149. *See also* J. L. Garvin

Oliver, F. S., 158, 201, 213; and Coefficients, 94; and Compatriots Club, 114; on democracy and war, 252–253; in Lloyd George Government, 348; "Pacificus" articles, 180; and the Triumvirate, 339n

Orwell, George, 30

Osborne Judgment, 154–155

Parliament Bill of 1911, 223; "Die-Hard" resistance to, 200–201, 201n. *See also* House of Lords

Pearson, Karl, 8

Pember Reeves, W., and Coefficients Club, 79ff, 79n; and Compatriots, 121; on Pollock Commission, 122

Perks, Robert, and Liberal League, 61

Pollock, Frederick, Pollock Commission, 122

Primrose League, 69, 127

Reconstruction, 4, 307; Ministry of Reconstruction, 10, 308, 347;

Index

recruiting for, 348–350, 348n, 353–354
Redmond, John, Irish Nationalists and the Lords' Veto, 155–156; isolation of, 169. *See also* Irish Home Rule
Reserved Occupations Committee, 277
Rosebery, Earl of, 4; on Boer War, 34n; Chesterfield speech, 54–56, 58; on Germany, 57, 57n; and Home Rule, 55–56; as leader, 33; and origins of Liberal-Imperialism, 29–32; on party system, 44–45; and reform of House of Lords, 168; and Social-Imperialism, 7; and the Tariff Reformers, 73–74; and the Webbs, 36ff
Round Table, 13, 110, 110n; and crisis of 1910, 158; and Lloyd George Plan, 207, 207n
Runciman, Walter, on compulsion, 316–317
Russell, Bertrand, 9; and Coefficients Club, 79ff; on Coefficients, 88

Shaw, George Bernard, 77; *Fabianism and the Empire*, 36–39, 50–51. *See also* Fabian Society
Smith, F. E., Earl of Birkenhead, 223, 228; "Balfour Must Go," movement, 230; Lloyd George's intermediary, 237; and Lloyd George Plan, 203–206, 213; and Unionist Business Committee, 294 and Unionist Social Reform Committee, 213–215
Snowden, Philip, 246–247
Social-Imperialism, 8ff, 37n, 190, 220, 222–223, 245–246, 249, 264, 312, 315; and classes, 10; and Halsbury Club, 224; Labor and unconditional surrender, 343–344; in Lloyd George Government, 346; in Ministry of Reconstruction, 275; and postwar reconstruction, 4; and "remodernization," 24–27; and Second Industrial Revolution, 23–24; and status quo, 305; and the war, 17, 253
Stead, W. T., as Lloyd George's emissary, 176–178.
"Supplementary Memorandum," 196, 196n. *See also* Criccieth Memorandum, Appendix B

Tariff Reform League, 9, 95, 214, 275; colonial section of, 108, 108n; and Edwardian counter-revolution, 20–21; and Lloyd George, 139, 342; "New Crusade," 342; platform of, 104–107; and Union of Democratic Control, 342–343; and Unionist Business Committee, 319; and working men, 98–100, 102–103. *See also* Tariff Reformers
Tariff Reformers, attacks on Asquith, 283; and fall of Balfour, 228; in Coefficients Club, 85ff, 95; compulsory military service, 130; and "Die-Hards," 223n; election of 1905, 113, 124–125; ethic of leadership, 129–130; and Irish Question, 230; and labor, 98–99; and Liberal-Imperialists compared, 97; and Lloyd George, 5, 66, 139ff, 225, 291; and Lloyd George Plan, 203; Minority Report, 190–191; "Monthly Notes," 283n; National Insurance Bill, 213, 221; parliamentary strength, 113; Social-Imperialist doctrine of, 92; and Socialism, 109; Territorial Force Associations, 136. *See also* Tariff Reform League
Tennant, H. J., and Liberal League, 62
Trades Union Congress, Bristol Conference, 267–270
Treasury Agreement, 267

415

Unionist Business Committee, 283; Nigerian properties debate, 318–321; Shell crisis, 254, 254n
Unionist Free Traders, 113; dispute over tariff, 178
Unionist Party, factions in, 223; and Lloyd George, 274–275; loss of leadership, 119–120
Unionist Social Reform Committee, 163, 213–214, 248, 248n, 275; on Germany, 214, 214n; and National Insurance Bill, 214–215, 221, 227
United States, financial influence on policy, 344–345

War Committee, 326ff
Webb, Beatrice and Sidney, 7, 37, 104; and Coefficients Club, 79ff; on Evolution, 53–54; efficiency in government, 126–127; industrial conscription, 269; industrial controls, 310; on Japan, 106–107; and the Left, 11; and "Limps," 60; Lloyd George and "Imperialist Nationalist Party," 261; and Lloyd George Government, 311–312, 346–347; 359–360; and Milner, 106; Minority Report, 147, 190–191, 193, 193n, 321; National Efficiency, 48ff; National Insurance Bill, 215, 215n; National Minimum, 51–52, 90, 215, 231; "permeation," 38–40, 67, 142, 311–312; political dinners, 76–77; Reconstruction Committee, 351–353; break with Rosebery, 77–78; "Lord Rosebery's Escape from Houndsditch," 42, 42n, 43; the "Servile State," 271–272; and Social-Imperialism, 7; and Tariff Reformers, 231. *See also* Fabian Society
Wells, H. G., 9, 10, 246; and Coefficients Club, 79ff; *The New Machiavelli*, 225–226; *The New Machiavelli* and the Coefficients, 84–85; split with the Webbs, 85n
Wilson, Henry (Field Marshal), attacks on government, 288–289

Library of Congress Cataloging in Publication Data

Scally, Robert J
   The origins of the Lloyd George coalition.

   Bibliography: p.
   1. Great Britain—Politics and government—1901-1936.
2. Lloyd George, David Lloyd George, 1st Earl, 1865-
1945. I. Title.
DA570.S25   320.9′41′083   74-25608
ISBN 0-691-07570-0